The Hulbert Financial Digest
Annual Review of
Investment Newsletters

The Hulbert Financial Digest Annual Review of Investment Newsletters

Mark Hulbert
Joel Bludman Wittenberg

Reston Publishing Company, Inc.
A Prentice-Hall Company
Reston, Virginia

ISBN: 0-8359-2945-0

Copyright 1985 by
The Hulbert Financial Digest, Inc.

All rights reserved.
No part of this book may be reproduced
in any way, or by any means,
without permission in writing
from the publisher.

From an electronically transmitted
manuscript, the galley proofs
for this book were composed on a
TYXSET 1000 System by TYX Corporation
in Reston, Virginia, and output using
a Canon LBP-10 Laser Beam Printer.
The repro galleys were also composed
on a TYXSET 1000 System and output
using a Mergenthaler 101.

TYXSET 1000 is a trademark of TYX Corporation

10 9 8 7 6 5 4 3 2 1

Printed in the United States of America.

Contents

Preface ix

1 Methodological Prologue 1

2 Answers to the Questions Most Frequently Asked About Newsletters 9

3 Choosing a Newsletter: The place of newsletters in your overall financial planning 15

4 Choosing a Newsletter: Tax considerations 27

5 Choosing a Newsletter: Which newsletters are best at timing the stock market? 39

6 Choosing a Newsletter: The use of telephone hotlines, or how much time do you want to devote to following a newsletter's recommendations? 49

7 Analysis of Each Newsletter's Performance   57

The Addison Report   61
The Cabot Market Letter   67
California Technology Stock Letter   71
The Charted Course   75
The Chartist   79
Dessauer's Journal   85
The Dines Letter   89
Dow Theory Forecasts   103
Dow Theory Letters   113
The Granville Market Letter   119
Green's Commodity Market Comments   123
Growth Fund Guide   127
Growth Stock Outlook   135
Harry Browne's Special Reports   139
Heim Investment Letter   143
High Technology Investments   147
The Holt Investment Advisory   153
Howard Ruff's Financial Success Report   159
Indicator Digest   165
The International Harry Schultz Letter   169
Market Logic   175
New Issue Investor   179
New Issues   183
The Nicholson Report   189
The Option Advisor   197
The Outlook   203
The Peter Dag Investment Letter   213
The Professional Investor   217
The Professional Tape Reader   227
Professional Timing Service   233
The Prudent Speculator   237

The RHM Survey of Warrants, Options and Low-Price Stocks   243

Robert Kinsman's Low Risk Advisory Letter   247

The Speculator   251

Successful Options Investing   255

Switch Fund Advisory   259

Systems and Forecasts   263

Telephone Switch Newsletter   269

Tony Henfrey's Gold Letter   275

United Business and Investment Report   279

The Value Line Investment Survey   287

The Value Line OTC Special Situations Service   293

The Zweig Forecast   297

Zweig Performance Ratings Report   303

Appendix A	**Newsletter Performance**	**307**
Appendix B	**Risk-Adjusted Performance**	**321**
Appendix C	**Newsletter Directory**	**329**
Appendix D	**A Short Guide to Using Discount Brokers**	**337**

Preface

"Shortages come and go, but one commodity never seems in short supply: investment advice."

—*The Wall Street Journal*

The number of Americans who invest in the stock market has increased dramatically in recent years, especially in the wake of the most powerful bull market in 50 years. The latest count by the New York Stock Exchange puts the number at 41 million, in fact, about one in every six men, women and children in the U.S.! Not surprisingly, with this growth in the number of investors has come an explosion in the investment advisory industry. Seemingly everyone is offering financial advice—commentators on television and columnists in the financial press, personal and business acquaintances, stockbrokers, and investment advisory newsletters.

How are you to choose? While this book will help you choose between various investment advisory newsletters, you may be asking, "Why should I look to any newsletters at all?" We address this question in this preface.

What about newspapers, television, and the financial press as sources of investment advice? In recent years, they have greatly improved and expanded their coverage and analysis of the economy and of financial developments and trends. Public television's "Wall

Street Week" is now one of the most popular shows in all of television; *Barron's* is so widely followed and respected that a positive or negative report on a stock can send the stock soaring or plunging. Nevertheless, television programs, financial magazines, and newspapers of general circulation are probably better thought of as good sources of factual information and investment ideas than of specific and systematic investment advice. As a rule, they do not provide a specific model portfolio for you to follow or consistent follow-up on the securities they mention.

Financial advice may also be forthcoming from any of your personal or business acquaintances. Everyone from your banker, accountant, lawyer, business partner, golf buddy, dentist, or neighbor may volunteer investment advice. As with television and the financial press, however, personal and business acquaintances are better seen as sources of ideas than of systematic investment strategies. The frequency with which such acquaintances offer their advice, for example, is often a function of how well the market has done recently. At market tops, everyone is offering advice and giving examples of his latest winnings. At market bottoms, on the other hand, the stock market is not to be mentioned in polite company!

STOCKBROKERS VS. NEWSLETTERS

Two other, more traditional, and often more informed and more systematic, sources of investment advice are stockbrokers and investment newsletters. In deciding between them, the following factors should be kept in mind.

With respect to stockbrokers, you should realize that their incentives to make money for you sometimes can conflict with their desire to make money for themselves. The source of this conflict is the fact that they are compensated on a commission basis; they are paid according to how many shares of stock have been bought and sold by their clients, not according to how much money they have made for them. The incentive they have to make money for you—gaining more and wealthier clients to the extent their advice is profitable—is therefore indirect and long-term compared to the direct and immediate incentive to generate commission income.

For example, when a brokerage firm has in its inventory a large block of stock that it wants to unload, it offers "special compensation" for those of its brokers that sell the most shares of that stock. Typically, this compensation includes an increased portion of the commission that is charged or an all-expenses-paid trip to Hawaii. Does your stockbroker tell you how he is being compensated for pushing this stock, or why his firm is so anxious to unload it?

Brokerage Firms' Research

Another factor you should consider in comparing brokers with newsletters is that many firms forbid their brokers to make their own recommendations—requiring them instead to choose their recommendations from the "recommended list" compiled by the firm's research department. While the stocks on the recommended list may very well turn out to be more profitable than the stocks the broker himself would have chosen, this arrangement has several drawbacks. First, firms' research departments rarely offer sell advice. Because brokers too easily begin to believe their own sales pitches, this may lead them to become permanently bullish on the market. Your broker therefore is likely to be far more silent on what or when to sell than about what or when to buy.

Another drawback with firms' limitations on what their brokers can recommend is that you are just one of your broker's many clients, and your broker is just one of his firm's many brokers. In all likelihood, therefore, you are nowhere near to being the first client of the firm to receive the particular recommendations. In fact, a recommended stock's price will already have been bid up substantially by the firm's "major" clients by the time you hear about it through your broker.

Finally, if the research that brokerage firms perform is valuable, why are these firms virtually always reluctant to publish their performance results? What, for example, is the average change in price of a stock recommended by Merrill Lynch? And is that better or worse than Dean Witter, Paine Webber, or their competitors? Don't you think that these firms would be sure to document their superior stockbroking ability if their advice was profitable?

Investment Newsletters

To be contrasted with brokers is the other important source of investment advice—advisory newsletters. Currently, approximately 10,000 investment advisors are registered with the Securities and Exchange Commission (SEC), and we estimate that about 500 of them publish investment newsletters. No more than about two dozen of those, however, have 5000 or more subscribers.

The performance incentives of investment newsletters differ from those of stockbrokers in several significant respects. First and foremost, investment newsletter editors charge directly for their advice. Consequently, the size of their subscriber base and their profitability are highly dependent upon the value of that advice; renewal rates for newsletters are extremely sensitive to their editors' success in devising a profitable strategy. The newsletter industry is filled with examples of newsletters which have lost many of their subscribers and much or all of their profitability when their advice has been consistently or substantially off-base. Indeed, there have been some cases where this has led to a newsletter going out of business.

In addition, newsletters ordinarily have no immediate incentive to generate stock transactions. Unlike brokers, they are not compensated according to the number of shares that their clients have bought or sold. Their income is directly related to how many investors are convinced that the advice contained in the newsletter is profitable.

Finally, unlike brokers, performance data are available for most of the widely followed investment newsletters. These figures, calculated by the *Hulbert Financial Digest* (referred to throughout this book as the HFD), enable an investor to select an advisor with a proven record from the many seeking attention (and your dollars) in the marketplace.

This book is based upon our conviction that you would do well to consider newsletters as a source of investment advice. Because the incentives they have to make profitable recommendations differ from the incentives under which brokers operate, newsletters are a refreshing source of advice. They can make recommendations that are rare within the brokerage community and lead you in directions where brokers are unlikely to take you.

Just because newsletters operate under different incentives than do stockbrokers, however, does not mean that those incentives are all to the good—and a preface to any comparison of newsletters would be amiss if it did not point this out. For example, newsletter editors often feel they must continually recommend new investments—even when market conditions are not optimum—in order to convince their subscribers that they are receiving their money's worth. Some editors have complained that they have lost subscribers during periods when their recommended strategy was to remain in cash—even when such a strategy was more profitable than that advocated by most other newsletters. According to such editors, their subscribers felt they were not getting enough "action" for their subscription dollars; they felt that they did not pay someone up to $300 per year to be told to keep their money in cash. Potential newsletter subscribers therefore need to be on their guard for newsletters which generate more transactions than are paying off—after taking commissions and taxes into account (see discussions of these two topics later in this book).

Exaggerated Advertising Claims

Another less-than-desirable consequence of the incentives under which newsletters operate is exaggerated advertising claims. As with any industry, the newsletter industry contains both honest and less-than-honest members, and it is too much to expect that each editor will be objective about his track record when such objectivity can be so devastating to his own fortunes. A random sampling of the direct mail advertising we receive for various newsletters reveals claims of the following sort:

(a) a letter that "regularly" earns profits of 1602% in just 48 months;

(b) a letter that turned $8,750 into $405,125 in only 13 weeks;

(c) a report on how you can "regularly" earn 4000% annual profit;

(d) a report on how to earn "spectacular" profits of "950% better than the Dow" while "reducing your risks";

(e) an advisor who has helped subscribers earn "consistent profits of 922% during the last few years."

While the HFD has not tracked the performance of the newsletters making these specific claims, we doubt them. During the four years the HFD has been tracking investment newsletters, we have found no service that can live up to such claims. In fact, consistent average annual gains of more than 20% to 30% are extremely rare over long periods of time.

Because of these unfortunate consequences of newsletters' incentives, it is important that you choose between letters with care. Can you look to SEC registration as a way to choose? No! The SEC does not place any education, training, or experience standards on becoming registered as an adviser. In fact, almost anyone—other than convicted felons—could become registered upon doing little more than filling out several forms and paying the $250 filing fee.

In choosing between investment newsletters, you must examine closely their performance—and this is exactly what this book does. Relying upon their advertising claims is too dangerous, and it is too risky to assume that newsletters never recommend an imprudent number of transactions. By utilizing an objective rating system such as that devised by the HFD, one can counteract the negative effects of newsletters' incentives and take maximum benefit from what those services do have to offer.

NEWSLETTERS AND "RANDOM WALKS"

Another potential source of investor skepticism towards newsletters may be the growing debate among academic economists over whether the market can be beaten over long periods of time. If the movement of securities' prices is random—as some contend—then there is no reason to pay for the advice of any newsletter, or more crucially, no reason to invest one's assets according to a letter's advice.[1] While we believe the market can be beaten, we think it is important for investors to be aware of and familiar with the dispute.

The "random walk" theory, and its closely related "efficient market hypothesis," bases much of its confidence in the fact that the stock market very quickly and efficiently assimilates new information. By the time you or I read about a company's new earnings report in the newspaper, for example, it is invariably too late to profit from it. The stock's price has already adjusted to the news. And to the degree that information is quickly and efficiently reflected in the marketplace, it follows that, at any given time, a stock is neither "overvalued" nor "undervalued." Stock prices of course will go up or down over time, so the theory concludes, but their behavior will be random. Those who try to predict and profit from alleged trends in the market will inevitably meet with failure.

Is The Market Efficient For Every Stock?

The stock markets are indeed very efficient, and in disputing the conclusion of the theory, one cannot deny that efficiency. But the markets are not equally efficient for all stocks. With thousands of researchers from brokerage firms devoting themselves to scrutinizing IBM, for example, one would expect the market for IBM's stock to be far more efficient than the market for a tiny OTC stock with no following among the brokerage community. In the former case, there is very little likelihood that you or I could hope to discover some salient fact about IBM that has not already been analyzed hundreds of times. In the latter case, however, the likelihood is much greater. And, in fact, some academic research conducted recently indeed suggests that the average stock with no brokerage following has outperformed the average stock with such a following!

Apart from the presence or absence of a brokerage following, academic research has located a number of other areas where the market's efficiency is less than complete. These areas include companies that are in a strong capital position, stocks that are low-priced, stocks of smaller companies, stocks that are trading at a low price-earnings ratio, and companies with recent high profit increases.[2]

---

[1] Of course, doubts about newsletters arising from the efficient market hypothesis would extend to any source of advice—not just newsletters.

[2] These are not the only stock selection criteria that have shown promise, and each of these must be qualified in various ways. For a good discussion of these issues, see "Stock Screens: A Review of the Indicators," by James Cloonan, in the *American Association of Individual Investors Journal*, May 1984, pp. 31–2.

Apart from these academic studies is the performance of stock rating systems which have in fact beaten the market over significant periods of time. Most prominent of such systems is that devised by the Value Line Investment Survey (published by Arnold Bernhard & Co.) which has rated 1500 stocks each week since 1965 from Group I (the 100 best bets to outperform the market over the next six months to one year) to Group V (the 100 worst bets). During each year since 1965, it turns out that, with few and minor exceptions, those stocks rated "I" have outperformed those rated "II," which in turned have outperformed those rated "III," and so forth. This is a record one cannot ascribe to chance.

The Market's Efficiency and You

Why is this debate something you should be aware of? Because it points out what you should be looking for in a newsletter. To justify subscribing to a service and investing your assets according to its advice, a newsletter must show convincingly how and why there is reason to believe it can beat the market. Does it base its recommendations on an already proven method (such as a stock selection method based on the criteria listed above) or on a method devised by it and on which sufficient research has been conducted to verify its effectiveness? Can the newsletter persuasively demonstrate that the factors on which it bases its advice have not already been discovered by other market participants and thus already discounted by the market? You should approach newsletters with the attitude of the skeptic; make each service convince you that it has sufficiently increased the odds of beating the market to justify subscribing to it and risking your assets by following its advice.

Several examples illustrate what you should be on guard against. Several services give great weight each year to the so-called January Indicator, which holds that, if the market is up in January, it will be up for the year as a whole, and vice versa. In December 1981, several services—acting out of their belief that January 1982 was going to be an up month—used the January indicator to justify becoming bullish for the year as a whole. As it turned out, however, that month was down, not up. If these services genuinely believed in their reasoning of one month earlier, they would have turned bearish in February. But they did not. Instead, they merely focussed on another indicator that allegedly justified a bullish posture.

In our mind, such reasoning is a dead give-away that the service in question has a predetermined view of the market that they will maintain—regardless of what happens in the market. Needless to say, following such advice can be dangerous. The profitability of such newsletters' advice will be purely random. If services can so easily disregard their own arguments of a previous month, then why should you accord that advice any greater respect?

How Accurate is the January Indicator?

This example of some newsletters' use of the January indicator is a good example of another common pitfall—failure to conduct enough historical research on which to base a confident conclusion. It turns out, according to this indicator's adherents, that the indicator has a good success ratio. (It supposedly was successful in 10 out of the 14 years from 1969–1982, for example.) But how has such a success rate been calculated? According to an analysis of the matter which appeared in the March 12, 1984, issue of *Barron's*, this success rate is based on erroneous reasoning. In determining whether the market was up or down for the year—and thus whether the indicator was a success—such calculations look at the period from January 1 to December 31, not from February 1 to December 31. Thus in years when the market went up 100 points in January and fell 90 points thereafter through December 31, the indicator was judged a success when it in fact was a failure. It appeared to be a success because January was up by 100 points and the year was up by 10 points, even though you would have lost 90 points by acting upon the indicator. When this bias is removed from the calculations, according to the *Barron's* article, January's record as an indicator is little better than random and, in any case, is worse than the records of four other months of the year! Needless to say, advice that is based on inadequate or inconsistent research holds no promise of being more profitable than random stock picks. You may or may not make money by following its advice, but whether or not you do has nothing to do with the reasons advanced by the letter.

The example of the January indicator points up yet another thing to look for in judging between various indicators. Look to see that an indicator has been tested in "real time," so to speak. The problem arises because it is all too easy—especially with the advent of computers allowing more historical comparisons—to look back through history, picking and choosing among hundreds of potential indicators until one "discovers" one that has an "uncanny" record of accuracy. While such historical research has some validity, it does not provide as strong a foundation as do real time tests. All too often, an indicator judged to be a success by non-real time tests begins to break down the moment you start to follow it.

Yet another type of reasoning which you need to guard against is the sort which appears to enjoy a strong foundation in historical research but which, upon examination, does not. In 1980, for example, several newsletters developed an argument based on the fact that, every time in this century when a Republican president was in office during certain sets of circumstances, the market crashed. This appeared to be a strong, historically based argument, but what these letters did not tell you is that there was only one year in this century which fit its preconditions—1930! The market did not do well in the years following 1930, of course, but a historical argument based on a sample size of just one has no validity whatsoever.

CONCLUSION

These examples, by pointing out what to avoid, also show what sort of approach to take to newsletters. Scrutinize them and the arguments they put forth. Make them convince you that they are worthy of your investment dollars. Just as you do not accept at face value every advertising claim you read, do not turn off your critical faculties and follow blindly the advice given in any letter. Beating the market is never easy, and it requires all the insight and hard-nosed analysis you can muster.

The Hulbert Financial Digest
Annual Review of Investment Newsletters

I

Methodological Prologue

The performance figures published in this book are derived from calculations made by the *Hulbert Financial Digest* (HFD), the nationally recognized, pre-eminent newsletter-rating service. The figures reflect the gains and losses of hypothetical model portfolios which were set up in accordance with the advice contained in each newsletter. In so doing, the HFD endeavored to be as faithful as possible to what each newsletter was telling its subscribers to do. Because of ambiguities in the investment advice provided by some newsletters, however, it was often difficult to know for sure what each letter's advice really was. To deal with each case of ambiguity impartially, since the HFD has no stake in one letter or another doing well, the HFD set down in advance various rules and procedures that would be followed automatically in the event a newsletter was silent or vague about this or that aspect of constructing a model portfolio. This prologue discusses those rules and procedures. It is important for you to be aware of them, for only through that awareness can you hope to make the most use of this book.

The most important point for you to be aware of is that there is no one right way for a newsletter rater to deal with vague and ambiguous investment advice. One of the inevitable consequences of ambiguity is that different subscribers, each faithfully following such advice, may nevertheless invest their portfolios in quite different ways, with some making handsome profits and others losing money. To the extent one were to follow newsletters' performance under different rules and procedures for dealing with ambiguity, different results would be obtained than those published by the HFD.[1] This is not to say that we believe the methodology chosen by the HFD is unfair or unrevealing; on the contrary, as we discuss below, we think it is eminently fair. Our point is merely that because there is no one correct way to deal with ambiguities, you should not assume that the way the HFD resolves them is the only way that could be chosen by fair and reasonable people. As long as this is kept in mind, we believe the performance figures herein constitute significant information of use to investors in selecting an investment newsletter.

The HFD's Rules

What are the rules the HFD follows when dealing with ambiguous advice? Basically, the HFD constructs a portfolio for each newsletter that has the following characteristics, unless the newsletter advises specifically to the contrary:

1. is fully invested;
2. employs no margin;
3. gives equal weight to each position;
4. includes just those securities most highly recommended at any given time.

If a newsletter wants to have a certain percentage of its subscribers' portfolios out of the market and in cash, wants positions to be purchased on a certain margin, or wants unequal allocation of the portfolio between its various components, and so on, then the HFD requires the newsletter to specifically say so.

---

[1] A good example of how changed rules can lead to different results is provided by the figures calculated by the HFD for the years 1980–1982 assuming: (1) that commissions and dividends offset each other and that stocks recommended on telephone hotlines can be bought at the price prevailing when the hotline message is recorded; and (2) that a 2% round-trip commission cost is debited, dividends are credited, and telephone hotline recommendations are executed at the average of their high and low prices in trading during the day following the hotline. (These two methods correspond to how the HFD used to calculate its performance ratings [up to 1982] and how they have been since then; all the figures in this book, however, reflect the second approach.) For those services that had many transactions and utilized telephone hotlines the most—for which the difference in the rules would have the most relevance—the changes were substantial. The 1981 performance for the Zweig Forecast under the first approach was 37.8%, for example, while under the second it was 24%. For 1982 the difference was 80.1% vs. 24.6%. The difference for the 1981 performance of the Professional Tape Reader, furthermore, was between a gain of 6.9% and a loss of 6.7%. For 1982 it was 56.7% vs. 30%.

Implicit in this approach is that the HFD takes a "total" portfolio approach to rating newsletters. In other words, the best way to measure a newsletter's performance, it is assumed, is by trying to translate each of its recommendations into a portfolio—thus having to decide how much to keep in cash, what weight to give to each position, and so on. To put it another way, it is not enough to say "the average recommendation of newsletter ABC gained X%." Such a statement does not take into account the fact that a security's weight in a portfolio is a crucial factor in newsletter performance. How a stock behaves when there are only 10 stocks in the portfolio should have a different impact on a newsletter's track record than how it behaves when there are 100 stocks in the portfolio.

Also implicit in the rules listed above is that the hypothetical portfolios set up by the HFD undertake transactions that no one subscriber to a newsletter is likely to undertake. Take, for example, a service which recommends that you purchase a new stock without also recommending that you sell a currently held position. Where are you to get the money to buy the new stock? Each subscriber to this service will no doubt deal with this question differently, some selling out this or that security, some selling out partial positions in several securities, and some deploying new amounts of cash not previously invested according to the advice of the newsletter. New subscribers whose first issue of the newsletter is the one that contains the "buy" recommendation for the new security will not have this problem. They will simply buy all recommended securities in more or less equal portions. How can the HFD best reflect the diverse experiences of these different subscribers? By assuming that, as a new stock is recommended, its weight in the portfolio is made equal to all others also in the portfolio. This means that, when a new stock is recommended, the HFD rebalances the portfolio so that thereafter no position carries greater weight than another. In other words, if a stock has gained enough in value to have greater-than-equal weight, a portion of it is sold to bring it back into line with the others. And if a stock has declined in value so that it has less-than-equal weight, more shares are purchased to bring it back to the same weight as others. While these many rebalancing transactions are unlikely to be undertaken by any single investor, they are necessary to make the portfolio representative of a diverse group of subscribers.

Buys vs. Holds

Another consequence of the attempt to be representative of a broad group of subscribers is the rule that only those stocks most highly recommended will be included in the portfolio the HFD constructs.

In other words, if 50 stocks are rated "good" and 25 are rated "best bets," the portfolio will include just the 25 best. This rule is made necessary in large part because of the nebulous category of "hold." How long should the HFD carry a "hold"-rated stock in a portfolio that is supposed to be representative of a wide variety of subscribers— three months, six months, one year, or longer? Take for example a letter that, on January 1, 1980, recommends IBM and rates it a "buy." Assume further that it downgrades IBM to a "hold" on February 1, 1980, and continues to carry it as a hold in every issue up to the present. How many subscribers to that letter would have this stock in their portfolios today? If they faithfully follow the advice in the letter, only those who were subscribers during that one-month period during early 1980 would. For all other subscribers, the performance of IBM is irrelevant.

This tension between "buy" and "hold" is made even worse because sell recommendations are far rarer than buy recommendations. The worst that most analysts can manage to say about a stock is that it should be "held." *The Wall Street Journal*, in a recent article on the subject (May 29, 1984, p. 33), wrote, "Wall Street seems to have a built-in bias to be positive." One money manager was quoted as saying that, out of 200 newsletters analyzing a given stock, "175 of them would be 'buy' reports." This was particularly evident in analyses of Continental Illinois before its liquidity problems became apparent in May 1984. One analyst was quoted as saying that, despite being quite negative on the bank for some time, he continued to rate the stock a "weak hold." How representative would the HFD figures have been for such newsletters' subscribers had the model portfolios included Continental Illinois during the years it was rated "hold"?

This discussion leads to an important insight into the tracking of newsletters. Model portfolios set up to track a service's performance must of necessity be hypothetical in order to be representative. Because of this, you should recognize that your particular performance in following a given letter may vary from that reported here. This, again, is the inevitable consequence of the ambiguous advice in some newsletters.

There is only one type of letter for which there will be no discrepancy between the performance of each individual subscriber and that reported by newsletter raters such as the HFD. Such a service is one that contains absolutely no ambiguity in its advice; it tells you where to get the proceeds to purchase new positions, where to put proceeds of sold positions, how much weight should be placed in each position, how much—if any— should be kept in cash or money market funds, etc. In short, the clearest newsletter is one whose model is an actual portfolio.

The HFD's Clarity Ratings

The HFD rates each one of the newsletters it monitors on the basis of the clarity and completeness of its advice, and those ratings are reproduced below. They give you an indication of the extent to which the HFD had to resort to its methodology in resolving the ambiguities contained in the letter. An "A" rating is for the clearest letters, and these had relatively little or no ambiguity in their advice. Those rated "D"—the lowest rating—had more ambiguity, and the ratings to that extent are more tentative for such letters. (In looking over the list, you should realize that in rating clarity, there is no completely objective way to determine that one newsletter is clearer than another. Because of this subjective component to rating clarity, you should be aware that they are based in part on the opinions of the authors).

Newsletters Rated "A" For Clarity

(These newsletters offer their advice in the form of actual model portfolios, specifically and completely covering all aspects of translating their advice into an actual portfolio.)

Cabot Market Letter
California Technology Stock Letter
Charted Course
Chartist's Actual Cash Account
Dines Letter (all portfolios)
Green's Commodity Market Comments
Growth Stock Outlook
Harry Browne's Special Reports
Heim Investment Letter
High Technology Investments
Kinsman's Low-Risk Advisory
Option Advisor*
Peter Dag Investment Letter
Professional Tape Reader*
Prudent Speculator
Successful Options Investing*
Switch Fund Advisory
Zweig Forecast

Newsletters Rated "B" For Clarity

(These newsletters offer advice on how to allocate a model portfolio between cash and the market but not advice on what to buy or sell in order to bring a portfolio into line with that allocation.)

Dessauer's Journal
Holt Investment Advisory
Howard Ruff's Financial Success Report*
Indicator Digest*
International Harry Schultz Letter*
Market Logic
Systems & Forecasts

Newsletters Rated "C" For Clarity

(These newsletters offer no specific percentage allocation advice on the proper division of a model portfolio between cash and the market but instead recommend a list of favored investments.)

Addison Report†
Chartist's Portfolio of Stocks for Traders
Dow Theory Forecasts
Granville Market Letter
Growth Fund Guide
New Issue Investor
New Issues
Nicholson Report
Outlook
Professional Investor
Professional Timing Service
RHM Survey of Warrants, Options, & Low-Priced Stocks
Speculator's Selected Stocks of the Week
Telephone Switch Newsletter
Tony Henfrey's Gold Letter's Long-Term Gold Share Portfolio
United Business & Investment Reports
Value Line Investment Survey
Value Line OTC Special Situations Survey
Zweig Performance Ratings Report

Newsletters Rated "D" For Clarity

(These newsletters only occasionally recommend specific percentage allocations for the division of a model portfolio between cash and

---

* Denotes newsletters which at some point during period monitored by HFD were rated lower in clarity than current rating.

† The *Addison Report* does provide allocation advice about the proper division of a portfolio between cash and equities, but it does not apply that advice to the two portfolios the HFD monitors. See the write-up about the *Addison Report* later in this book.

the market and sometimes recommend only categories of investments rather than specific securities.)

Dow Theory Letters

Other Rules

In addition to the above rules—which deal with ambiguous advice—there are some which the HFD follows for all letters. For example, the HFD buys and sells recommended securities at their closing prices on the day the issue making the recommendation is received by the HFD in the mail. If the recommendation is made on a telephone hotline, then the trade is executed at the average of the security's high and low prices in the day's trading following the hotline. These rules should insure that the figures we publish are based on prices you could have obtained.

In addition, the HFD debits a 1% commission on all purchases and sales (2% round-trip) of stocks and bonds, and 0.05% round-trip for commodity futures. Dividends are credited on the day the underlying security goes ex-dividend. Taxes are not included in the calculations.

II

Answers to the Questions Most Frequently Asked About Newsletters

We feel that the best way to begin to guide a diverse readership through the book's charts and graphs is to start with a series of questions about newsletters, pointing out which sections of the book are essential for all readers and which can be skipped by those already familiar with the subject being discussed.

I'm happy with my present full-service broker; Why should I look to a newsletter for my investment advice?

If your broker is giving you enough profitable advice to justify paying full-service brokerage rates, then by all means stay with him. We suspect, however, that in many cases when you analyze how much you are actually paying for his advice your enthusiasm may wane. But even if your enthusiasm remains undiminished, you should still take a look at newsletters because they may provide you with better advice for your investment advisory dollars.

To get an idea of how much you are paying for investment advice with your current broker, you should first add up all the full-service commissions you paid over the last year. The amount you paid for the advice of your broker last year is about 70% of this figure! This is the average amount you could save by using a discount broker over the typical full-service broker (according to Mark Coler and Ellis Ratner, in their book *70% Off*; see Appendix D for a discussion of their book and the use of discount brokers in general).

How many newsletters could you subscribe to for this "premium" you paid to get the advice of your broker? The average subscription price of an investment newsletter is about $150 per year—less than the annual amount of commission premiums paid by many investors to a full-service broker. In addition, subscription fees paid for investment newsletters usually are tax deductible, which means that their real cost to you is less than their full subscription rate.

In appendix C at the end of this book, you will find the subscription rates to the major investment advisory newsletters. As you will see, most have very inexpensive trial offers.

I'm too busy to manage my own investments. I much prefer to let my broker handle my account.

If you really are too busy to do it yourself, then some of the more active trading newsletters may not be for you. But you can still tell your broker what investment strategy to pursue; for example, you could subscribe to a newsletter and have it mailed to him and instruct him to follow its advice.

In any case, not all newsletters require the same amount of attention in order to follow their advice. The newsletter the HFD calculated to be the top performer during 1983, for example, sold only one stock from its portfolio during the year; reading (in this case) the once-every-three-weeks newsletter and calling a discount broker when it made a change in its portfolio would have required less than an hour each month. Are you really so busy that one hour per month is worth the amount you pay your full-service broker?

In Section IV we divide up the newsletters monitored by the HFD according to how much time we think it would take you to follow their advice. We think you will be surprised at how little time it takes for some of the better-performing letters.

Which is the best investment newsletter?

This crucial question is not nearly as simple as it appears. To begin with, we feel that the question itself is poorly formulated. You might just as well ask, "Who is the best lawyer in the U.S.?" or "Who is the best physician?" Far more worthwhile is the question, "Which adviser is the best for what I want to achieve?"

Because different subscribers are striving for different goals through their investing, there is no one single best investment adviser. An excellent option newsletter, for example, is of little use to someone seeking primarily to preserve capital. Advisory newsletters specialize in various segments of the investment markets, and rarely will you find that the adviser who is best at calling turns in one area is also the best in another.

The question of which is the best investment adviser would be appropriate in the event that you had to choose just one of the many investment newsletters available. But, happily, that is not the case. In fact, most newsletters have relatively inexpensive trial offers enabling you to become exposed to a wide number of investment approaches with very little effort and at reasonable cost. Appendix C gives you a complete list of leading newsletters, their addresses, whether trial subscriptions are available, and at what cost.

What will this book do for me?

This book will help you formulate the most useful criteria to choose an investment strategy and help you choose the newsletters that best fulfill those criteria. Obviously, while proven performance is the single most important factor to consider when selecting an investment adviser, other considerations must be taken into account. For example, how important are tax considerations to you? After-tax investment results are what count; a newsletter that makes 40% per year in short-term trading may not in fact prove to be a better choice than one that generates 30% per year in long-term capital gains. Are you in a high tax bracket where getting long-term (as opposed to short-term) capital gains treatment is essential, or are tax considerations relatively less important (investing for an IRA or KEOGH plan, for example, or having offsetting short-term capital losses, etc.)? In Section IV, we discuss various tax considerations of which you should be aware and we will rank the major newsletters according to the average holding period of positions they have closed out over the past year and the percentage of those close-outs which were long-term.

What is your risk threshold? How much of a gambler are you? Do you roll the dice and participate in the office football pool, or are you risk-averse, unable to sleep nights when an investment moves only a few points against you? Is your worst nightmare receiving a margin call, or are you willing to risk a lot in some of your investments in the hopes of catching a really big winner? No amount of information about performance can decide for you what amount of risk you are willing to incur. That is something you must decide for yourself—taking into account your age, financial status, family situation, sense of security, etc. Only after answering these questions can you pick a newsletter intelligently; even a well-performing newsletter may be inappropriate for you if it exceeds your risk threshold. Section III discusses a prudent approach to take towards risk and ranks the newsletters according to their relative riskiness/volatility.

Another consideration is the clarity of the advice given. Some newsletter writers (as well as some other purveyors of financial advice, for that matter) are notorious for their ambiguous statements, talking out of both sides of their mouths at once. Some letters, for example, will discuss in each issue both the bullish and bearish cases for the stock market—and in the next issue quote only that portion making them look clairvoyant. Others will not consistently follow up each of the stocks mentioned in earlier issues, instead mentioning just those which have performed the best in the interim.

The HFD specifically rates the clarity and completeness of the advice contained in each newsletter. For a complete listing of each newsletter's rating, you should turn to the end of the methodological prologue that appears earlier in this book. In addition, the write-up about each of the newsletters that appears later in this book includes a discussion of how clear and complete its advice is.

I'm interested only in market timing for my mutual fund switch program, not stock selection. Which newsletters are best for me?

Some newsletters are geared specifically to mutual fund investors, making no specific stock selections at all and concentrating only on timing. But you should not rule out other letters just because they include advice on individual securities; some of the best market timers around also focus on stocks. In Section V, we rank all the newsletters on the basis of their market timing alone. This should help you choose which adviser to follow for your fund switching.

The ranking in that section can also help you pick and choose from the best features of several letters. As you will see, some of the newsletters are much better at market timing than they are at selecting stocks, and vice versa. You could thus devise a particularly profitable strategy using the market timing of one letter with the stock prices of another.

I once compared the HFD ratings with mutual fund performance and found—at least then—that there were more high-performing funds than newsletters. Why shouldn't I just invest in mutual funds?

You would still have to decide which mutual funds to invest in, when to invest in them, and when to have your money in other market funds or other cash equivalents, such as T-Bills. There are many newsletters that you would find beneficial in making those decisions—not just the few letters which concentrate exclusively upon mutual funds.

In any case, comparisons between newsletters and mutual funds can be misleading. Funds are often part of "families" of funds—for example, the Fidelity funds or the T. Rowe Price funds—and a fairer comparison for newsletters would be with the average of all funds within a family. The same is true for comparisons between newsletters, some of which have numerous recommended portfolios. The fairest basis for such comparison is the average performance of their portfolios. Otherwise, newsletters could always be on top by offering numerous different portfolios, one of which always would do well no matter what the market. A family of mutual funds can also be thought of as having "many shots" at being the best, and just as with newsletters, the fairest basis of comparison is the average of all funds within a family.

Having said this, however, many, if not most, newsletter subscribers would do well to invest in one mutual fund or another. Unless you have substantial amounts to invest in individual stocks, it is very difficult to achieve adequate portfolio diversification on your own. Through purchases of shares in mutual funds, however, you can achieve that diversification for as little as the minimum purchase amount set by the fund.

Another advantage of some mutual funds is that they are "no-load" meaning that no salesperson charges a commission for selling you shares in the fund. You can trade in and out of no-load funds as often as you want without incurring any commission costs at all—a significant advantage over buying and selling stocks. But be careful; recently a number of so-called "no-load" funds have started to charge redemption fees and similar charges. Be sure to read each fund's prospectus very carefully before investing in it.

I've read a lot recently about so-called "dart funds"—portfolios whose stocks were picked at random, by the throw of a dart against the page of stocks in the newspaper. Some people claim that these funds stand just as much chance of success as newsletters do.

If you really believe this to be the case, then you have bought the wrong book. The premise behind this book is that you can increase your odds of success dramatically by taking an objective, intelligent approach to the markets and to a major source of independent market advice in this country—the newsletters. Some newsletters have excellent records at beating the odds in the market, and we believe that you stand a better chance of profit by following them than by following those whose record is poorer. (The efficient market hypothesis is discussed at greater length in our preface.)

Ask yourself this question: if you had to choose between two newsletters, one with a consistent record of underperforming the market and one with an equally consistent record of superior performance, which would you choose?

Choosing a Newsletter:
The place of newsletters in your overall financial planning

Investment newsletters are designed to do, and people subscribe to them for, dramatically different things. Some newsletters are designed for only the most speculative of accounts and carry a substantial risk that everything could be lost. Only that portion of investable funds which you can afford to lose, therefore, should be invested in the recommendations of such a letter. Other newsletters, however, take a very low-risk approach.

The situation of an investor choosing between such diverse newsletters is much like that of someone who, after walking in on the middle of a poker game, is asked to bet on which of the present players will win. In such a case, would you automatically bet on the player with the largest pile of chips in front of him? Not necessarily. You would ask certain questions about the playing habits of the players; for example, how did the current leader win his chips? Did he win them with one "lucky" bet that overcame round after round of losing bets, or did he rack up his gains with a series of more consistent, though less spectacular, gains? The answers to these questions are crucial to predicting which player will ultimately have the most chips.

Unless you like losing sleep at night, the same considerations are relevant to choosing an investment newsletter. Yet, curiously enough, when it comes to choosing an investment strategy, many people lose their well-founded instincts that protect them so well in gambling situations. Instead of asking which adviser has the most consistent record, too many investors want to know which one has made the most money, period. Too few of them realize that winning the Irish Sweepstakes would provide them with larger winnings than virtually any found in the stock market, but that does not mean you should invest your company's pension fund in the Irish Sweepstakes.

Risk vs. Return

Consistency and risk are two sides of the same coin, and an understanding of the relationship between risk and return shows why consistency is a virtue. Of two portfolios that have performed similarly over a period of time, the one that did so with the least risk (most consistency) would be the better bet for future performance. Conversely, of two portfolios with the same degree of risk (equal consistency), the one with the greater performance would be the better bet for future performance. To choose otherwise would mean you were needlessly sacrificing security and/or performance for, literally, nothing in return.

Statisticians have come up with a number of good measures of risk and consistency that allow us to use the insight gained from the poker example. One measure is known as the standard deviation[1], and Table I lists the newsletters monitored by the HFD according to the standard deviations (risk) of their monthly performance since January 1983. (January 1983 was used as the starting point because the HFD began following many letters at that date. For those letters that were followed for a longer period of time, there are additional tables comparing their volatility and risk later in this section.) Those listed at the top of the list—the ones with the highest volatility—were the most risky and the ones at the bottom were the least risky.

At the bottom of the list, for example, is the "T-Bill Portfolio," showing how much risk would have been associated with investing entirely in Treasury bills. The very low standard deviation shows that very little risk was associated with such a strategy. In fact, it is so close to zero that a portfolio consisting entirely of T-Bills is often referred to as a "riskless" portfolio. At the top of the list, in contrast,

---

[1] The standard deviation measures volatility. If a portfolio gained 1% each and every month, for example, its performance would have no volatility at all. Its standard deviation therefore would be 0.0. This is to be contrasted with another portfolio that gains 20% or 30% each month, only to lose about as much the next. Its standard deviation would be in the 20%–30% range.

Choosing a Newsletter: The place of newsletters in your overall financial planning

TABLE I. Newsletters Ranked According to Their Risk

(From highest risk to lowest)
(On basis of performance from 1/1/83 to 3/31/84)

Newsletter	Standard Deviation
1. Option Advisor (Aggressive Portfolio)	35.909
2. Option Advisor (Conservative Portfolio)	28.895
3. Dines Letter List #6 (Trading Portfolio)	27.493
4. Dines Letter List #2 (Speculative Portfolio)	22.174
5. Successful Options Investing (Hedged Portfolio)	20.976
6. Tony Henfrey's Gold Letter (Long-term Gold Share Portfolio)	11.476
7. Holt Investment Advisory	10.826
8. Dines Letter List #4 (Growth Portfolio)	10.521
9. Dines Letter List #5 (Precious Metals Portfolio)	10.515
10. Howard Ruff's Financial Success Report	10.049
11. RHM Survey of Warrants, Options & Low-Priced Stocks	9.700
12. New Issues	9.067
13. Value Line OTC Special Situations Service	8.735
14. New Issue Investor	8.589
15. Prudent Speculator	8.552
16. Speculator (Selected Stocks of the Week)	8.255
17. Cabot Market Letter (Model Portfolio)	7.527
18. Chartist (Stocks for Traders)	7.123
19. Telephone Switch Newsletter (Gold/Equity/Cash Switch Plan)	6.786
20. Dines Letter List #1 (Moderate Risk Portfolio)	6.634
21. California Technology Stock Letter (Model Portfolio)	6.521
22. Professional Investor (Investment Grade)	6.335
23. International Harry Schultz Letter (U.S. Stocks Portfolio)	6.327
24. Addison Report (Speculative Stocks)	6.309
25. Professional Timing Service	6.254
26. Green's Commodity Market Comments (Portfolio for Traders)	6.207
27. Value Line Investment Survey (Stocks rated "I" for timeliness)	5.952
28. Indicator Digest	5.935
29. Growth Fund Guide (Aggressive Growth Funds)	5.683
30. Zweig Performance Ratings	5.662
31. Telephone Switch Newsletter (Equity/Cash Switch Plan)	5.479
32. United Business & Investment Reports (Cyclical Stocks)	5.341
33. Professional Investor (AMEX Scan)	5.097
34. Outlook (Speculative Stocks)	4.895

35. Chartist (Actual Cash Account)	4.583
36. Market Logic (Master Portfolio)	4.544
37. Outlook (Growth Stocks)	4.446
38. Outlook (Foundation Stocks)	4.434
39. Growth Fund Guide (Special Situations Funds)	4.370
40. Professional Investor (OTC Scan)	4.335
41. Granville Market Letter	4.306
42. Dow Theory Forecasts (Speculative Stocks)	4.187
43. Zweig Forecast	4.186
44. Outlook (Income Stocks)	4.135
45. Growth Stock Outlook (Supervised Portfolio)	4.014
46. Dow Theory Forecasts (Growth Stocks)	3.949
47. High Technology Investments (Long-term Portfolio)	3.880
48. Growth Fund Guide (Growth Funds)	3.759
49. Dow Theory Forecasts (Investment Stocks)	3.538
50. Professional Investor (NYSE Scan)	3.415
51. Systems & Forecasts	3.388
52. Nicholson Report (Stocks for Traders)	3.306
53. Professional Tape Reader (Model Portfolio)	3.253
54. Dow Theory Letters	3.231
55. United Business & Investment Reports (Growth Stocks)	3.221
56. Charted Course (Model Portfolio)	3.174
57. Addison Report (Conservative Stocks)	3.113
58. Nicholson Report (Stocks for Investors)	2.965
59. Harry Browne's Special Reports (Variable Portfolio)	2.857
60. Standard & Poor's 500 (including dividends)	2.852
61. Dessauer's Journal (International Portfolio)	2.571
62. United Business & Investment Reports (Income Stocks)	2.488
63. Dow Theory Forecasts (Income Stocks)	2.374
64. High Technology Investments ("Trigger Price Advisory" trading portfolio)	2.333
65. Growth Fund Guide (Quality Growth Funds)	2.268
66. Dines Letter List #3 (Income Portfolio)	2.199
67. Switch Fund Advisory (Model Portfolio)	2.168
68. Heim Investment Letter	1.385
69. Kinsman's Low-Risk Advisory Letter	1.286
70. Peter Dag Investment Letter (Model Portfolio)	0.994
71. T-Bill Portfolio	0.045

are several portfolios made up of options, and their very high standard deviations are indicative of the riskiness of investing in options.

The first should be first and the last should be last

In Table II, we have listed the portfolios in the same order as they were in Table I, but instead of their standard deviation we show what their place in the list would be if they were to be ranked on the basis of their performance. What these rankings allow you to discover is whether those newsletters with riskier strategies earned sufficiently more to justify incurring that risk. If all newsletters were to have done so, then their ranking in the performance column of Table II would be the same as their ranking on a risk basis. In other words, assuming all newsletters were equally good at exploiting risk, the lowest risk portfolio—#71 on the list, the T-Bill portfolio—would have earned the least of any of the portfolios and be ranked the lowest in the performance column. Similarly, if all newsletters were equally good bets, then the portfolio with the highest risk—#1 on the list, the Option Advisor's Aggressive Portfolio—would have been ranked the highest on a performance basis.

As you can see, however, there is no such correlation. The lowest risk portfolio is not the lowest performer; in fact, it is ranked #26 on a performance basis. In other words, for the 15-month period covered by this analysis, all newsletters ranked below #26 on a performance basis (second column of Table II) incurred greater risk than a Treasury bill portfolio but actually earned less money. Similarly, the highest-risk portfolio was not the highest-performing portfolio. Indeed, the two portfolios with the greatest risk (#1 and #2 on the table), far from having the greatest performance actually had the least performance (ranked #70 and #71).

Some of the riskier newsletters, however, did perform sufficiently better to justify their greater risk. The Dines Letter portfolios listed near the top of Table II, for example, are ranked near the top on a performance basis. This is exactly what you should look for when moving to a riskier strategy.

Table II also allows you to pick which newsletter did the best in each risk category. Take, for example, the lowest-risk newsletters—those in positions #61 to #71 on the table. Which newsletter performed the best within this low-risk category? The table shows that Switch Fund Advisory's model portfolio, Growth Fund Guide's quality growth funds portfolio, and Dow Theory Forecasts' income stocks portfolio were the best performers.

Or take a group of newsletters in the middle ranges of risk—say those from position #30 to #40 in Table II. Within this average-risk category, the best-performing portfolios were two recommended by the Professional Investor (its AMEX and OTC Scans) as well as Market Logic's master portfolio.

In similar fashion, you can define your own risk category by choosing a group of newsletters bunched together on Table II. Then, within that group, you can choose those ranked the highest on a performance basis. The newsletters thus identified would be those that performed the best for your chosen level of risk.

TABLE II. Newsletters Ranked According to Their Risk and Their Performance
(1/1/83 to 3/31/84)

Newsletter and Rank on Basis of Risk (from highest to lowest)	Rank on Basis of Performance
1. Option Advisor (Aggressive Portfolio)	70
2. Option Advisor (Conservative Portfolio)	71
3. Dines Letter List #6 (Trading Portfolio)	1
4. Dines Letter List #2 (Speculative Portfolio)	2
5. Successful Options Investing (Hedged Portfolio)	69
6. Tony Henfrey's Gold Letter (Long-term Gold Share Portfolio)	8
7. Holt Investment Advisory	56
8. Dines Letter List #4 (Growth Portfolio)	3
9. Dines Letter List #5 (Precious Metals Portfolio)	28
10. Howard Ruff's Financial Success Report	60
11. RHM Survey of Warrants, Options & Low-Priced Stocks	27
12. New Issues	54
13. Value Line OTC Special Situations Survey	45
14. New Issue Investor	59
15. Prudent Speculator	5
16. Speculator (Selected Stocks of the Week)	52
17. Cabot Market Letter (Model Portfolio)	61
18. Chartist (Stocks for Traders)	41
19. Telephone Switch Newsletter (Gold/Equity/Cash Switch Plan)	53
20. Dines Letter List #1 (Moderate Risk Portfolio)	6
21. California Technology Stock Letter (Model Portfolio)	62
22. Professional Investor (Investment Grade)	68
23. International Harry Schultz Letter (U.S. Stocks Portfolio)	37
24. Addison Report (Speculative Stocks)	4
25. Professional Timing Service	42
26. Green's Commodity Market Comments (Portfolio for Traders)	9
27. Value Line Investment Survey (Stocks rated "I" for timeliness)	18
28. Indicator Digest	46
29. Growth Fund Guide (Aggressive Growth Funds)	35
30. Zweig Performance Ratings	43
31. Telephone Switch Newsletter (Equity/Cash Switch Plan)	23
32. United Business & Investment Reports (Cyclical Stocks)	57
33. Professional Investor (AMEX Scan)	7
34. Outlook (Speculative Stocks)	31

Choosing a Newsletter: The place of newsletters in your overall financial planning

35.	Chartist (Actual Cash Account)	22
36.	Market Logic (Master Portfolio)	14
37.	Outlook (Growth Stocks)	47
38.	Outlook (Foundation Stocks)	44
39.	Growth Fund Guide (Special Situations Funds)	17
40.	Professional Investor (OTC Scan)	11
41.	Granville Market Letter	66
42.	Dow Theory Forecasts (Speculative Stocks)	48
43.	Zweig Forecast	50
44.	Outlook (Income Stocks)	25
45.	Growth Stock Outlook (Supervised Portfolio)	10
46.	Dow Theory Forecasts (Growth Stocks)	39
47.	High Technology Investments (Long-term Portfolio)	49
48.	Growth Fund Guide (Growth Funds)	21
49.	Dow Theory Forecasts (Investment Stocks)	29
50.	Professional Investor (NYSE Scan)	38
51.	Systems & Forecasts	51
52.	Nicholson Report (Stocks for Traders)	65
53.	Professional Tape Reader (Model Portfolio)	64
54.	Dow Theory Letters	58
55.	United Business & Investment Reports (Growth Stocks)	55
56.	Charted Course (Model Portfolio)	36
57.	Addison Report (Conservative Stocks)	12
58.	Nicholson Report (Stocks for Investors)	63
59.	Harry Browne's Special Reports (Variable Portfolio)	33
60.	Standard & Poor's 500 (including dividends)	15
61.	Dessauer's Journal (International Portfolio)	13
62.	United Business & Investment Reports (Income Stocks)	34
63.	Dow Theory Forecasts (Income Stocks)	20
64.	High Technology Investments ("Trigger Price Advisory" trading portfolio)	67
65.	Growth Fund Guide (Quality Growth Funds)	16
66.	Dines Letter List #3 (Income Portfolio)	24
67.	Switch Fund Advisory (Model Portfolio)	19
68.	Heim Investment Letter	40
69.	Kinsman's Low-Risk Advisory Letter	32
70.	Peter Dag Investment Letter (Model Portfolio)	30
71.	T-Bill Portfolio	26

The HFD has been following some newsletters for longer periods of time, of course, and comparisons of newsletters' riskiness gain more and more credence as the duration of the comparison increases. Tables III, IV, and V are constructed exactly as was Table II—ranking newsletters on the basis of their risk and showing what their rank would be on a performance basis. They differ from Table II only in that each covers a different period of time. (As the length of time increases, the number of portfolios compared reduces because fewer services were monitored by the HFD when it began in 1980.)

TABLE III. Newsletters Ranked According to Their Risk and Their Performance
(1/1/82 to 3/31/84)

Newsletter and Rank on Basis of Risk (from highest to lowest)	Rank on Basis of Performance
1. Dines Letter List #6 (Trading Portfolio)	1
2. Dines Letter List #2 (Speculative Portfolio)	4
3. Tony Henfrey's Gold Letter (Long-term Gold Share Portfolio)	2
4. Dines Letter List #5 (Precious Metals Portfolio)	38
5. Value Line OTC Special Situations Service	10
6. Howard Ruff's Financial Success Report	29
7. RHM Survey of Warrants, Options & Low-Priced Stocks	21
8. Dines Letter List #4 (Growth Portfolio)	3
9. Holt Investment Advisory	43
10. Speculator (Selected Stocks of the Week)	17
11. Cabot Market Letter (Model Portfolio)	33
12. United Business & Investment Reports (Cyclical Stocks)	35
13. Dines Letter List #1 (Moderate Risk Portfolio)	7
14. Green's Commodity Market Comments (Portfolio for traders)	5
15. Granville Market Letter	44
16. Professional Investor (Investment Grade)	42
17. Zweig Forecast	25
18. Professional Timing Service	39
19. International Harry Schultz Letter (U.S. Stocks Portfolio)	40
20. Chartist (Actual Cash Account)	9
21. Market Logic (Master Portfolio)	8
22. Dow Theory Forecasts (Growth Stocks)	30
23. Professional Investor (AMEX Scan)	6
24. Dow Theory Forecasts (Speculative Stocks)	31
25. Outlook (Speculative Stocks)	15
26. Professional Investor (OTC Scan)	12
27. Outlook (Growth Stocks)	32
28. Professional Investor (NYSE Scan)	18
29. United Business & Investment Reports (Growth Stocks)	37
30. Professional Tape Reader (Model Portfolio)	36
31. Dow Theory Forecasts (Investment Stocks)	16

32. Standard & Poor's 500 (including dividends)	13
33. Outlook (Foundation Stocks)	28
34. Growth Stock Outlook (Supervised Portfolio)	10
35. Outlook (Income Stocks)	24
36. Dessauer's Journal	14
37. United Business & Investment Reports (Income Stocks)	27
38. Dow Theory Forecasts (Income Stocks)	19
39. Heim Investment Letter	41
40. Dow Theory Letters	34
41. Harry Browne's Special Reports (Variable Portfolio)	23
42. Dines Letter List #3 (Income Portfolio)	20
43. Kinsman's Low-Risk Advisory Letter	22
44. T-Bill Portfolio	26

TABLE IV. Newsletters Ranked According to Their Risk and Their Performance
(1/1/81 to 3/31/84)

Newsletter and Rank on Basis of Risk (from highest to lowest)	Rank on Basis of Performance
1. Dines Letter List #6 (Trading Portfolio)	1
2. Dines Letter List #2 (Speculative Portfolio)	3
3. Dines Letter List #5 (Precious Metals Portfolio)	38
4. Value Line OTC Special Situations Service	22
5. RHM Survey of Warrants, Options & Low-Priced Stocks	37
6. Howard Ruff's Financial Success Report	24
7. Green's Commodity Market Comments (Portfolio for Traders)	4
8. Cabot Market Letter (Model Portfolio)	28
9. Speculator (Selected Stocks of the Week)	23
10. Holt Investment Advisory	34
11. Dines Letter List #4 (Growth Portfolio)	2
12. Dines Letter List #1 (Moderate Risk Portfolio)	11
13. United Business & Investment Reports (Cyclical Stocks)	33
14. Granville Market Letter	39
15. International Harry Schultz Letter (U.S. Stocks Portfolio)	36
16. Professional Investor (Investment Grade)	32
17. Professional Investor (AMEX Scan)	6
18. Dow Theory Forecasts (Growth Stocks)	21
19. Zweig Forecast	9
20. Dow Theory Forecasts (Speculative Stocks)	29
21. Outlook (Speculative Stocks)	12

22. Market Logic (Master Portfolio)	5
23. Professional Investor (OTC Scan)	10
24. United Business & Investment Reports (Growth Stocks)	35
25. Outlook (Growth Stocks)	17
26. Professional Investor (NYSE Scan)	19
2B. Dow Theory Forecasts (Investment Stocks)	16
28. Standard & Poor's 500 (including dividends)	15
29. Professional Tape Reader (Model Portfolio)	31
30. Dow Theory Forecasts (Income Stocks)	20
31. Outlook (Foundation Stocks)	18
32. Growth Stock Outlook (Supervised Portfolio)	7
33. Outlook (Income Stocks)	14
34. United Business & Investment Reports (Income Stocks)	26
35. Heim Investment Letter	30
36. Harry Browne's Special Reports (Variable Portfolio)	27
37. Dow Theory Letters	25
38. Dines Letter List #3 (Income Portfolio)	8
39. T-Bill Portfolio	13

TABLE V. Newsletters Ranked According to Their Risk and Their Performance
(6/30/80 to 3/31/84)

Newsletter and Rank on Basis of Risk (from highest to lowest)	Rank on Basis of Performance
1. Dines Letter List #6 (Trading Portfolio)	1
2. Dines Letter List #2 (Speculative Portfolio)	3
3. Dines Letter List #5 (Precious Metals Portfolio)	33
4. Value Line OTC Special Situations Service	8
5. Green's Commodity Market Comments (Portfolio for Traders)	4
6. Howard Ruff's Financial Success Report	28
7. Holt Investment Advisory	32
8. Dines Letter List #4 (Growth Portfolio)	2
9. Dines Letter List #1 (Moderate Risk Portfolio)	18
10. International Harry Schultz Letter (U.S. Stocks Portfolio)	27
11. United Business & Investment Reports (Cyclical Stocks)	26
12. Granville Market Letter	34
13. Professional Investor (Investment Grade)	30
14. Dow Theory Forecasts (Growth Stocks)	19
15. Professional Investor (AMEX Scan)	5
16. Dow Theory Forecasts (Speculative Stocks)	23

Choosing a Newsletter: The place of newsletters in your overall financial planning

17.	Zweig Forecast	9
18.	Outlook (Speculative Stocks)	11
19.	Professional Investor (OTC Scan)	10
20.	Market Logic (Master Portfolio)	7
21.	United Business & Investment Reports (Growth Stocks)	31
22.	Outlook (Growth Stocks)	16
23.	Professional Investor (NYSE Scan)	20
24.	Standard & Poor's 500 (including dividends)	12
25.	Dow Theory Forecasts (Income Stocks)	22
26.	Dow Theory Forecasts (Investment Stocks)	14
27.	Outlook (Foundation Stocks)	17
28.	Outlook (Income Stocks)	15
29.	Professional Tape Reader (Model Portfolio)	25
30.	Growth Stock Outlook (Supervised Portfolio)	6
31.	United Business & Investment Reports (Income Stocks)	24
32.	Heim Investment Letter	29
33.	Dines Letter List #3 (Income Portfolio)	13
34.	T-Bill Portfolio	21

As a cursory overview of Tables II through V reveals, the relative riskiness of the portfolios we monitor changes depending upon the period of the comparison. This is due to a number of reasons, but one is worth noting here. Newsletters change their strategies over time, recommending investment approaches with significantly greater or lesser risk than before. That in itself is no crime, but it makes it more difficult for you to discover which newsletter is best suited for your particular preferences about risk. The *Dines Letter*, for example, used to take a very long-term approach to investing; according to introductory material which as recently as 1983 was sent to new subscribers, their recommended portfolios "are geared to the 5–10 year pull." In mid-1983, however (see the write-up about the *Dines Letter* later in this book), it took a significantly more short-term approach, with some of its recommended portfolios focussing exclusively on options. The HFD found that some of the *Dines Letter* portfolios evolved over a year's time from being approximately as risky as the market as a whole to being more than ten times riskier. There is thus no one answer to the question, "Are the *Dines Letter* portfolios very risky or not?"

Risk-adjusted performance

To compare newsletters when some of them change their approaches so dramatically, it is helpful to examine them on a risk-adjusted basis. When performance figures are adjusted for risk[2], newsletters are being measured on the basis of how much they earned per unit of risk—regardless of how much risk they have incurred. So whether one newsletter is very risky and another is not, or whether a single newsletter changes its strategy over time, this measure allows you to see which newsletter made the most use of the risk it incurred.

Appendix B at the end of this book ranks the newsletters over four different time periods on a risk-adjusted basis. Examine it carefully in conjunction with the tables reproduced in this section. Newsletters may change dramatically over time in the riskiness of their approaches, but their ability to make money per unit of risk does not change nearly so much. It is this latter measure which you can be most confident about extrapolating from past to future performance.

---

[2] By "risk-adjusted performance" we mean "performance per unit of risk." Consider two portfolios, one of which incurred ten times as much risk as the other and earned ten times as much profit. Per unit of risk, these two portfolios would have performed equally. For the calculation of risk-adjusted performance, we used the standard deviation as the measure of risk. And because you can earn the Treasury bill rate while incurring no risk whatsoever, we credited the newsletters only for that performance they achieved above and beyond the T-Bill rate. The ratio of this premium above the T-Bill rate to the standard deviation shows the amount earned per unit of risk. As an example, assume that newsletter ABC earned an average of 11% each month with a risk measure of 2%, while newsletter XYZ earned an average of 21% each month with a risk measure of 10%. Assume also that you could have earned 1% each month in Treasury bills. The risk-adjusted performance figure for newsletter ABC would be 5% (11% less 1%, divided by 2%), while for newsletter XYZ it would be 2% (21% less 1%, divided by 10%). Looked at in this way, you can see that newsletter XYZ, even though it earned more money than newsletter ABC, did so with an inordinate level of risk—and is therefore not as good a bet for future performance.

IV

Choosing a Newsletter: Tax considerations

Taxes (along with death) may be one of the two certain things in life, but how much you pay in taxes and when you pay them are not certain at all. In the investment arena, for example, your choice of a newsletter can have a large, direct bearing on your eventual tax liability, and regardless of newsletter there are a few simple rules you can follow to keep your tax bill down and paid in years most advantageous to you.

In this section, we discuss some of the basics of tax planning and point out what can easily be done to reduce or defer taxes. It is written for those with little background in tax planning; those with such a background can turn directly to the second half of the section where each of the newsletters is ranked according to the percentage of their closed-out positions which would have qualified for long-term capital gains treatment. (The tables also show what the average holding periods for those close-out positions were.)

Holding period

The most significant factor as far as taxes on stock and bond[3] transactions are concerned is the holding period. If your gains come on positions held for longer than six months, the tax code as amended in mid-1984 allows you to deduct 60% of the gain before adding it to taxable income. If your gains come on positions held for less than six months, however, no such deduction is allowed. Therefore, short-term gains in a 50% tax bracket are taxed at 50% while long-term gains are taxed at 20%. (This 20% represents 50% of the 40% of the gain remaining after the 60% capital gains deduction.)[4] If by following newsletter "A" you could have made $1,000 profit on positions all held for less than six months, and if by following newsletter "B" you could have made $1,000 profit on positions all held for longer than six months, newsletter "B" would be a better after-tax performing newsletter than "A." After taxes, the subscriber in the 50% tax bracket to "A" would have $500 left, whereas the subscriber to "B" would have $800 left. In the 50% tax bracket, it takes 1.6 times as much short-term as long-term profit to give you the same after-tax return.

The situation with tax losses is the reverse of the situation with gains. While a long-term gain is clearly preferable to a short-term gain, a short-term loss is more advantageous than a long-term loss. This is because short-term losses can shelter more taxable income than can long-term losses. In fact, only half of long-term losses can be used to offset income, while 100% of short-term losses can be so used. In other words, it takes $2 of long-term losses to do the work of $1 of short-term losses.

If at the end of your taxable year you have a combination of both short- and long-term gains and losses, the tax code requires you to consolidate them before calculating your taxes. Depending upon whether you have greater gains than losses in the short- or long-term category, these tax rules can appear a bit complicated. But an understanding of them is an important part of keeping your tax bill low.

Short vs. Long; Gain vs. Loss

You must first group your gains and losses into short-term and long-term categories to determine whether you have a net loss or a net

---

[3] The tax treatment of commodity futures and some options is different from the tax treatment of stocks and bonds. The tax law requires you to automatically treat 60% of all gains or losses realized on futures contracts as long term and 40% short term, regardless of how long in fact you had held the positions when closed-out; the same holds for gains and losses on various options. (Which options qualify is too complicated to go into here, so you should consult a tax professional.) And if there are any of these commodity or option positions open at the end of the taxable year, the tax laws require you to value them at the market, treating 60% as long term and 40% as short term, regardless of how long in fact you have held each position. Because of these provisions applying to commodities and options, the discussion that follows only applies to stocks and bonds.

[4] The amount of the capital gains deduction is known as a "preference item" for the calculation of the alternative minimum tax, so depending upon your tax situation, the maximum tax on long-term gains may be higher than 20% . Consult a tax professional for details.

gain in each category. You must then use whichever of the following rules applies to your situation:

1. If you have a net long-term gain, you must subtract any net short-term loss. If there is long-term gain remaining after netting against short-term loss, you can deduct 60% of it before adding it to your taxable income.
2. If you have a net long-term loss, you must subtract any net short-term gain. Any remaining long-term loss is reduced by one-half and then used to reduce taxable income.
3. If you have a net short-term loss, it is first applied against net long-term gain (per #1 above). If there is short-term loss remaining, it is used to reduce taxable income.[5]
4. If you have a net short-term gain, it is first applied against net long-term losses (per #2). If there is any short-term gain remaining, it is added to taxable income.

Rules of Thumb

Because of the different tax treatment of long- and short-term gains and losses, and because of the rules about how they must be consolidated on your tax return, there are several rules of thumb that you should keep in mind when planning your investments. First, you should let short-term gains mature into long-term gains whenever possible. Unless you envision your security dropping dramatically in price during the period remaining before it matures to long term, it may very well be more sensible for you to wait rather than sell now. A decision in your particular case depends upon your tax bracket and whether you have realized any other gains or losses that year.

Second, it is better to take short-term losses than long-term losses. Unless you believe that the security currently held at a loss holds promise to become profitable within six months, it is probably more sensible for you to take the loss now rather than wait. Again, a decision in each particular case depends upon your tax bracket and other gains or losses you may have realized that year.

Third, you should avoid taking substantial long-term capital gains in the same year that you have substantial short-term losses. If you were to take them in the same year, you would be using the short-term losses to shelter income that was already in large part sheltered. It is far more efficient to use short-term losses to reduce short-term gains or other fully taxable income.

---

[5]You only can use $3,000 of net short-term losses to offset other income in one year. But you can carry those losses forward to other taxable years indefinitely.

Finally, you should avoid taking long-term gains in years when you have substantial short-term gains and long-term losses. When you have long-term losses, they are most advantageously used to offset short-term gains, but first those long-term losses must be used to offset long-term gains (see #2 above). So if you are planning to use long-term losses to offset short-term gains, you should either avoid taking long-term gains or defer those gains to a future year. (See the discussion below about how to defer gains.)

The accompanying chart is a good summary of these and other tax-planning rules. It was prepared by Deloitte, Haskins & Sells as part of their *1983 Personal Tax & Financial Planning Guide*, and we gratefully acknowledge their work and thank them for the right to reproduce it here. (Though the table refers to tax planning for 1983, it has equal applicability to 1984.)

Tax deferral[6]

Generally, tax and investment experts seem to agree that, in most cases, economic and investment factors should take precedence over tax matters. "Don't let Uncle Sam manage your portfolio," many of them will say. But there are some simple methods by which you can follow the rules of thumb outlined above without violating the economic and investment factors behind your investment strategy. Most of these methods revolve around ways in which you can defer the realization of gains and losses from one year to the next.

A common technique for locking in the profit you have in a position without taking the gain in the current taxable year is known as "shorting against the box." What you can do is sell short an equivalent number of shares of the stock whose gain you want to freeze. Thereafter, every loss in your original position will be offset dollar for dollar by gains in your short sale, and vice versa. But because you have not sold your original shares, the gain is unrealized. You can preserve this hedge until it is more advantageous for you to pay tax on it. If, for example, in the current taxable year you want to use your long- term losses to offset short-term gains, you do not want to realize any long-term gains. (See the discussion above.) If you are following a newsletter that recommends the sale of a position which

---

[6] As this book goes to print, the impact of the 1984 tax bill is still being debated by tax professionals. While every effort was made to ensure that the tax deferral strategies discussed here are consistent with the new bill, you should consult a tax professional before assuming that a given strategy is consistent with the tax code or with treasury regulations that may be issued in the interim.

Choosing a Newsletter: Tax considerations

Planning Year-End Securities Transactions

Results to Date	Unrealized Portfolio Gains and Losses	Possible Action To Be Taken Before Year-End
Short-term gain only	Losses and gains	Cover short-term gain by first taking long-term losses, then short-term losses. Take additional losses to offset ordinary income. See Notes 1, 2, and 3.
Short-term gain only	Gains only	Taxwise, nothing need be done.
Short-term loss	Gains only	Generally, no advantage to realizing additional gains. See Note 3.
Long-term gain	Losses and gains	Cover long-term gain by taking long-term losses then short-term losses, if applicable. Take additional losses to offset ordinary income. See Notes 2 and 3.
Long-term gain	Gains only	Taxwise, nothing need be done.
Long-term loss	Gains only	Opportunity exists to realize short-term gain at minimum tax cost—see Note 1. Any remaining long-term loss will offset ordinary income—see Note 3. Remainder will carry forward.
Long-term loss	Losses only	Nothing need be done—see Notes 2 and 3. Consider taking short-term loss to offset ordinary income and carrying over full long-term loss to offset future short-term gains.
None	Losses and gains	Generally, no advantage to realizing gains. Consider taking short-term loss to offset ordinary income. See Notes 2 and 3.

Notes:

1. Long-term losses are used most advantageously against short-term gains, but must first be used against long-term gains, if any. If long-term gains are also contemplated, it may be advantageous to defer the long-term gains to 1984 by delaying the sale or by selling short against the box (page 9).

2. It may be advantageous to take additional losses. Many investors build a "loss-carryover bank"—especially for short-term losses. This loss bank provides them with a means of realizing tax-free cash in the future. Gains realized on a future sale can be offset by losses in the bank.

3. You may use $3,000 of short-term loss, or $6,000 of long-term loss, to offset $3,000 of ordinary income.

Also: Fifty percent of net long-term losses may still be used to offset up to $3,000 of ordinary income each year even though only 40% of long-term gains are taxed. Therefore, tax savings result (a maximum of $300 for 1983 for top-bracket individuals) by recognizing up to $6,000 of net long-term losses in 1983 and net long-term gains in 1984, rather than offsetting them in the same year.

Reprinted with permission from *1983 Personal Tax & Financial Planning Guide*, prepared by Deloitte, Haskins & Sells.

would result in long-term gains, your best course of action might be to "short against the box" in this stock rather than sell your shares.

You also can use call and put options to lock in your gain on a position. For example, on the date when you otherwise would have sold a stock, you could purchase a put option on that stock. (A put option is the right to sell stock at a certain price for a specified length of time.) Assuming you purchase a put option whose strike price is the price at which the stock is currently trading, you will have locked in your profit. If your stock declines in price between when you originally wanted to sell it and the next taxable year, you merely exercise the option and sell it at that original price. (An options strategy that has similar effects as purchasing a put is selling a call option on the stock you would otherwise sell. This is known as "covered call writing.")

Consider, for example, that in December of a given year you want to sell your 100 shares of IBM at $120/share, but you do not want to realize the gain on those 100 shares until the next year. You could purchase a January 120 put on IBM, which gives you the right to sell IBM at $120 per share at any time up until the third Friday in January. If IBM declines between December and the third Friday in January, you can exercise your put and sell the stock at $120/share—the only difference being that the gain is realized in the next taxable year.

One thing that such tax-deferral strategies will not do, however, is convert a short-term into a long-term gain. The tax law holds that if the holding period on your stock is short-term at the point when you enter into one of these tax deferral strategies, then any gain or loss on the position will always be treated as short-term—no matter for how long you defer the payment of tax. This is because, in the words of the tax law, in locking in your profit you have in effect sold a stock that is "substantially identical" to that you already own. If you want to avoid this consequence of these deferral strategies—and attempt to convert a short- to a long-term gain—the stock on which you enter into an options strategy or with which you "short against the box" must be different from the stock you already own (such that they are not "substantially identical"). If you must continue to own Exxon for two more months in order to have your profit on the position considered long term, but you want to lock in your profit in the interim, you could for example sell short an equal dollar amount of Mobil's stock (or any other stock of a company whose stock's behavior you suspect will closely mirror that of Exxon's). While such strategies have the potential to convert all short-term to long-term gains, they are also risky in that the stock you choose to lock in your profit may behave differently than the stock you already own.

Choosing a Newsletter: Tax considerations

Average Holding Period of Positions Closed Out by Newsletters

In addition to reducing and deferring your taxes by the above methods, you can also maximize your after-tax performance by choosing an investment newsletter with tax considerations in mind. Does the newsletter concentrate on short-term trading, for example, with most or all of its gains taxed at the higher rate? Or does the newsletter concentrate more on a long-term strategy, with its gains taxed at the lower capital gains rate? In Tables VI and VII we list for each newsletter the percentage of its closed-out positions which were long term (more than six months), the average holding period for positions closed out, and the number of positions closed out. Table VI is for 1983 and Table VII is for 1982 (Table VI covers more newsletters than Table VII because the HFD added a number of newsletters in 1983 to the lists of those it monitors.) Both tables look only at stock and bond positions, because, as discussed above, 60% of all gains and losses on commodity and some options transactions are automatically treated as long term, with 40% short term, regardless of how long you actually held the positions.

TABLE VI. Portfolios Ranked According to Percentage of 1983 Stock and Bond Closeouts Which Were Long Term (Greater Than Six Months)

Newsletter	% of Closeouts Long Term	Average Holding Period (days)	Total Number of Closeouts
1. California Technology Stock Letter (Model Portfolio)	100%	> 6 mos.	10
2. Dessauer's Journal	100%	> 6 mos.	4
3. Dow Theory Forecasts (Income, Investment & Growth Stocks)	100%	> 6 mos.	3
4. Growth Fund Guide (Aggressive Growth Funds, Growth Funds, and Quality Growth Funds Portfolios)	100%	> 6 mos.	3
5. Market Logic (Master Portfolio)	100%	> 6 mos.	1
6. New Issue Investor	100%	> 6 mos.	5
7. Outlook (Foundation, Growth, and Speculative Stocks)	100%	> 6 mos.	3
8. Prudent Speculator	100%	> 6 mos.	1
9. Switch Fund Advisory (Model Portfolio)	100%	> 6 mos.	5
10. Tony Henfrey's Gold Letter (Long-term Gold Share Portfolio)	100%	> 6 mos.	14

11.	United Business & Investment Reports (Growth and Cyclical Stocks)	100%	> 6 mos.	26
12.	RHM Survey of Warrants, Options & Low-Priced Stocks	93.8%	> 6 mos.	16
13.	Speculator (Selected Stocks of the Week)	93.3%	> 6 mos.	15
14.	Chartist (Actual Cash Account)	81.8%	> 6 mos.	6
15.	New Issues	80.0%	> 6 mos.	5
16.	Holt Investment Advisory	76.7%	> 6 mos.	30
17.	High Technology Investments (Long-term Portfolio)	75.0%	> 6 mos.	4
18.	Growth Stock Outlook (Supervised Portfolio)	74.1%	> 6 mos.	14
19.	Dines Letter List #2 (Speculative Portfolio)	72.7%	> 6 mos.	11
20.	Peter Dag Investment Letter (Model Portfolio)	71.7%	> 6 mos.	2
21.	Growth Fund Guide (Special Situations Funds Portfolio)	66.7%	> 6 mos.	3
22.	Howard Ruff's Financial Success Report	66.6%	> 6 mos.	6
23.	Value Line OTC Special Situations Survey	66.7%	> 6 mos.	6
24.	Chartist (Stocks for Traders)	66.0%	> 6 mos.	50
25.	Dines Letter List #1 (Moderate Risk Portfolio)	61.5%	> 6 mos.	13
26.	Charted Course (Model Portfolio)	59.2%	> 6 mos.	79
27.	Nicholson Report (Stocks for Investors)	57.1%	> 6 mos.	28
28.	Dines Letter List #4 (Growth Portfolio)	53.8%	> 6 mos.	13
29.	Professional Investor (OTC Scan)	53.6%	> 6 mos.	28
30.	Dines Letter List #3 (Income Portfolio)	50.0%	> 6 mos.	14
31.	Dines Letter List #6 (Short-term Portfolio)	50.0%	178	12
32.	Telephone Switch Letter (Gold/Equities/Cash Switch Plan)	50.0%	141	8
33.	Addison Report (Conservative Stocks)	46.7%	> 6 mos.	15
34.	Professional Investor (AMEX Scan)	42.3%	> 6 mos.	26
35.	Indicator Digest	39.1%	176	23
36.	Value Line Investment Survey (Stocks rated "I" for timeliness)	38.8%	169	219
37.	Cabot Market Letter (Model Portfolio)	37.5%	154	8
38.	Dines Letter List #5 (Precious Metals Portfolio)	35.7%	> 6 mos.	14
39.	Kinsman's Low-Risk Advisory (Model Portfolio)	33.3%	162	3
40.	Zweig Performance Ratings Report	32.3%	160	65
41.	Professional Investor (Investment Grade Stocks Scan)	21.4%	145	14

Choosing a Newsletter: Tax considerations

42. International Harry Schultz Letter (U.S. Stocks Portfolio)	21.4%	107	28
43. Professional Timing Service	20.0%	114	20
44. Professional Investor (NYSE Scan)	17.3%	112	104
45. Granville Market Letter	17.2%	64	99
46. Addison Report (Speculative Stocks) (Hedged Portfolio)	13.3%	102	30
47. Systems & Forecasts	12.7%	88	55
48. High Technology Investments ("Trigger Price Advisory" Trading Portfolio)	10.0%	88	10
49. Zweig Forecast	7.1%	70	99
50. Professional Tape Reader (Model Portfolio)	4.1%	75	193
51. Nicholson Report (Stocks for Traders)	0.0%	62	32

The following portfolios closed-out no stock or bond positions in 1983:

Dow Theory Forecasts (Speculative Stocks)
Heim Investment Letter
Outlook (Income Stocks)
Telephone Switch Newsletter (Equity/Cash Switch Plan)
United Business & Investment Reports (Income Stocks)

TABLE VII. Portfolios Ranked According to Percentage of 1982 Stock and Bond Closeouts Which Were Long Term (Greater Than Six Months)

Newsletter	% of Closeouts Long Term	Average Holding Period (days)	Total Number of Closeouts
1. Cabot Market Letter (Model Portfolio)	100%	> 6 mos.	8
2. Dow Theory Forecasts (Income, Investment, Growth, and Speculative Stocks)	100%	> 6 mos.	28
3. Granville Market Letter	100%	> 6 mos.	27
4. Market Logic (Master Portfolio)	100%	> 6 mos.	5
5. Outlook (Foundation, Growth and Speculative Stocks)	100%	> 6 mos.	12
6. Speculator (Selected Stocks of the Week)	100%	> 6 mos.	21
7. United Business & Investment Reports (Growth and Income Stocks)	100%	> 6 mos.	17
8. Dines Letter List #5 (Precious Metals Portfolio)	92.7%	> 6 mos.	55
9. Dessauer's Journal	91.7%	> 6 mos.	12
10. Value Line OTC Special	90.0%	> 6 mos.	30

Choosing a Newsletter: Tax considerations

	Situations Survey			
11.	United Business & Investment Reports (Cyclical Stocks)	85.7%	> 6 mos.	7
12.	Holt Investment Advisory	80.8%	> 6 mos.	52
13.	Outlook (Income Stocks)	75.0%	> 6 mos.	4
14.	Growth Stock Outlook (Supervised Portfolio)	61.5%	> 6 mos.	13
15.	Kinsman's Low-Risk Advisory (Model Portfolio)	50.0%	> 6 mos.	2
16.	RHM Survey of Warrants, Options & Low-Priced Stocks	40.0%	> 6 mos.	5
17.	Professional Investor (AMEX Scan)	40.0%	180	40
18.	Professional Timing Service	38.1%	155	32
19.	Professional Investor (OTC Scan)	23.4%	138	47
20.	International Harry Schultz Letter (U.S. Stocks Portfolio)	18.8%	> 6 mos.	30
21.	Professional Investor (Investment Grade)	18.8%	105	16
22.	Dines Letter List #3 (Income Portfolio)	16.7%	68	6
23.	Professional Tape Reader (Model Portfolio)	8.3%	77	157
24.	Dines Letter List #2 (Speculative Portfolio)	7.7%	74	13
25.	Dines Letter List #1 (Moderate Risk Portfolio)	7.1%	84	14
26.	Chartist (Actual Cash Account)	6.0%	151	16
27.	Professional Investor (NYSE Scan)	5.4%	90	74
28.	Zweig Forecast	1.8%	53	136
29.	Dines Letter List #6 (Short-term Portfolio)	0.0%	45	42
30.	Dines Letter List #4 (Growth Portfolio)	0.0%	68	11
31.	Heim Investment Letter	0.0%	50	17

The following portfolios closed out no stock or bond positions in 1982:

Tony Henfrey's Gold Letter (Long-term Gold Share Portfolio)

Qualifications on Tables VI and VII

Several things should be kept in mind while interpreting the data in these tables. First, only holding periods of stock and bond transactions were included in the calculations for Tables VI and VII—not the holding periods for any commodity futures contracts or options that may have been recommended by the newsletter. This, as discussed above, is because the tax treatment of commodity futures contracts and options does not depend upon the period of time the contracts were held. There were two options newsletters that did not therefore appear on the tables at all—*The Option Advisor* and *Successful Options Investing*, as well as several services which recommended only commodities during the periods covered by the tables—*Harry Browne's Special Reports* and *Green's Commodity Market Comments*.

Second, you should be on guard against drawing too hasty a conclusion from the data in the tables. A longer holding period is not always better than a shorter one when the position is closed at a loss. Some of the lower averages in the tables, in fact, resulted from conscious attempts to take advantage of this.

Another qualification on these figures is that they are most revealing for those letters that closed out the most positions during the year. For example, the *Professional Tape Reader* had the second highest number of closeouts in Table VI, and we calculated that the average holding period for those closeouts was almost identical to the average for it in 1982 (Table VII)—75 days vs. 77 days. If the number of positions closed out is very low (listed in the last column of each table), however, one needs to be somewhat more cautious about drawing conclusions about the holding periods for future closeouts.

V

Choosing a Newsletter: Which newsletters are best at timing the stock market?

For a growing number of investors, market timing advice alone is most important. Whether they are investing in a family of mutual funds and want to know when to switch out of an equity fund into a money market fund, or whether they already know which stocks they wish to purchase when the "market is right," such investors are less interested in the stock selection abilities of newsletter editors than in their timing. This section should help identify which newsletters have the best record at market timing, regardless of their abilities to select stocks.

The basis of this section's analysis is a series of hypothetical portfolios based on trading the NYSE Composite. If a given newsletter recommends for its model portfolio that it should be, say, 70% in stocks and 30% in cash, the hypothetical portfolio constructed for the purposes of this section's analysis will have 70% "invested" in the NYSE Composite and 30% earning the Treasury bill rate. Or, if a newsletter recommends that you be 100% short the market, the hypothetical portfolio constructed here will be invested 100% on the short side in the NYSE Composite. For the purposes of this analysis, therefore, an advisor who is much better at stock selection than another will have no advantage. To come out on top, an advisor has to be in the market at the right times and out of it and in cash at the right times. Tables VIII through XV show the results of this analysis, each table differing only in the time period of the comparison (and, of course, in the number of newsletters compared, as the HFD followed more letters in later years).

Which Newsletters Were Included

In order to be included in this analysis, a newsletter's advice had to be specific in its recommendation about the proper portfolio allocation between the equity markets and cash. Those portfolios rated less than a "B" in clarity by the HFD (see the methodological prologue) were therefore excluded from this analysis. In addition to those portfolios rated "B" or above in clarity, several other portfolios were constructed for purposes of this study. These additional portfolios were based on the timing indicators maintained by several of the newsletters— *Professional Tape Reader's* "Group Intensity," *The Dines Letter's* "Trading Signals," *Dow Theory Letter's* "Primary Trend Index," *Systems & Forecasts'* "Time Trend," and *Professional Timing Service's* "Supply/Demand Formula." While portfolios based on these indicators frequently are similar to the model portfolios recommended in each of the respective newsletters, it is important to distinguish them. For example, I may subscribe to the *Professional Tape Reader* solely in order to trade in and out of mutual funds on "Group Intensity" signals. I may or may not do better following that portfolio than I would by following the newsletter's model portfolio; the data presented below allows me to find out for sure.

In constructing portfolios on the basis of these indicators, sell signals were interpreted to be a recommendation to be 100% in cash, not to go short the market. This was to replicate the experience of a mutual fund trader who is unable to "short" a mutual fund. The only exceptions to this were in the cases of *Professional Tape Reader's* "Group Intensity" (because editor Stan Weinstein sometimes recommends that a relatively weak bullish or bearish reading be reflected in a 50% equity/50% cash position), and the *Dines Letter's* "Trading Signals" and *Professional Timing Service's* "Supply/Demand Formula" (because these newsletters specifically recommend going short when the indicator flashes a sell signal).

Other than the substitution of the NYSE Composite for the stock portion of the model portfolios of each letter, the calculations in Tables VIII through XV were made in the same way as those for the HFD's Performance Ratings. (See the methodological prologue for a discussion of how those ratings were calculated.) There is one additional rule worth noting, however. The percentage of the portfolio that was invested on the long side of the NYSE Composite included both the percentage in stocks and the portion in call options; similarly, the percentage on the short side included both outright short sales and any portion invested in put options. In addition, no commissions were charged, on the assumption that those trading the market would use no-load mutual funds.

Intriguing Patterns

The write-ups about each of the individual newsletters later in this book will include discussions about their timing records, but there are some patterns worth noting here. One is that more newsletters outperform the market in down years than up years. In 1981, for example, the only calendar year since 1980 when the market was down, all newsletters outperformed the NYSE Composite (see Table XII). This is because the best course of action in a down market is to have at least some portion of funds out of the market. To the extent that a portfolio does—and all those followed in 1981 did—have at least some funds out of the market for some length of time during the year, the portfolio will do better than the market as whole.

The situation is reversed during bullish years. Then, to the extent a portfolio is out of the market, it will underperform a portfolio that is fully invested throughout. The fact that there have been more bullish than bearish years since 1980 is one reason why fewer newsletters outperformed the market in the years other than 1981. In bullish years, the few newsletters that did better than the NYSE Composite were those that successfully got out of the market during corrections and back in when those corrections were over.

Trading vs. Buy-and-Hold Strategies

Can those newsletters which attempt to trade in and out of the market do it consistently well and, over time, do better than those newsletters that advocate more of a buy-and-hold strategy? Tables VIII through XV can help us answer this question. Look first at Table VIII, which covers the 45-month period ending March 31, 1984. Of the portfolios listed on this table *Growth Stock Outlook, Market Logic, Dow Theory Letters'* "Primary Trend Index," *Holt Investment Advisory* and *Granville Market Letter* would probably be classified nearer the buy-and-hold end of the spectrum than the trading end. (The distinction is not hard and fast, of course, but depends on the frequency of trades. And these portfolios have changed their recommended equity-to-cash allocation less frequently than the others on the list.) The trading strategies on the list are represented by the *Dines Letter* List

#6, the *Dines Letter's* "Trading signals," *Zweig Forecast, Professional Tape Reader,* and *Professional Tape Reader's* "Group Intensity." Of the six portfolios that bettered the NYSE Composite for this 45-month period, three were buy-and-hold strategies and three were trading strategies.

When tax considerations are taken into account (see the discussion in Section IV), the scale tips in the direction of the buy-and-hold strategies. In the 50% tax bracket, as the discussion about taxes pointed out, profits on short-term trading have to be more than 60% greater than the profits from long-term strategies in order to outperform them on an after-tax basis. Of the three trading strategies that outperformed the NYSE Composite over the 45-month period, only one would still be an outperformer on an after-tax basis—the *Dines Letter List #6.* The others most likely would have inferior after-tax returns than a strategy which simply invested in the market and held that position for the 45 months.

The resolution of the "buy-and-hold vs. trading" debate is not as easy as this, unfortunately. As editors of trading newsletters will point out, the 45 months ending March 31, 1984, were on balance very bullish—and thus the period of comparison is biased in favor of buy-and-hold strategies. If the period of comparison included more bearish years, they predict, then trading strategies would be shown to outperform the buy-and-hold strategies.

The longer the period of time over which various strategies are compared, of course, the more confident one can be of the conclusions. While granting that the period since 1980 has been a period when buy-and-hold strategies would be expected to do the best, the important point to remember is that, regardless of market conditions, it is very difficult and rare for an adviser to consistently get out near market tops and in near market bottoms. A cursory overview of Tables VIII through XV shows a number of trading strategies which outperformed the market in one year only to underperform it in the next.

Market Timing vs. Stock Selection

Another use to which these tables can be put is pinpointing which newsletters' stock selections outperformed the market and which did not. Because the portfolios in these tables were constructed almost exactly as were their corresponding model portfolios—except for the substitution of the NYSE Composite for the stock portion—a comparison of the performance of the timing portfolios with the performance of the corresponding model portfolios can be very revealing. If a portfolio constructed for this timing analysis does better than the newsletter's model portfolio itself, then that means that the newsletter's stock selections underperformed the NYSE Composite. Or, conversely, if a newsletter's model portfolio does better than the portfolio constructed out of the NYSE Composite, then that newsletter's stock selections have outperformed the market. In Tables VIII through XV, those portfolios whose stock selections outperformed the market are denoted by an "*."

TABLE VIII. Records of Newsletters Trading the NYSE Composite (June 30, 1980, to March 31, 1984)

Newsletter	Gain	Stocks vs. Market
1. Dines Letter (Short-term Portfolio)	+84.5%	*
2. Growth Stock Outlook (Supervised Portfolio)	+56.1%	*
3. Market Logic (Master Portfolio)	+53.3%	*
4. Dow Theory Letters (Primary Trend Index)	+51.6%	n/a
5. Zweig Forecast	+50.1%	*
6. Professional Tape Reader (Model Portfolio)	+49.8%	
7. NYSE Composite	+40.3%	n/a
7. Professional Tape Reader (Group Intensity)	+40.3%	n/a
9. Dines Letter (Trading Signals)	+21.7%	n/a
10. Holt Investment Advisory	+ 1.0%	
11. Granville Market Letter	− 4.6%	

TABLE IX. Records of Newsletters Trading the NYSE Composite (January 1, 1981, to March 31, 1984)

Newsletter	Gain	Stocks vs. Market
1. Dines Letter (Short-term Portfolio)	+65.7%	*
2. Market Logic (Master Portfolio)	+36.3%	*
3. Growth Stock Outlook (Supervised Portfolio)	+35.8%	*
4. Zweig Forecast	+32.1%	*
5. Professional Tape Reader (Model Portfolio)	+32.0%	
6. Dines Letter (Trading Signals)	+31.3%	n/a
7. Dow Theory Letters (Primary Trend Index)	+27.2%	n/a
8. Professional Tape Reader (Group Intensity)	+24.2%	n/a
9. Cabot Market Letter (Model Portfolio)	+22.8%	
10. NYSE Composite	+17.7%	n/a
11. Holt Investment Advisory	+ 8.3%	
12. Granville Market Letter	−20.0%	

Choosing a Newsletter: Which newsletters are best at timing the stock market?

TABLE X. Records of Newsletters Trading the NYSE Composite (January 1, 1982, to March 31, 1984)

Newsletter	Gain	Stocks vs. Market
1. Dines Letter (Short-term Portfolio)	+42.3%	*
2. Growth Stock Outlook (Supervised Portfolio)	+36.7%	*
3. Market Logic (Master Portfolio)	+33.4%	*
4. NYSE Composite	+28.9%	n/a
4. Professional Tape Reader (Model Portfolio)	+28.9%	
6. Chartist (Actual Cash Account)	+28.8%	*
7. Professional Tape Reader (Group Intensity)	+27.7%	n/a
8. Cabot Market Letter (Model Portfolio)	+27.5%	
9. Zweig Forecast	+26.4%	
10. Dow Theory Letters (Primary Trend Index)	+25.2%	n/a
11. Dines Letter (Trading Signals)	+ 9.9%	n/a
12. Professional Timing Service	+ 2.6%	
13. Holt Investment Advisory	− 2.7%	
14. Granville Market Letter	−23.8%	

TABLE XI. Records of Newsletters Trading the NYSE Composite (January 1, 1983, to March 31, 1984)

Newsletter	Gain	Stocks vs. Market
1. Professional Timing Service	+36.0%	
2. Dines Letter (Short-term Portfolio)	+20.4%	*
3. Telephone Switch Letter (Equity/Cash Switch Plan)	+18.9%	
4. Dines Letter (Trading Signals)	+17.3%	n/a
5. Peter Dag Investment Letter (Model Portfolio)	+16.8%	
6. Professional Tape Reader (Group Intensity)	+16.6%	
7. Systems & Forecasts (Time Trend)	+16.4%	n/a
8. Growth Stock Outlook (Supervised Portfolio)	+15.3%	*
9. Chartist (Actual Cash Account)	+14.9%	*
10. High Technology Investment ("Trigger Price Advisory" Trading Portfolio)	+13.9%	
11. Charted Course (Model Portfolio)	+13.8%	
12. Market Logic (Master Portfolio)	+13.1%	*
12. NYSE Composite	+13.1%	n/a
14. Indicator Digest	+13.0%	
15. Cabot Market Letter (Model Portfolio)	+11.9%	
15. Prudent Speculator	+11.9%	*
17. Switch Fund Advisory (Model Portfolio)	+11.8%	*
18. Dow Theory Letters (Primary Trend Index)	+11.5%	n/a
19. Zweig Forecast	+11.4%	

Choosing a Newsletter: Which newsletters are best at timing the stock market?

20. California Technology Stock Letter (Model Portfolio)	+11.0%	
21. Professional Tape Reader (Model Portfolio)	+ 6.7%	
22. Systems & Forecasts	+ 6.4%	
23. Holt Investment Advisory	− 6.5%	*
24. Granville Market Letter	−12.5%	

TABLE XII. Records of Newsletters Trading the NYSE Composite (June 30, 1980, to December 31, 1980)

Newsletter	Gain	Stocks vs. Market
1. Dow Theory Letters (Primary Trend Index)	+19.2%	n/a
1. Granville Market Letter	+19.2%	
1. NYSE Composite	+19.2%	n/a
4. Growth Stock Outlook (Supervised Portfolio)	+14.9%	*
5. Zweig Forecast	+13.6%	*
6. Professional Tape Reader (Model Portfolio)	+13.5%	*
7. Professional Tape Reader (Group Intensity)	+12.9%	n/a
8. Market Logic (Master Portfolio)	+12.5%	*
9. Dines Letter List #6 (Short-term Portfolio)	+11.3%	*
10. Holt Investment Advisory	− 6.7%	*
11. Dines Letter (Trading Signals)	− 7.3%	n/a

TABLE XIII. Records of Newsletters Trading the NYSE Composite (Calendar year 1981)

Newsletter	Gain	Stocks vs. Market
1. Dines Letter (Trading Signals)	+19.4%	n/a
2. Dines Letter List #6 (Short-term Portfolio)	+16.5%	
3. Holt Investment Advisory	+11.4%	
4. Granville Market Letter	+ 5.0%	
5. Zweig Forecast	+ 4.5%	*
6. Professional Tape Reader (Model Portfolio)	+ 2.4%	
7. Market Logic (Master Portfolio)	+ 2.2%	*
8. Dow Theory Letters (Primary Trend Index)	+ 1.6%	n/a
9. Growth Stock Outlook (Supervised Portfolio)	− 0.6%	*
10. Professional Tape Reader (Group Intensity)	− 2.7%	n/a
11. Cabot Market Letter (Model Portfolio)	− 3.7%	*
12. NYSE Composite	− 8.7%	n/a

TABLE XIV. Records of Newsletters Trading the NYSE Composite (Calendar Year 1982)

Newsletter	Gain	Stocks vs. Market
1. Professional Tape Reader (Model Portfolio)	+20.8%	*
2. Growth Stock Outlook (Supervised Portfolio)	+18.5%	*
3. Dines Letter List #6 (Short-term Portfolio)	+18.1%	
4. Market Logic (Master Portfolio)	+17.9%	*
5. NYSE Composite	+14.0%	n/a
6. Cabot Market Letter (Model Portfolio)	+13.9%	*
7. Zweig Forecast	+13.5%	*
8. Dow Theory Letters (Primary Trend Index)	+12.3%	n/a
9. Chartist (Actual Cash Account)	+12.1%	*
10. Professional Tape Reader (Group Intensity)	+ 9.5%	n/a
11. Holt Investment Advisory	+ 4.0%	
12. Dines Letter (Trading Signals)	− 6.3%	n/a
13. Granville Market Letter	−12.9%	
14. Professional Timing Service	−24.5%	n/a

TABLE XV. Records of Newsletters Trading the NYSE Composite (Calendar year 1983)

Newsletter	Gain	Stocks vs. Market
1. Professional Timing Service	+25.7%	n/a
2. Prudent Speculator	+24.4%	*
3. Systems & Forecasts (Time Trend)	+18.7%	n/a
4. Growth Stock Outlook (Supervised Portfolio)	+17.6%	*
5. Dow Theory Letters (Primary Trend Index)	+17.5%	n/a
5. Market Logic (Master Portfolio)	+17.5%	*
5. NYSE Composite	+17.5%	n/a
5. Telephone Switch Newsletter (Equity/Cash Switch Plan)	+17.5%	*
9. Indicator Digest	+17.0%	
10. Cabot Market Letter (Model Portfolio)	+16.4%	
11. Professional Tape Reader (Group Intensity)	+16.3%	n/a
12. Chartist (Actual Cash Account)	+16.2%	*
13. Peter Dag Investment Letter (Model Portfolio)	+15.9%	
14. California Technology Stock Letter (Model Portfolio)	+15.4%	
15. Dines Letter List #6 (Short-term Portfolio)	+15.2%	*
16. Switch Fund Advisory (Model Portfolio)	+14.6%	*
17. Zweig Forecast	+14.3%	
18. Charted Course (Model Portfolio)	+13.6%	
19. High Technology Investments ("Trigger Price Advisory" Trading Portfolio)	+12.0%	

Choosing a Newsletter: Which newsletters are best at timing the stock market?

20. Professional Tape Reader (Model Portfolio)	+ 8.6%	
21. Systems & Forecasts	+ 8.2%	
22. Dines Letter (Trading Signals)	+ 6.9%	n/a
23. Holt Investment Advisory	− 6.6%	
24. Granville Market Letter	−15.2%	

*Denotes portfolio whose stock selections outperformed market. See text for discussion.

VI

Choosing a Newsletter: The use of telephone hotlines, or how much time do you want to devote to following a newsletter's recommendations?

It used to be that one of the factors distinguishing newsletters from other sources of investment advice was the fact that they arrived by mail. Whereas brokers might call up anytime with the latest "hot tip" that had to be acted upon "immediately," newsletters would be waiting in the mail when you got home. This permitted you to examine their recommendations with the perspective provided by thinking about them over night—a perspective too often missing when investors follow so-called "hot tips."

Many newsletters no longer have this distinguishing characteristic, however. The number of newsletters that now make the majority of their-buy-and sell recommendations over the telephone has grown dramatically. When the HFD first began monitoring newsletters in mid-1980, for example, there were only a couple of newsletters which offered telephone hotlines at no extra charge to their regular subscribers. Now, as many as 50% of them do.

One of the advantages of such updates is that subscribers need not wait for the mail to be delivered to have the immediate benefit of the newsletter's recommendations. This can be particularly important for those services which focus on short- term recommendations. The price movement during the period beginning when the adviser first

49

makes the recommendation until his newsletter is printed, mailed, and delivered to you, may well exhaust much of the potential first envisioned when the stock was recommended.

But the use of telephone hotlines also has various drawbacks, two of which we discuss in this section. The first is that it increases the amount of time it takes to follow the advice of an advisory service. You should be aware of this factor in choosing a newsletter, and we attempt to rank the services on the basis of how much time it would take to follow them. The second potential drawback results from the fact that thousands of other investors receive the advice at the same time as you do, which makes it difficult to secure a good price.

Time it Takes to Follow Newsletters

In the accompanying ranking of the newsletters, we attempt to rank them according to how much time it would take for you to faithfully follow the advice contained in them. In devising the ranking, in addition to whether the newsletter has a telephone hotline we also looked at the number of transactions they recommend. While you may feel that it is unnecessary to call *every* hotline of a newsletter to benefit from its advice (perhaps because recommendations come infrequently), we assume that, to follow each service faithfully, you must do so. The rankings we devised are based on that assumption.

In ranking one category higher than another, we also assumed that a newsletter with a telephone hotline takes more time to follow than a newsletter with no telephone hotline—even if the former has very few transactions and the latter has many. The assumption behind this is that, even when there are relatively few transactions, you must nevertheless call each telephone hotline in the unlikely event that any given hotline might contain a change in recommended strategy. Compare, for example, the time it takes to follow *Market Logic* and the *Value Line Investment Survey*. *Market Logic* made only one change in its portfolio during 1983, but it has a twice-weekly hotline and its issues come out every two weeks. *Value Line Investment Survey* has no hotline and comes out weekly, but it sold 219 stocks from its portfolio during 1983—an average of four each week.* We assume that it takes more of your time to call *Market Logic's* twice-a-week hotline, read its twice-a-week newsletter, and call your broker with the occasional new recommendation than it takes to read *Value Line's* once-a-week issue and call your broker with any new recommendations. We raise this comparison here because we acknowledge that it is a close call. For this reason, in the listing below we provide you with the data with which we made our decisions, so you can check for yourself whether one letter would be easier for you to follow than another.

Choosing a Newsletter: The use of telephone hotlines

Ranking of Newsletters According to How Much Time It Takes to Follow Their Advice

I. Newsletters Taking the Most Time to Follow

These services make all or almost all their recommendations via telephone hotlines, and have a relatively large number of transactions.

Newsletter	Total Number of Closeouts in 1983	# of Hotlines Week
Charted Course (Model Portfolio)	95	2+
Option Advisor (Aggressive Portfolio)	102	1+
Option Advisor (Conservative Portfolio)	102	1+
Professional Tape Reader (Model Portfolio)	193	1
Systems & Forecasts	74	2
Zweig Forecast	99	3+

II. Newsletters Taking the Second Most Time to Follow

These newsletters, while making all or almost all their recommendations via a telephone hotline, have relatively few transactions.

Newsletter	Total Number of Closeouts in 1983	# of Hotlines Week
Addison Report (Conservative Stocks)	15	2
Addison Report (Speculative Stocks)	30	2
Chartist (Actual Cash Account)*	6	<1*
Chartist (Stocks for Traders)*	50	<1*
Growth Stock Outlook (Supervised Portfolio)	14	1
Howard Ruff's Financial Success Report**	10	10**
Indicator Digest	23	2
Kinsman's Low-Risk Advisory (Model Portfolio)	7	1
Market Logic	1	2
New Issues	5	1
Nicholson Report (Stocks for Investors)	29	2
Nicholson Report (Stocks for Traders)	33	2
Professional Timing Service	23	2
Speculator (Selected Stocks of the Week)	15	2
Telephone Switch Newsletter (Equity/ Cash Switch Plan)	0	1
Telephone Switch Newsletter (Gold/Equity/ Cash Switch Plan)	8	1

Choosing a Newsletter: The use of telephone hotlines

Tony Henfrey's Gold Letter (Long-term Gold Share Portfolio)	14	2

* The *Chartist*'s hotlines are activated at least every two weeks, coinciding with its publishing schedule, but they also have more frequent hotlines in the event transactions are recommended.
** Howard Ruff's Financial Success Report maintains a hotline which is updated twice daily.

III. Newsletters Taking the Third Most Amount of Time to Follow

These newsletters make none of their recommendations via telephone hotlines but have a relatively large number of transactions.

Newsletter	Total Number of Closeouts in 1983
Granville Market Letter	99
Dines Letter (All Portfolios)	87
Holt Investment Advisory	79
International Harry Schultz Letter (U.S. Stocks Portfolio)	28
Professional Investor (All Portfolios)	173
Successful Options Investing	91
Value Line Investment Survey	219
Zweig Performance Ratings	65

IV. Newsletters Taking the Least Amount of Time to Follow

These newsletters make no recommendations via telephone hotlines and have relatively few transactions.

Newsletter	Total Number of Closeouts in 1983
Cabot Market Letter (Model Portfolio)	8
California Technology Stock Letter (Model Portfolio)	10
Dessauer's Journal	4
Dow Theory Forecasts (All Portfolios)	3
Growth Fund Guide (All Portfolios)	6
Harry Browne's Special Reports	2

Heim Investment Letter	0
High Technology Investments (Both Portfolios)	14
New Issue Investor	5
Outlook (All Portfolios)	3
Peter Dag Investment Letter (Model Portfolio)	3
Prudent Speculator	1
RHM Survey of Warrants, Options & Low-Priced Stocks	16
Switch Fund Advisory	5
United Business & Investment Reports (All Portfolios)	26
Value Line OTC Special Situations Service	6

Profiting from Telephone Hotlines

The second potential problem associated with telephone hotlines is that it is more difficult to execute buy and sell orders at a good price. This, as mentioned above, occurs because, with a well-followed hotline, you are just one of thousands of subscribers who also called the hotline and are attempting to execute the transaction at the same time. The skill with which you place your orders to buy or sell stocks recommended over hotlines can make a large difference in the profitability of a newsletter's advice.

A few simple procedures can be used to avoid many of these difficulties. To discover what is the best procedure to follow in buying or selling hotline-recommended stocks, the HFD conducted a study of the relationship between the opening price of such stocks and their best price of the day (which is the day's low if you are buying, the day's high if you are selling). The HFD examined the price behavior of stocks recommended to be bought or sold during 1982 on the hotline of Martin Zweig's *Zweig Forecast*, which is probably the most widely followed hotline in the industry. More than 100 stocks were scrutinized.

The most important finding of the study was that, in the large majority of cases, the opening price was not the best price of the day. On the buy side, for example, stocks opened at their low of the day in only 24% of the cases; on the sell side, stocks opened at their high of the day in only 26% of the cases. In the other 76% and 74% of the cases, you could have received a better price by avoiding the opening. The pattern that emerged from the study was one where the majority of investors following the hotline jump in before the opening with market orders, causing the opening price to be bid up or down to an unsustainable degree. As a result, in most cases, the prices ease back later in the day—giving the wary the opportunity to buy or sell at a better price.[1]

The Rewards for Patience

How much better a price could be obtained by waiting until after the opening? In the case of the *Zweig Forecast*, stocks recommended for purchase traded at some point during the day at a price 1.6% lower than the prices at which they opened. Conversely, sale candidates on average traded at some point during the day 1.9% higher than their respective openings. On a $50 stock, this corresponds to differences ranging from $0.50 to $1.00. With annual portfolio turnover of between six and seven times, which was the average for the *Zweig Forecast* for 1982 and 1983, the lucky investor who got the best price would have made about 25% more for the year than the investor who automatically executed each transaction at the opening price. While the chances of being so lucky are small, this shows the potential gains from not buying or selling at the opening.

An intelligent course of action in such cases, it would appear, would be to wait until after an opening price has been established (the price that allows the specialist to clear his books of all buy and sell orders that have accumulated overnight), and then enter a limit order perhaps one-quarter or one-half lower or higher (depending upon whether you are buying or selling). In a large percentage of cases, depending upon how much lower or higher you set your limit, you will catch these stocks at the better prices.

The Risks in Waiting

Waiting until after the opening carries some risk, of course, since the opening price is rarely the worst price of the day. If your limit is set too strictly and your order is not executed, you might have to settle for a worse price than the opening. But the risk is not so large as to make it not worthwhile to try. During the day's trading following

---

[1] The results of the HFD's study about Zweig's hotline recommendations are confirmed by another HFD study looking at the stocks recommended to be bought or sold over the hotline by Stan Weinstein's *Professional Tape Reader* (PTR) during the third quarter of 1982. While the sample size was not as large as the 100+ stocks in the study of Zweig's recommendations, the results were strikingly similar. On the buy side, for example, the HFD found for PTR's recommendations that in only 27% of the time did they open at the low of the day (as compared to 24% in Zweig's case); on the sell side, in only 25% of the cases did the stocks open at their high for the day (as compared to 25% in Zweig's case).

hotline recommendations, it turned out in the study of Zweig's hotline recommendations, even the average of the stock's high and low prices was a better price than its opening. On the buy side, for example, the average of the high and low prices was 0.4% lower than the opening; on the sell side, the average was 0.1% higher. So even if you have no better than random luck in getting a price close to the day's best price, chances are you nevertheless still would be better off than if you were automatically to buy or sell at the opening.

In any case, at least when stocks are recommended purchase, you may not be interested in buying all of them anyway. Since many newsletters recommend more stocks than the average investor would be interested in purchasing, a stricter and stricter limit rule of the above nature makes sense because it provides an intelligent way to narrow down the potential buy list to a manageable number. If you choose a limit of one-fourth better than the opening and find that you still are buying too many stocks for your account, then you could try using a limit of 3/8's better, and so forth.

VII

Analysis of Each Newsletter's Performance

If the reader has survived to this point, he has narrowed down the list of newsletters to which he might want to subscribe according to degrees of risk and has further narrowed down that list according to tax considerations and the amount of time it takes to follow each newsletter's advice. Nevertheless, it is likely that the list of potential newsletters has not been narrowed down to just one service. What should be the investor's next step?

The next step should be to review the analysis we have provided for each newsletter. We discuss what each letter does and does not offer and provide more insight into its performance than can be given by a line item in a table. For each newsletter we also include a graph of its performance, comparing it to the market as a whole.

In addition to studying the newsletter write-ups that follow, we strongly recommend that the investor take out trial subscriptions to those newsletters surviving the winnowing process described in previous sections. Fortunately, as Appendix C shows, most newsletters have fairly inexpensive trial offers. These allow you to become exposed to each of your newsletter candidates with a minimum of cost.

What should you look for after receiving the trial? A particularly crucial thing to look for is clarity of advice. As discussed in detail in

Analysis of Each Newsletter's Performance

the methodological prologue, does the newsletter offer specific advice on all elements of constructing a portfolio—telling you how much you should keep out of the market in a money market fund, how much to put into their recommended investments, and so forth? Do some of the stocks that are recommended in one issue never get mentioned again, or do you find complete follow-up advice on each stock in each issue, including follow-up on those stocks that happen to have gone down in price? Investors can often be looking for different sorts of advice when looking at a newsletter, so the above questions are not meant to provide a conclusive basis for accepting or rejecting a newsletter. But we often find that subscribers are frustrated at the ambiguity and vagueness found in many letters, so you should be aware of the clarity of a newsletter's advice before subscribing.

Another aspect worth looking at is the investment philosophy underlying the letter. As discussed in the preface, you should approach each letter with the attitude of a skeptic, making each one convince you that it sufficiently increases your odds of beating the market to justify risking your assets. If a letter cannot convince you that it does, then that is a good basis for further narrowing down the list of letters to which you would want to subscribe.

Following the discussion of each newsletter we have included a small table which lists some of the salient characteristics of that newsletter's performance for different periods. In addition to performance in each year for which the HFD has tracked the service, this table also gives a "risk ranking" for each letter and shows the percentage of their stock and bond closeouts in 1983 and 1982 that were long term as currently defined by the tax law (more than six months). These percentages are not meant to reflect the portion of each service's closeouts that actually were long term (since the tax law just redefined "long term"); instead, they are calculated to help you choose between the newsletters under the current tax situation. The "risk ranking" comes directly from Table I in Section II above, and we refer the reader to that table for an explanation of how the ranking is calculated. The percentage of each newsletter's stock and bond closeouts that are long term is also listed in Tables VI and VII in Section IV.[*]

In each of the tables following the discussions, we also rank the newsletter according to its quintile. If a newletter's performance for a given year is in the top 20%, then we indicate that it is in the "Best 20%" quintile, and so on. If the percentage of a service's closeouts

---

[*] As discussed in Section IV, the new tax law treats options and commodities differently than stocks and bonds. In the write-ups that follow, the percentages listed for long-term closeouts refer *only* to stocks and bonds. When it is indicated that no positions were closed out, this also refers just to stocks and bonds; of course, the service may or may not also have closed out some options or commodity positions.

Analysis of Each Newsletter's Performance

is in the middle 20% of letters (having a percentile between 40% and 60%), we indicate that it had the "Third highest 20%" quintile. By ranking each service in this way, you can immediately ascertain how the service compared to other newsletters during the same period. (In the event a newsletter recommended several portfolios, we show how each individual portfolio ranked alongside other individual portfolios, as well as how the newsletter as a whole (based on the average of its several portfolios) ranked alongside other newsletters).

A NOTE ON THE GRAPHS

Accompanying the write-up for each newsletter that follows is at least one graph of its performance along with the change in an appropriate market index. In the cases of some newsletters, you will find that the plot of its performance extends only partially across the graph. This is due to the fact that the HFD has been monitoring some newsletters for less time than others; since we wanted all graphs to cover the same time frame (June 30, 1980, to March 31, 1984), we had no choice but to leave blank some portions of the graphs for newsletters followed for less than this 3-3/4 year period.*

Not only is the time frame covered by each graph the same, so is the scale for the performance (from −100% to +400%). If we had chosen different scales for different graphs, of course, smaller percentage changes on one graph might appear more substantial than larger changes on another. One consequence of drawing graphs this way, however, is that the plots of the performance for unvolatile newsletters cover only a small range of the graph, leaving a lot of it blank. While some may think this is a waste of space, its effect is intended; it is a graphic way of illustrating the difference between a volatile and risky newsletter (whose performance would cover much of the graph) and a conservative newsletter (that leaves much of the graph untouched). The extremes of newsletter performance over the past four years range from a nearly 90% loss to a nearly 400% increase, which is why each graph covers such a large range.

---

* Even when a newsletter's performance covers only a portion of the graph, however, we nevertheless extended the plot of the market average across the entire graph, configuring that market average to cross the 0% line at the point the newsletter began being monitored by the HFD.

The Addison Report

P.O. Box 425 Quincy, Massachusetts 02269

COPYRIGHT © 1983

Audison Investment Mgmt. Co.   Registered under the S.E.C. as an Investment Advisor   Published and Edited by: Andrew L. Addison

November 23, 1983

Performance

New figures tabulated by THE HULBERT FINANCIAL DIGEST through October 31 show that our Monitored List of Speculative Stocks attained the #1 showing of any investment letter in the country. Our Speculative List has appreciated +74.5%. When combined with the +30.3% gain in our Monitored List of Conservative Stocks, our combined performance was +52.4%. This continues to place us in the #2 spot on a combined basis. (Past performance is no guarantee of future performance.)

QUICK TAKES

Our market opinion remains basically unchanged, although with a slightly more positive bias. Since late Spring, we have been telling you to expect a choppy, transitional market, with an 1160-1280 trading range. While we still believe that this trading range will continue through year-end, we want to alert you to an increasing possibility that the market could score at least a minor breakout above 1280. For that reason, we are urging Traders to move to a 60% Long/40% Money Market position. Long-term Investors should remain in our Monitored Stocks. With most of the Secondary and Tertiary stocks "Sold Out" for now, and with many of the Blue Chips and "Big Caps" now undergoing corrections, the Corrective Process could be nearing an end. We continue to favor the Blue Chips, Utilities, and our "Stay-at-Home" stocks for the long-term. These groups are the beneficiaries of a continuing decline in Inflation rates, and an eventual shift to Deflation. Because the Correction has now caught up with the Blue Chips, we believe that we are near the end in time of the Correction. Bond yields should continue their irregular rise, with prices declining to test their August lows.

COMMODITY CORNER

We continue to believe that the Commodity Market's message is that we are in a transition from Inflation to Deflation. Recent actions serve to reinforce our opinion. The Dow Jones Spot Commodity Index has now broken below its March 1983 reaction low. This indicates the increasing strength of the emerging Deflationary trend. Further Deflationary evidence is the fact that oil prices broke decisively (again) last week. Crude oil prices have now fallen below the OPEC benchmark price of $29. We have been Bearish on the outlook for oil prices for more than 1½ years. The recent break below the OPEC benchmark during an economic recovery is powerful evidence that Deflationary trends are increasing in strength, and that OPEC and other Third World countries continue to be hard-pressed for cash.

GOLD - continues its steady erosion. As we wrote last issue, Spot prices' break below 395 has extremely Negative long-term implications. If Spot prices decisively pierce 370, that would break a 13-year Uptrend, and prompt still greater selling. Should 370 hold, then we could see a rally back to the 400-410 area.

SILVER - has been firmer than Gold lately. December has been forming a trading range between 8.40 and 9¼. If 9¼ can be broken on the upside, prices could then rally back to the 10-10½ level. Long-term, we still expect to see prices test their $5 low of June 1982.

The Addison Report

The *Addison Report* is published and edited by Andrew L. Addison, who handled some bond trading accounts for Shawmut Bank for five years before founding his newsletter. An annual subscription costs $185; an eight issue (semi-annual) subscription costs $100; and a free sample copy is available upon request. The address is P. O. Box 425, Quincy, Massachusetts 02269. A telephone hotline and a glossary are included with each subscription at no additional cost. Due to its excellent record in 1983, the *Addison Report* has begun to attract media attention, including a lengthy interview of Addison in the October 3, 1983, issue of *Barron's*.

In each issue, Addison offers capsule commentaries on the commodities, bond, and stock markets. He then briefly reviews the price behavior of several stocks, specifically mentioning target sale prices and mental stop loss points. His general market timing appears to be based solely on technical factors such as advance-decline lines, moving averages of advance-decline lines, numbers of new highs and lows, whether any of the most active stocks are trading at new highs or lows for the year, and other measures of relative price strength and trading volume. His analysis of particular stocks focuses heavily on upside-to-downside volume. Addison then maintains two "Monitored Lists"—one of conservative stocks and one of speculative stocks. In addition, Addison specifically advises subscribers what percentage of their investable funds to invest in stocks at any given time. Both lists of recommended stocks are tracked by the HFD.

Performance

The HFD has only calculated the performance of those stocks recommended for purchase in Addison's Monitored Lists since the start of 1983. The performance of other stocks recommended in the newsletter for purchase have not been calculated, since it is inferred that Addison's most highly recommended stock selections are included in one of his two Monitored Lists. In fact, a few of the stocks receiving favorable commentary in the newsletter are later added to one of the Monitored Lists. Though Addison does provide advice on the proper allocation of assets between the market and cash, he does not apply it to the Monitored Lists. Therefore, the gains the HFD has calculated for Addison's Monitored Lists assume they were fully invested throughout.

In 1983, the list of conservative stocks gained 28.9% and the list of speculative stocks surged 89.6%, while the S & P 500 rose 22.5% (see accompanying chart). On the basis of the average performance of these two lists, the *Addison Report* was the second best performing newsletter in 1983 among those monitored by the HFD. Both portfolios were among the few that continued to make money during the market decline in late 1983.

On a risk-adjusted basis, the *Addison Report* was also a top performer. (For a discussion of risk-adjusted performance, see Appendix B.) The volatility of the Monitored List of conservative stocks over the 15 months from January 1, 1983, to March 31, 1984, was only slightly more than that of the Standard & Poor's 500, for example (making it one of the 20% least volatile portfolios followed by the HFD), yet its performance was about one-and-one-third times better than that of the S & P. Although the speculative stock list had a volatility a bit more than double that of the S & P 500, its performance was 4-1/2 times as good! On a risk-adjusted basis, in fact, Addison's list of speculative stocks was the single best portfolio among those monitored by the HFD, and on the basis of the average of both of Addison's lists, his letter was the best-performing newsletter for this 15-month period.

Of course, it should be remembered that one year's results will not necessarily be repeated in any subsequent period. In fact, during the first three months of 1984, the *Addison Report's* conservative list dropped 4.4% in value and the speculative list gave up 5.5%. Even this loss, however, was better than the 6.4% drop in the DJIA.

THE ADDISON REPORT

Monitored List of Speculative Stocks

Period	Gain	Quintile
1983	+89.6%	Highest 20%
Risk ranking	6.309	Second highest 20%
% 1983 Closeouts long term	13.3%	Shortest 20%

Monitored List of Conservative Stocks

Period	Gain	Quintile
1983	+28.9%	Highest 20%
Risk ranking	3.113	Lowest 20%
% 1983 Closeouts long term	46.7%	Second shortest 20%

Average of Both Lists

Period	Gain	Quintile
1983	59.3%	Highest 20%

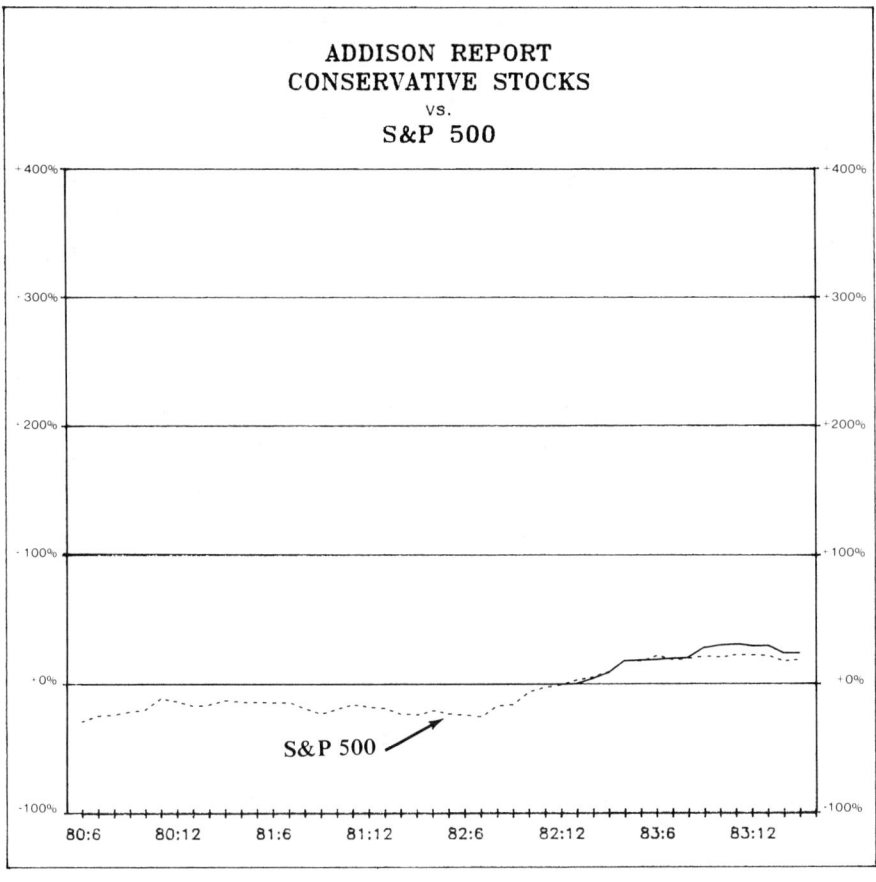

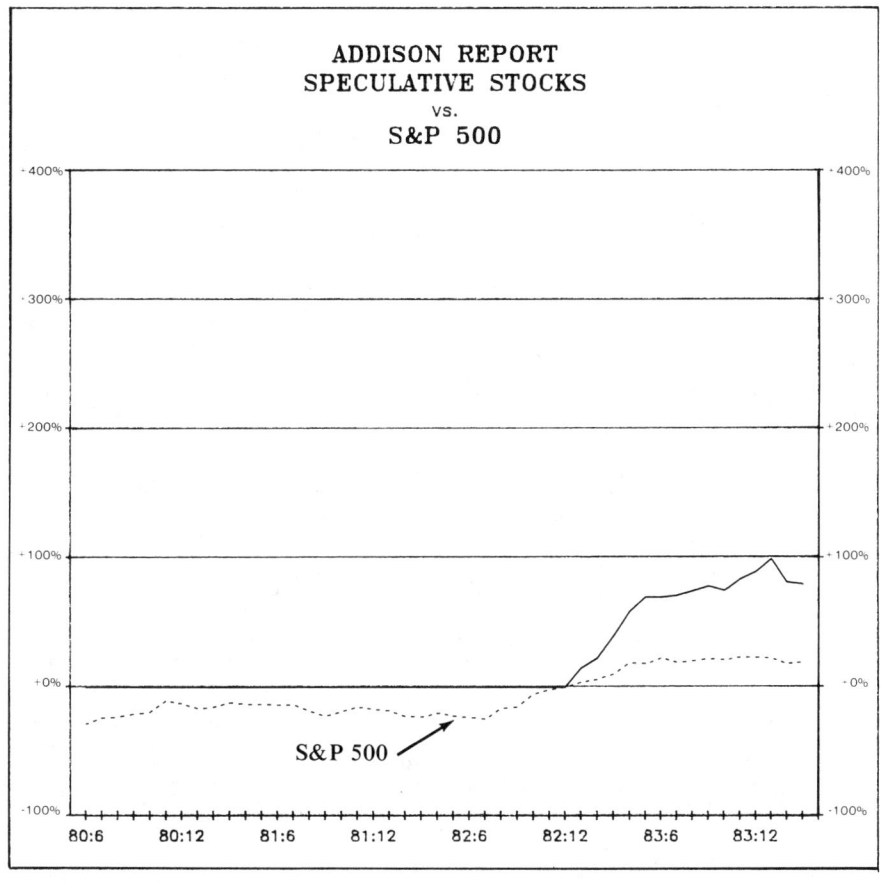

The Cabot Market Letter

Post Office Box 1013, Salem, Massachusetts 01970

Carlton G. Lutts, Editor

Letter No. 516   April 22, 1983

Dow Industrials — 1188.27   Dow Transports — 531.13

BEING RIGHT.....AND.....SITTING TIGHT

PRESENT MARKET POSITION   Back on July 23 of last year when the Dow Industrials were at 832, our important POWER INDEX flashed a major new buy signal. And we wrote, "You should adopt a very positive attitude toward the market. If you are not fully invested you should become so at once." We also wrote, "We are deadly serious when we say that you will probably *never again* in your lifetime be able to buy stocks while the Dow Industrials are in the low 800 area." Since then the Dow Industrials have blasted ahead a magnificent 360 points.

We are proud of that market call. At the time it was made, both business conditions and the outlook for the stock market couldn't have looked much worse. But making a correct call on the coming market direction is only half of the job. *Being right.....and then sitting tight is the really difficult task.* We believe there were a lot of investors who turned bullish at just the right time last July and August. Some have an uncanny knack of knowing just when the market will turn for the better. They seem to correctly sense that the "moment is right." Not only that, but they have the courage and conviction to make a major commitment at the precise moment.

But the next step is the truly difficult one. It's sitting tight once you are right. It is rare. Men who can both be right and sit tight are uncommon. Why is this so? We have thought a great deal about this. And it seems to us that most investors lack STAYING POWER.....or persistence. It is difficult enough to persist on a given course (staying with a specific stock) over the months and years without outside influences. But none of us operates in a vacuum. External news bombards each one of us in an incessant stream and in many forms: newspapers, magazines, radio, television, annual reports, financial letters, books, friends, brokers and others. These forces tend to alter our thinking. They make us more bullish or more bearish. They make us more optimistic or pessimistic about a given stock. *In effect, they can induce us to action when no action is warranted.*

Here's an excellent current example. Think back over the past few months. How many times and in how many different ways were you informed that an important market correction would, in all likelihood, get underway soon? How many pronouncements did you receive from authoritative and irreproachable sources suggesting the sale of stocks? The new bull market is only seven months old and yet we think you will agree that so far there have been at least two major attempts to dislodge your winning stocks from your possession. Naturally all the negative news associated with these attempts occurred during market weakness when all of us are most susceptible. As for the market we remain firmly bullish. Will there be corrections? Of course. One could get underway at anytime.

WHAT TO DO NOW   Remain 80% to 85% invested in equities. The balance should be invested in a money-market fund for now. You should have sold *Kasler* when our mental stop was reached. (See details on page 6.) There are now two empty spots in the Model Portfolio. We think this is a good time for you to stand aside with these spare funds. Let the other investors get emotionally involved. Let's wait for things to cool down a little. The bubbly enthusiasm we are presently witnessing in the investors we talk with is a far cry from their dismay and discouragement of last summer when the Dow was in the 850 area. If you do have any weak stocks, we feel this is an excellent time to sell them. Set the funds aside in preparation for new commitments in the not-too-distant future. But hold onto your strong stocks with grim determination, regardless of the severity of any tumbles that may occur.

Copyright 1983 Cabot Heritage Corporation

Registered with the Securities and Exchange Commission as an Investment Adviser. Subscriptions: $150 annually, $85 for six months. Twenty-four issues a year. We may or may not hold securities mentioned. Sources of information are believed to be reliable but they are in no way guaranteed to be complete or without error. Recommendations, opinions or suggestions are given with the understanding that subscribers acting on information assume all risks involved.

The Cabot Market Letter

The Cabot Market Letter is published 24 times each year and is edited by Carlton G. Lutts. An annual subscription costs $150; a semi-annual subscription is available for $85. The newsletter does not have a supplementary hotline. The address is P. O. Box 3044, Salem, Massachusetts 01970.

Each six-page issue contains commentary on market trends and indicators, specific advice to subscribers on which stocks to buy and which to sell, a review of Cabot's Model Portfolio, financial news with respect to recommended issues, and technical analysis of the market in general and individual stocks in particular.

Lutts limits the size of his model portfolio to just 12 stocks, which is less than the average size of the portfolios maintained by other letters. In addition to recommending which stocks to include in the model portfolio, Lutts also gives advice as to how to allocate funds between cash and each of the stocks in the model portfolio. Lutts takes a relatively long-term approach to the market, adding or selling positions to the portfolio fairly infrequently and varying his recommended division of assets between the market and cash only occasionally. All of the positions closed out by the portfolio in 1982 would have qualified for long-term capital gains treatment, as 37.5% would have in 1983.

Performance

The HFD has tracked the performance of *The Cabot Market Letter's* Model Portfolio since 1981, and calculates that it made a profit of 2.5% in 1981, 32.8% in 1982, 7.3% in 1983, and lost 22.7% in the first three months of 1984. For the 39-month period from January 1, 1981, to March 31, 1984, CML's model portfolio gained 13.0%, putting it in fourteenth place out of the 21 newsletters the HFD has tracked for that period of time. The Standard & Poor's 500, including dividends, appreciated 38.3% over the same period. An investor could have made 41.3% over the same period by investing solely in Treasury bills.

During this period when it has underperformed the market, the model portfolio has been significantly more risky than the market as a whole. This greater risk is due to CML's focus on stocks of smaller growth companies. Over the 15-month period beginning January 1, 1983, for example, it was 2.3 times more volatile than the Standard & Poor's 500, making it the seventeenth riskiest of the 70 portfolios followed by the HFD during the period. This increased risk was reflected in the portfolio's 22.7% loss in just the first three months of 1984.

Because CML's model portfolio has underperformed the market despite being more risky, it has also underperformed the market on a risk-adjusted basis. And because it has underperformed the Treasury bill rate—the riskless rate of return—its performance per unit of risk is negative.

CABOT MARKET LETTER
(Model Portfolio)

Period	Gain	Quintile
1981	2.5%	Third highest 20%
1982	32.8%	Second highest 20%
1983	7.3%	Third highest 20%
Risk ranking	7.527	Second highest 20%
% 1983 Closeouts long term	37.5%	Second lowest 20%
% 1982 Closeouts long term	100%	Highest 20%

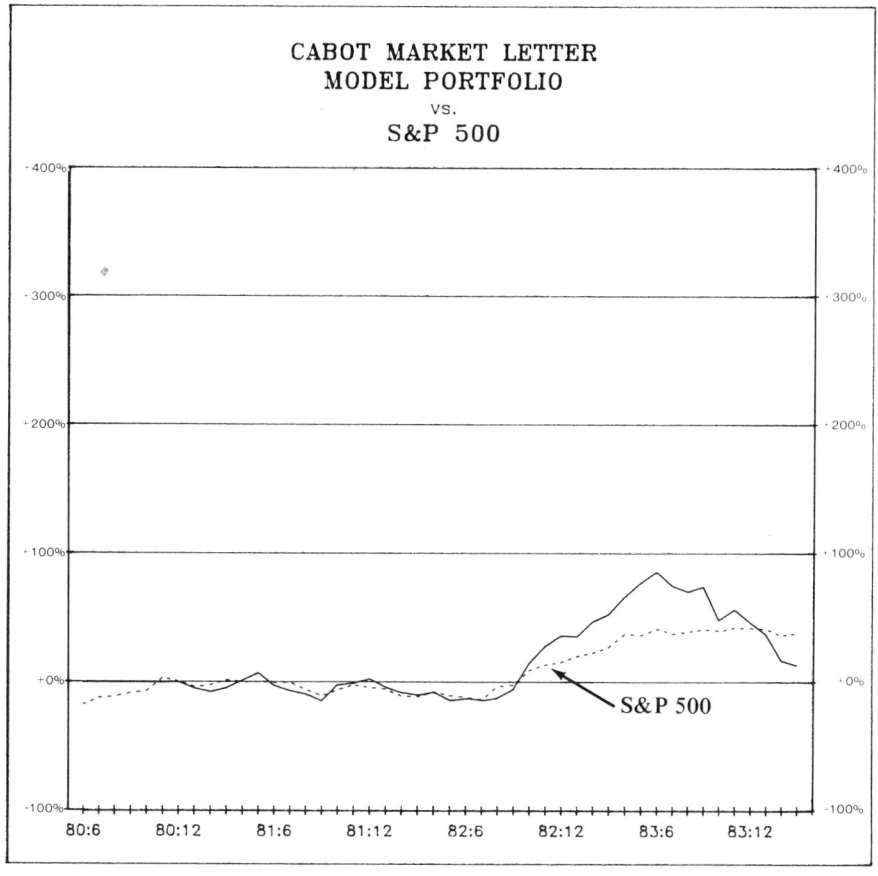

California Technology Stock Letter

JULY 1, 1983   ISSUE NO. 38   CTSL INDEX: 193.44

This Issue: Computer Assisted Design   DJIA: 1225.25

MARKET REVIEW & OUTLOOK: Patience Pays

During the last two weeks we've seen continued volatility in the technology stocks, with any bad news resulting in sharp price declines. For example, Televideo was $39 1/4 two weeks ago and hit a low of $27 this week, including a drop of $7 1/4 on Tuesday. Victor Technologies was $20 1/8 last Friday and hit a low yesterday of $12. Both of these microcomputer companies have attractive long-term prospects, but short-term disappointments resulted in sharp price declines. On Tuesday, many of the overvalued technology stocks had price declines of 5-10% with no news. While most bounced back on Wednesday, we believe these fluctuations emphasize the risk that still exists in most technology stocks. The DJIA was down 1.4% for the two weeks while our CTSL Index was down 0.1%.

INVESTOR PSYCHOLOGY:

The short-term market climate is changing, and we must look at investor's emotions to understand the change. As we've said many times, the two most important emotions affecting the stock market are fear and greed. In the last two weeks we've seen some fear as a factor in the market again. The two-day 30% drop in Texas Instruments two weeks ago reminded many investors there are still risks in the stock market. The sharp drops this week in some other technology stocks have caused more investors to begin worrying about losing some of their profits.

Emotions are important because stock prices change when investors make decisions to buy or sell; most of the time those decisions are strongly influenced by emotions. Greed remains the strongest emotion in the current market. Many investors missed this market's big move and are eager to grab opportunities created by price declines. It is this remaining greed that could cause a new market rally -- even to new highs on the averages -- but we believe the resurgence of fear will play a more and more important role in coming weeks. We think increasing fear will bring a correction before the third quarter is over.

Another way of analyzing the short-term market climate is to look at who the buyers and sellers are. Although this kind of analysis is always imprecise, it has real value. Within the technology sector, we have a strong impression stocks have been moving from strong hands into weak hands. For example, we've talked to a number of successful professional investors who generally hold stocks for the long term but have been selling in recent weeks. As one of them said: "I've already had a good year, why should I keep taking a lot of chances?" On the other side, we hear from brokers about individual investors eager to buy stocks for the "easy profits". The large amount of insider selling in recent weeks is another sign of stocks moving into weaker hands. We don't mean to imply that insiders are always right, but they do tend to be patient long-term holders of their companies' stocks. It's a danger signal when they sell. The new, weaker holders will add momentum to the decline when it gets underway, so be patient.

©Venture Capital Management, Inc. 1982, a Registered Investment Adviser with the Securities & Exchange Commission and the State of California. Address: 155 Montgomery Street, Suite 1401, San Francisco, California 94104 USA. Telephone: (415) 982-0125. Published every other Friday at $220 per year, usually tax-deductible. You may cancel at any time for a pro-rata refund. Your subscription is not assignable without your consent.

California Technology Stock Letter

The California Technology Stock Letter, a bi-weekly newsletter, is the brainchild of Michael Murphy and Jim McCamant, managers of Venture Capital Management, Inc. 1984. A three-issue trial subscription is available for $25, and an annual subscription costs $220. Beginning in the spring of 1984, the letter was supplemented with a telephone hotline, which is free to annual subscribers. The address is 155 Montgomery Street, Suite 1401, San Francisco, California 94104. The newsletter's first issue was on January 29, 1982.

Each very readable and clear issue is typically eight pages long and is divided into eight sections: "Market Review & Outlook," "Investor Psychology," "Window on Silicon Valley," "Recommended Stocks," "Notes on New Issues," "Current Recommendations," a list of all issues followed by CTSL, and a review of CTSL's model portfolio. "Window on Silicon Valley" reviews developments in the microprocessor/electronics/silicon chip industry; this feature in recent issues has focused on floppy disks, integrated software, desktop computer suppliers, artificial intelligence, computer-aided engineering, and solar energy. In the review of recommended stocks, CTSL gives specific buy-hold-sell advice for each. The number of stocks for which such advice is given has ranged from 21 to its current high of 28. The model portfolio is made up of a subset of the stocks reviewed and has ranged from 9 to 15 stocks.

Focus on Technology

As its name suggests, CTSL concerns itself exclusively with technology stocks, principally firms involved in the computer, electronics, and biotechnology fields. (In early 1984, Murphy and McCamant started a companion publication, the *Medical Technology Stock Letter*, and it appears that the emphasis within CTSL upon such companies will diminish). The stocks reviewed in the newsletter during the period the HFD was monitoring it were not cheap; they typically sold at a price/earnings ratio of 20 or more, and not infrequently sold at a P/E in excess of 40. In addition, the companies that CTSL concentrates on are extremely volatile. They tend to be young companies with low earnings predictability but exciting growth prospects, just the type of stocks and industries in which purportedly expert information and advice might prove most helpful. CTSL's track record is too short to draw any definitive conclusions, but the record over the 15 months during which the HFD was monitoring it have proven disappointing, particularly in light of the high-beta characteristics of most of the recommended stocks.

Performance

According to performance figures compiled by the HFD, in 1983 *California Technology Stock Letter's* model portfolio gained 4.6% in value, while the S & P 500 gained 22.5%. In the first three months of 1984, CTSL's model portfolio fell 20.8% during a period when the S & P 500 dropped 2.4%. The cumulative gain for this fifteen-month period for the CTSL model portfolio is a loss of 17.1%, compared to a 19.6% gain for the S & P 500. On a risk-adjusted basis, their performance was also less than the market, having underperformed the S&P 500 despite having more than twice as much risk.

According to CTSL, from the inception of the letter in January 1982, their model portfolio had (through the end of March 1984) gained about 30%. Because during the period the HFD has monitored the service its calculations have closely matched those of CTSL, we see no reason to question those figures. During the same period of time, for comparison, the S & P 500 (including dividends) gained about 47%.

CALIFORNIA TECHNOLOGY STOCK LETTER
(Model Portfolio)

Period	Gain	Quintile
1983	4.6%	Second lowest 20%
Risk ranking	6.521	Second highest 20%
% 1983 Closeouts long term	100%	Highest 20%

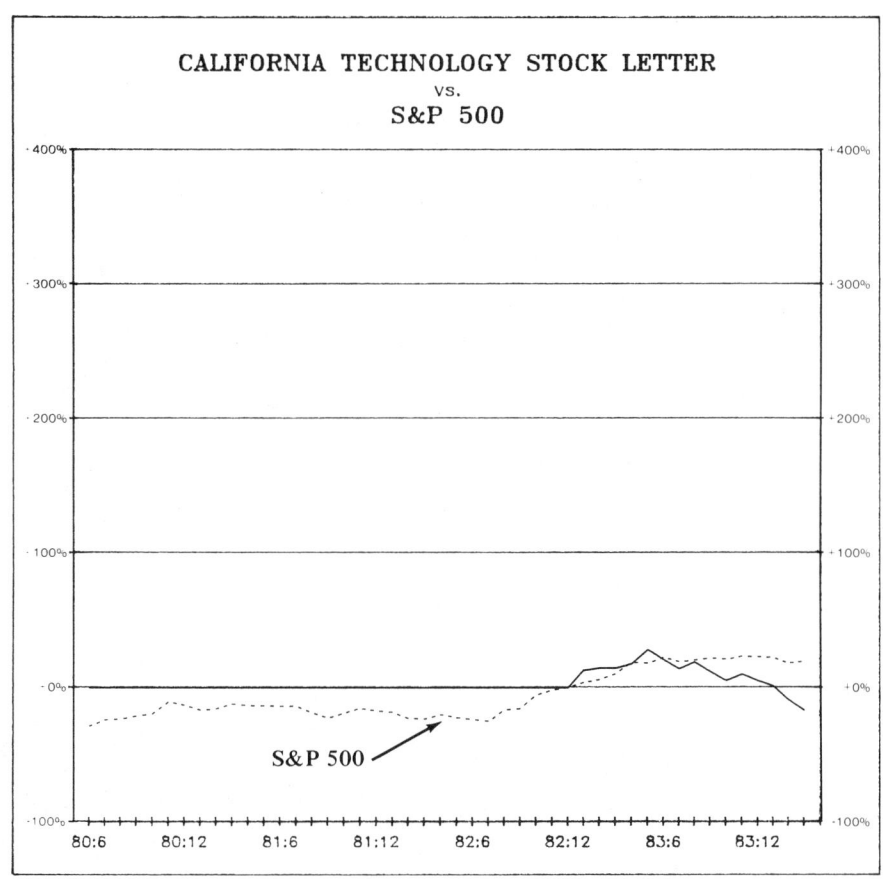

THE CHARTED COURSE

Market Timing and Stock Selection for Traders and Investors

Issue Number 34 October 6, 1983 Carl A. Cascella, Editor

DJIA: 1250.20

The Dow Average is near a new high. But underlying market tone is weak. Use stops & remain defensive.

Current Posture: 56% Long, 1% in Puts, and 43% in Money Markets.

Crowds Don't Think, They React !

Last year, during the Laker-Sixer playoffs, the TV announcer turned to Bill Russell and asked him: " Russ, did you ever get affected by what the crowd thought ? " In an instant, the ex-Celtic answered: " Crowds don't think, they react ! "

Now, you may wonder, what does this all have to do with the stock market ? Why are we talking about crowds? The reason is that Human Nature is the one CONSTANT- the thing that never changes. Indicators may come and go, analysts may come and go, computers may come and go. But human nature stays pretty much the same. Here are three recent examples of crowd reactions.

August 1982   Dow breaks " critical support area at 780 "
Reflex reaction is to call for " third leg in the bear market "
Dow immediately turns around and starts new Bull move.

August 1983   Dow breaks " critical support area at 1180 "
Reflex reaction is to think that Bull Market correction is at hand.
But Dow immediately turns around and closes at new high above 1250.

September 83   Dow closes above previous high on September 20
Reflex reaction is to call for " new upleg in Bull Market "
That brings us to the present.

Last summer, when The Dow fell below 780, the reflex response was to get MORE bearish. Now, with The Dow at new highs, the reaction is to get MORE bullish. However, we do not think this is what you should do. The chart to your left shows The Dow from May '82 to the present. We marked-off the past several months, starting in April. Note that the Dow has been contained in the 1180-1250 area for 24 weeks. 24 Weeks is a long-time.! What is happening during this " sideways " action ?

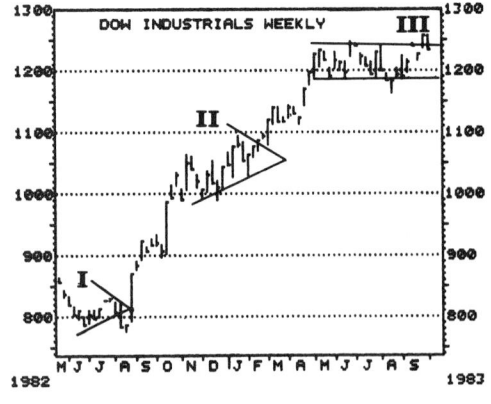

Market-wise, the underlying tone of the market is weakening, as we explain on page two. Quite a different situation from last summer, and even from the December-January congestion zone. At zones I & II, while The Dow went sideways, the underlying market was getting stronger. Now, at zone III, while The Dow is travelling in the 1180-1250 area, the underlying market is getting weaker. (continued on back pg)

EQUITY & INVESTMENT ANALYSIS, INC. P.O. BOX 88 WESTPORT, CT. 06881 • 203-334-5102
Copyright © 1983 by Equity & Investment Analysis, Inc. All rights reserved.

The Charted Course

The Charted Course is published 24 times a year by Equity and Investment Analysis, Inc. The newsletter's editor is Carl A. Cascella. An annual subscription costs $180; a semi-annual subscription costs $95; and a three-issue trial subscription is available for $25. All subscriptions include a twice weekly telephone hotline and any special "flash" bulletins and expanded issues. The address is P. O. Box 88, Westport, Connecticut 06881. *The Charted Course* is a relatively new newsletter, having only been published since May, 1982. Editor Cascella, who was previously a stockbroker, occasionally conducts stock market workshops at New York's New School for Social Research.

  Each issue of *The Charted Course* contains four pages of technical analysis of the stock market generally and of individual stocks in particular. Each issue also includes a two-page summary of positions held short or long in *The Charted Course's* model portfolio, which was begun on June 1, 1983.[*] In each issue, a one-sentence summary is provided of the recommended strategy for each stock in that model portfolio, often stating a stop loss point or a technical comment. The advice contained in *The Charted Course* is ranked in the highest category for clarity.

---

[*] Prior to June 1, 1983, Cascella maintained portfolios for both traders and investors and did not have one model portfolio. The gain the HFD reports for the first five months of 1983 is based on an average of the performance of these two portfolios.

The model portfolio consists mostly of round lots of recommended stocks. The percentage weight enjoyed by each of the stocks in the portfolio is not the same. For example, the model portfolio recently included the following holdings: 300 shares of Champion Home Builders @ $4 having a market value of $1,200 but also 300 shares of Chrysler @ $26-1/2 having a market value of $7,950, almost seven times as much; 100 shares of Uniroyal @ $13 worth $1,300 dwarfed in portfolio weight by 500 shares of U. S. Steel @ $27 worth $13,500—more than ten times as much! In February 1984, 38 different stocks were held in the model portfolio, whose value was about $200,000. Duplicating the portfolio's performance depends upon adhering to the specific allocation that is recommended.

Performance

The HFD calculates that *The Charted Course* would have made 5.9% in 1983 while the S & P 500 rose 22.5% (see accompanying chart). In the first three months of 1984, *The Charted Course* bucked the 2.4% decline in the S & P 500 and gained 0.1%. This success was due in large part to the newsletter's advice to engage in active short selling, recommending as many as 11 stocks for short selling at one time. The cumulative performance for the portfolio for the fifteen-month period was 5.9%, which places it at #20 on the ranking of the 44 newsletters the HFD tracked for that period. Over the same period, an investor could have made 11.6% by staying in Treasury bills.

The volatility of *The Charted Course's* model portfolio during this 15-month period was about equal to that of the S & P 500. On a risk-adjusted basis, therefore, the portfolio underperformed the market. And because it did less well than the riskless rate of return on Treasury bills, its return per unit of risk was negative over this period.

Unlike many of the newsletters aimed at active traders, *The Charted Course* is cognizant of the different federal tax treatment of capital gains and losses and endeavors to keep its gains long term and its losses short term. The average holding period of positions closed out in 1983 by *The Charted Course* was over six months.

THE CHARTED COURSE
(Model Portfolio)

Period	Gain	Quintile
1983	5.9%	Second lowest 20%
Risk ranking	3.174	Second lowest 20%
% 1983 Closeouts long term	59.2%	Second lowest 20%

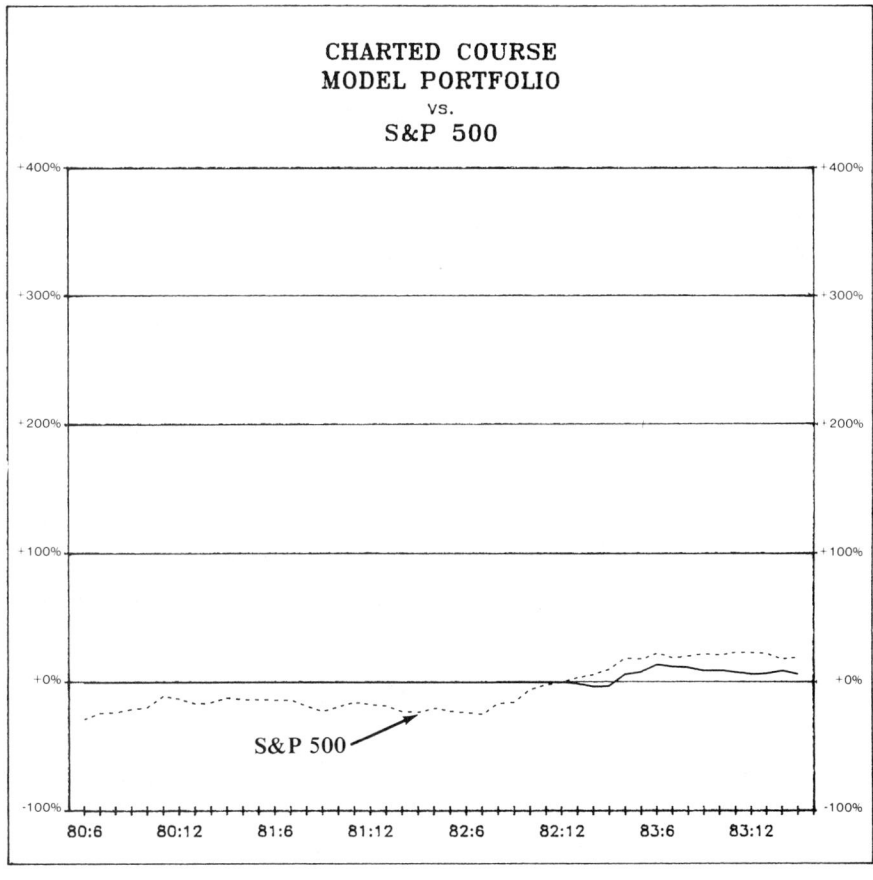

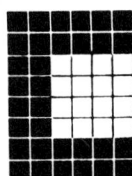

THE CHARTIST

P.O. BOX 3160, LONG BEACH, CALIFORNIA 90803
EDITOR: DAN SULLIVAN

January 6, 1983

DJIA: 1070.91	AMEX: 358.97
TRN: 456.63	NYSE: 83.71
UTL: 123.66	OTC: 236.01

     Since early December we have advised a cautious stance for the intermediate term, and that is how we would continue to approach the market at the present time. Looking further out, we feel that we are in the early stages of a long term bull market that has many months to run. The recent all time high recorded by the Dow on December 27, at 1070, put it some 37% above its 776, August 12 bear market lows. The nine previous bull markets since 1949 lasted an average of 32 months, with average gains of 63%. This current bull market has only been under way for a little over four and a half months, so if history is any criteria it still has a long way to go in appreciation and duration.

     The reason for our caution over the short to intermediate term is multi-faceted. To begin with, the market has lost a great deal of its internal momentum in recent weeks. When the Dow recorded an historic high of 1065 on November 3, there were 527 new highs on the NYSE, and 146 new highs on the AMEX. At the 1070 high on December 27, there were only 74 new highs on the NYSE and 24 new highs on the AMEX. You can readily see the glaring shrinkage of the number of new highs recorded on December 27 versus the previous peak. The internal deterioration is most obvious. The weekly figures tell the same story. There were 934 new highs (NYSE) during the week of November 3, versus only 181 for the week of December 27. The Advance/Decline Line gives us virtually the same information in that it failed to better its early November peak in unison with the Dow.

     In essence, fewer and fewer issues have been participating on each upward probe, signifying sub-surface deterioration which the Dow has been masking. On top of this, there has been a definite shrinkage in volume. The 10-day moving average of NYSE daily volume was running at 95 million shares at the November 3, 1065 peak, versus 74.5 million shares at the most recent peak of 1070 on December 27. Add to this the fact that there was a non-confirmation in that the Dow Transports failed to confirm the December 27 breakout of the Dow.

     Unfortunately, the problems the market has to deal with do not end here. The 8-week moving average of Insiders Selling versus Buying is now up to an extremely bearish 4.76 to 1. Normally Insiders sell more shares on balance because they have obtained their shares through stock options, etc. Whenever selling exceeds buying by a ratio of 2-1/2 to 1, it is considered bearish, while readings of 1 to 1-1/2 are bullish. The current reading is just about as bearish as it can get, but this does not mean that the market is going to go into an immediate tailspin, primarily because the Insiders, although extremely accurate, often act prematurely. In 1974 they were buyers on balance (a rare occurrence) for several months right in the face of a 300 point decline. However, the current reading does tell us, as we have been stating since early December, that the best gains are now behind us as far as the intermediate term is concerned. Back in mid-August when the Dow was 250 points lower than today, the 8-week moving average of Insiders Sales versus Buying was a highly bullish 1.18 to 1. All in all, the Insiders have produced an enviable record over the years, and it certainly pays to heed what they are doing.

     QUESTION: What about today's dramatic surge, with the Dow up 26 points, hitting a new all time high; with new NYSE highs expanding to 135? This is significantly higher than the 74 new highs recorded back on December 27. Could it be that the internal condition of the market is actually getting stronger and another buying stampede is now under way that is going to take the Dow well over 1100?

The Chartist

The Chartist, edited by Dan Sullivan and published bi-weekly, is unabashedly technical in its approach to the stock market. The newsletter's address is P. O. Box 3160, Long Beach, California 90803. An annual subscription costs $115, and a semi-annual subscription is available for $70. A telephone hotline service is included with each subscription. *The Chartist* has been published since 1969.

As its name suggests, each issue of *The Chartist* is filled with charts, graphs, and tables. These charts depict price patterns in individual stocks, stock market averages, and various technical indicators. Almost half of each eight-page issue is devoted to Sullivan's technical analysis of the current prospects for the stock market. Another page or more gives *The Chartist's* proprietary "Relative Strength Ratings" for two dozen or so stocks that the service finds most attractive. Most of these stocks are NYSE or Amex Listed. The company's line of business and the stock's price, price/earnings ratio, yield, growth rate, earnings comparisons, common stock outstanding and institutional ownership are also provided. *The Chartist* maintains two portfolios: an "Actual Cash Account" oriented toward long-term investors, which is an actual brokerage account, and, unlike most newsletters' model portfolios, is not hypothetical, and a list of recommended stocks for short- to intermediate- term traders.

Though each issue of *The Chartist* reports on the shares held in the "actual cash account," it is sometimes difficult to ascertain what portion of the account is in cash. Only occasionally does Sullivan mention what that portion amounts to. Not only does this make it difficult for newsletter raters to replicate the portfolio's performance, it can also lead to headaches for subscribers who are trying to recreate the portfolio for their own account.

Performance

The value of the Actual Cash Account at its inception on September 9, 1969, was $64,458. In addition, approximately $50,000 was subsequently invested in this account in 1975 and $44,000 was later withdrawn. According to Sullivan's records, the Actual Cash Account generated a net profit of $164,180 between September 1969 and March 1981, including brokerage commissions, margin interest paid, dividends and money market interest earned, but excluding unrealized gains and losses on open positions. We have been unable to calculate the compounded rate of return for this account, but assuming that the $164,180 is properly compared to the initial value, this implies a more than tripling in value over this 12-year period. The Wilshire 5000 total return index (which includes dividends), by way of comparison, has been calculated since December 1970, and through March 1981 it had more than doubled in value.

The HFD has tracked the performance of *The Chartist's* Actual Cash Account since the start of 1982. This portfolio gained 35.4% in 1982, advanced 25.1% in 1983, but fell 7.7% in the first quarter of 1984, for an aggregate 27-month gain of 56.3%. The S & P 500, in comparison, appreciated 21.6% in 1982 and added another 22.5% in 1983, before receding 2.4% in the first three months of 1984, for an aggregate gain of 45.4%. A portfolio of Treasury bills, in contrast, would have made 23.7% over the same period.

This portfolio's performance was turned with about a third more risk than the S & P 500, and so just barely outperformed the S & P 500 on a risk-adjusted basis.

Since the beginning of 1983, the HFD has also calculated a performance rating for *The Chartist's* stock picks for traders. This portfolio racked up a 30.5% gain in 1983 but plummeted 20.1% in the first quarter of 1984, for an aggregate 15-month gain of just 4.2%, compared to a 19.5% advance by the S & P 500 over the same period and an 11.6% return on Treasury bills. Because this portfolio underperformed the market with more than twice the risk of the S & P

500, it underperformed the market on a risk-adjusted basis (and, by underperforming the Treasury bill rate, had negative return per unit of risk).

THE CHARTIST

Actual Cash Account

Period	Gain	Quintile
1982	35.4%	Highest 20%
1983	25.1%	Highest 20%
Risk ranking	4.583	Third highest 20%
% 1983 Closeouts long term	81.8%	Second highest 20%
% 1982 Closeouts long term	6.0%	Lowest 20%

Portfolio of Trading Stocks

Period	Gain	Quintile
1983	30.5%	Highest 20%
Risk ranking	7.123	Second highest 20%
% 1983 Closeouts long term	66.0%	Third highest 20%

Average of Two Portfolios

Period	Gain	Quintile
1983	27.8%	Highest 20%

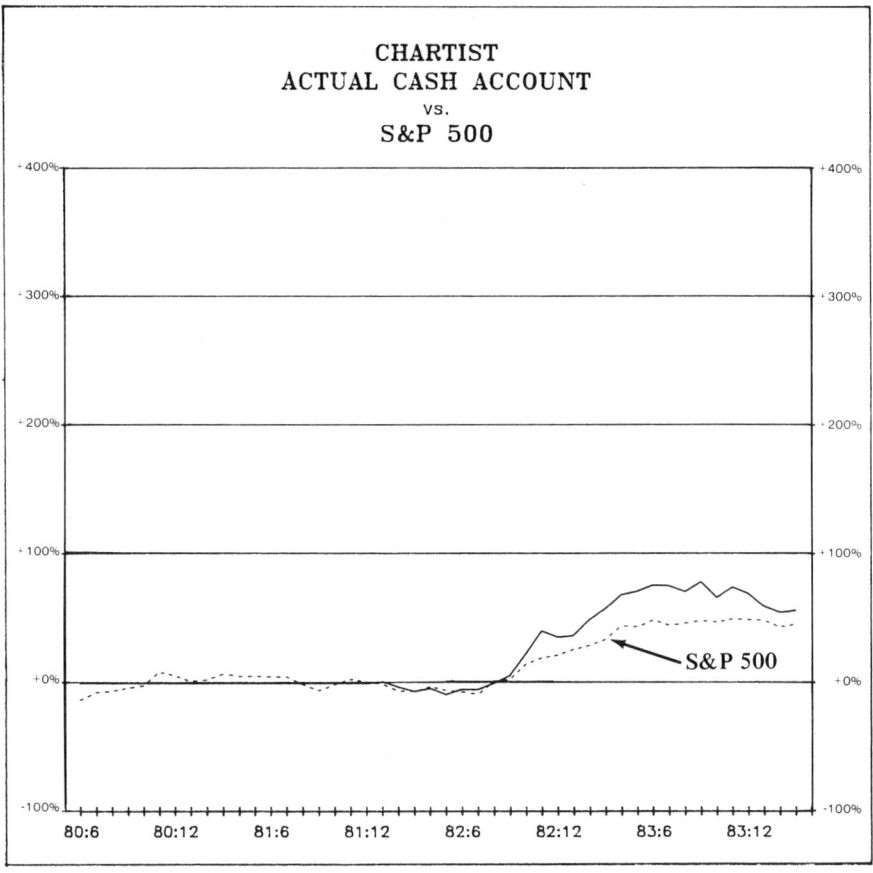

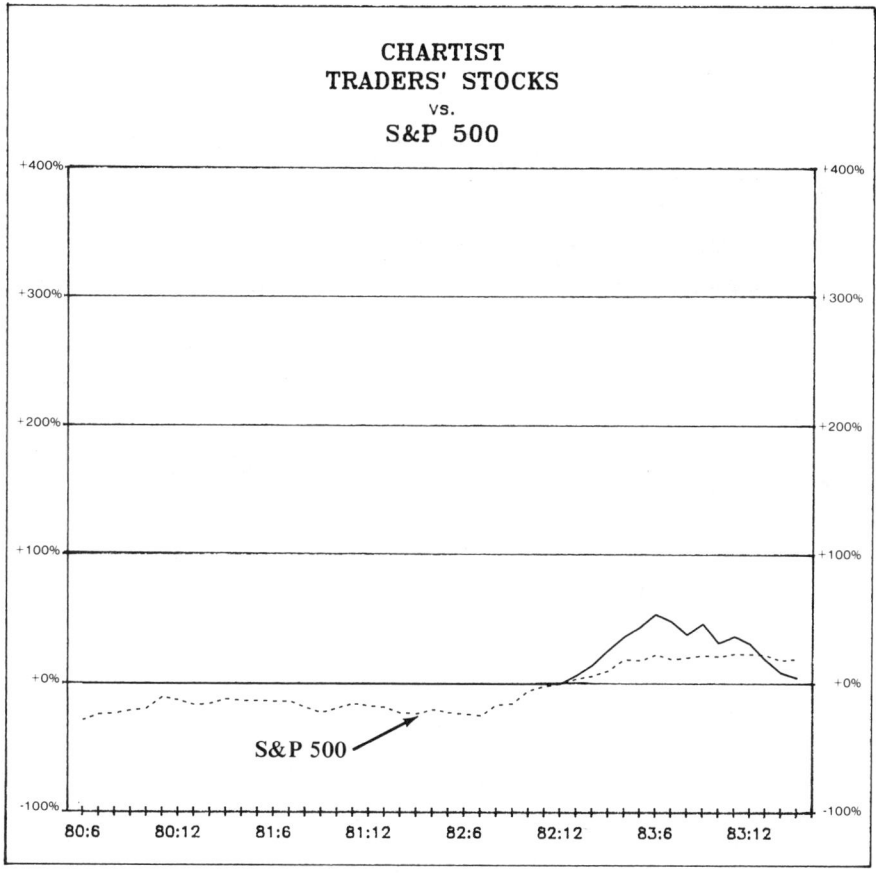

Dessauer's Journal OF FINANCIAL MARKETS

AUTHENTIC DEVELOPMENTS FROM AN UNTRODDEN POINT OF VIEW June 22, 1983

TIMING THE STOCK MARKET: WHERE WILL THE U.S. MARKET RISE END?

FOR 17 YEARS SELLING WAS EASY. 1,000 ON THE DOW WAS A TOP FROM 1966 TO 1982. IN THOSE DAYS THE HARD PART WAS KNOWING WHEN TO BUY.

THE SITUATION IS NOW REVERSED. BUYING WILL BE EASY. BUY WHEN THE DOW REACHES 1,000. SELLING WILL TAKE PATIENCE, CAREFUL OBSERVATION OF WORLD EQUITY TRENDS AND NERVES OF STEEL.

A backward glance at the DOW reveals that virtually no one wanted to buy stocks just prior to a market advance. Last summer, for example, most were caught by surprise when the DOW exploded in August. The same was true at 730 in 1980 and 736 in 1978.

Finding the buy points below 1,000 was a challenge that frustrated many investors. Watching world equity trends, paying close attention to foreign investors in the U.S. market and using common sense psychology were the techniques that worked.

We have reached a major watershed in the stock market. The DOW has passed 1,000 and moved into new record high territory. Investors are more optimistic about the future for American business.

The new challenge for investors is picking the sell points.

There is no formula that will guarantee success. Those who believe we are in a new long term bull market will be

To page 2

INSIDE

THE CONTINUING MONEY FLOOD
    AT THE U.S. TREASURY .... page 3

POPULAR FALLACIES ABOUT GOLD .... page 4

THE IMPLICATIONS OF
    MARGARET THATCHER'S LANDSLIDE .. page 5

A STOCK WELL BELOW ITS HIGH,
    WITH AN ATTRACTIVE DIVIDEND AND
    IMPROVING FUNDAMENTALS .... page 6

Profitable Perspectives

TO PROFIT IN THE U.S. STOCK MARKET; SIMPLY FOLLOW IN THE RIGHT FOOTSTEPS.

For twenty years the American cash buyer of common stocks had the best performance record. He (and she) bought at market lows and sold at the top. Profits were made by following in the footsteps of the cash stock buyer.

Last year that record was broken. The American cash buyer stayed on the sell side after the market turned in August.

U.S. institutions did begin buying shortly after the market's August explosion. The problem with following in the footsteps of the institutions is that their long term track record is dismal. They are more often wrong than right.

The best footsteps to have followed the past few years are those made by foreign investors. They sold near the top in 1981 and were major buyers right at the bottom last August.

Foreign investors have become an increasingly significant force in the U.S. market. Gross purchases of U.S. stocks by foreigners during the first quarter of this year totaled $17.6 billion. That is impressive by any standard.

World markets are integrated. Many American investors are still groping to understand that fact of modern economic life. Foreign investors have been living with that idea for a long time. That may explain why their footsteps have led to profits in recent years.

In any case, until there is evidence to the contrary, the best footsteps to follow are those of foreign investors in the U.S. stock market.

You can follow foreign investor activity through publications from the U.S. Treasury, the Federal Reserve and through the "Foreign Investor Watch" section in every issue of this Journal.

NEXT ISSUE JULY 13TH

Dessauer's Journal

Dessauer's Journal of Financial Markets is published and edited twice monthly by John P. Dessauer. Dessauer worked for Citibank in Switzerland prior to starting his newsletter. An annual subscription costs $150; a semi-annual subscription costs $85; and a three-month trial subscription is available for $45. The address is P. O. Box 1718, Orleans, Massachusetts 02653.

In each eight-page issue, Dessauer reviews both American and foreign economic stock markets; discusses interest rates, inflation, and foreign exchange rates; discusses the prognosis for gold; updates prior recommendations, makes new ones, and specifically recommends how an invester should internationally diversify his investments. For example, in his February 22, 1984, issue, Dessauer recommended that his subscribers place 45% of their investable assets in U.S. common stocks; another 15% in U. S. long-term bonds; 10% each in German/Swiss, Japanese, and French stocks; 2.5% in Eurodollars; and 2.5% each in British, Hong Kong, and Canadian stocks. This diversification reveals Dessauer's approach to investing; he is constantly aware of the interchangeability of international assets and the opportunity for profit created by these relationships. Recent articles have discussed the price of oil in terms of grams of gold, the Dow in Swiss francs, the dollar versus the Swiss franc, and gold in terms of Swiss francs. An unusual statistic that Dessauer follows closely is first-hour volume on the New York Stock Exchange, which he believes reflects foreign buying and selling of American stocks, as gauged by the market movement in the first hour of trading.

Dessauer takes a relatively long-term view of the markets and, as a rule, does not engage in short-term trading. The average holding period for positions closed out by his international portfolio was over six months in both 1982 and 1983.

Performance

According to calculations by the HFD, Dessauer's approach has proven moderately profitable in each of the last two years. In 1982, Dessauer's international portfolios rose 20.1% compared to a 21.6% rise in the Standard & Poor's 500. In 1983, Dessauer gained another 21.0%, compared to a 22.5% gain in the S & P 500. All told for the 27-month period from January 1, 1982, to March 31, 1984, Dessauer's international portfolio gained 44.3%, compared to a 45.4% gain for the S&P 500, and a 23.7% gain which could have been obtained by staying in Treasury bills.

Though Dessauer's international portfolio slightly underperformed the S & P 500, on a risk-adjusted basis it slightly outperformed the market. This was due to the fact that the portfolio's performance—which was only slightly less than the market—was achieved with about 10% less risk. Per unit of risk, therefore, Dessauer's international portfolio is ranked sixth among the 26 newsletters the HFD has been tracking since January 1982.*

DESSAUER'S JOURNAL
(International Portfolio)

Period	Gain	Quintile
1982	20.1%	Third highest 20%
1983	21.0%	Second highest 20%
Risk ranking	2.571	Lowest 20%
% 1983 Closeouts long term	100%	Highest 20%
% 1982 Closeouts long term	91.7%	Third highest 20%

---

* In the interests of full disclosure, we should point out that a public relations firm owned by an individual who is a director, shareholder, and publisher of *The Hulbert Financial Digest*, has done work for *Dessauer's Journal*. To avoid a conflict of interest, his shares of the *HFD* were converted to non-voting shares.

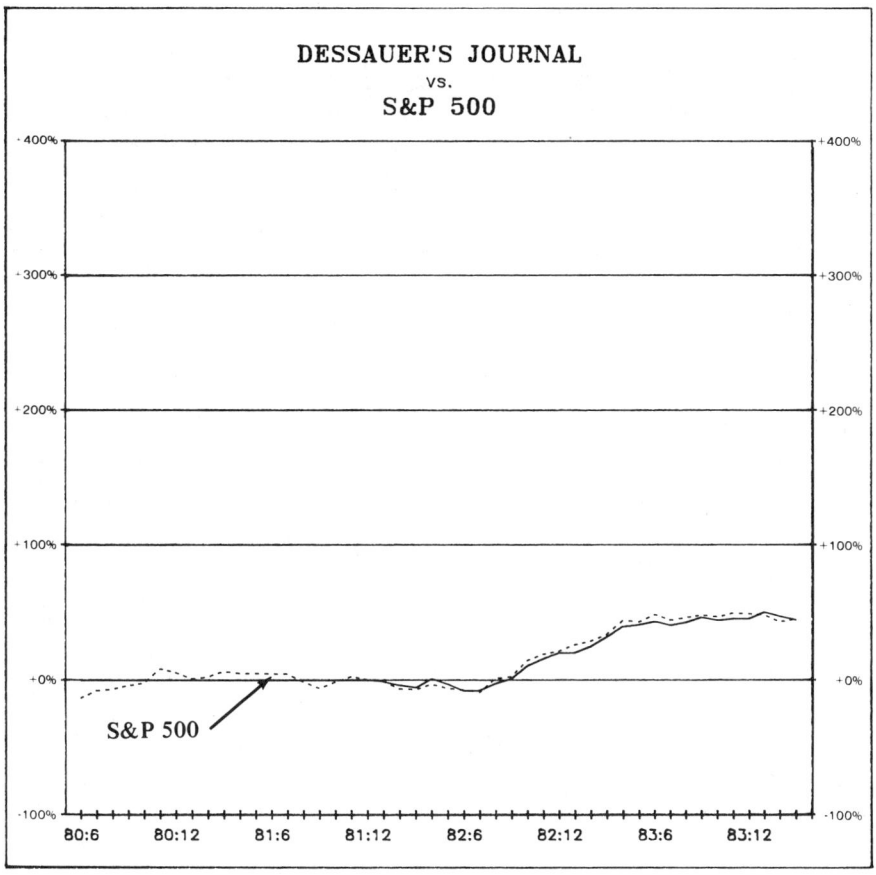

The Dines Letter

advice and information for traders and investors

14 October 1983
VOL CXX, No 11

What we need are soulless barometers, price indexes and averages to tell us where we are going and what we may expect. The best, because the most impartial, the most remorseless of these barometers, is the recorded average of prices in the stock exchange.

Dow's theory is fundamentally simple. He showed that there are, simultaneously, three movements in progress in the stock market. The major is the primary movement.

This primary movement tends to run over a period of at least a year and is generally much longer. Coincident with it, or in the course of it, is Dow's secondary movement, represented by sharp rallies in a primary bear market and sharp reactions in a primary bull market.

Concurrently with the primary and secondary movement of the market, and constant throughout, there obviously was, as Dow pointed out, the underlying fluctuation from day to day. It must here be said that the average is deceptive for speculation in individual stocks.

The market represents everything everybody knows, hopes, believes, anticipates, with all that knowledge sifted down to what Senator Spooner once called, in quoting a Wall Street Journal *editorial in the United States Senate, the bloodless verdict of the market place.* **WP HAMILTON, 1922**

TDL'S CURRENT MARKET ANALYSIS:
THE "COMING YEAR-END MASSACRE"?

We have been intensely optimistic on the economy and correspondingly bullish on the Major (or Primary) movement since our controversial switch out of gold and into the DJI at 796 over a year ago. Many fine market observers have been tricked out of this bull market by expecting a Technical Correction (secondary reaction) all the way up. Thus, in a bull market it pays to err on the side of bullishness, waiting for time and the Major movement to bail out instances of inopportune timing.

Nonetheless, having gone all year without flashing a single sell signal, we are understandably fidgety and find ourselves worrying about a possible Technical Correction. As demonstrated in the chart below, the closest we came was to warn of a "shallow Correction" that we expected to end in July. We did not advise selling out because we did not think it would be deep enough for people to repurchase at a profit after taxes. This judgment proved correct as the DJI in fact made a Bottom on 9 Aug 83, which we clearly pinpointed in our 12 Aug 83 issue (page 4).

Since our Aug 9th buy signal, the DJI has moved irregularly higher, and when the DJI made a new all-time high confirmed by Upside Breakouts in all other leading Averages the result was a "Confirmed" Dow Theory buy signal. The NYSE Advance/Decline Line has not yet made a new high, but the accompanying chart shows that it is in an Uptrend, and provided that Line (U) is not penetrated yet another Confirmation will take place.

It is vital for Security Analysts to ascertain and become aligned with the Major trend. Don't fight the tape. Don't try to stem the tide; move the beach! Nonetheless, great Technical Analysts from the past, such as WP Hamilton, do not tell you how to discern between the beginning of a secondary reaction and the end of the primary movement! Thus, as we sense the market approaching some kind of Top in October or November, we naturally struggle with the question as to whether it will be a sharp secondary decline or the beginning of a bear market. After all, this is a year where one had to be crazy to go to the gambling casinos with the stock market so bullish. Not since the 1950s has it been so easy to make money. Call options have proved to be a bonanza and might even become more so before the final Top is registered.

The tail end of a rise is the most tempting time to buy. Those who scorned stocks at the 9 Aug Bottom have now heard about this or that stock and are finally prepared to take their "plunge." Such readiness

© *1983* **James Dines & Co., Inc.** P.O. Box 22, Belvedere, California 94920

The Dines Letter

Now in its twenty-fourth year of publication, *The Dines Letter* (TDL) published by James Dines & Co, Inc. P. O. Box 22, Belvedere, California 94920, is one of the best-known investment newsletters. An annual subscription costs $150; a six-month subscription is awarded for $85. The newsletter is not supplemented with a telephone hotline.

Subscribers to TDL receive two mailings per month. One is the 16-page newsletter itself, and the other is what Dines calls his "Bimonthly Update" (but which actually is monthly), which is four pages long. The 16-page newsletter typically contains a number of regular features, including a three- to four-page analysis of the stock market's current trend, a two- to three-page analysis of the precious metals market, three to four pages of specific trading advice for commodity futures (which may or may not be followed up), a page showing an hourly point-and-figure chart of the Dow Industrials, and a page reviewing and updating Dines' portfolios (which he calls "Supervised Investment Lists"). The reporting for each of the portfolios shows each individual security, the price and date at which it was bought, any stop-loss advice, and the percentage of the portfolios that should be placed in cash.

Editor Dines attended the University of Chicago and graduated from Columbia Law School. He served two years in military intelligence and then became a security analyst before starting TDL in 1961. Dines is the author of two well-respected books, *How the*

Average Investor Can Use Technical Analysis for Stock Profits and *The Invisible Crash*. Dines bills himself (and enjoys a considerable reputation) as the "Original Goldbug," first recommending the purchase of gold in 1961 when its price was fixed at $35 per ounce. He accurately foresaw the phenomenal appreciation in the price of gold, the devaluation of the dollar, the depreciation of paper currencies vis-a-vis physical commodities, and the sharp decline in the stock market in nominal as well as real terms. These prescient predictions gained Dines a prominent reputation as an advocate of a gold standard as the only way to avoid monetary collapse.

"Much-Vaunted" Gold Sell Signal

After 21 years, Dines finally issued his much-vaunted gold sell signal on June 15, 1982, when gold was trading at $315 per ounce, up ninefold from its recommended price in 1961, but down $485 per ounce from its high of more than $800 per ounce in early 1980. The price at which Dines gave his sell signal for gold turned out to be the bottom, at least for the the bear market cycle of 1981 to 1982. Dines received a lot of adverse publicity for flashing a sell signal at the bottom, but he did write at the time that, regardless of gold's action, he thought the stock market would be a better place for subscribers. In terms of relative strength, at least, he was right; gold is trading around $370 per ounce as this book goes to press, while the Dow Industrials are some 350 points higher than they were in mid-1982.

Change of Orientation

The issues of *The Dines Letter* in 1982 reflected Dines' growing disheartenment with what he perceived was the press' failure to appreciate his successes and a bias to exaggerate his mistakes. One of his letters that year, for example, was headlined "The Numbering of TDL's Days," and concluded that subscribers should "enjoy your monthly TDL now as someday this pointless exercise will disappear forever." In the July 1982 issue of TDL, Dines announced a shift in the nature of advice provided in the newsletter from long term to short term:

> "On Fundamentals, nothing has changed, as outlined in the blueprint we gave in *The Invisible Crash*, and we still believe the world is in an ongoing monetary crisis that will culminate in tragedy. For those who wish to maintain long-term precious metal positions, we will continue to offer long-term advice, but we have gotten the message that very few are interested. Too few are willing to maintain a passive posture in the face of broad

advances and declines. We will, therefore, shift our focus to a short-term outlook but there is no change whatsoever in our expectation that the world is headed first for an economic crash and then for a gold standard at far higher prices."

TDL's change in orientation was clearly evident in the make-up of Dines' recommended portfolios. Dines used to maintain six "Long-Term Lists" for various risk categories, as well as a short-term trading portfolio. Over the 1980–81 period, for example, only one of the six lists was fully invested in stocks; the other five were either totally or substantially in cash. And the one list that was fully invested was in precious metals mining stocks, most of which had been held in the list for over five years. In the months following TDL's change in orientation, however, all of Dines' portfolios became fully invested. As of the last issue of 1982, only one of the stocks in any of the portfolios had been held for more than six months.

The shortening of TDL's investment horizon continued into 1983 and 1984. By late 1983, for example, half of the positions in Dines' portfolios were call or put options; by May 1984, options represented some 75% of all of Dines' recommended positions. And the two Dines' lists that were least volatile and whose securities were held longer than those in other lists were dropped. According to a study conducted by the HFD in early 1984, the volatility and risk of Dines' portfolios grew dramatically from 1982 through 1984—from being about equal to the market's to being as great as ten times riskier.

Performance

The HFD has data for six Dines portfolios, including the two which subsequently have been deleted from his newsletter, from mid-1980 through the end of 1984. Subscribers should be aware that, with the deletion of two of the lists, Dines has renumbered the remaining ones; what is called List #6 here is now numbered #4, and what is called List #4 here is now numbered #3. Rather than review the percentage gains and losses for each of the portfolios for each year here in the text, we refer you to the accompanying tables and graphs. You can clearly see the dramatic effect of Dines' increasing focus on options in increasing the volatility of Dines' portfolios; each list has been ranked in the bottom 20% in at least one period or another that the HFD has been monitoring newsletters, and each list also has been ranked at the top at least once. Collectively, they are near to being the riskiest of any of the portfolios currently being monitored by the HFD.

One thing worth noting is that the risk rankings for these portfolios coincide with Dines' announced goals for each. In other words, the trading portfolio is intended to be the riskiest of the portfolios and is; it, in turn, is riskier than Dines' speculative portfolio, as one would expect, which, in turn, is riskier than Dines' growth portfolio, and so on, with the least risky of the six being Dines' income portfolio. Dines does not tell you how you should divide up your investable assets between his various portfolios, so that is a decision you must make yourself.

The Importance of Risk-Adjusted Analysis

The increasing riskiness of these portfolios over time underlines the need to compare these portfolios and those of other newsletters on a risk-adjusted basis. With one exception, the riskier Dines portfolios have, in fact, earned more money than have the less-risky portfolios. One has every right to expect greater profits in return for greater risk, but as was shown in Section III, many newsletters do not justify incurring the greater risk. The only exception in Dines' case is his precious metals portfolio, which has incurred greater risk but performed less well than some of Dines' less-risky portfolios. On a risk-adjusted basis, the average performance of Dines' six portfolios has bettered the market (see Appendix B) and been above average as compared to the other newsletters monitored since mid-1980.

Good Timing

Though greater risk is part of the reason that Dines' trading portfolio has done so well, it is not the only reason. As shown in Section V, on timing grounds alone, Dines' trading portfolio was the best-performing portfolio of those monitored by the HFD—bettering the NYSE Composite in the last six months of 1980, 1981, and 1982, and underperforming it only in 1983. Cumulatively over the 45-month period from mid-1980 to March 1984, a portfolio that bought or sold the NYSE Composite according to the percentages used by Dines' trading portfolio (to go long or short, respectively) would have made 84.5%, compared to 40.3% for the NYSE Composite.

In addition to the timing that is implicit in his short-term trading portfolio, Dines also offers explicit short- to intermediate-term buy and sell signals on the market. As Section V shows, a portfolio that went long or short the market on such signals would have underperformed the market. Why is this so? The primary reason is that, while the portfolio based on Dines' trading signals went 100% short on sell signals (per Dines' instructions), he usually recommended that his short-term portfolio remain in cash. What this divergence suggests is that Dines' buy signals have been more profitable than his sell signals. In addition, it suggests that you might do better to vary your market exposure according to Dines' trading portfolio than his trading signals.

THE DINES LETTER

List #1: Moderate Risk Portfolio

Period	Gain	Quintile
7/1 to 12/31/80	10.2%	Second lowest 20%
1981	−20.4%	Lowest 20%
1982	15.1%	Second lowest 20%
1983	43.5%	Highest 20%
Risk ranking	6.634	Second highest 20%
% 1983 Closeouts long term	61.5%	Third highest 20%
% 1982 Closeouts long term	7.1%	Lowest 20%

List #2: Speculative Portfolio

Period	Gain	Quintile
7/1 to 12/31/80	5.8%	Lowest 20%
1981	15.5%	Highest 20%
1982	9.1%	Lowest 20%
1983	8.6%	Third highest 20%
Risk ranking	22.174	Highest 20%
% 1983 Closeouts long term	72.7%	Third highest 20%
% 1982 Closeouts long term	7.7%	Lowest 20%

List #3: Income Portfolio

Period	Gain	Quintile
7/1 to 12/31/80	5.8%	Lowest 20%
1981	14.2%	Highest 20%
1982	20.1%	Third highest 20%
1983	13.2%	Third highest 20%
Risk ranking	2.199	Lowest 20%
% 1983 Closeouts long term	50.0%	Second lowest 20%
% 1982 Closeouts long term	16.7%	Second lowest 20%

List #4: Growth Portfolio

Period	Gain	Quintile
7/1 to 12/31/80	5.8%	Lowest 20%
1981	14.2%	Highest 20%
1982	25.1%	Second highest 20%
1983	7.0%	Second lowest 20%
Risk ranking	10.521	Highest 20%
% 1983 Closeouts long term	53.8%	Third highest 20%
% 1982 Closeouts long term	0.0%	Lowest 20%

List #5: Precious Metals Portfolio

Period	Gain	Quintile
7/1 to 12/31/80	28.9%	Highest 20%
1981	−39.4%	Lowest 20%
1982	−8.4%	Lowest 20%
1983	9.1%	Third highest 20%
Risk ranking	10.515	Highest 20%
% 1983 Closeouts long term	35.7%	Second lowest 20%
% 1982 Closeouts long term	92.7%	Second highest 20%

List #6: Trading Portfolio

Period	Gain	Quintile
7/1 to 12/31/80	19.3%	Third highest 20%
1981	−13.2%	Lowest 20%
1982	−4.3%	Lowest 20%
1983	90.1%	Highest 20%
Risk ranking	27.493	Highest 20%
% 1983 Closeouts long term	50.0%	Second lowest 20%
% 1982 Closeouts long term	0.0%	Lowest 20%

Average of Six Lists

Period	Gain	Quintile
7/1 to 12/31/80	12.6%	Second lowest 20%
1981	−4.8%	Second lowest 20%
1982	9.4%	Second lowest 20%
1983	28.6%	Highest 20%

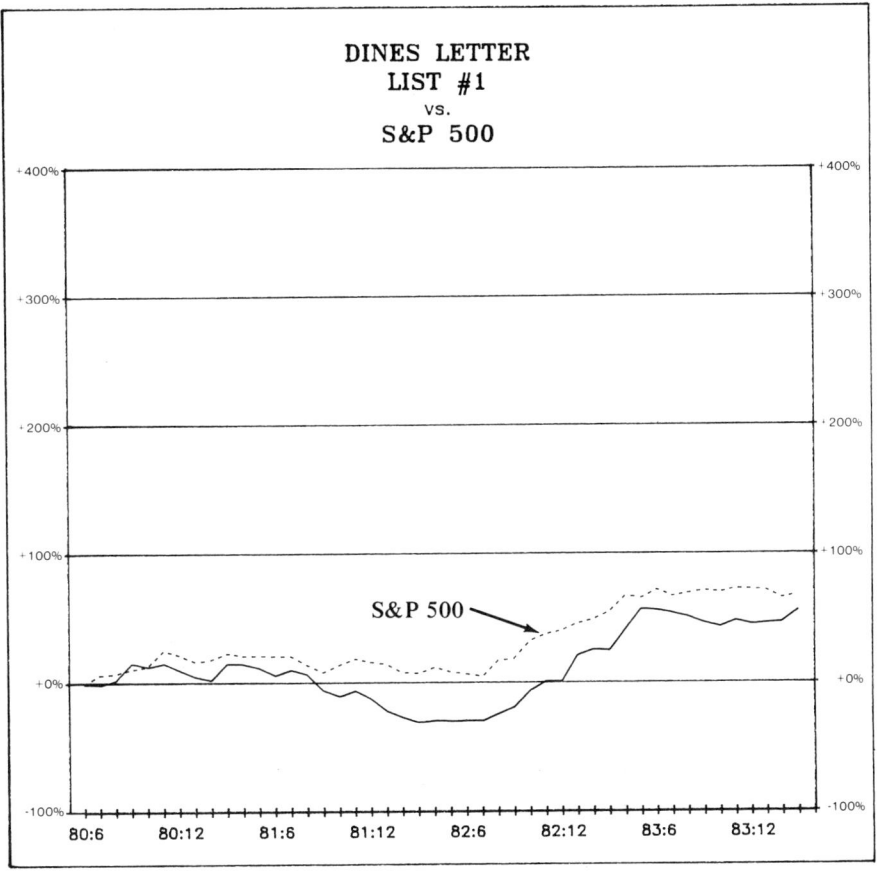

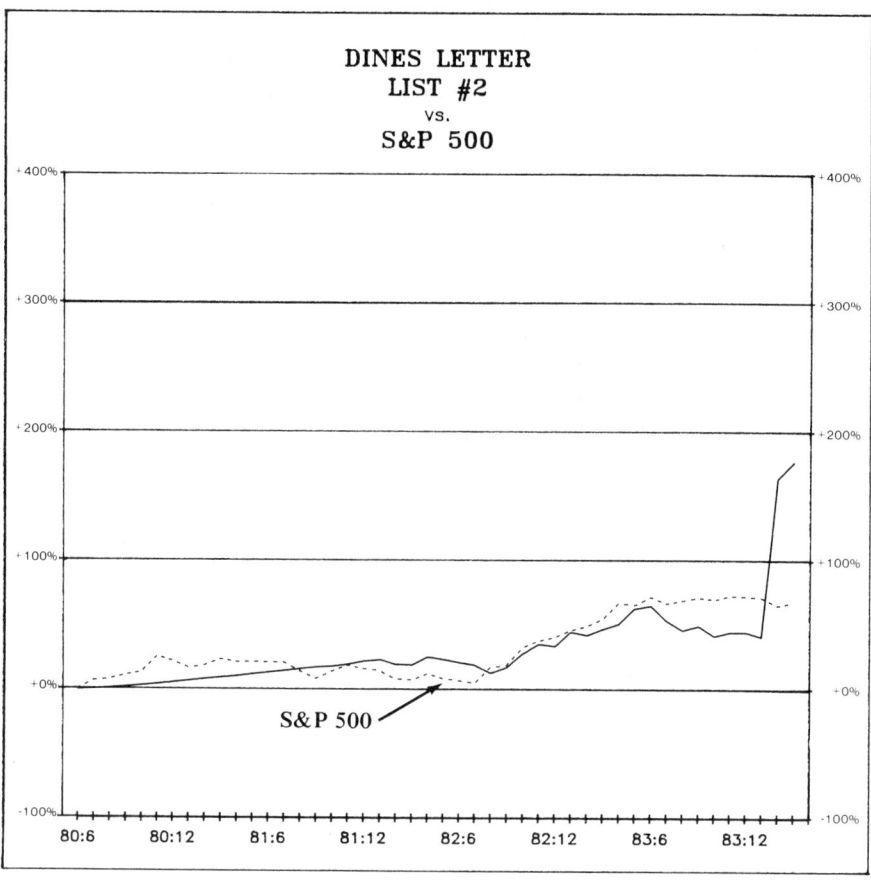

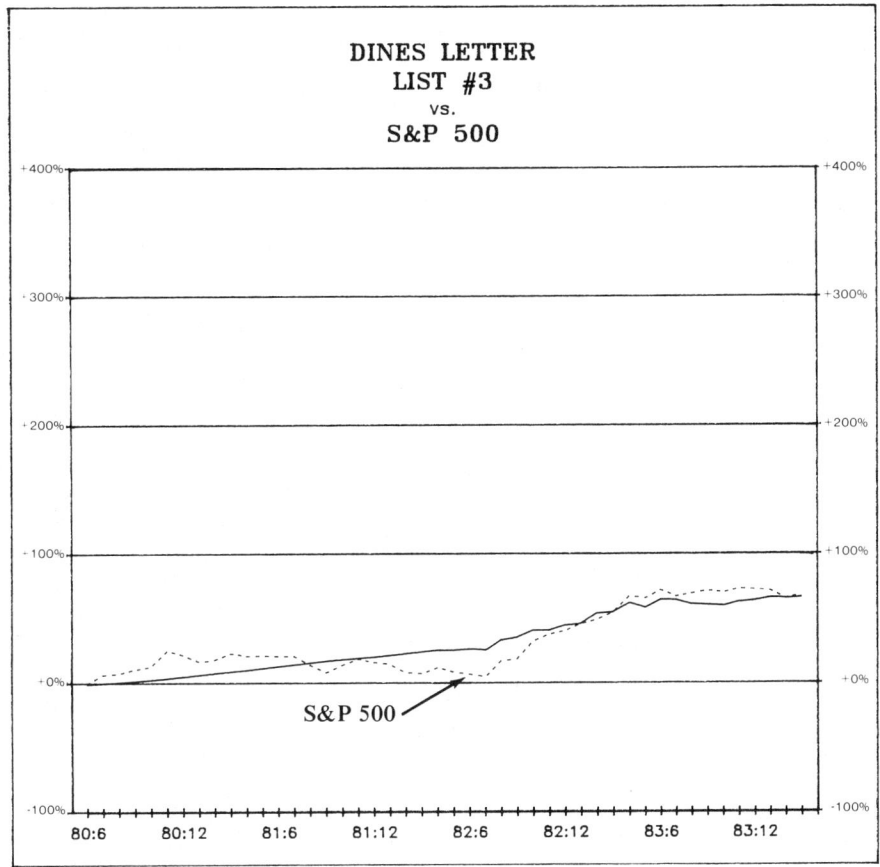

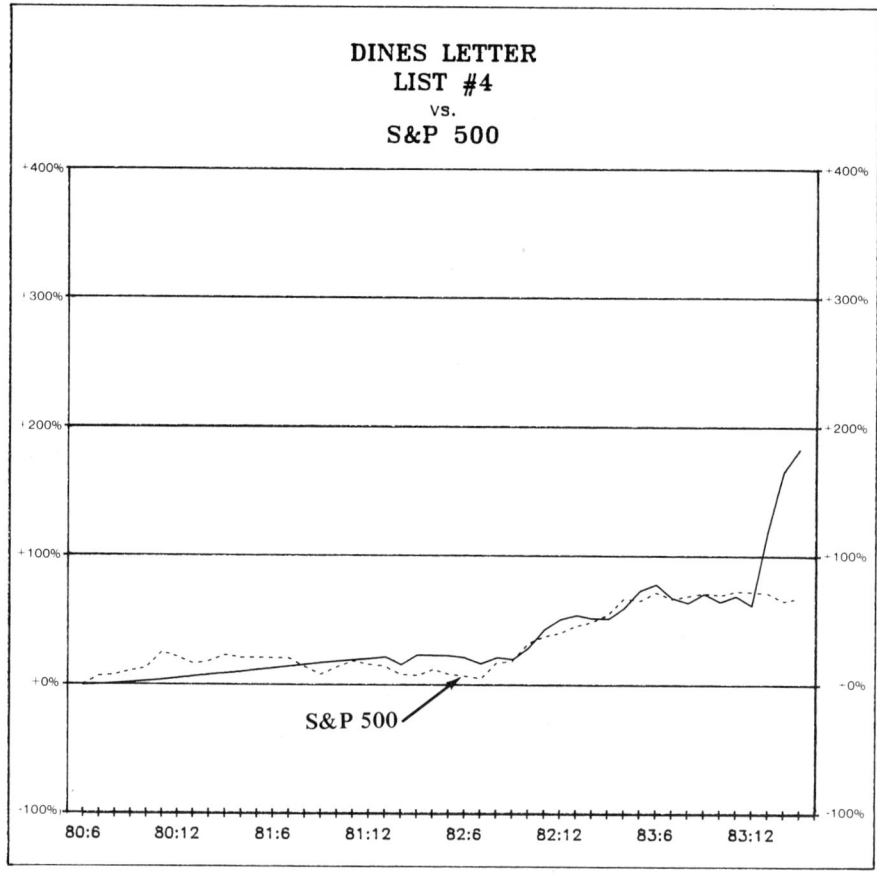

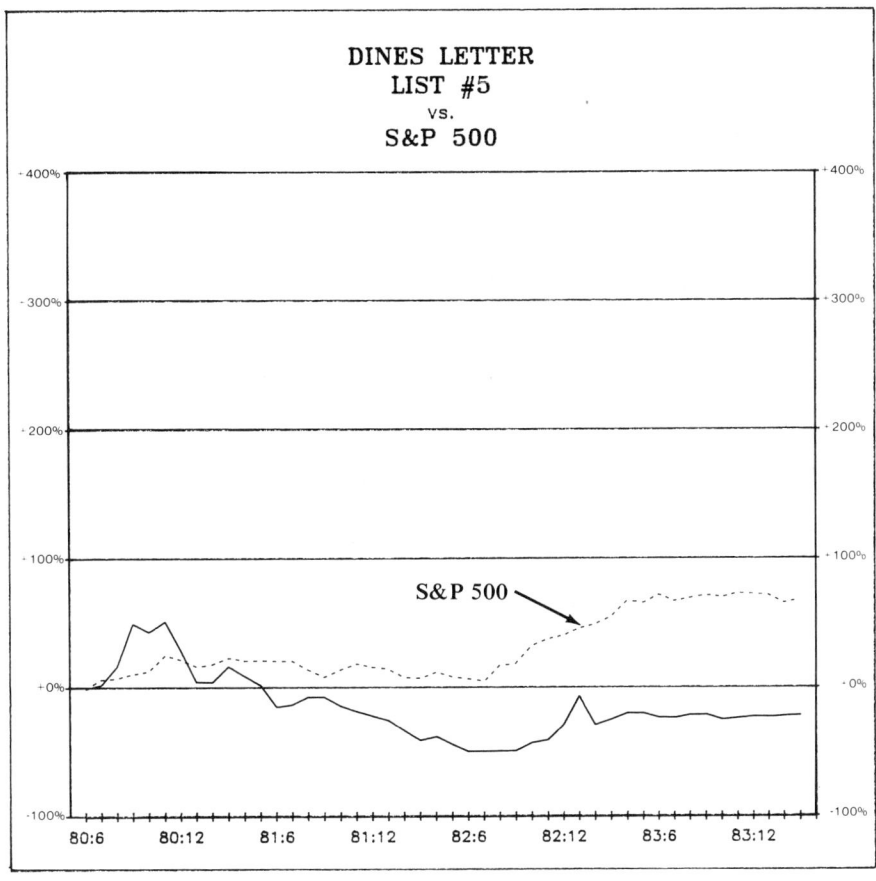

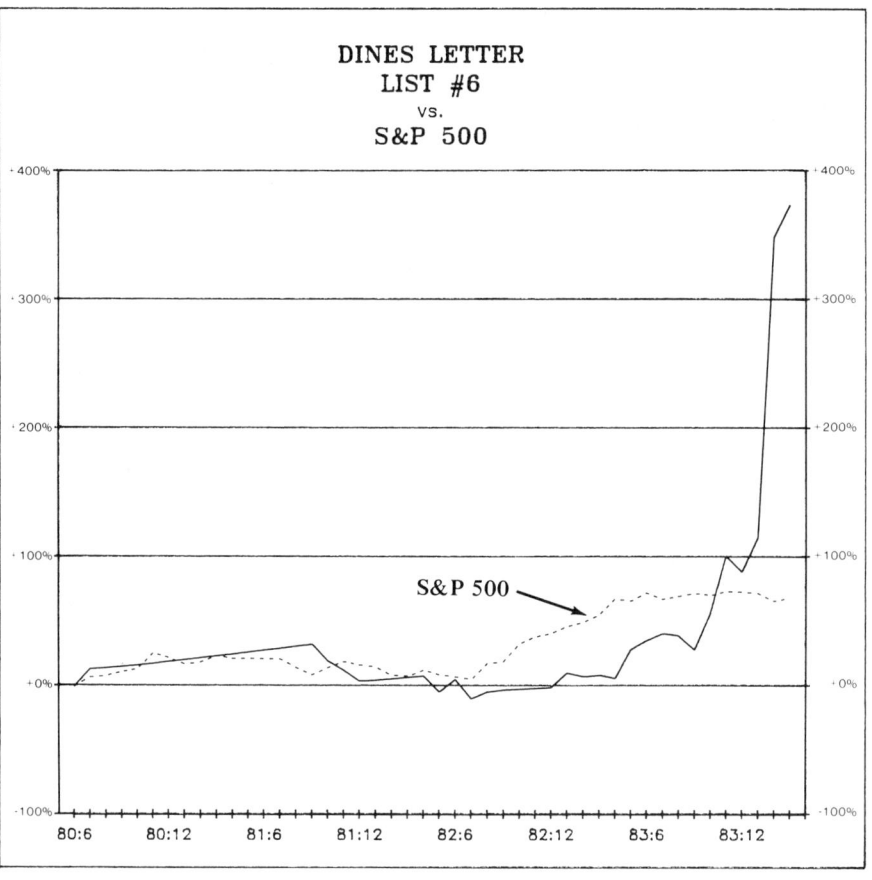

Dow Theory Forecasts

STOCK MARKET TRENDS AND SECURITIES REPORTS

November 28, 1983   Vol. 39, No. 48

IN THIS WEEK'S FORECASTS: Page

Stock Service Digest   2
Optimism Spreads

Stocks In The News   2

Market Commentary   3

Special Report   4
Capital Gains Create Opportunities

Tax Talk   6
Year-End Tax-Saving Strategies For Individuals

Analysts' Choice   8
Payless Cashways: Building For The Future

UPCOMING TOPICS
Light-Blue Chip Review

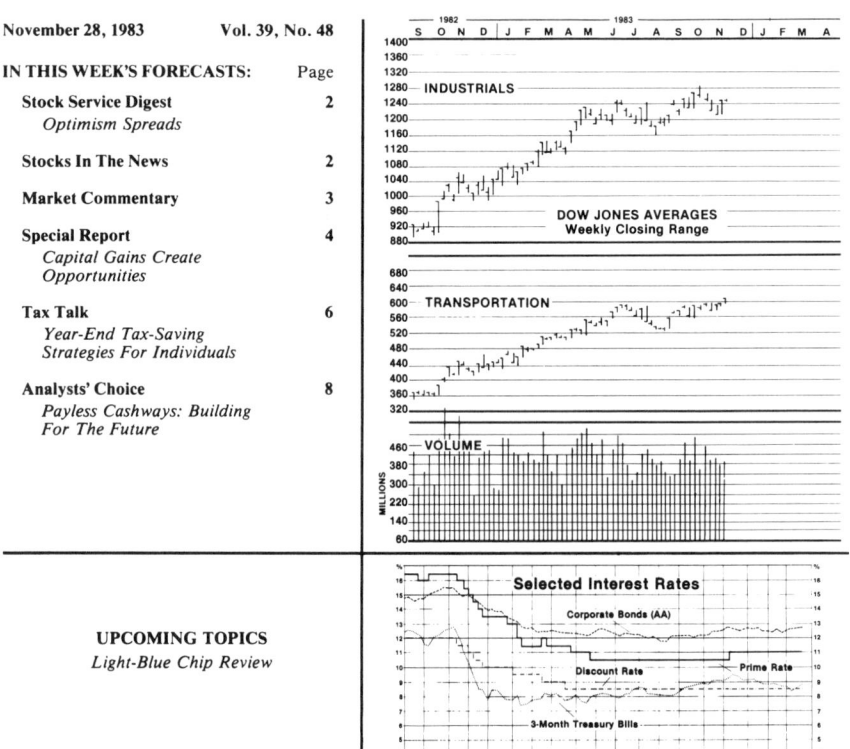

Dow Theory Forecasts is an independent Investment Adviser and makes no commissions on the stock transactions of its subscribers.

Dow Theory Forecasts

Dow Theory Forecasts, now in its fortieth year of publication, is published weekly by Dow Theory Forecasts, Inc. , 7412 Calumet Avenue, Hammond, Indiana 46324-2692. A year's subscription costs $157, and shorter-term subscriptions such as a six-month subscription for $79.50 and a three-month trial for $47.50, are often advertised in *Barron's* and elsewhere. The newsletter is sent by second class mail, and the service is not supplemented by a telephone hotline service.

Each eight-page issue of *Dow Theory Forecasts* includes a page of stock market commentary (which gives the service's current opinion of what the Dow Theory holds for the market), a "stock service digest," which reports on the consensus among 30 leading advisors (giving which percentage of them are recommending that subscribers "buy," which are recommending that subscribers "hold," and so forth, though who the 30 services are is not revealed), and an update of one of the service's recommended portfolios (of which there are five: income stocks, investment stocks, growth stocks, speculative stocks, and low-priced stocks).

These updates indicate which stocks on the lists (which typically number 25 or more) are "especially recommended." Typically, 10 to 15 issues on each list are especially recommended. Once a month, the Service also gives its "Performance Ratings" for 792 stocks. These ratings are based on a three-month and a twelve-month analysis of each stock's relative strength compared to the other issues.

Each issue of *Dow Theory Forecasts* typically also includes a page or two of analyses of individual companies. While the service's market timing appears to be based exclusively on technical analysis, their stock selection is heavily weighted to fundamental factors such as price/earnings ratios.

While *Dow Theory Forecasts* does devote a page of each issue to timing the market, they do not translate that timing into a specific allocation of portfolios between the market and cash. In May 1984, for example, when they were somewhat negative on the market's intermediate trend, they wrote, "a cautious stance is warranted." Several months earlier, in contrast, when they were more bullish, their advice was, "continue to purchase selectively the better-quality issues for the higher prices we anticipate in the months ahead." Pursuant to its established methodology, the HFD therefore assumed that *Dow Theory Forecasts'* recommended portfolios were fully invested.

Performance

The HFD has tracked the performance of four of the service's five portfolios since mid-1980. The fifth, their low-priced stock portfolio, used to be broken down into subsets on the basis of whether the low-priced stocks were income-oriented, growth-oriented, and so on. During that period, the HFD added the stocks on the low-priced list to the other four portfolios according to this breakdown. Since 1981, however, no such breakdown of the low-priced list has been provided, and the list has not been monitored by the HFD. In accordance with HFD's goal to follow those securities most highly recommended by a newsletter (see the methodological prologue), the four portfolios constructed for Dow Theory Forecasts were composed of those issues "especially recommended" at any given time.

Over the last six months of 1980—during which the S & P 500 was up 21.7%, the portfolio of speculative stocks was up 27.5%, the growth stocks up 22.5%, the investment stocks up 21.8%, and the portfolio of income stocks was up 14.9%—the average of the four was 21.7%, equal to the broad market. During 1981—when the S & P 500 was down 4.9%, the growth stocks gained 5.2%, investment stocks lost 4.2%, speculative stocks lost 5.9%, and income stocks lost 8.2%—the average of the four portfolios was −3.3%, slightly better than the market. In 1982, the investment stocks did the best, gaining 28.4%, while the S & P 500 was up 21.6%. The income stocks were up 20.2%, growth stocks were up 14.9%; and the speculative stocks were up 13.4%. The average of the four this year was 19.2%, slightly lower than the broad market's return. Over the next 15 months—during which the S & P 500 was up 19.6%, the income stocks were up 17.0%, the investment stocks were up 10.4%, the growth stocks were up 5.1%, and the speculative stocks were up 0.9%—the average of the four lists for this period was 8.4%. Cumulatively for the 45-month period from mid-1980, *Dow Theory Forecasts'* portfolio of investment stocks was the best performer, gaining 65.5%; second was the portfolio of growth stocks (up 55.7%); third was the portfolio of income stocks (up 48.3%); and fourth was the speculative stock portfolio (up 37.3%). None of the four portfolios outperformed the S & P 500 over this period, however, which gained 68.2%. The average gain of the four portfolios was 51.7%.

DOW THEORY FORECASTS
Investment Stocks

Period	Gain	Quintile
7/1 to 12/31/80	21.8%	Second highest 20%
1981	−4.2%	Third highest 20%
1982	28.4%	Second highest 20%
1983	15.6%	Second highest 20%
Risk ranking	3.538	Second lowest 20%
%1983 Closeouts long term	100%	Highest 20%
%1982 Closeouts long term	100%	Highest 20%

Income Stocks

Period	Gain	Quintile
7/1 to 12/31/80	14.9%	Second lowest 20%
1981	−8.2%	Second lowest 20%
1982	20.2%	Third highest 20%
1983	20.5%	Second highest 20%
Risk ranking	2.374	Lowest 20%
%1983 Closeouts long term	100%	Highest 20%
%1982 Closeouts long term	100%	Highest 20%

Growth Stocks

Period	Gain	Quintile
7/1 to 12/31/80	22.5%	Second highest 20%
1981	5.2%	Second highest 20%
1982	14.9%	Second lowest 20%
1983	11.7%	Third highest 20%
Risk ranking	3.949	Second lowest 20%
%1983 Closeouts long term	100%	Highest 20%
%1982 Closeouts long term	100%	Highest 20%

Speculative Stocks

Period	Gain	Quintile
7/1 to 12/31/80	27.5%	Second highest 20%
1981	−5.9%	Second lowest 20%
1982	13.4%	Second lowest 20%
1983	11.7%	Third highest 20%
Risk ranking	4.187	Third highest 20%
%1983 Closeouts long term	(No positions closed out)	
%1982 Closeouts long term	100%	Highest 20%

Average of Four Portfolios

Period	Gain	Quintile
7/1 to 12/31/80	21.7%	Third highest 20%
1981	−3.3%	Third highest 20%
1982	19.2%	Third highest 20%
1983	14.9%	Second highest 20%

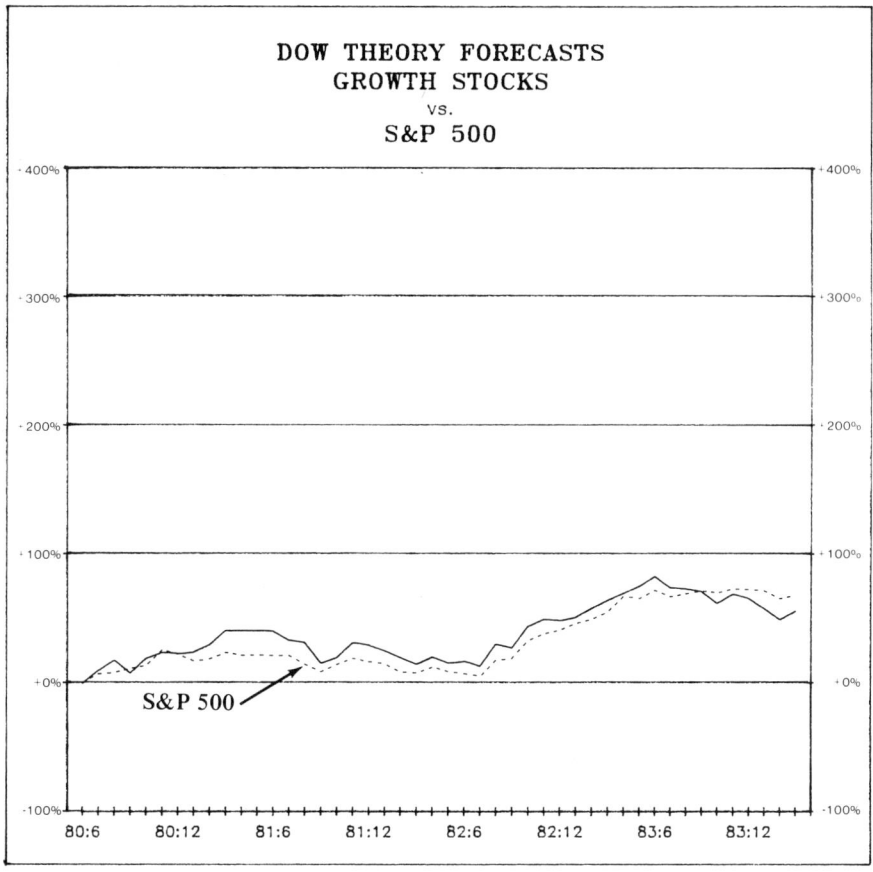

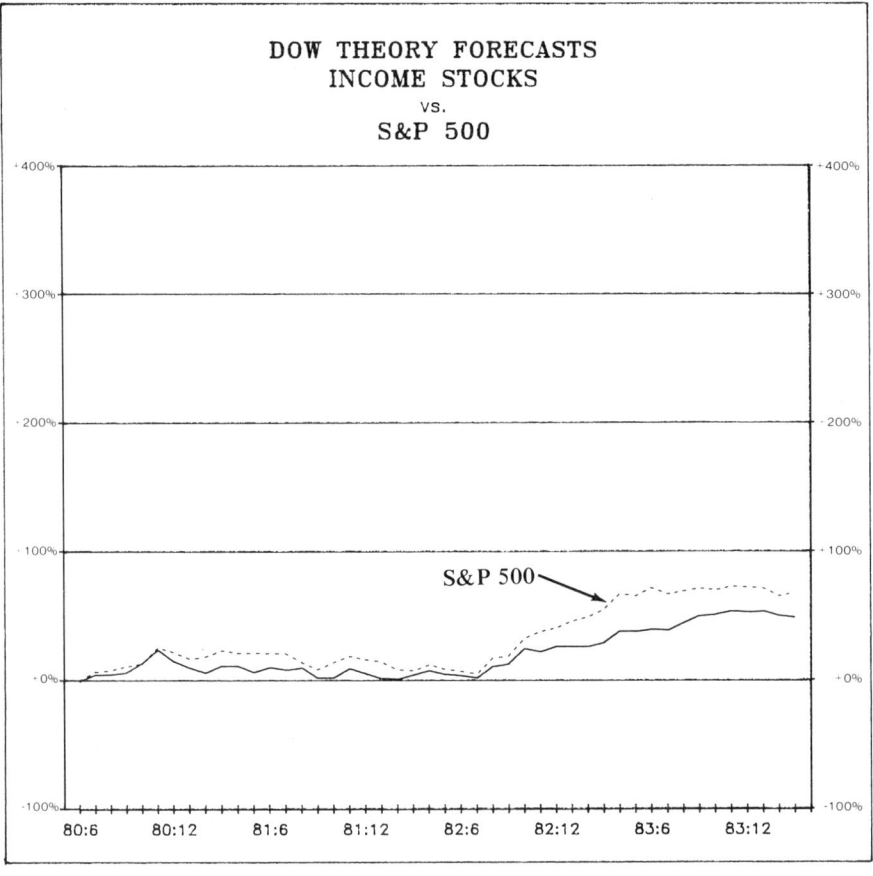

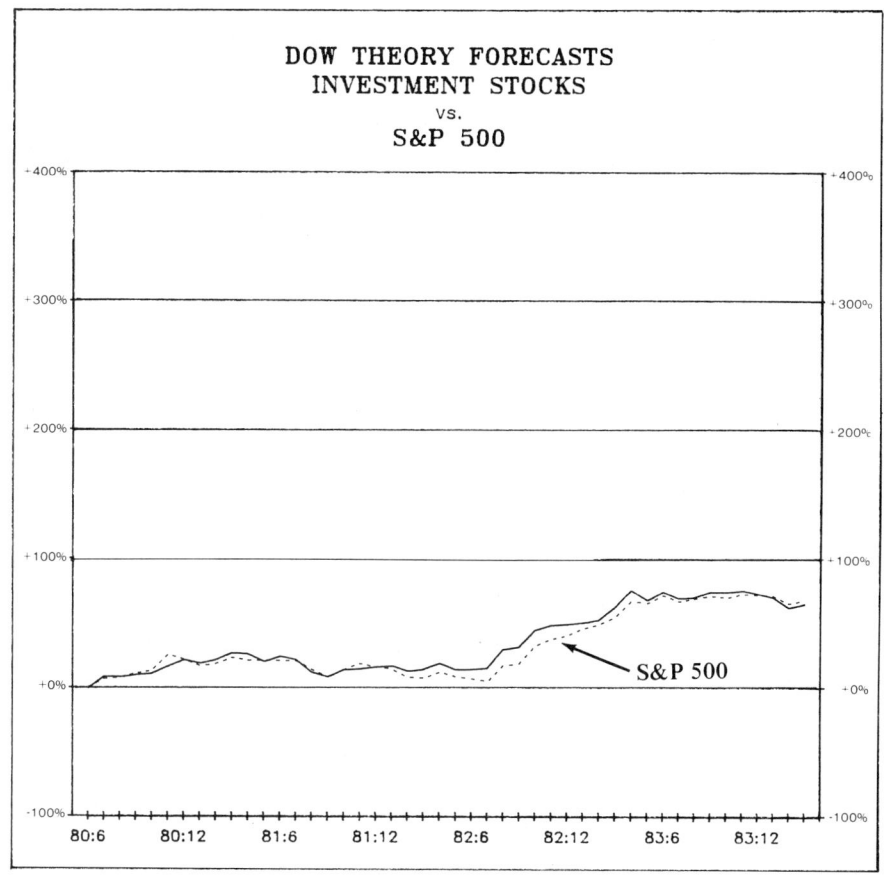

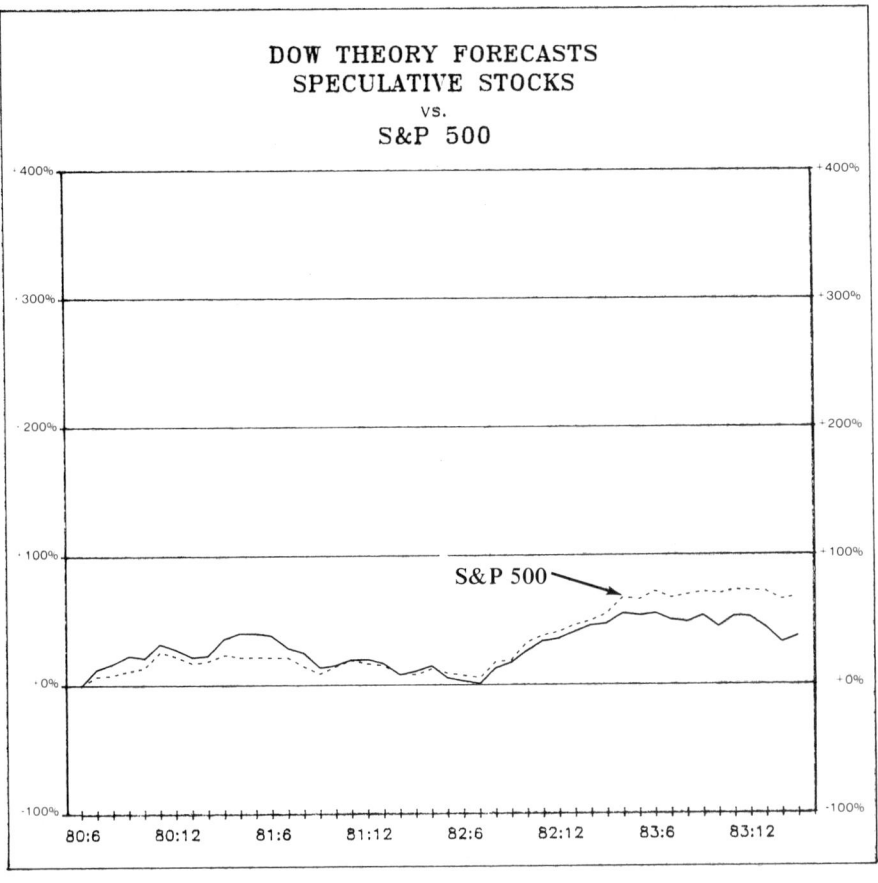

RICHARD RUSSELL'S DOW THEORY LETTERS, INC.

P. O. Box 1759, La Jolla, California 92038
Minimum of 26 Letters per year — $185 Annually
Registered with the Securities and Exchange Commission

June 15, 1983   LETTER 863

June 3, DJIA 1213.04; PTI 1637; A-D Ratio −12.89
June 10, DJIA 1196.11; PTI 1641; A-D Ratio −13.13

THE MARKET: In the last two Letters I stressed the basic Dow Theory non-confirmation thesis. This is the "rule" (it should really be termed an observation) that *a penetration by one Average, unconfirmed by the other, is USELESS for predictive purposes and more than likely apt to be DECEPTIVE.*

In the last Letter I showed (page 1 chart) that on May 3 the two D-J Averages recorded lows, Industrials at 1204.35 and Transports at 515.80. Later in May the Industrials broke below their May 3 low. At that time they recorded a new closing low of 1190.02. But as you will note (see chart), the Transports didn't even begin to confirm (a confirmation would have entailed a Transport break below 515.80). On June 8 the Dow sank to a new closing low (below 1190.02) but again the Transports totally refused downside confirmation.

Since late-May the Industrial action has been ragged, but that's perfectly all right in a bull market. After all, if the action was too good, too easy to read, then everybody would love the market. They'd ALL climb aboard simultaneously, and the bull market would be over in a few days! But it doesn't happen that way. The bull always gives the customers something to worry about, and currently it has been the weak and erratic action of the D-J Industrial Averages.

But look at the strength in the Transports! We see on the WSJ chart that there have been five successive higher Transport bottoms, bottoms occurring on March 14, April 6, May 3, May 19 and May 31. This is hardly the profile of an Average which is about to fall apart. It is hardly the profile of an Average that is about to confirm on the downside. And as I said, if Transports persistently refuse to confirm the weak indications of the Industrials, we have a market that is not going to collapse. More importantly, we have a market that, in due time, is going to move higher.

So my feeling is that at worst this market is going to do some consolidating. And in time (given Transport strength) the Averages are going to move to new highs. Actually, the longer the Averages back and fill in this area, the better I like it. A consolidation often serves to convince the bears that the market is "about to cave in." Consequently, new rounds of shorts are put out, and the technical condition of the market improves.

Conclusion: The refusal of the Transportation Average to weaken is a bullish indication. Sit tight with your no-load funds and defense stocks. Time is on the side of the bulls. Someone once said (thanks to Peter Bernstein for this one) that "a bull market is a market where you can buy late and still be a hero." That's the kind of market I think we're in.

At it's recent June peak of 1641 the Primary Trend Index (PTI) was not only at a record high, but it was extraordinarily far above its 21-week moving average (see chart). Since last August, each time the PTI has climbed too far above the moving average, the market has pulled back and the PTI has declined towards its rising trendline.

FRONT PAGE COMMENT: The predictions of "a new round of inflation" are coming through thick and fast. Me, I'm skeptical. Gold has cracked along with silver and the precious metals, the dollar is super-strong. Farm land has dropped an average of 6% over the last year, the sharpest fall-off since 1932. Commodity prices are going nowhere, business is halting in many areas (particularly the smoke-stack areas). Real interest rates have held in a high area, and if there's any real inflation coming up I don't see it yet. To top it off, the year-to-year rate of inflation in the US has cracked a rising trendline going back to the mid-1950s. So that's the "non-inflation story," as I see it.

I always take a cold and unemotional view of the PTI action. So far, as you can see on the chart, the bull trend in the PTI is intact. When that changes, the market will be in its first major corrective phase.

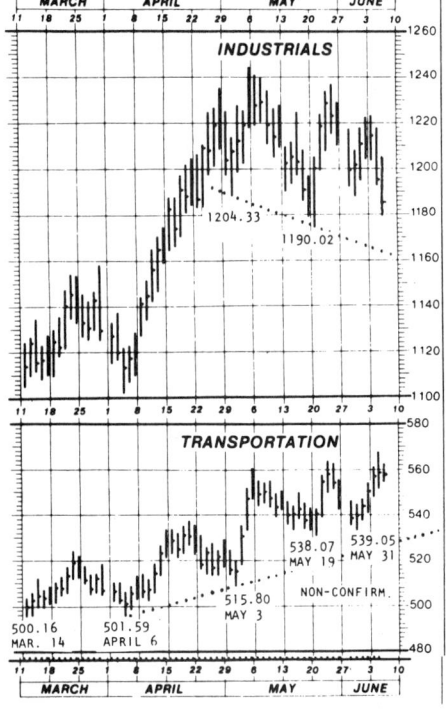

Dow Theory Letters

Dow Theory Letters, published and edited by Richard Russell, is one of the oldest investment newsletters that has been continuously written by one person, having been written by Russell since 1958. A yearly subscription of 26 issues costs $225; a three-issue trial costs $5; and a one-issue-for-one-dollar offer is frequently advertised in *Barron's*. The address is P.O. Box 1759, La Jolla, California 92038. The telephone number is (714) 454-0481. The newsletter is not supplemented by a telephone hotline, though Russell on occasion has been known to send a one-page update to subscribers between issues if he feels that market conditions so warrant.

Russell was an officer in the Army Air Force from 1944 to 1945, and he graduated in 1947 from New York University with a major in English. Robert Gross, editor of the *Professional Investor*, refers to Russell as "the modern father of Dow Theory," and Russell has written two books about Dow Theory—*Dow Theory Explained* and *Making the Dow Theory Work*. In addition to publishing the books and the newsletter, Russell also gained wide recognition through a series of 17 articles on Dow theory and technical forecasting that appeared in *Barron's* from 1958 through 1961.

What Each Issue Contains

Each six-page issue of DTL includes a number of regular features: an analysis of the stock market's current trend, an analysis of the interest rate and money markets, and a discussion of gold and the precious metals. Russell's investment advice appears in an "Investment Position" box that summarizes Russell's opinion about the stock market and offers general guidance in the construction of a portfolio. (See the discussion below about difficulties in interpreting his advice.)

In addition to these regular features, Russell also devotes a portion of each issue to his observations about the world at large, some related to investing and some not. For example, in his April 4, 1984, issue, Russell offered readers a number of observations from his recent visit to New York City. He mentioned a Picasso exhibit at the Guggenheim, restaurants where he ate, buildings he visited, the quality of shopping, and the hotel he stayed at. "It's a great hotel, and the service is excellent," he wrote. "The elevators are speedy, and we never waited for a thing." In his May 16, 1984, issue, Russell offered his theory about what is the world's biggest problem: lying. "We lie to our husbands, our wives, our kids, our bosses... We lie by ommission, we lie by cover up, we lie as easily as we breathe the air. But I'm firmly convinced that if everyone lived by the truth, the painful truth, the bitter truth, the absolute truth, ALL the world's problems would disappear within a generation."

An appreciation of what is contained in DTL is necessary before deciding whether the service is right for you. There are no doubt many reasons why investors are interested in subscribing to a service, and clearly one of the reasons why subscribers renew Russell's newsletter is the chatty, conversational approach to topics including, but not limited to, investment analysis. DTL subscribers have on several occasions relayed to the authors that they regard the receipt of an issue of DTL as akin to a visit by an old friend; they look forward to curling up in an armchair to read it.

Interpreting Russell's Advice

Tracking the performance of DTL has been difficult because Russell does not recommend a specific model portfolio nor does he consistently follow up the advice he might make in each issue. In early 1981, Russell established an "Investment Position" box that would appear in each issue and provide specific portfolio advice, but unfortunately what is said in one issue does not necessarily relate to what is said in a subsequent one. Consider, for example, the sequence of recommendations that appeared in five issues during March and April 1983. In his March 9 issue, Russell recommended reducing the gold and gold share portion of your portfolio, and said he liked utility stocks (mentioning seven in particular) as well as defense issues (mentioning nine in particular). In his March 23 issue, Russell says that, "this is a time to be conservative. Money rates have been creeping higher with the 91-day bills now yielding an attractive 8.30%." Russell then said he felt comfortable "with a limited exposure in no-load funds and a very minimum core position in gold coins." No mention was made in the Investment Position box of the utility shares or defense stocks. In his April 6 issue, Russell, in the Investment Position box, said, "the mix is T-bills, defense stocks, some utilities and no-load funds... The situation today is unfavorable for gold so any gold position should be minimal. And that's it." The April 20 Investment Position box said to "hold all your no-load funds, hold your defense portfolio, and hold a solid position in Treasury bills." Finally, in his May 4 Investment Position box, Russell wrote "my suggestion is to ride it [the bull market] with well-managed no-load funds."

Several things are clear from this summary, which is typical of Russell's investment advice. First, Russell rarely if ever recommends a particular allocation of a model portfolio between the various investments he mentions. Second, investments mentioned in one issue may or may not be followed up in the next or subsequent issues. Third, recommendations often come in the form of categories of investments rather than individual securities. For these reasons, the HFD rates DTL the lowest in clarity of any of the newsletters it monitors.

Performance

Within these limitations, the HFD has constructed a portfolio from the advice contained in DTL's Investment Position box. Data are available from 1981. In 1981, according to HFD calculations, DTL gained 10.2% while the S & P 500 lost 4.9%. In 1982, DTL gained 19.2% while the S & P 500 gained 21.6%, and from January 1983 through March 1984, DTL lost 9.1% while the S & P 500 was tacking on another 19.6%. Cumulatively over this 39-month period, the HFD shows DTL gaining 19.3%, in contrast to the 38.3% turned in by the S & P 500 and the 41.3% obtainable from Treasury bills. Though, according to the HFD, DTL was about half as risky as the S & P 500 during this period, it still underperformed the Treasury bill rate and thus had a negative return per unit of risk.

One of the features Russell's letter is most known for is his proprietary "Primary Trend Index"(PTI), which attempts to call turns in the market's major trend. The HFD also has calculated the returns you could have obtained by trading in and out of the market according to signals from the PTI (see section IV). According to the HFD, over this 39-month period if you traded the NYSE Composite on the basis of the PTI, investing in Treasury bills on PTI "sells," you would have made 27.2%, as compared to a 17.2% gain in the NYSE Composite itself.

DOW THEORY LETTERS

Period	Gain	Quintile
1981	10.2%	Second highest 20%
1982	19.2%	Third highest 20%
1983	−6.8%	Lowest 20%
Risk ranking	3.231	Second lowest 20%
% 1983 Closeouts long term	*	

* Due to the low clarity of the newsletter's recommendations, it was impossible to calculate an average holding period of the service's recommendations; see text.

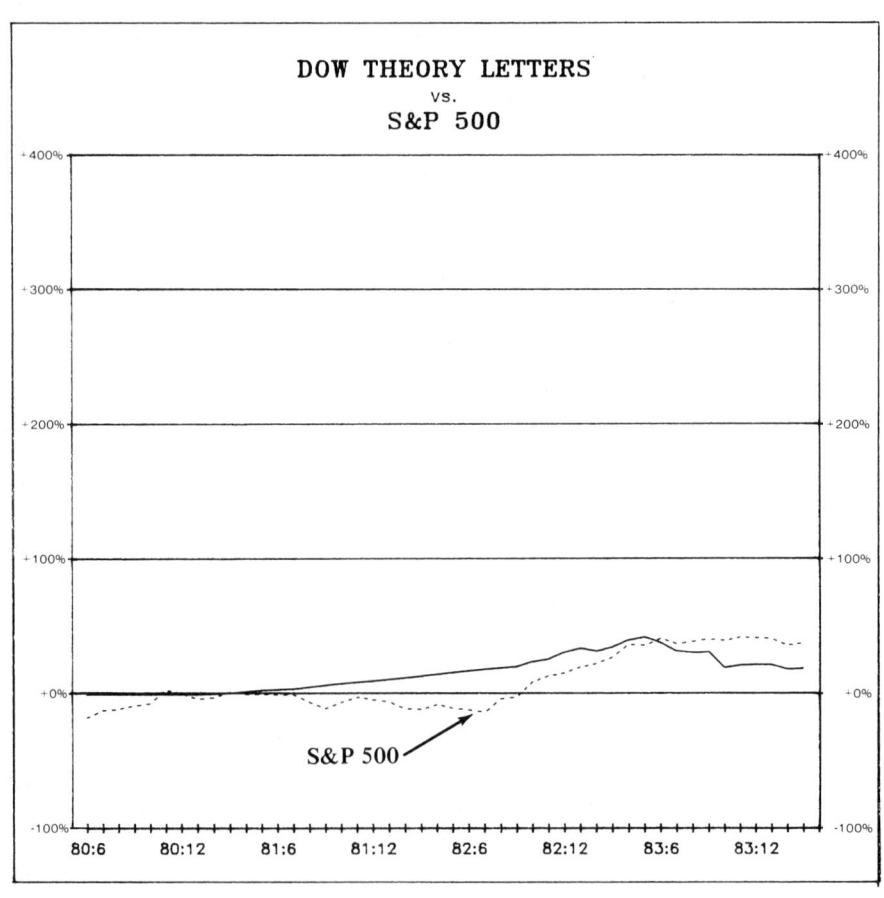

THE GRANVILLE® MARKET LETTER

©1983 The Granville Market Letter, Inc. All Rights Reserved.   P.O. DRAWER 23006, KANSAS CITY, MISSOURI 64141

Volume XXI, Number 27   July 30, 1983   Whole Number 916
Registered with the S.E.C.   Written solely by Joseph Granville

SHADES OF '73

I had stated in the 1976 Strategy book, that when the Net Field Trend Indicator gets up into the +17 to +20 area, that that is the best single indication of the true internal market peak. That precedes the external peak in the Dow-Jones industrial average that occurs on a much lower Net Field Trend Indicator reading. Also accompanying the lower NFI reading on the Dow peak is a cluster of Climax Indicator upside non-confirmations. That technical combination is unbeatable in homing in on major market peaks. The 1973-74 period comprised a severe bear market in stocks. The warnings came from the NFI and the CLX. The Net Field Trend Indicator peaked at +17 on December 6, 1972, when the Dow-Jones industrial average stood at 1027.54. The Dow then declined to exactly the 1000 level and then rallied sharply to 1051.70 by January 11, 1973. On that rally the NFI had declined from +17 to +10 and had only rallied back to +11 by the time the Dow peaked out. Just before the Dow peak the Climax Indicator peaked at +16 and then recorded CLX upside non-confirmations at +14, +9, +8 and +9. Generally, the NFI leads the Dow on market peaks by anywhere from five to seven weeks. The lead time on the 1973 Dow peak was five weeks. Those signals were followed by a severe bear market.

Is a similar signal now being recorded? The answer is emphatically, yes. Here are the figures: On April 29th the Net Field Trend Indicator topped out at +19. The Dow-Jones industrial average closed that day at 1226.20. That was the best single indication of the true internal market peak. Subsequent Dow rallies saw the Dow peak out at 1248.30 on June 16th, seven weeks after the NFI peak. While the Dow was making the final bull market run, the NFI had dropped from +19 to +8, rallying weakly to +10 on the final Dow peak. The Climax Indicator had reached +15 on the day of the top. When it reached the +15 reading again on July 20th, the day of the 30-point Dow rally, the NFI was down to -3, lower than it was at the end of January, 1973. There are no indications now whatsoever that the Dow could make a meaningful new high. The latest attempts to do this following the 30-point rise of July 20th saw a bearish cluster of Climax Indicator upside non-confirmations. This is why the call went out for a straight down market. What we are seeing here are major technical upside failures, and following such major signals, it would be a miracle if the developing decline was contained within Wall Street guidelines.

One might argue that the NFI had declined last December to -9 and had fully recovered, and so why be overly concerned about a -3 reading? The difference is like night and day. Last December the public had only started to stream back into the market, and the warnings stemming from new issues, stock splits, low-priced stocks, mutual

(continued on page 4)

The Granville Market Letter

The Granville Market Letter is published 46 times a year and is written solely by Joseph E. Granville, who for a period enjoyed a reputation as perhaps the foremost market technical analyst. Granville does supplement his newsletter with a telephone hotline service, but it is available only for an extra fee. An annual subscription costs $250; a semi-annual subscription costs $150; and a four-issue trial subscription is available for $25. The address of the Granville Market Letter is P. O. Drawer 23006, Kansas City, Missouri 64141. Granville has been writing his newsletter for 22 years, beginning in 1963. This is among the longest periods of publication of any of the major investment newsletters.

Granville is a self-proclaimed 100% technician: "Earnings have nothing to do with market timing, and market timing is everything." Granville devotes two pages of each issue to reviewing the technical picture of each of the 30 stocks making up the Dow Jones Industrial Average and giving the readings for several of his trademarked technical indicators—several of which have become widely respected among market technicians over the years. Three pages of a typical issue are devoted to general market commentary, and another page advises new subscribers what to do and reviews past recommendations.

Subscribers are not told what percentage of investable funds they should invest in the market and what portion to keep in cash. Instead,

The Granville Market Letter

Granville's advice typically has been couched in all-or-nothing terms; either a subscriber should be completely on the long side of the market or completely short. If an advisor has you hedged, Granville has often said, then that is tantamount to admitting he does not know what he is doing.

Writing Style

Typical of this black vs. white, right vs. wrong attitude towards the market is the style of Granville's market commentary, which often takes on a religious fervor. For example, in support of his conviction that we are in a bear market, Granville wrote, "the days of the bulls are numbered and private arks should be ready now before the rains come, rains that promise to be a flood drowning the majority." To further his case that you should not listen to what "Wall Street" is telling you, he wrote, "the financial Merlins have appeared invincible in their investment advice and, at the worst of times, the public naively places their substance at the altar of the shrine of Broad and Wall." It would not be entirely unfair to say that Granville sees the Market and the Tape as the only gods worthy of worship—and himself one of the anointed high priests.

Beginning in late 1983, Granville's letter took on a more short-term focus than previously. In addition to offering general market commentary of the above sort and recommending which stocks to buy or sell short, Granville now recommends two additional portfolios, one which trades stock index futures and one which trades gold futures. The performance rating the HFD has calculated for *The Granville Market Letter* back to mid-1980 is based on his stock recommendations—what he now calls his Aggressive Traders Portfolio.

Performance

The accompanying chart depicts the monthly fluctuations of Granville's stock recommendations. In the last six months of 1980, Granville's picks were up 10.6%, and during 1981 they lost 3.3%. They lost 29.8% in 1982 and 25.2% in 1983. During the first quarter of 1984, his stocks gained 8.2%. Cumulatively for the 45-month period from mid-1980 to March 31, 1984, Granville's stock picks have lost 39.2%, placing him at the bottom of the list of newsletters that the HFD monitored for that period of time. Over the same 45-month period of time, for purposes of comparison, the S & P 500 was up 68.2% while a portfolio of Treasury bills would have gained 49.5%.

This poor performance was due to a combination of both poor timing and sub-market performance of his recommended stocks. As shown in Section V on newsletters' market timing abilities, Granville's market timing over this 45-month period would have led to a loss of 4.6% —if Granville's stocks had all performed exactly as had the NYSE Composite index. While this 4.6% loss puts *The Granville Market Letter* at the bottom on market timing grounds, the 39.2% loss actually turned in by Granville's stock selections means that his recommended stocks underperformed the market.

GRANVILLE MARKET LETTER

Period	Gain	Quintile
7/1 to 12/31/80	10.6%	Second lowest 20%
1981	−3.3%	Third highest 20%
1982	−29.8%	Lowest 20%
1983	−25.2%	Lowest 20%
Risk ranking	4.306	Third highest 20%
% 1983 Closeouts long term	17.2%	Lowest 20%
% 1982 Closeouts long term	100%	Highest 20%

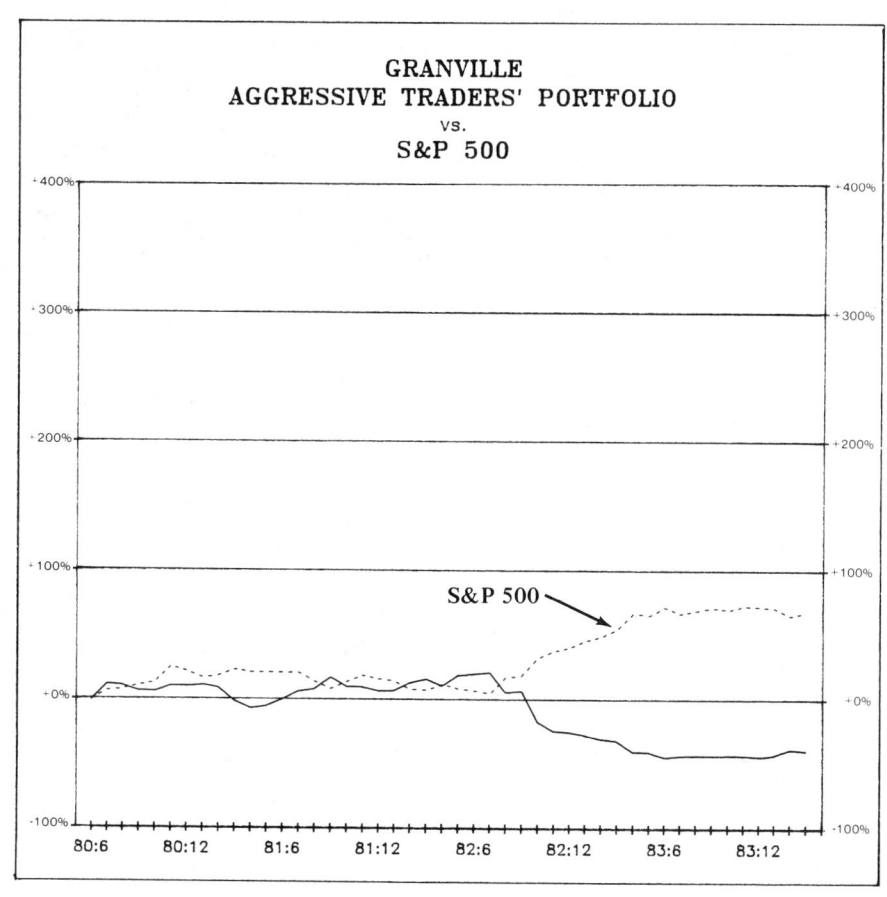

US ISSN 0017-4076

Head Office: 565 Fifth Avenue, New York, N.Y. 10017 • Mailing Address: P.O. Box 174, Princeton, New Jersey 08540

Phone (609) 921-6594 Telex 84 34 01

European Head Office: 12 Petersham Place, London SW7 5PX, England

GREEN'S COMMODITY MARKET COMMENTS

FEATURING
PRECIOUS METALS AND MONETARY MATTERS

BIWEEKLY REVIEW PUBLISHED BY ECONOMIC NEWS AGENCY, INC. EST. 1949

Vol. XVIII No. 19

October 5, 1983

GOLD   Since our last Comments were written, spot gold on Comex reached an intraday high of $416.50 on September 23, from where it declined to an intraday low of $397 on September 30. As of this writing, September 30, it closed at $401.90, and the London afternoon fix was $405. Traders and investors are long without a stop. Investors, who are long only 15% of their intended position at $412, should add 30% between that price and $370, in other words 15% at $391 and another 15% around $370. The recent decline in the price of gold was prompted by weakness in silver, and occurred despite the fact that interest rates were lower and the dollar weaker.

The 38th annual meeting of the International Monetary Fund concluded without resolving the problem of the debts of developing countries, which now approach the $700 billion mark. Despite some optimistic statements by IMF officials and U.S. Treasury Secretary Regan, the fact remains that creditor nations and commercial banks sooner or later will have to absorb substantial losses on those loans. Fritz Leutwiler, Chairman of the Swiss National Bank and President of the Bank for International Settlements, who attended the meeting, in a speech at the National Press Club luncheon, stated among other things that "the world debt problem will leave deep marks [on banks' balance sheets.]" Mr. Leutwiler also suggested that further rescheduling of the repayment of those loans is inevitable, and that the interest due on them is not really collectible, unless new loans are granted for that purpose, all this assuming that IMF will be allowed to increase its quotas. The failure to increase IMF's financial resources, according to Mr. Leutwiler, would "disastrously worsen the debt problem." Therefore a lot now hinges on whether Congress will finally approve the $8.4 billion contribution increase to IMF.

In our opinion Brazil, which was the main topic of conversation at this year's IMF meeting, will default (actually it has already done so), despite all the press notices to the contrary, and will declare a moratorium on its debts before the IMF meeting convenes next September. When the majority of the participants in gold trading finally perceive this inevitable outcome, there will be fireworks in the gold pits around the world.

The Gold Institute recently released its 1982 coinage statistics, which show that a total of 5,896,110 oz. of gold was used for minting gold coins last year, representing about $2.2 billion. South Africa remained the largest user of gold for that purpose, with 3,328,888 oz.; Canada was in second place, having used 1,015,972 oz., and the United Kingdom third, having used 1,012,566 oz. The 1982 gold consumption for coinage minting declined 25% from the 7,909,983 oz. used for that purpose in 1981. 192 different gold coins were issued in 1982, versus 168 in 1981. The above totals do not include production of U.S. gold medallions, which are not coins of the realm. However that will change this year, since on September 13 the U.S. Mint began production of a $10 gold coin to commemorate the Olympic Games, the first time in 50 years that a U.S. gold coin is minted which will be a coin of the realm.

In September, the average price of gold on the London afternoon fix was $411.80, versus $416.23 in August and $437.31 in September of last year.

© Economic News Agency, Inc. - 1983

Green's Commodity Market Comments

Green's Commodity Market Comments has proven to be one of the best-performing investment newsletters monitored by the HFD. The newsletter is published bi-weekly by Economic News Agency, Inc. and is edited by Charles Stahl, a renowned technical analyst of the precious metals markets. Stahl, 63 years old, was originally trained as an architect and is a concentration camp survivor with close to 30 years experience in gold trading. An annual subscription costs $240; a semi-annual subscription is available for $150; and a three-month trial subscription is offered for $65 from P. O. Box 174, Princeton, New Jersey 08540. The telephone number is (609) 921-6594. Despite the newsletter's focus on gold and silver, two frequently volatile commodities, a telephone hotline is not offered to subscribers (though he has been known to answer subscribers' phone calls to his office). Each four-page issue of *Green's Commodity Market Comments* (GCMC) contains specific commentaries and short-term forecasts on the gold and silver bullion markets. Stahl also provides refineries' production statistics, consumption figures, and estimates of world precious metals supplies.

Sophistication May Be Required

Though *Green's Commodity Market Comments* is a relatively clear newsletter, it does assume a certain sophistication. Editor Stahl's recommendations occasionally require you to study the markets and make a decision as to whether the prerequisites for a given trade have been met. For example, in early 1981, Stahl recommended that traders attempt to play a technical rally after gold and silver reached his specified targets on the downside. Stahl's advice was to sell out with only a small profit if the rally off the lows was "swift," but to hold on for a greater profit if the rally initially was "belabored."

Gold did rally in the trading sessions following trading a low as Stahl had forecast, but was its rally "belabored?" Stahl wrote in his next issue, "of course it was. Any trader worth his salt could have seen that the rally was belabored." The consequences of a "right" or "wrong" answer to this question in this case included profits of some $50 per ounce of gold traded.

We bring this up here not to dispute Stahl's contention but instead to alert you to the level of sophistication that may be needed to fully utilize the trading rules set out in GCMC. Having started his service in 1949, Stahl brings a wealth of experience and sophistication to the precious metals market, and he understandably can become impatient with the uninitiated. (In the above-mentioned reply to the "belabored" issue, Stahl seemed to be scolding those of his subscribers who had called him asking whether or not the rally was in fact belabored.)

Another judgment you must make in translating Stahl's advice into actual trades concerns when to reinstate positions after profit targets have been hit. Stahl often recommends that positions be reinstated "after any correction." Unfortunately, the best price at which to buy during such correction is only clear in hindsight. The HFD, for example, immediately reinstates the position when the price first corrects as little as $1 from Stahl's specified profit targets. Though this admittedly is a very conservative rendering of Stahl's record, it is based on the assumption that, in the event the price corrected just $1 and then catapulted to new profits, Stahl would want to claim credit for those profits. Again, the point of bringing this up here is that, depending upon your sophistication, you could in such cases attempt to estimate how great a correction would ensue. Insofar as you do so successfully, the gains realized from GCMC would be even greater than those reported here.

Performance

The HFD has calculated GCMC's performance since July 1, 1980. The statistics that follow assume Stahl's advice was implemented on a non-margined basis. It is worth noting that this is an unrealistic assumption—commodities trading typically only requires a small good faith deposit of 10% or less. It is this leverage of 10 or even 20 times one's investment that characterizes the frenetic world of commodities trading. An investor who always employed leverage of 10:1 would have enjoyed gains 10 times larger than those reported below.

According to the HFD, GCMC gained 21.3% during the second half of 1980, added another 11.6% in 1981, surged 48.4% in 1982, advanced 20.2% in 1983, and profited 13.0% in the first quarter of 1984. GCMC shows an aggregate unleveraged gain of 172.7% over this 45-month period—the very best performance of the 30 portfolios tracked by the HFD over this period.

GREEN'S COMMODITY MARKET COMMENTS

Period	Gain	Quintile
7/1 to 12/31/80	21.3%	Third highest 20%
1981	11.6%	Highest 20%
1982	48.4%	Highest 20%
1983	20.2%	Second highest 20%
Risk ranking	6.207	Second highest 20%

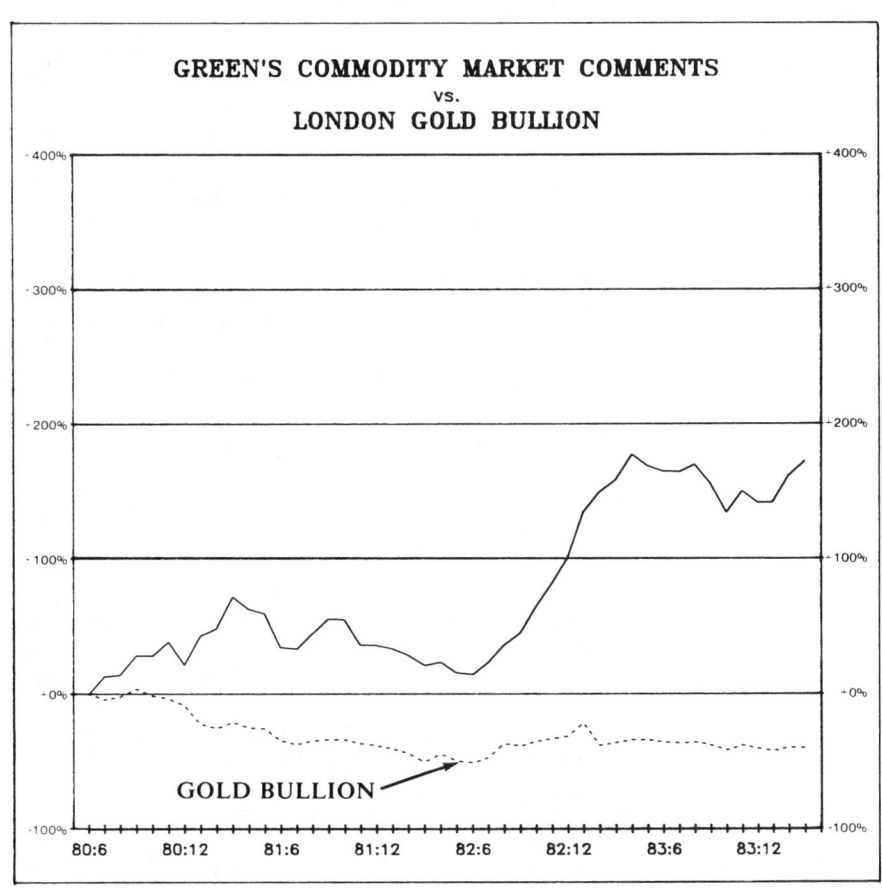

THE INVESTORS GUIDE TO DYNAMIC GROWTH FUNDS

JANUARY 1980   VOLUME 12   NO. 7

IN REVIEW

<u>1979 Was Another Good Year For GFG Funds</u> - On average, the 28 funds now on the GFG list were up a solid 48.7%. .... page 2

<u>An Automatic Investment Plan Update</u> - The Investment Plan is simple in design and easy to apply. It has just three rules and they do not require judgment type decisions where emotions can easily dictate choices.   ..... page 3

<u>Indicator Corner</u> - For the fifth time in mutual fund history, the cash position of the industry has climbed above 10%. In the not too distant future, this should help to trigger a strong market rise.   ..... page 5

<u>Top Performing GFG Funds for December</u> - were Sherman Dean (+28.1%), United Services (+20.2%), 20th Century Growth (+13.7%) and Constellation (+12.4%).   ..... page 7

<u>Current Highest Rated Funds</u> - are 20th Century Growth and Constellation on the Aggressive List, Weingarten and Dreyfus Number Nine on the Growth List, Price New Era and Energy on the Quality List and 20th Century Select and Dreyfus Third Century on the Special Situations List. ..... page 8

<u>The Relative Strength Report</u> - tries to show which funds are apt to do well in the months ahead.   ..... page 10

<u>Fund Group Comments</u> - A look at the strongest funds in four growth categories, a discussion of good buy opportunities and a gold fund comment.   ..... page 22

<u>Dreyfus Third Century</u> - A fund that invests in companies that are considered to be 'socially responsible' has been added to the Special Situations List.   ..... page 24

Also See

    Forecast 6   Centerfold Data Sheet...12
    Persistency Guide........7   Performance Charts..... 14
    Most Desirable Funds.... 9   Developing Funds.......24

Copyright 1980 by Growth Fund Research, Inc., Growth Fund Research Building, Yreka, Calif. 96097. All rights reserved. Issued Monthly - Annual U.S. Subscription - $52.00

Growth Fund Guide

Growth Fund Guide has been published monthly since July 1968 by Growth Fund Research, Inc., Growth Fund Research Building, Box 6600, Rapid City, South Dakota 57709. The telephone number is (605) 341-1971. An annual subscription costs $79. A sample copy is provided free upon request.

Each 24-page monthly issue of *Growth Fund Guide* contains an abundance of historical performance data for a large number of no-load equity mutual funds, subdivided by the investment aim of the fund and the time period examined. *Growth Fund Guide* also presents approximately three dozen semi-logarithmic graphs of the changes in net asset value for individual equity funds.

Rating Mutual Funds

Each month *Growth Fund Guide* rates 31 equity mutual funds and four money market funds on their potential for intermediate to long-term growth. Their ratings are derived from a number of historical factors including performance and volatility, size, inflow of capital, and a "management evaluation quotient." A forecast is provided of each fund's volatility and its performance in rising and in declining markets. The cash position of each fund is also reported. A supplementary list identifies the best-performing no-load and load stock funds over the preceding 12-month period, irrespective of whether these funds are among the ones followed on a continuing basis by the newsletter. The newsletter reviews nine technical indicators in each issue. In addition it has developed a forecasting tool that it labels "The No-Load Fund Composite Oscillator," which provides projections for both the long-term trends of the market and the secondary moves within long-term trends, and which can also be used to evaluate the strength of individual funds.

Although *Growth Fund Guide* provides some market timing, it has tended to adopt a long-term bullish perspective. Because of this investment posture, the newsletter makes few changes in its "Select Supervised List of Funds." It does not try to catch small market oscillations but rather focuses on long-term growth. It is therefore less useful to traders seeking to switch aggressively between extremely volatile stock mutual funds and money market funds.

Performance

Growth Fund Guide's "Supervised List" is subdivided into four types of funds: aggressive growth, growth, quality growth, and special situations. The HFD has calculated the performance of each of these four portfolios for the January 1, 1983 to March 31, 1984, period. The portfolio of aggressive growth funds edged up 6.3%; the group of growth funds increased in value 16.0%, the recommended quality growth funds increased in value 18.9%, and the special situations funds showed the best performance, gaining 18.9%. In comparison, the S & P 500 (including dividends) gained 19.6%, and a Treasury bill portfolio appreciated 11.6%.

The volatility of these groupings has been in accord once with what one would expect from the investment goal of each of them: the aggressive growth funds were twice as risky as the market; the growth funds experience 1.3 times the volatility of the S & P 500; the quality growth funds were 20% less volatile than the S & P 500, making this the fifth least volatile portfolio of the 69 portfolios followed by the HFD for this period; and the special situations funds proved to be 1.5 times as risky as the general stock market. Though all four GFG portfolios underperformed the S & P 500 over this 15-month period, the fact that the gain on the quality growth funds came on lower volatility gave it a risk- adjusted return greater than the market. In addition, only the Aggressive Growth Funds portfolio underperformed the T-Bill rate, so three of the four portfolios had positive return per unit of risk. (See the discussion of risk in Section III.)

GROWTH FUND GUIDE

Aggressive Growth Funds

Period	Gain	Quintile
1983	22.4%	Second highest 20%
Risk ranking	5.683	Third highest 20%
% 1983 Closeouts long term	100%	Highest 20%

Growth Funds

Period	Gain	Quintile
1983	24.2%	Second highest 20%
Risk ranking	3.759	Second lowest 20%
% 1983 Closeouts long term	100%	Highest 20%

Quality Growth Funds

Period	Gain	Quintile
1983	22.4%	Second highest 20%
Risk ranking	2.268	Lowest 20%
% 1983 Closeouts long term	100%	Highest 20%

Special Situations Funds

Period	Gain	Quintile
1983	30.3%	Highest 20%
Risk ranking	4.370	Third highest 20%
% 1983 Closeouts long term	66.7%	Third highest 20%

Average of Four Portfolios

Period	Gain	Quintile
1983	24.8%	Highest 20%

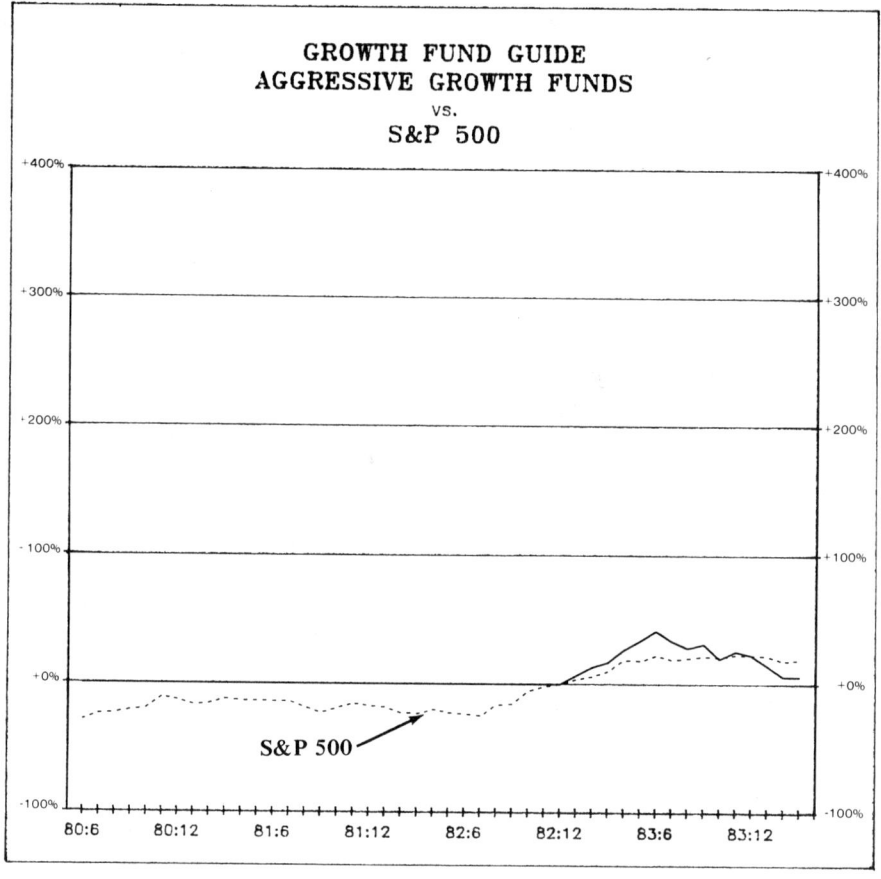

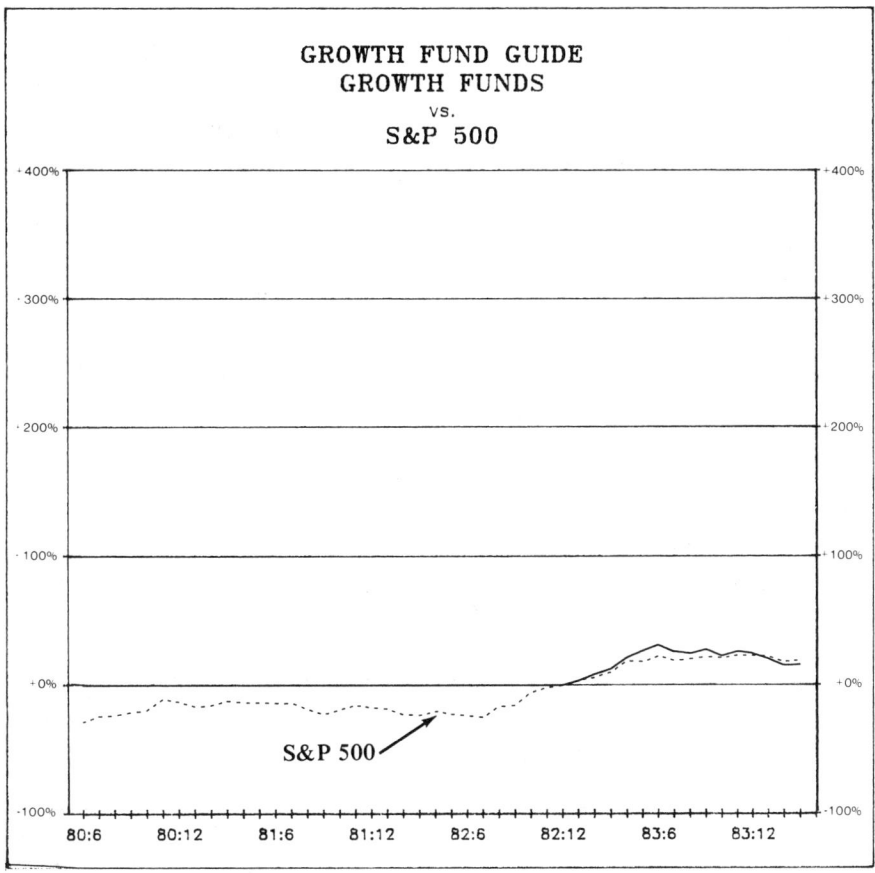

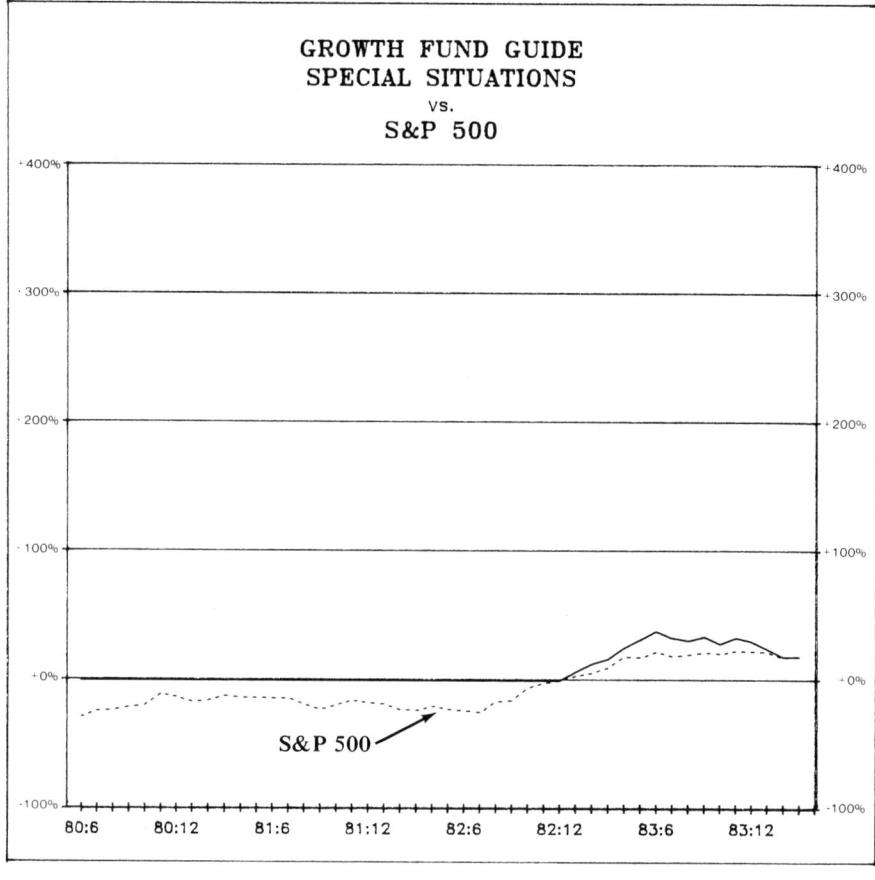

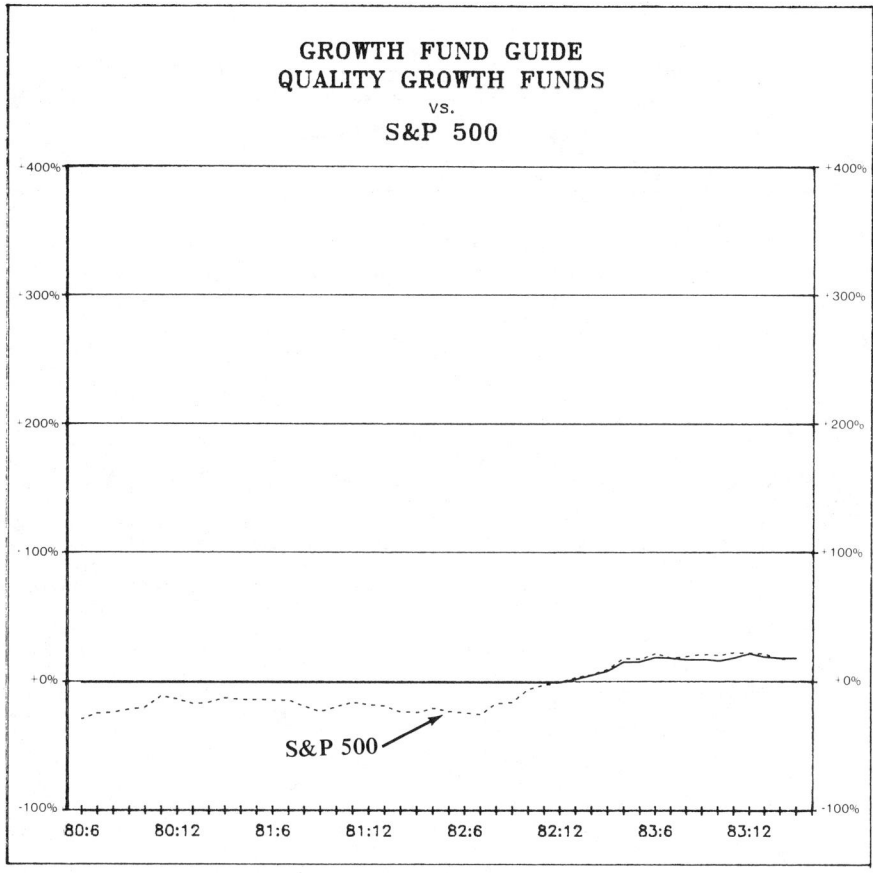

Growth Stock Outlook

P. O. Box 9911 CHEVY CHASE, MARYLAND 20815

Twice Monthly • $95.00 Per Year   Registered under the S.E.C. Investment Advisors Act.   • NINETEENTH YEAR

SEPTEMBER 15, 1983
VOL. 19, NO. 23

©Growth Stock Outlook, Inc., 1983
Reproduction Prohibited

"A conference is just an admission that you want someone to join you in your troubles." — Will Rogers

OIL ON THE ROCKS, OR SKY-HIGH? — Wall Street tongues began wagging several months ago as computers tracking oil stocks did a flip-flop, and chart followers couldn't believe their eyes. Oil stocks began to climb smartly in price, yet no one seemed to care why or bothered to examine prospects ahead. They could pay dearly for their folly if the scenario suddenly reverses and the price of oil heads down in earnest. From where we sit, it appears that the price of oil could move to $45 per barrel, or plunge to $18.

For a thousand years, inhabitants of the Middle East have been fighting a battle which seemingly has no end. Leaping over the moon might be a lot easier than settling various feuds in the Middle East. First, let's look at that nasty Iran-Iraq war. If and when the war is settled, it seems highly likely that 5,000,000—8,000,000 barrels per day of Iran-Iraq oil will begin pouring into the world oil market within eighteen months. This, in turn, could sink the price of oil to $18—$22 per barrel. Nobel economist Milton Friedman thinks the price of oil could drop to $8. We dismiss this highly unlikely premise because Friedman is an economist, not a hard-nosed businessman — more theoretical than practical.

What's behind that nasty little war is something else. As you know, the Soviet Union sells arms to both sides, ostensibly at a nice profit. More importantly, the Soviets are the world's second biggest oil producer behind Saudi Arabia. Therefore, we do not look for an early settlement of the war because the Soviets have much to lose from arms sales, but far more from lower oil prices. So the Soviets may somehow manage to keep things hot for a long time. One well-known news columnist stated in late July that the Soviets have 24 divisions on the Iranian border. This is an invasion force, not customs agents.

Let's examine the possibility for sky-high oil prices. Iraq will soon acquire French Super Etendard high-performance aircraft equipped with Exocet air-to-ground missiles which gave the British such a fit during the Falklands furor. These aircraft will be used to smash Iranian oil installations. Esmat Quitani, Iraq's deputy foreign minister, said in early September, "If we have the capacity to bomb their oil facilities, we will do it." Who's paying part of the bill for the Iraqi war? Saudi Arabia, according to most estimates.

Now comes the $64 question. Iran already has stated that they'll smack Saudi Arabia a big blow if Iranian facilities are blasted with those Exocet missiles. Will the Saudis retaliate, and with what? Mr. Khomeni stated in late July that Iran just might block the Strait of Hormuz. The United States already is on record that it will not tolerate such an act. Will the U.S. smash Iran in event Hormuz is plugged? Will the Soviets move into Iran in force by invitation? If the Saudis are attacked, or Hormuz is blocked, oil could quickly escalate to $45 per barrel. Trying to contain such a flap once it starts in the Middle East may not be easy. With Khomeni gone, saner heads should prevail in Iran. But who knows what he will do, or how long he will last. Whatever happens, do keep your eye on the Middle East where anything could evolve.

NO DEFLATION? — When we spoke at investment conferences in San Francisco and Hawaii in July, we noted that inflation was accepted as a foregone conclusion — except for one speaker. We stated that such a lopsided consensus invariably is wrong and that investors are not prepared for no inflation or, their biggest horror, genuine deflation. It would be simply wonderful for the stock market, and devastating for real estate gamblers and gold bugs. Will it happen? Your guess is as good as any, but we feel genuinely uneasy that inflation psychosis remains rampant. Do look at the potential for losing your shirt in today's new investment climate.

PLAY IN DEFENSE STOCKS — Richard Russell, one of the old-timers in the investment letter business, reports that "roughly 30% of all world spending now goes into defense. Roughly 45% of all the stocks on the NYSE are engaged in some form of defense production or high technology production that is defense oriented."

As noted above, the Middle East tinderbox could soak up a lot of hardware if things really get hot. A few GSO companies, **Pacific Scientific, TSI** and **Zero**, offer some exposure in the defense area. TSI could be a real sleeper because it has a wealth of technology for such a small company.

NO GOLD BOOM ON HORIZON — What's cooking with the Consumer Price Index (CPI)? Plenty. At midyear (June) the CPI was up a modest 2.6% in the latest twelve months (6-30-82 to 6-30-83). In June 1983 alone, the CPI was up a meager 0.2%. This continued low inflation rate was reflected in a sluggish gold price, which is going nowhere.

A passel of gold bugs are forecasting gold at $3,000—$4,200 the ounce by 1986. That's not far off. Those gold guessers may have about as much success in teaching a frog to sing opera!

INTERSTATE HIGHWAY SYSTEM BECKONS — Quite a ruckus was stirred up when that highway bridge in Connecticut fell apart and triggered an incredible traffic snarl. Although the interstate highway system accounts for only 1% of all roads in our country, the system carries 20% of our nation's traffic.

Think of all the repairs needed in this decade, plus bridge replacements. We hope to come up with a candidate or two in this area which, hopefully, could grow for years. The two top cement-consuming states are Texas and California, so keep an eye on companies operating there. If any of our readers have viable candidates with good growth records, do let us know.

Information presented here was obtained from sources believed to be reliable but accuracy and completeness and opinions based on this information are not guaranteed. Under no circumstances is this an offer to sell or a solicitation to buy securities suggested herein. The publisher may have an interest in companies mentioned which we disclose so that you may judge the possibility and extent of bias on our part. It should not be assumed that recommendations will be profitable or will equal the performance of securities listed here or recommended in the past. All data and information, and opinions expressed, are subject to change without notice. Published by GROWTH STOCK OUTLOOK, INC., a Maryland corporation.

Growth Stock Outlook

Growth Stock Outlook is published twice monthly by Charles Allmon. He supplements his newsletter with a weekly hotline. An annual subscription costs $125; a three-month trial subscription is available for $40. The address is P. O. Box 15381, Chevy Chase, Maryland 20815. *Growth Stock Outlook* has been published since 1965.

Growth Stock Outlook provides the following performance statistics, which we have no reason to believe are untrue. Between January 1, 1976, and February 1, 1984, GSO recommended 93 new stocks, an average of just under one per month. Forty of these 93 doubled or more in price. Impressively, 78 of the 93 recommendations increased in price, while only eight of the recommendations declined more than 25% in price. It should be remembered, of course, that this remarkable performance occurred during a period marked by a sustained bull market in secondary (second-tier) stocks, during which the NASDAQ OTC Composite Index more than tripled.

As of February 15, 1984, GSO followed a total of 105 stocks in its "Stock Selection Guide"; 47 of these stocks traded on the NYSE, 10 on the Amex, and 48 over the counter. With respect to each of these companies, GSO provides an earnings history back to 1977 along with a 1984 estimate, book value, return on equity, revenues, dividend yield, institutional ownership, price-earnings ratio, a GSO rating from A to C, and the number of consecutive years of uninterrupted growth enjoyed by that company. In the first issue of each month, GSO reports on its "$50,000 Supervised Portfolio."

Consistently Good Performance

GSO is the sole investment newsletter tracked by the HFD that has outperformed all six of the major market indexes (DJIA, NYSE Composite, Amex Market Value Index, S & P 500, NASDAQ OTC Composite, and the Wilshire 5000 Equity Index) during each of the four periods for which the HFD has calculated performance data for newsletters: July to December 1980, 1981, 1982, and 1983. A graph detailing the particulars of GSO performance since July 1, 1980 in comparison to the S & P 500 is shown on page 000.

On a risk-adjusted basis, *Growth Stock Outlook* ranks first among the letters we have monitored since mid-1980. GSO's cumulative gain for this 45-month period of 133.2% is almost double the total return of the S & P 500, yet GSO turned in this gain with 10% less risk (volatility) than the S & P. (See the appendix that ranks all letters on absolute and risk-adjusted performance at the end of this book.)

GSO takes a relatively long-term view of the markets, not attempting to trade in and out to avoid any corrections. This keeps transaction costs down and a significant portion of gains in the long-term capital gains category. In 1982, 61.5% of the positions closed out by GSO in its Supervised Portfolio were held for longer than a year; in 1983 the figure was 74.1%.

GROWTH STOCK OUTLOOK
(Supervised Portfolio)

Period	Gain	Quintile
7/1 to 12/31/80	+34.0%	Highest 20%
1981	+11.8%	Highest 20%
1982	+24.0%	Third highest 20%
1983	+33.1%	Highest 20%
Risk ranking:	4.014	Second lowest 20%
% 1983 Closeouts long term	74.1%	Third highest 20%
% 1982 Closeouts long term	61.5%	Third highest 20%

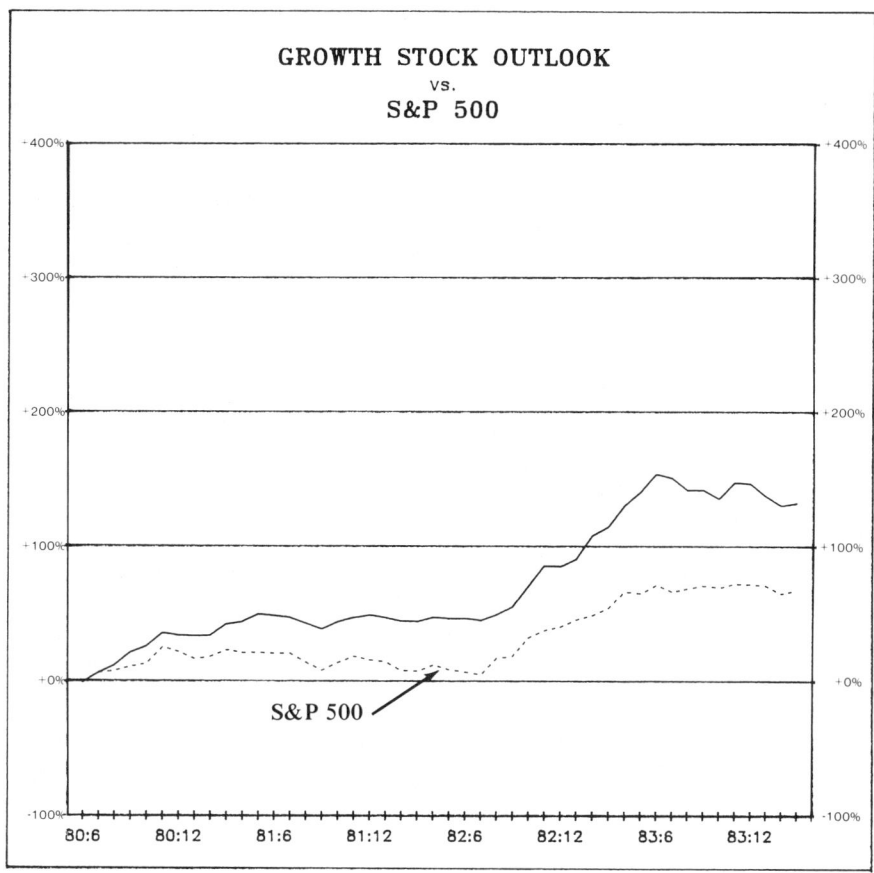

Harry Browne's SPECIAL REPORTS

HARRY BROWNE SPECIAL REPORTS, INC.   (512) 453-7313   BOX 5586   AUSTIN, TEXAS 78763

INFLATION-DEFLATION UPDATE

May 16, 1983

File under: **Economic Conditions**

This article is an update of recent articles on the question of whether a new cycle of monetary inflation began last summer.[1]

The common assumption has been that the Federal Reserve "threw in the towel" last summer — forsaking its money-supply growth targets in order to force interest rates downward. However, the data have indicated that monetary stimulation wasn't the cause of last summer's interest rate drop.

It's more likely that interest rates fell because of the continuing downturn in the inflation rate and because the demand for business loans leveled off. From July 14, 1982, to April 13, 1983, the volume of business loans grew at an annual rate of only 2.6%.[2]

The M1 money supply grew rapidly during the last half of 1982, but this had been expected. The introduction of new types of bank checking accounts caused transfers of money into M_1 from savings and time deposits — which are counted in M_2 but not in M_1. Growth rates for M_2 and M_3, as well as for bank reserves and the monetary base, were normal during the last half of 1982.

However, all the monetary aggregates have grown rapidly since the beginning of this year. Most likely, the Fed will take measures to offset whatever is causing the rapid growth. But there's no guarantee of that, and no way to know how long this rapid growth will continue.

The table on page 68-9 shows the growth rates of various monetary aggregates for various recent periods.[3]

---

[1] "Has a New Inflationary Cycle Started?", February 16, 1983, page 66-5, filed under *Economic Conditions;* and the Front Page for issue 67.

[2] *U.S. Financial Data,* Federal Reserve Bank of St. Louis, April 22, 1983.

---

[3] In a recent issue, I mentioned that the Fed had revised a great deal of old data, and that I wasn't sure whether the old data I was presenting was fully compatible with the new. As far as I can tell, all the data in the table in this issue are from the new, revised series.

CHANGES IN THE MONEY SUPPLY & ITS COMPONENTS
(Percentage changes converted to annual rates)

	March 1982 to March 1983	August 1982 to March 1983	August 1982 to December 1982	December 1982 to March 1983
M1	+10.9%	+15.2%	+13.6%	+17.3%
M2	+13.0%	+15.1%	+ 9.1%	+23.6%
M3	+10.5%	+ 9.5%	+ 7.9%	+11.5%
Monetary base	+ 9.4%	+10.6%	+ 7.5%	+14.7%
Bank reserves	+ 9.7%	+13.3%	+ 6.9%	+22.1%
All checkable deposits	+11.7%	+17.4%	+18.9%	+16.4%
All time & savings deposits	−10.7%	−22.1%	− 1.7%	−42.8%

Sources: M2, M3, and time deposits from *Federal Reserve Statistical Release H6(508),* February 25, 1983; all other data from Federal Reserve Bank of St. Louis *U.S. Financial Data,* February 25, 1983.

Monetary base and bank reserves data are from Federal Reserve Bank of St. Louis *U.S. Financial Data,* April 1, 1983. Monetary base figures are for March 31-March 30, September 1-March 30, September 1-December 29, and December 29-March 30. Bank reserve figures are for March 24-March 23, August 25-March 23, August 25-December 22, and December 22-March 23.

All other data are from *Federal Reserve Statistical Release H6 (508),* April 15, 1983. Checkable deposits and time & savings deposits data include both banks and thrift institutions.

© Harry Browne Special Reports, Inc., P.O. Box 5586, Austin, Texas 78763

Harry Browne's Special Reports

Harry Browne's Special Reports are published by Harry Browne's Special Reports, Inc., P. O. Box 5586, Austin, Texas 78763. The subscription rate is $225 for ten issues. This is not necessarily an annual subscription; rather, it is for whatever length of time it takes Browne to publish ten issues—and Browne varies the length of time between issues according to how much he has to say. Usually, the issues are published every five or six weeks. A limited form of telephone hotline service is made available to subscribers at no extra charge. When any recommended investment nears its recommended stop-loss point, a taped telephone message will provide updates on the status of the recommendation—whether to sell or hold and whether to change one's stop-loss order. In addition, Browne occasionally sends to subscribers a special investment bulletin or mailgram. A one-issue trial subscription costs $5.

Harry Browne is the well-known author of several bestselling financial books, including *How You Can Profit From the Coming Monetary Crisis*, *New Profits From the Monetary Crisis*, *How You Can Profit From the Coming Devaluation*, and *Inflation-Proofing Your Investments* (which was co-authored with Terry Coxon). The accuracy of many of the financial predictions made in these books established Browne's reputation and made him a familiar face at investment conferences and the like.

Model of Clarity

Harry Browne's Special Reports are a model of clarity. His analyses are well-written, insightful, and clear, and his graphs are well-drawn and easy to read. Browne is known for his concern about paper money and his advocacy of gold, silver, and Swiss bank accounts. Not surprisingly, therefore, a portion of his newsletter is devoted to these topics, as well as to making general observations, reporting on foreign exchange fluctuations, and making unambiguous investment recommendations.

Browne believes that a prudent investor should divide his capital between two portfolios—a permanent portfolio and a variable portfolio. In the Variable Portfolio, Browne actively trades investments in an attempt to profit from changing market trends. The Permanent Portfolio ignores changes in market trends and seeks to remain unchanged over many years. Investing in a diversified group of investments, including gold, silver, Swiss francs, common stocks, stocks of real estate and natural resource companies, and cash equivalents such as U.S. Treasury bills and bonds, the Permanent Portfolio aims to at least preserve its real value regardless of economic scenario.

Performance

The HFD has only tracked the performance of Browne's Variable Portfolio, not his Permanent Portfolio.* Unfortunately, the Variable Portfolio has significantly underperformed the return available from either T-Bills or the stock market. It lost 6.9% in 1981, gained 17.2% in 1982, and advanced 8.6% between January 1, 1983, and March 31, 1984, for an aggregate gain of 18.5% in the 3-1/4 years since the HFD began evaluating Browne's Variable Portfolio. In comparison, the S & P 500 dropped 4.9% in 1981 but surged 21.6% in 1982 and increased in value another 19.6% in the following 15 months, for a composite 39-month gain of 38.3%. A Treasury bill portfolio would have gained 41.3%.

Part of this lower gain was due to the low risk incurred by the portfolio—only slightly more than half the risk of the S & P 500 over the 39-month period. For large periods of time during this period, Browne recommended that the variable portfolio be invested entirely

---

* Since early 1983, a mutual fund known as the Permanent Portfolio Fund has been in operation, based on Browne's concept of a permanent portfolio. Since it first offered shares publicly on December 1, 1982, by May 4, 1984, the fund had appreciated by 2.1%. This performance was better than gold, silver, or the major foreign currencies, but worse than the average performance of the stock market or the return obtainable on Treasury bills.

in Treasury bills. Deviations from that strategy have been relatively infrequent, such as a late-1982, early-1983 foray into silver and late-1983 speculations in the Swiss Franc and silver. But because it underperformed the Treasury bill rate, the Variable Portfolio's return per unit of risk was negative.

HARRY BROWNE'S SPECIAL REPORTS
Variable Portfolio

Period	Gain	Quintile
1981	−6.9%	Second lowest 20%
1982	17.2%	Second lowest 20%
1983	8.0%	Third highest 20%
Risk ranking	2.857	Lowest 20%

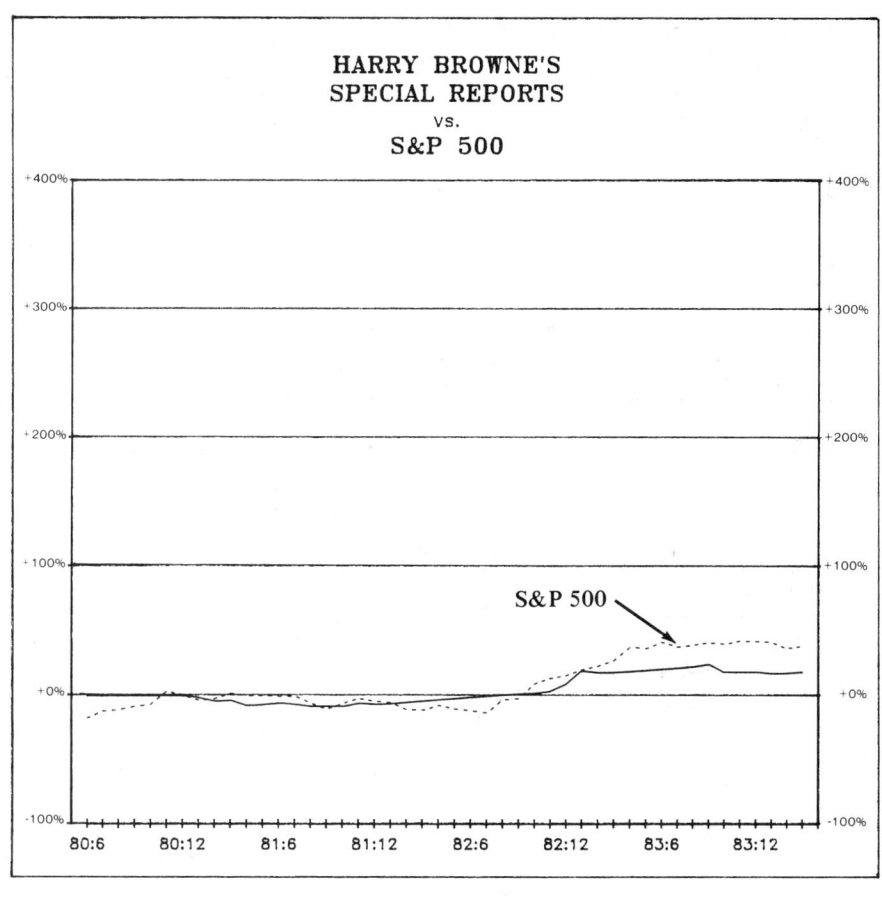

HEIM INVESTMENT LETTER

Published twice-monthly by: HEIM INVESTMENT SERVICES, INC., 729 S.W. Alder Street, Suite 420, Portland, Oregon 97205. Tel. (503) 228-9555. Send subscriptions to above address. 1 year subscription rate $150. $165 outside North America.

VOLUME 10   NOVEMBER 25, 1983   NUMBER 22

PRICES ON NOVEMBER 23, 1983

```
D.J. INDU. . . . . . . . . . . . 1275.61
D.J. TRAN. . . . . . . . . . . . .607.53
D.J. UTIL. . . . . . . . . . . . .137.72
LONDON P.M. GOLD . . . . . . . . $375.75
H&H SPOT SILVER  . . . . . . . . .$8.585
```

* * * * * *

* GOLD AND SILVER CONTINUE TO GIVE US THE IMPRESSION THAT THEY WILL MAKE A MOVE ON THE UPSIDE SOON. POSITIVE TECHNICAL FACTORS ARE IN PLACE. OUR IMAP FOR GOLD GAVE A BUY SIGNAL ON 10-28-83.

* THE STOCK MARKET APPEARS TO BE IN A RATHER UNCERTAIN CONDITION AT THIS TIME. INTEREST RATES SEEM TO BE MOVING THE PRICE OF STOCKS, AND THEIR DIRECTION IS ALSO UNCERTAIN. WE SUGGEST THAT YOU MAINTAIN A NEUTRAL POSITION ON STOCKS.

* RECOMMENDED INVESTMENT POSITIONS:

THE CONSERVATIVE AND THE AGGRESSIVE INVESTOR SHOULD HAVE 20% OF INVESTABLE ASSETS IN BULLION TYPE GOLD COINS, AND 10% IN SILVER (BULLION OR COINS). 70% OF INVESTABLE ASSETS SHOULD BE IN CASH (T-BILLS OR EQUIVALENT), EARNING INCOME. 13-WEEK T-BILLS CAN GIVE YOU ABOUT A 8.8% INCOME.

* IT IS GENERALLY EXPECTED THAT NEW SUBSCRIBERS WILL WAIT UNTIL WE MAKE NEW INVESTMENT CHANGES, RATHER THAN SHIFTING OVER IMMEDIATELY TO OUR CURRENT POSITION.

* OUR TOLL FREE NUMBER, 800-547-1680, IS AVAILABLE FOR ANYONE WHO WANTS TO BUY GOLD OR SILVER COINS OR OBTAIN INFORMATION.

Gold and Silver

We still see bullish or positive price patterns showing on the short-term charts for gold and silver. Perhaps the potential upside price action will arrive next week--it is long overdue in our opinion. A move of $3 is all that it would take to cause gold to break out above a 2-1/2 month downtrend line. If this happens, technical analysis suggests that a trip to $390 would occur immediately, then, after a short pause, we should find gold above $400 again.

On the long-term chart for gold, we continue to show the massive multi-year flag down formation that has proved so useful to us in predicting major gold price moves. We are confident that the

© 1983 Heim Investment Services, Inc.

Heim Investment Letter

The Heim Investment Letter is edited twice monthly by Lawrence H. Heim and Truman C. Pagh and published by Heim Investment Services, Inc., 729 S. W. Alder Street, Suite 420, Portland, Oregon 97205. The telephone number is (503) 228-9555. An annual subscription costs $150 (although on several occasions recently they have offered a "special" discount rate of $95/year); a six-month subscription is available for $80; and a one-month trial subscription is offered for $10. The newsletter is not supplemented by a telephone hotline. In its eleventh year of publication, the *Heim Investment Letter* is one of the longer-lived letters in the industry.

Each six-page issue summarizes the recommended investment posture for subscribers and then employs technical analysis to review current trends in the stock, gold, and silver markets. Changes in investment advice are relatively infrequent; for much of the period since mid-1980 when the HFD first began monitoring the service, the *Heim Investment Letter* has recommended that its subscribers invest 70% or more of their investable assets in T-Bills or other money market instruments. This steady income flow has made this newsletter one of the least risky of the 70 followed by the HFD.

Conservative Approach

As the low-risk nature of his advice would suggest, Heim orients his newsletter to the conservative investor. Beginning in 1983, Heim expanded his newsletter's orientation to include a portfolio for aggressive investors as well. As of May 1984, however, the aggressive portfolio has never differed from Heim's conservative portfolio.

According to HFD performance figures, the *Heim Investment Letter* gained 2.6% during the second half of 1980, added another 10.5% during 1981, lost 8.4% in 1982, and picked up another 4.7% from January 1, 1983, through March 31, 1984. The cumulative gain for the 45-month period was 8.8%. This places the *Heim Investment Letter* in the bottom 20% of newsletters we have been monitoring for this period. In comparison, one could have made 49.5% by staying in Treasury bills throughout.

Unprofitable Call

In 1982, Heim made an extremely unprofitable call, wiping out what at the time was one of the top performances for the year. In an issue dated August 6, 1982, and received by subscribers on or around August 9, 1982, the *Heim Investment Letter* urged its readers in a large, bold headline to "SELL!", arguing that "a modern-day DEPRESSION had begun." Subscribers were told to short stocks heavily. Within two weeks, the most powerful bull market in 50 years had taken off. Undaunted, Heim did not throw in the towel until mid-October, by which time his short sales had lost heavily. As a result, his newsletter's loss for the entire year was 8.4%.

HEIM INVESTMENT LETTER

Period	Gain	Quintile
7/1 to 12/31/80	2.6%	Lowest 20%
1981	10.5%	Highest 20%
1982	−8.4%	Lowest 20%
1983	2.6%	Second lowest 20%
Risk ranking	1.385	Lowest 20%
% 1983 Closeouts long term	(There were no closeouts in 1983)	
% 1982 Closeouts long term	0%	Lowest 20%

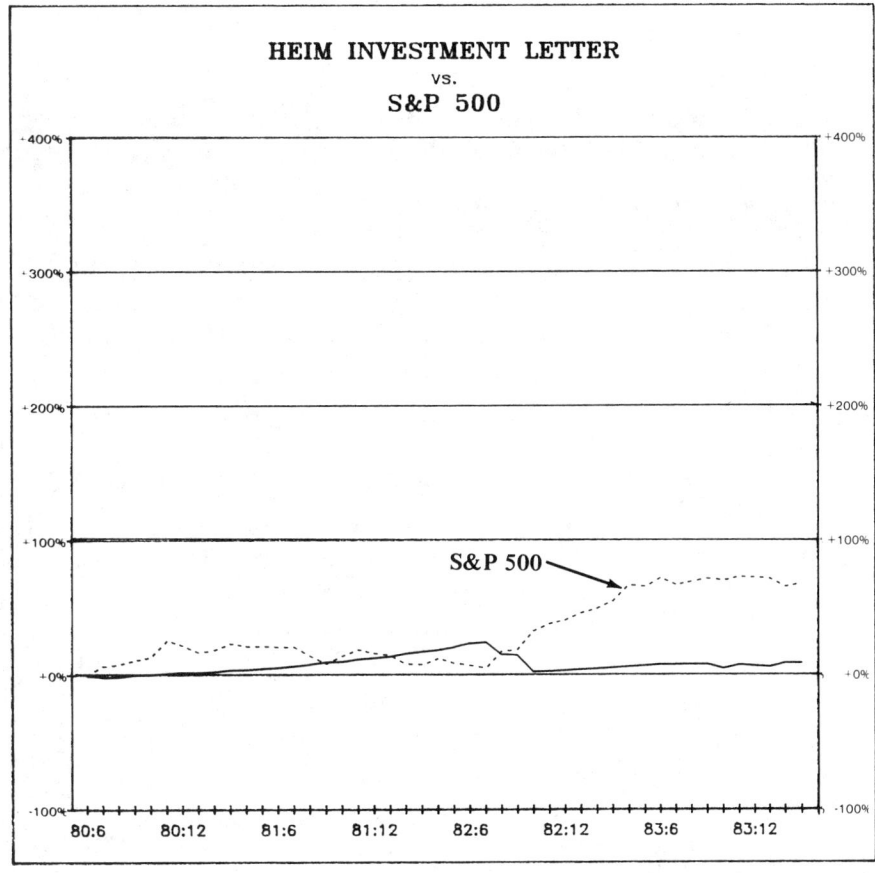

May, 1983   Volume III, No. 8

High Technology Investments™

REGISTERED WITH THE S.E.C. AS AN INVESTMENT ADVISER

"How dangerous it is to attempt new Discoveries, either for the length of the voyage, or the ignorance of the language, the want of Interpreters, danger of thieves and robbers, darkness of sudden falling fogges..."
— from Hakluyt's Voyages

Systematics, Inc. (SYST)

As of the close of the fiscal year 1982, last May, Systematics' President Walter V. Smiley was able to report "The company is now the unquestioned leader in bank data processing in the United States." In February of this calendar year they reported cumulative 9-months revenues of $47.1 million and revenues for the third quarter of $16.5 million. The corresponding quarter in the prior year showed revenues of $12.77 million. They have been public since August, 1981. There was a second stock offering last autumn.

As you may recall from last month's letter, we have been reviewing the analytical literature on and talking to people in the field of software for banks. Systematics markets software, but does so as an adjunct endeavor to the thier main business, which is to provide data processing services. Revenue from services has in the past accounted for around 95 percent of the total; Like Hogan, Systematics emphasizes their integrated approach to the creation of software systems, and their prospectus description of

Pursuant to the provisions of Rule 206 (4) of the Investment Advisers Act of 1940, we advise all readers to recognize that they should not assume that all recommendations made in the future will be profitable or will equal the performance of any recommendations referred to in this issue. The information presented in this issue has been obtained from sources believed to be reliable, but its accuracy is not guaranteed. The security portfolios of our employees, officers or affiliated companies may, in some instances, include securities mentioned in this issue.

The Adviser, its officers, directors, employees and members of their families (hereafter referred to as "associated persons") are not permitted to act upon advice before subscribers have had a reasonable opportunity to act first. Neither the advisor nor any associated person functions as a broker-dealer or is involved in the buying and selling of securities or commodities on a commercial basis.

All opinions expressed are our own, unless otherwise stated, and are given with the understanding that 1) subscribers or others acting upon the material presented assume all risks involved and 2) said opinions are not based on the individual needs or investment objectives of any individual subscriber.

what this means is succinct and helpful: "Each of the company's software systems is fully integrated, i.e., the systems may be used individually or in combination with each other. System integration permits data entered into one system to automatically flow to other appropriate systems, without manual re-entry of the data."

The alternative -- the way much conventional banking programs have grown up, has been with individual and functionally isolate program modules, each dedicated by account. One for savings, one for checking and so on, with no common data base and multiple entries of the same data required.

Systematics has evidently been working on the integrated approach for a number of years, and their package appears mature. Hogan has an integrated concept in their UMBRELLA, and into it they have plugged a Deposits application program and, more recently, a Loan system. At this stage, the Hogan product appears less complete than that offered by Systematics.

The technical difference between the two approaches appears (to me) to arise and matter when the program packages are to be installed, that is, tailored to serve the needs of a particular bank.

Hogan uses an adapter to make the customers computer receptive to its standard packages of software. Systematics has designed all their software to be adaptable in its several aspects. "All of the company's software uses a common system run flow, file organization, program logic and programming language (COBOL)." The finished, installed program, from Systematics, will be customized in detail to meet the requirements of the particular bank. If I were a Big banker, the decision I might weigh in choosing between the two would probably take into account the present completeness of the Systematics software vs probably higher downstream costs in maintenence and adaption to future changes.

If I were any other banker, small to large, I would probably be delighted to simply drop the whole data processing problem into the capable and experienced hands of Systematics. In this light, it seems clear the two companies are not head-to-head competitors at this point, except in that segment of business attributible to outright software licensing. It might appear that in its willingness to permit banks to license its proprietary software, in lieu of using the company's complete data processing service, that Systematics is undercutting its own main business. On scrutiny, however, it appears that the software licenses could either a) salvage revenues from business which would otherwise go away into do-it-yourself processing, b) appeal straight to the richest component of the market.

We remarked last month on the exceedingly short tenure -- less than a year -- of employment of data processing professionals in banks. Systematics has seized this problem and is solving it by creating, through a thoroughgoing education program, a body of data processing professionals immersed in the technology of data processing for banks. This is not a casual project of the company. They have established a campus and make substantial committments of funding to the effort. The people who attend are learning the Systematics System, of course, so whether they remain within the company or move out into banks, they are going to secure and assure future business.

The company was originally funded by the Stephens, Inc., in 1968, and they retain a substantial ownership position in the company. You might wish to refer to The Wall Street Journal's front page for 4/26/83 for a story on this firm, run beneath the slugline "Quiet Approach."

We added Systematics to the TPA portolio on 4/25/83 at an asked price of $42.25. It is in the trader's portfolio for the nonce because of the current uncertainty about a presidential veto and/or possible override, of the repeal of July 1 witholding provision. Such a veto is not now expected, but I somehow feel it is not out of the question. There could be some turbulence in the stock in the meantime, howev-

High Technology Investments, Copyright © 1983 by Gianturco & Michaels, Inc., 5009 Caroline, Suite 207, Houston, Texas 77004. All rights reserved. Permission to reprint any material herein is expressly prohibited without the consent of the publisher. Subscription, monthly newsletter, $36. Complete service, $194.

High Technology Investments

High Technology Investments, now in its sixth year of publication, is edited by Michael C. Gianturco, a former writer for NASA who earned an M.S. degree in biochemistry. In 1982, Gianturco wrote a 275-page guide to using a comPAQ computer. The newsletter focuses principally, as its names suggests, on a relatively narrow market segment, mostly computer and bio technology stocks. An annual subscription costs $119, and includes twelve monthly four-page newsletters and 48 one-page computer print-outs. A quarterly 18-page database is offered for $14 per printout. This database maintains data for 102 high-technology companies. The newsletter's address is 5925 Kirby Drive, Suite 219, Houston, Texas 77005.

The Utility of Studying a New Stock's Past Performance

Because *High Technology Investments* seeks to analyze the likelihood of scientific breakthroughs at a number of high- technology companies and the prospective marketability of any such scientific breakthrough, it believes that the statistical history of a stock's performance is "utterly useless" to its approach. Gianturco instead relies upon his ability to expertly analyze each company's prospects, frequently visiting the company himself. Each informative four-page monthly issue of the newsletter describes the prospects for various segments of the high technology industry and the position of a number of companies in that evolving technology. Each weekly computer update simply restates which stocks are held in each of two portfolios—its "Long-Term Portfolio" and its "Trigger Price Advisory Portfolio" for traders—and how many shares of each stock were purchased on what date at what price. Tentative target prices and stop-loss points are given for stocks included in both portfolios, although subscribers are asked to call a specified telephone number to receive an updated recommendation for any stock that reaches its target or stop. (More often than not, during the period the HFD tracked the performance of these portfolios, Gianturco chose not to sell out when a stop was hit, lowering the stop instead.)

Performance

The HFD has calculated the performance of the two portfolios of stocks recommended by *High Technology Investments*. According to HFD performance data, the Long-Term Portfolio edged up 3.5% in 1983 but receded 2.8% during the first quarter of 1984, for an aggregate gain of 0.6%. The Trigger Price Advisory Portfolio plummeted 19.2% in 1983 and dropped 1.4% more in the first three months of 1984, for a composite loss of 20.4%. In comparison, the S & P 500 soared 22.5% in 1983 and backtracked just 2.4% in early 1984, making its aggregate 15-month gain 19.6%, after adjusting for dividends paid. A Treasury bill portfolio would have gained 11.6% over the same period. Because most of the stocks recommended by *High Technology Investments* are traded over the counter, a more apt market measure might be the NASDAQ OTC Composite Average, which rose 19.9% in 1983 but dropped 10.0% in the first quarter of 1984, for an aggregate 15-month gain of 7.9%. These last figures are not adjusted for dividends.

Risk-Adjusted Performance

Despite the newsletter's concentration on high-risk stocks, the risk measurements for its two portfolios show that their risk was relatively low. This was caused by the high proportion of the two portfolios that was invested in cash during much of the 15- month period. The Long-Term Portfolio was 1.4 times as volatile as the S & P 500 but only 0.8 times as volatile as the NASDAQ OTC Composite over this period. The Trigger Price Advisory Portfolio was only 0.8 times as volatile as the S & P 500 and less than half as volatile as the NASDAQ OTC Composite. The fact that the performance of these two portfolios was so low despite this low risk means that, on a risk-adjusted basis, their rankings were even lower. For this 15-month period, in fact, their risk-adjusted performance places the newsletter in the bottom 10% of newsletters monitored by the HFD.

Although the two *High Technology Investments* portfolios have performed poorly since the beginning of 1983, the performance that Gianturco reports for them in 1982 was markedly better. The S & P 500 including dividends rose 21.5% in 1982; the NASDAQ OTC Composite Average, excluding dividends, increased 18.7%. The newsletter's own figures show a 1982 gain for its Long-Term Portfolio of 73% and a 13.9% gain in the traders' portfolio. The HFD has not independently calculated a performance rating for these portfolios for that year, but nevertheless, you should be aware that 15 months of data may not be enough to draw a firm conclusion.

HIGH TECHNOLOGY INVESTMENTS

"Trigger Price Advisory" Trading Portfolio

Period	Gain	Quintile
1983	−19.3%	Lowest 20%
Risk ranking	2.333	Lowest 20%
% 1983 Closeouts long term	10.0%	Lowest 20%

Long-Term Portfolio

Period	Gain	Quintile
1983	3.5%	Second lowest 20%
Risk ranking	3.880	Second lowest 20%
% 1983 Closeouts long term	75.0%	Third highest 20%

Average of Two Portfolios

Period	Gain	Quintile
1983	−7.9%	Lowest 20%

High Technology Investments

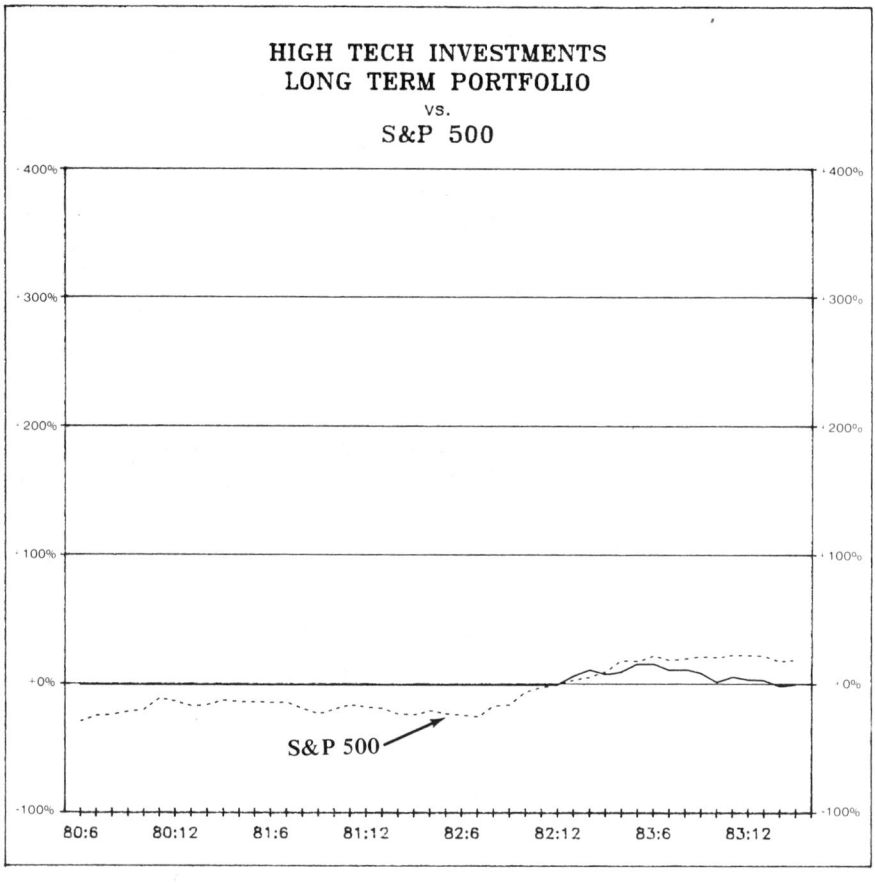

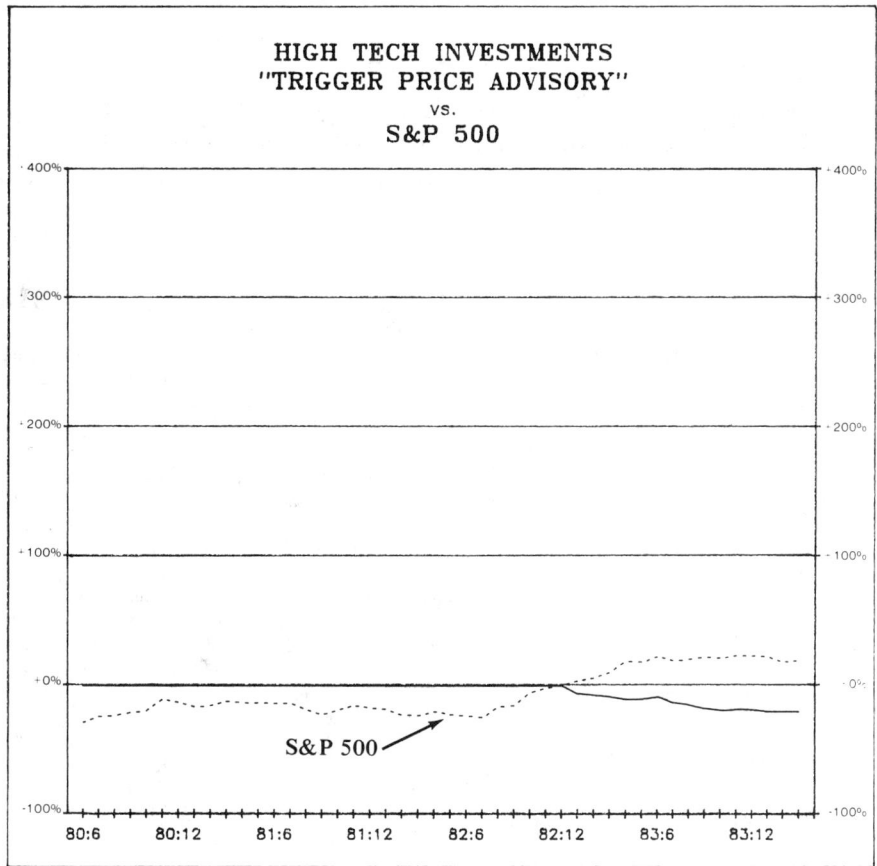

THE HOLT INVESTMENT ADVISORY

PUBLISHED BY: T.J. HOLT & COMPANY, INC., 290 POST ROAD WEST, WESTPORT, CT. 06880

RECOMMENDED INVESTMENT STRATEGY

JANUARY 7, 1983

Dow-Jones Industrials   *1045

NYSE Stock Index   *81.76

*1/5/83 closing

SPECULATORS HAVE
BEEN DOING MOST OF
THE BUYING OF LATE, AND
THEY CAN'T OFFSET
DEPLETED INSTITUTIONAL
COFFERS FOR LONG.
LOOK FOR A STEEP STOCK
SELL OFF............... 2

CONTINUED WORLDWIDE
ECONOMIC WEAKNESS
WILL SEND INTEREST RATES
SIGNIFICANTLY HIGHER,
CATCHING MOST
OBSERVERS COMPLETELY
BY SURPRISE............. 3

EVALUATION OF SELECTED
HIGHGRADE BONDS......... 6

RATING 100
WIDELY-HELD STOCKS 8

EIGHT KEY INDICATORS
OF THE MARKET'S
TECHNICAL POSITION 9

FOLLOW-UP REPORTS:
   AUTOMATIC SWITCH 11
   CSX PUT, FEB 50 11

FOR ALL PRACTICAL PURPOSES, the Administration now concedes that the budget deficit for both the 1983 and 1984 fiscal years will be a whole lot bigger than earlier projections. The handwriting has been on the wall for some time now. Actually, the figures to be submitted next week will probably be too low still. Government planners are again counting on an immediate and sustained, though modest, recovery to take hold. In short, the Treasury will have to borrow a lot more money this year than credit markets can readily accommodate.

Actually, yields of both Treasury bills and bonds have been nudging upward in the past two or three months—even before this year's massive borrowing gets under way. This is highly significant because (1) the Federal Reserve Board has repeatedly cut the discount rate during this period, and (2) the economy was noticeably weaker in the fourth quarter than in the preceding six months. Total business loans, seasonally adjusted, have dropped more than $5 billion from their October peak of $220 billion. Before that, they had trended upward.

The implications are serious. Most along Wall Street and in Washington are convinced that the liberal Fed and softening business loan demand will keep pushing interest rates down. But the evidence shows that the open market no longer succumbs to cuts in the discount rate. Nor will a slumping economy offset the pressure on rates from the Treasury's ballooning fiscal deficits and the mounting credit needs of illiquid debtors, notably the so-called less developed countries. We believe interest rates have touched bottom, and will move noticeably higher in the months to come.

Such an eventuality will no doubt catch Wall Street completely by surprise. Though many experts are looking for a technical correction, they are convinced that a brand new bull market is unfolding. More important, the tightening liquidity squeeze will erase any prospect for the beginning of a sound economic recovery.

Accordingly, industrial shares are definitely not the place to be right now; they are terribly overpriced. Instead, keep 50% of your portfolio in liquid assets such as Treasury bills and insured money market deposits. Continue to put 40% of available funds into the short sales of low-yielding, overpriced commons. The balance can be used for the purchase of put options.

CONFIDENTIAL REPORT TO SUBSCRIBERS — Reprinting Without Written Permission Strictly Prohibited

The Holt Investment Advisory

The Holt Investment Advisory has been published twice monthly since May 1967 by T. J. Holt & Company, Inc., 290 Post Road West, Westport, Connecticut 06880. Subscription rates are $180 per year; $98 for six months; and $25 for a three-month trial subscription.

Publicly Owned

T. J. Holt & Co., Inc. is one of only a handful of widely followed investment advisory subscription newsletters that are published by publicly owned corporations. The others include: Money Growth Institute, Inc., publisher of *The Speculator*; Arnold Bernhard & Co., the publisher of several Value Line publications which sold 19% of its stock to the public in mid-1983 for more than $30 million; and Standard & Poor's, a subsidiary of McGraw-Hill, which publishes *The Outlook* and *New Issue Investor*. Holt also handles managed accounts and publishes another newsletter entitled *Executive Wealth Advisory*. The fact that Holt's newsletter is publicly owned means that periodic reports must be filed with the SEC containing more information than is otherwise available for privately owned newsletters.

Holt, a prominent and long-term stock market bear, has made or lost money in trading for his company's account depending upon whether the market's action has been bullish or bearish. In 1980, a year which on balance was bullish, for example, Holt's realized and unrealized market trading losses amounted to −$272,682. In 1981, a bearish year, profits amounted to $889,000, and in 1982, the beginning of the most powerful bull market in 50 years, losses amounted to a whopping −$1,023,000. Despite this loss, Holt wrote in his newsletter in early 1983 that, "we believe the whole market rise since last summer has been an aberration."

What Each Newsletter Contains

In the first issue each month of *The Holt Investment Advisory*, which is 12 pages in length, Holt has eight regular features: "Recommended Investment Strategy," "Technically Speaking," "Behind the Market Facade," "The Holt Economic Analysis," "Evaluation of Selected Government and Listed Bonds," "Rating 100 Widely-Held Stocks," and graphs of eight medium- and long-term indicators. On the last page of this first issue of the month, Holt reviews all open recommendations and specifies which positions are currently attractive. In the second issue of the month, which is also typically 12 pages long, Holt presents market commentary, analyzes technical indicators, updates previous recommendations, reviews deep discount convertible bonds, writes about a selected stock group of interest, and devotes four pages to the following graphs: eight graphs depicting price movements and moving averages of four market indices; four weekly and four monthly graphs of gold and silver bullion and stock prices; five measures of the economy; and five measures of monetary and credit growth.

Holt views the international debt crisis with overriding concern and frequently discusses his expectation of declining economic liquidity, increased inflation coupled with deflation, and the likelihood of a major economic crisis. He presents cogent analysis and arguments in support of his unconventional forecasts. Not surprisingly, Holt's perspective strongly flavors his mix of recommended investments. For example, he often and sometimes exclusively recommends stocks to be sold short.

Performance

According to *The Holt Investment Advisory*'s own records, the newsletter has made 479 specific security recommendations since its inception in May 1967. As of April 6, 1984, these recommendations had appreciated an average of 10.9% each, compared to a 0.2% decline in the DJIA during the corresponding time periods. The average holding period was 20.3 months, so the average annualized gain per recommendation was 6.4%, excluding dividends, interests, commissions, and taxes.

According to the HFD, Holt's recommendations lost a composite of 16.2% from July 1, 1980, through March 31, 1984, declining 6.1% in the latter half of 1980, gaining 7.9% in 1981, dropping 11.8% in 1982, and edging down another 6.3% in the following 15 months. The S & P 500, in contrast, gained 68.2% over this 15-month period, while a Treasury bill portfolio would have gained 49.5%.

Risk-Adjusted Performance

The fact that Holt's portfolio underperformed the S & P 500 by a wide margin despite having a 65% higher risk placed *The Holt Investment Advisory*, on a risk-adjusted basis, near the bottom of the ranking of newsletters the HFD monitored for this period. Part of the higher volatility incurred by Holt's portfolio in recent years is due in part to his speculation with put options and in part to ambiguous advice on how much portfolio weight those puts should be given. In early 1983, for example, Holt recommended that 10% of a portfolio should be used to purchase puts—a fairly aggressive bet that the market was going to go down. (It did not.) In the next issue, Holt explains that this 10% was "on an annualized basis. Thus, the limit on any one quarter should be one fourth, or 2-1/2%." Since the percentage weight enjoyed by a portion of a portfolio is not a function of time, the HFD was unable to ascertain whether Holt wanted 10% or 2-1/2% in these puts.

On timing grounds alone, Holt's portfolio over this 45-month period should have showed a gain of 1.0%. The fact that the portfolio gain was less than this means that Holt's stock selections underperformed the market as a whole.

HOLT INVESTMENT ADVISORY

Period	Gain	Quintile
7/1 to 12/31/80	−6.1%	Lowest 20%
1981	7.9%	Second highest 20%
1982	−11.8%	Lowest 20%
1983	−8.2%	Lowest 20%
Risk ranking	10.826	Highest 20%
% 1983 Closeouts long term	76.7%	Second highest 20%
% 1982 Closeouts long term	80.8%	Third highest 20%

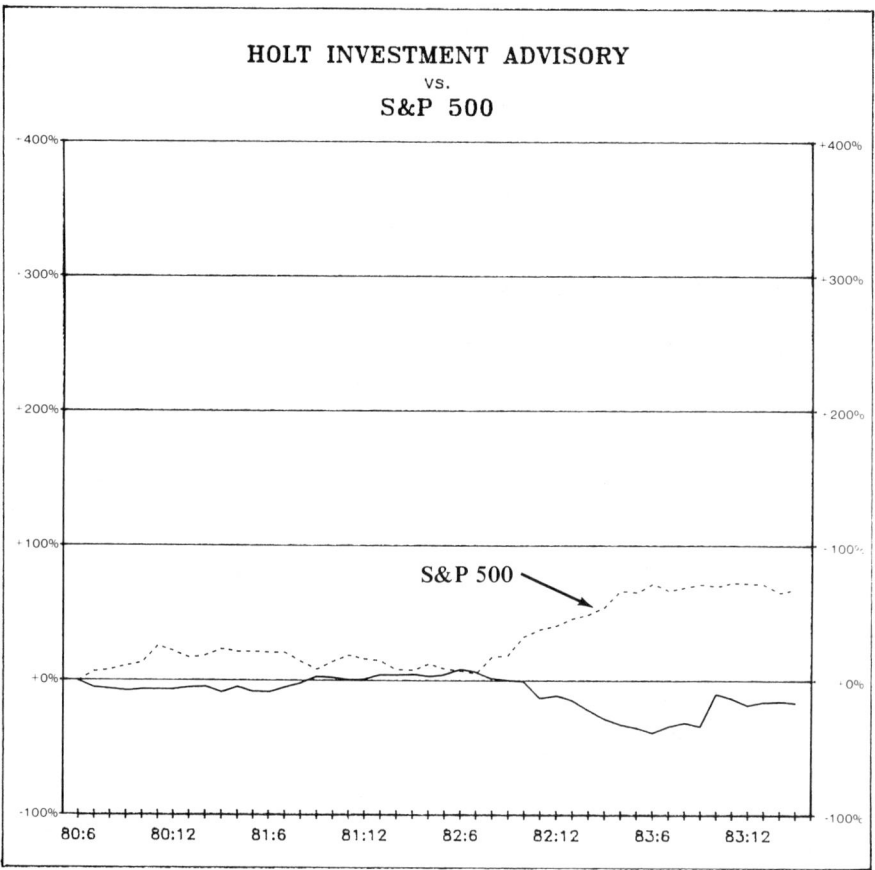

Volume IX, Issue 33   August 22, 1983

OPTION INSURANCE

HOWARD J. RUFF

All of our previous discussions of stock options have been about leveraged speculation in precious metals through gold shares, such as call options to bet on a market upmove. The emphasis has been on calls on ASA, Dome, and Homestake.

Options, however, can perform a conservative function for the smart investor, 180° away from speculation. Anyone who buys stocks would be crazy not to understand option strategies to reduce and limit risk, and increase income. You can actually use options to create income from a non-dividend paying stock.

To most people, buying put and call options is dressing up a crapshoot, but there is an insurance justification for options. Simply speculating with "puts" or "calls" is like owning a Swiss Army knife and only using one blade of ten. Let's look at some of the other blades.

Writing Call Options

Speculators buy calls because they expect a stock to go up. Put options are the opposite, a bet that the price of the underlying stock will fall. For a review of the basics of buying puts and calls, see my Sept. 3 letter.

The option page of The Wall Street Journal has thousands of options to choose from, on hundreds of stocks. But where did these options come from? Who created them? Who is on the other side of the deals? If you exercise a call option on ASA, who has to sell you the stock? Somebody like you, that's who.

For every buyer of a new call option -- the right but not the obligation to purchase the underlying stock for a specific price within a specified period of time --

IN THIS ISSUE...

Option Insurance	page 213
Buyer Beware:	page 215
Credit Is Due	page 217
Clarification	page 218
Scary Gold	page 218

Howard Ruff's Financial Success Report

Howard Ruff's Financial Success Report is the chief investment advisory newsletter mouthpiece for the charismatic and controversial Howard J. Ruff, perhaps the most widely known investment newsletter writer in the country. *The Financial Success Report*, formerly entitled *Howard Ruff's Financial Survival Report*, is the successor to *The Ruff Times* which Ruff founded in October 1975. *The Financial Success Report* is published 47 times per year by Target, Inc. , P. O. Box 25, Pleasanton, California 94566. The telephone number is (415) 463-2200. An annual subscription costs $89, but single copies are available for $3. In February 1983, this newsletter boasted 150,000 subscribers, which, if true, would have made it the most widely followed investment newsletter in the country at the time.

Ruff's diverse past (as reported in a January 11, 1982, article in *Fortune*) has included jobs as a stockbroker and as a soloist with an Air Force group called the Singing Sergeants. His business exploits have included an Evelyn Wood speed-reading franchise, a job as shoe salesman, and an attempt to sell dehydrated food to those looking for survival storage. Ruff is the author of *How to Prosper During the Coming Bad Years* (1979), which sold more than three million copies, making it the best- selling financial book in history. In this best seller, Ruff made a plea for national and international fiscal sanity and coupled his economic and political observations with investment ideas designed as inflation hedges. Ruff followed this bestseller with another success, *Survive & Win in the Inflationary Eighties*. In addition to financial matters, his newsletters and books frequently discuss ethical questions and related issues, such as proper codes of sexual behavior. The former host of his own television show, "Ruff House," Ruff has expanded his operation in recent years to include books, tapes, newsletters, seminars, conventions, publishing, and political lobbying. An article in *The Chicago Tribune* in March 1981 estimated that Ruff's activities at that time brought in $20–25 million per year.

What Ruff's Newsletter Contains

Ruff's newsletter is not easily described either. Ruff takes a more overtly political approach to finance than virtually any of the other letters monitored by the HFD, and at times, it seems that Ruff is most comfortable in a role as an educator about politics and finance. He has often said that his newsletter is not an investment "tipsheet." A review of the articles that appeared in the four May 1984 issues is a good way to acquaint you with what to expect in the letter. The May 7 issue included a three-page article on alleged plans by the government to replace the U.S. dollar with a new currency, a three-page article digesting news that appeared recently in various business and financial publications, a half-page each for an itinerary of one of Ruff's upcoming speaking tours and for a response to a subscriber's letter, with the remainder of the eight-page issue devoted to various announcements and other housekeeping chores. The four-page May 14 issue contained a two-page article on adjustable-rate mortgages, a page discussing the new tax bill in Congress, a half-page of Ruff's thoughts about South Africa following a two-day conference he had attended there, and another half-page itinerary of Ruff's imminent speaking tour. The eight-page May 21 issue devoted four pages to an interview with Ruff in which he answered a number of general questions about investment philosophy, a three-page article about Echo Bay Mining Warrants, and the remainder to yet another itinerary and various announcements. Finally, the four-page May 28 issue contained a one-and-one-half-page article on cellular radio, a one-page review of the scandal surrounding the Bullion Reserve of North America, a one-page response to a comment President Reagan had made after visiting China, a half-page on the lessons of the troubles then besetting Continental Illinois, and the remainder to another itinerary and various announcements. Not once in any of the four issues in May 1984 did Ruff review or update the composition of his recommended portfolio, alerting neither old nor new subscribers as to what portion of their investable assets should be in which investments.

Clarity

Determining the performance of Ruff's investment recommendations has not been easy. When the HFD began following this newsletter in 1980, it rated the letter poorly in terms of clarity because the HFD found the advice to be sketchy, with recommendations often coming in the form of categories of investments rather than particular securities. In the last half of 1982, Ruff changed the format of his letter to include an actual portfolio—his so-called "Phantom Investor"—making his advice easier to follow and implement. In early 1984, however, Ruff's advice again took on the characteristics that the HFD found originally. Ruff's "Phantom Investor" has taken its name seriously and is mentioned increasingly infrequently. In addition, the recommendations Ruff did make in early 1984 were in the form of categories of investments (such as penny mining shares or platinum shares) rather than recommendations of individual securities.

According to the HFD, a portfolio based on Ruff's advice would have lost 6.8% in the last six months of 1980, edged down 2.4% more in 1981, but surged 43.8% in 1982, before dropping 14.7% between January 1, 1983 and March 31, 1984. This is equivalent to an 11.5% gain over this 45-month period, as compared to the 68.2% earned by the S & P 500 during this period or the 49.5% which could have been obtained by investing in Treasury bills.

Risk-Adjusted Performance

In addition to underperforming the broad market averages, Ruff's recommended portfolio was one of the more risky of those monitored by the HFD. Over this 45-month period, in fact, Ruff's portfolio incurred 75% more risk than the S & P 500. On a risk-adjusted basis, therefore, Ruff's advice substantially has underperformed the market.

Though Ruff characterizes his investment strategy as taking a long-term perspective on the market, his actual recommendations have been much more oriented to the short-term, at least since the advent of his "Phantom Investor" in mid-1982. Of the stocks and bonds Ruff closed out of his Phantom Investor portfolio in 1983, for example, none had been held longer than just nine months.

HOWARD RUFF'S FINANCIAL SUCCESS REPORT

Period	Gain	Quintile
7/1 to 12/31/80	−6.8%	Lowest 20%
1981	−2.4%	Third highest 20%
1982	43.8%	Highest 20%
1983	−14.9%	Lowest 20%
Risk ranking	10.049	Highest 20%
% 1983 Closeouts long term	66.7%	Third highest 20%

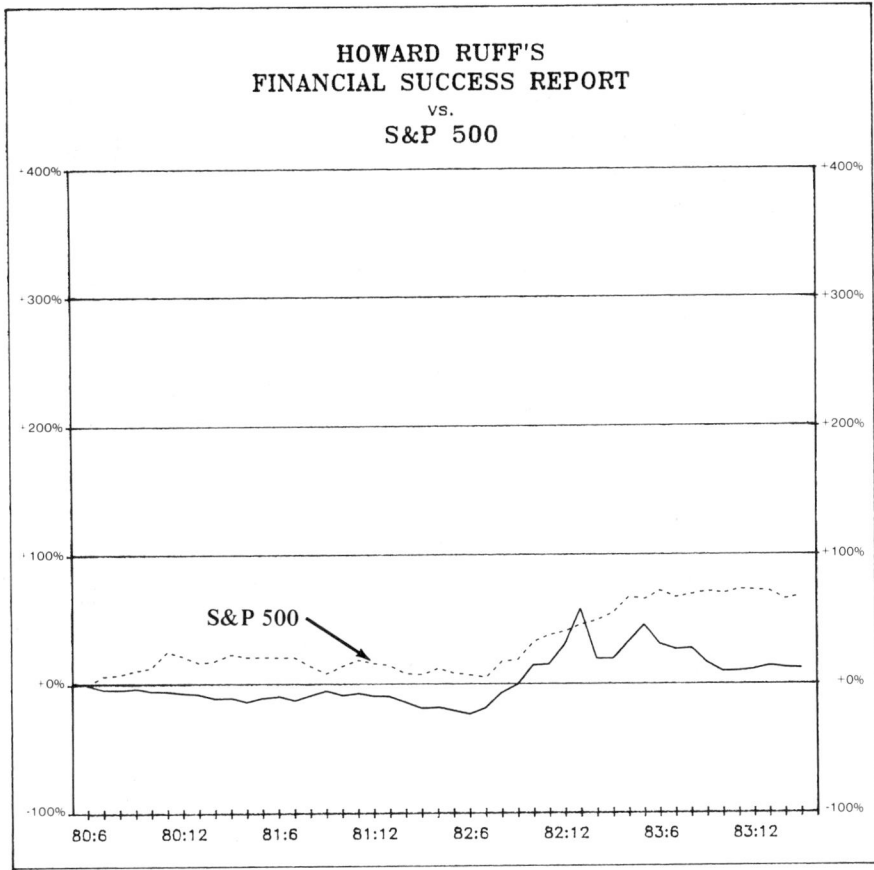

indicator digest

A COMPREHENSIVE GUIDE TO STOCK SELECTION AND MARKET TIMING

FIRST DECEMBER ISSUE   DECEMBER 2, 1983

IDA (11/30) 132.72   DJI 1276.01

MUTUAL FUNDS —
Choices For A Changed Market

That the last shall be first is more than a theological doctrine. Experienced investors know that it applies with great regularity in the stock market. Some stocks follow the economic cycle, some are driven by fads in the investment community. A rare few perform well for many years, inspired by unique products and superior management — but even these, like Xerox and Polaroid, eventually reach the end of the line and go into a period of stagnation. In this world, limitless growth is impossible.

Our first task is to time the market and let you know whether we think the overall trend is bullish or bearish. But even if we like the market, there's the essential question of *what* to buy. That's where our group studies, specialized averages and sentiment indicators come in. They help us pinpoint the stocks that are acting best and have the momentum to remain top dogs at least for a while.

Many Varieties

Many investors let experts do their stock picking through the use of mutual funds. The funds are convenient — particularly the no-loads, which allow you to move in and out of the market without any fees. But even going the fund route, you have to make some choices. These days, many funds specialize in particular types of investments. Even diversified funds vary in their concentration of assets and the degree of aggressiveness in their portfolios. So mutual funds offer investors more than ever before, but they also require study. There's just no way of getting around it — superior investment results come from paying attention.

However, we can help. We have already demonstrated that over a period

(Continued on Page 2)

STILL CAUTIOUSLY BULLISH

The Dow has pushed to a new high while the broad market is still lagging. Many indicators are favorable but some important ones like institutional cash positions and advisory sentiment are not. Some laggard stocks are coming to life in an encouraging way yet key issues such as IBM and General Motors (which had been strong) are now selling off.

What should you make of all this? Well, you shouldn't be particularly surprised — we've said many times that the easy money was made in this bull market's first 10 months. The mature stage is always harder, and there's even more reason this should be so after such an outsized first upleg. On our Hotline, before the Dow high, we said to do a little additional buying. But we didn't abandon caution, and we still wouldn't.

In troubled or confusing markets it always helps to keep the big picture firmly in mind. We think the major trend is still up. First, there's been no substantial evidence that it's not. Second, the majority of the fundamental, cyclical and technical forces now at work are favorable for stock prices. The bull market is no longer young, but it's far from a dotard. Most stocks are still reasonably priced by historical standards. While the institutions have spent a good part of their cash reserves, there is money available. So far the mutual funds are still experiencing healthy net inflows, cash balances in customer accounts at brokers keep hitting highs, and the foreigners haven't done much buying lately — suggesting that they might pile in if the market starts looking just a bit better.

One interesting thing is the ever-rising short interest. The number of shares sold short and not yet covered is at a record high. Even in terms of today's big volume, there's tremendous shorting going on. The NYSE Short Interest Ratio is at a multi-year high, though our special ratio for the Dow stocks has slipped a bit. Of course, arbitrage accounts for some of the shorting, but this activity still indicates considerable caution and pessimism, which is not what we see at market tops.

That's the favorable long-term picture. The near-term remains more cloudy, as it has been for months. At this writing the Dow has leaped to a new peak on good volume but then sold off on even higher volume. We could already be at an upside climax point for the very short term, but we don't see a lot of danger. The choppy and selective advance we expected all along is still alive.

On our Hotline we suggested moving up to an 80% invested position, but don't do it in a rush. Wait for dips to buy. This is not the market of a year ago when you had to worry about being left behind. If you miss one stock there are plenty of others. And if you wait out one rally there will probably be a dip soon to let you get aboard for the next upmove.

COPYRIGHT © 1983 BY INDICATOR RESEARCH GROUP
PALISADES PARK, NEW JERSEY 07650

Indicator Digest

Indicator Digest, which bills itself as, "a comprehensive guide to stock selection and market timing," is published 24 times a year by Indicator Research Group, Inc., Palisades Park, New Jersey 07650, which also publishes *Income Investor* and *International Gold Digest*. An annual subscription costs $125; a six-month subscription is available for $75; and individual copies are sold for $7. A telephone hotline is provided twice weekly to regular subscribers at no extra charge. Founded in 1961, *Indicator Digest* is among the most long-lived of investment newsletters. At least six persons who now publish their own investment newsletters have formerly worked at *Indicator Digest*, including Robert Gross, the editor of *Professional Investor* (who says that *Indicator Digest* "in a sense, is mother to us all").

Each semi-monthly eight-page issue contains a general stock market commentary. Twenty-two market indicators are tracked and analyzed and market timing advice is provided, based in part on the newsletter's proprietary "Short-Term Trading Guide," the product of *Indicator Digest's* original research into technical indicators. Each issue also reports the current results of its survey of 100 industry groups, specifying the ten strongest and the ten weakest groups and naming two stocks per group. *Indicator Digest* maintains a list of "current recommendations" and provides occasional updates of these stock picks, reporting corporate sales and earnings figures and commenting on the stocks' technical patterns.

The Stocks Most Highly Recommended

The HFD's performance figures for *Indicator Digest* are based on a portfolio constructed out of the "current recommendations"—on the assumption that these are the stocks most highly recommended by the service. But they are not the only stocks that are mentioned in the newsletter. In each issue, fundamental and technical advice with respect to a handful of other stocks is provided. These stocks are neither added to the list of current recommendations nor made the subject of subsequent reports. For example, the March 9, 1984, issue contained an article entitled "Best and Worst Stocks—More Current Picks," and the February 3, 1984, issue reviewed "Steady Stocks for a Mean Market." None of the stocks mentioned in these articles appeared in *Indicator Digest's* "current recommendations."

Prior to mid-1983, *Indicator Digest* did not advise subscribers on how to divide their assets between the stock market and cash. At that point, however, coinciding with the advent of their telephone hotline service, specific allocation advice was provided. The track record the HFD calculated for *Indicator Digest* was based on a fully invested portfolio up until mid-1983, after which a portion was kept in cash as recommended.

Performance

In 1983, a portfolio of *Indicator Digest's* stocks gained 11.8% while the S & P 500 advanced 22.5%; in the first quarter of 1984, the portfolio lost 9.2% during a market decline of 2.4%, as measured by the S & P 500. *Indicator Digest's* aggregate performance for this 15-month period was a gain of 1.6% while the S & P 500 moved up 19.6%.

On a risk-adjusted basis, *Indicator Digest's* portfolio also underperformed the market. For this 15-month period, its volatility (risk) was more than twice that of the S&P 500, but in return for that risk, subscribers received a sub-market rate of return.

INDICATOR DIGEST

Period	Gain	Quintile
1983	11.8%	Second highest 20%
Risk ranking	5.935	Second highest 20%
% 1983 Closeouts long term	39.1%	Second lowest 20%

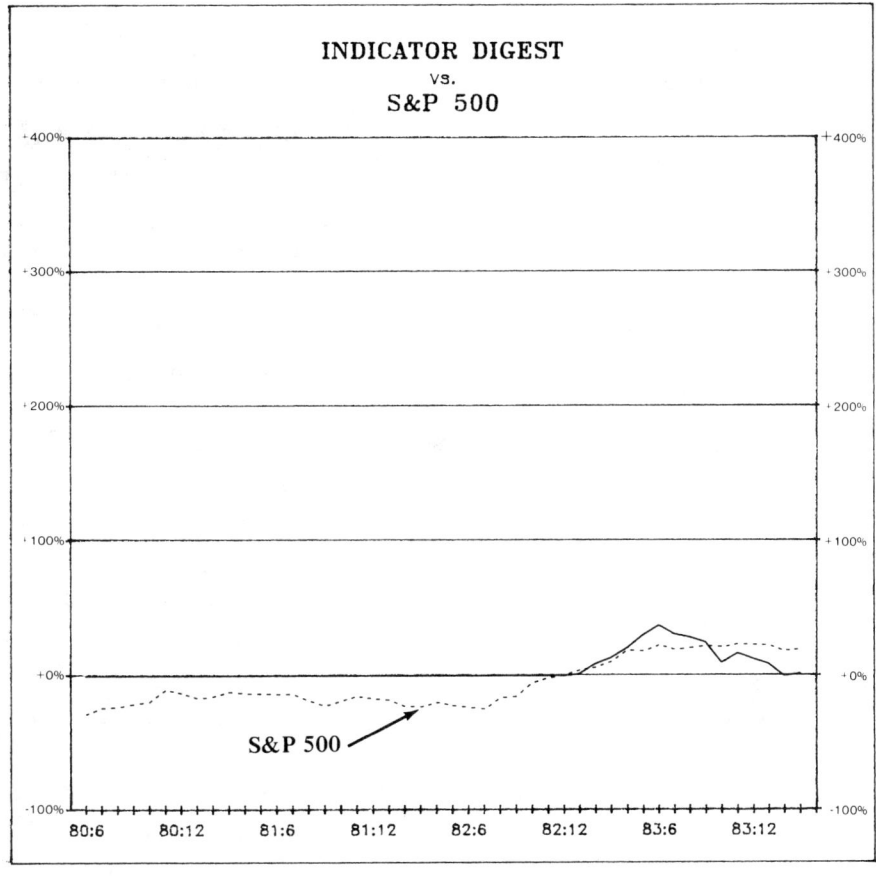

The International Harry Schultz Letter

The world's geo-political & money newsletter

Single copy : US$25 DM60 SwFr50 £16 Hfl68 A$28 C$30
HSL 448 -- April, 1983

APR. 1 1 1983

Did you hear a door slam?

The recent drop in gold from just over $500 to just under $400(followed by inconsequential movement since then) sounded like a door slamming. It may well have been the echo of the world economies taking a critical turn at/during a crossroads year.

Someone asked my Aussie friend Campbell Gorrie, R&D director at Richardson Mann, Sydney, some months ago: "What would a transition from disinflation to deflation <u>look</u> like? Last-week Campbell showed his client a chart of US M-l money-supply, rising over the last 6 months, & a chart of gold haemorrhaging recently. "<u>That</u>" said Campbell, "is what the transition to deflation looks like."

It's a chilling prospect. Cam & I wonder how many people realize that Volcker has fired his last bullets. For 8 months he's thrown everything he has into pump-priming. The gold market has carefully thought about it & handed in its verdict---not enough!

Yet, as I've said before, bond & stock mkts won't tolerate higher levels. Cam thinks Herr Volcker is terrified, as he knows that if his efforts over the last 8 months haven't worked, then the US economy is beginning to settle into a lower plane of economic life. If it does,so will the rest of the world. This is an early-warning. Any idiot can see if inflation re-ignites or if the business upturn is well-supported by economic indicators & sharply rising corporate earnings. What is much harder to perceive is if we are about to slip quietly into a second chapter of The Great Depression Mark II.

Old pal Vern Myers (Finance & Energy,PeytonBldg, Spokane, WA99201) says: "Markets seem to believe that once disinflation reaches zero,the process will automatically <u>stop</u>. But there is no built-in foundation at zero inflation. It is only an imaginary point that can easily be passed as the disinflation process proceeds into net DEFLATION." Vern (who used to publish "Oil Week" so he knows something about oil) feels it is wishful thinking to believe the oil decline will stop at $25 a barrel. With the disintegration of OPEC & a surplus of 13mil b/day, & based on historic fluctuations in oil prices, he doesn't see even $10 a barrel as impossible.

But even $24 (I have long predicted $25 or so) would mean a shortfall of $180bil a year. Just as oil price skyrocketing in the 1970's <u>created</u> money (which fostered inflation), so the oil price fall will <u>shrink</u> money supply. Just as we commonly explain inflation as too much money chasing too few goods, we can say deflation is a small amount of money for a large amount of goods. It means cheap goods & expensive money.

But we must wait & watch. Clues come from several areas. One is NBBR-- "non-borrowed bank reserves." While Ml was climbing, its <u>rate</u> of growth & more importantly the growth rate of NBBR, have been declining sharply. They've been saying the opposite of what most mkts were assuming. Inflation fires were being stoked in recent months not at a faster <u>rate</u>,but (surprize surprize) at a slower one. It affected money turnover rates, as I've mentioned before. When stock mkt traders realize this, the euphoria will dissipate quickly. Wall Street insiders apparently already realize it, for they've been shorting the mkt for many wks, while the public & institutions (same thing really) have been buying.

Another indicator is the gold mkt. If the $390-400 zone is broken,it is in the context of 8months of furious pump-priming having already taken place. Is it not curious that only now can we make definitive judgements? Previously it was theoretical, ie "if an extended recession/depression looked likely,the Fed would reflate & we would all get one more chance." For 30-40years it worked that way---when a real crunch point appeared, the Fed reflated & nothing nasty happened. Well, here we are. The Fed has done its act & apparently the gold mkt is warning us: <u>this</u> is the time it doesn't work. No syndrome, no cycle, ever repeats to perfection & indefinitely. To presume they do is irrational.

Only a fool would pre-empt the collective mkt-place's mighty decision, because for several decades the addiction has worked. But Campbell & I think we hear the sound of a door slamming----especially when viewing the gold chart. We have the curious feeling the world has left an era behind.

PS: Most people feel "Everything will be all right in the end." The depression is ending slowly,they feel, & somehow we'll sort

Chevalier Harry D. Schultz KHC. 'World's highest paid investment consultant' - GuinnessBookofRecords-1981-82-83 editions...Voted 'most outstanding Int'l newsletter' by American Economic Council--1978...Voted 'most outstanding Market Letter'--AEC-1979...Voted 'Man of the Year' by WorldGoldAssociation-1980...Voted 'Outstanding newsltr for profitability of advice' by Hard Money Digest--Jan 1981...Given the 'Liberty Award' by the Congress of Freedom...Declared 'Most Profitable advisory ltr'-by HulbertFinancialDigest--March 1981...Voted most prized newsltr by Flint School cadets... Awarded Benelux nations LibertarianSociety Man of the Year-1982... Given 'FreedomFighterExtraordinaire' award by CoalitionForPeace Through Security-1982...Voted most popular analyst by Australian Investors Digest-1982... Named favorite 'Pilot at the wheel' by 4R's Academic Method,1983.

The International Harry Schultz Letter

The International Harry Schultz Letter (IHSL), now in its twentieth year of publication, is written in a bold and unique style and is published monthly by FERC. An annual subscription costs $258; a six-month subscription is offered for $152; and IHSL charges $20 for a back issue. Subscription inquiries should be addressed to PM & S, Park Tremeland 12, 3120–Tremelo, Belgium. The telephone number in the United States for subscription inquiries is (203) 329-2066. Editor Schultz likes to bill himself (and *The Guinness Book of World Records* apparently concurs) as the "world's highest paid investment consultant," charging a rate of $2,000 per hour. It is not known how much consulting Schultz does. Schultz also offers TAS, a weekly commodity advisory service, for $150 per week. Schultz has written more than a dozen books, the first of which, *Bear Markets, How to Survive and Make Money in Them*, was published in 1964. He has also written *What the Prudent Investor Should Know About Switzerland and Other Money Havens* and *How to Keep your Money and Freedom*.

IHSL is more difficult than most investment newsletters to describe adequately. In part, this is because it covers an extremely broad variety of investments, is highly political in tone and advocacy, and, in its own words, is "[w]ritten in the abbreviated spelling of tomorrow." Harry Schultz views the standard spelling of English as "misguided" and "old fashioned" and advocates "Let's either pronounce English as we spell it, or spell it the way we pronounce it!" Although Schultz claims this enables him to cram more information into his newsletter, others may find this style difficult to read and use. For example, the full investment recommendation with respect to silver in the mid-December 1983 was written as follows: "U R out. Go long nr Mar 9.50. Sell some at 10, some at 10.50, then 10.80–11.00. Stop 1dc below 9.40, or use trailing stop. Also go long on 1dc over 10.00, more on 2nd day, for 10.50 & 10.80–11.00. Stop 2dc below 10. Go short on 2dc below 8.60 for 8.00 & 7.50. Out over 8.70."

Much of HSL is concerned with world politics, claiming to have "long spearheaded the drive to awaken the west to the Soviet menace." Schultz has lobbied hard in issue after issue for adoption of the Burnelli design for oversized air transport, warning readers to "[b]e prepared for the biggest scandal ever in U.S history," the suppression of an allegedly safer and more efficient technology for the manufacture of airplanes. Schultz shares the concern others have expressed over the international monetary crisis, writing recently that "[i]t's becoming increasingly likely that we are headed for a crash of once-a-generation proportions....What is not yet clear is whether it will be an inflationary crash or a deflationary crash..." A self-described "goldbug," Schultz recommends the purchase of gold in either case, although, unlike other goldbugs, Schultz is not wedded to gold as the be-all and end-all of investing.

Schultz's Claims About His Record

Schultz blows his own horn hard and consistently. On two occasions about which the authors are aware, this hornblowing has been deceptive. For example, on the first page of each issue of IHSL Schultz claims that IHSL was declared "Most Profitable advisory ltr" by the Hulbert Financial Digest in March 1981. We have been unable to discover what it was in the HFD which led Schultz to this conclusion, since in no period near March 1981 was the portfolio the HFD tracks for HSL the top-ranking newsletter. In the March 1981 issue of the HFD, for example, HSL ranked dead last—34th out of 34 portfolios tracked at that time—for the preceding month's performance. The April 1981 issue of the HFD ranked the performance of HSL 6th out of 37 portfolios for the month of March and 34th out of 37 for performance over the first quarter of 1981.

The second instance of deceptive hornblowing concerns Schultz's annual "prediction record." Though Schultz consistently claims to have a high success rate, we are unable to see how his actual success comes very close. Schultz claimed that his 1983 predictions were 66% correct, for example, yet we analyzed them to be no more than 48% correct, giving Schultz the benefit of the doubt in several instances. Another newsletter concluded its analysis of Schultz's 1983 predictions by concluding that only 30% of them were correct.

Performance

Since July 1, 1980, the HFD has calculated the performance of some of the American stock recommendations made by IHSL. IHSL also recommends stocks traded on exchanges throughout the world, precious metals, and other commodities, foreign currencies, and stock index futures. Up until February 1983, Schultz in each issue presented an "investment table," which usually contained American stocks but sometimes included foreign stocks and once had a currency futures contract. Because Schultz appeared to draw special attention to these selections by highlighting them in a separate box and because these recommendations were the subject of consistent follow-up advice, the HFD based its rating of IHSL on this list of recommendations until Schultz, in the February 9, 1983, issue of IHSL declared that, "this stock table has outlived its usefulness" and merged it into his review of the U.S. stock market. Since then, the HFD has restricted its evaluation to Schultz's American stock selections.

According to HFD's figures, IHSL outperformed the S & P 500 in the second half of 1980, gaining 41.2% versus an advance of 21.7% in the S & P 500, but has significantly underperformed the market ever since. In 1981, according to HFD figures, IHSL's stock picks lost 17.5% (the S & P 500 declined 4.9%), dropping 5.5% in 1982 (the S & P 500 gained 21.6%), and edging up 5.2% from January 1, 1983, through March 31, 1984 (the S & P 500 gained 19.6%). HSL's aggregate gain for this 45-month period was only 15.9%, whereas the S & P 500 advanced 68.2% over the same period, and a Treasury-bill portfolio gained 49.5%. IHSL's portfolio of (mostly) American stock picks was 55% more volatile (risky) than the market as a whole over this period. Because an investor could have gained a return of 49.5% with virtually no risk by investing in Treasury bills over the same period, IHSL's risk-adjusted performance is negative.

INTERNATIONAL HARRY SCHULTZ LETTER
U. S. Stock Picks (Formerly "Investment Table" Stocks)

Period	Gain	Quintile
7/1 to 12/31/80	41.2%	Highest 20%
1981	−17.5%	Lowest 20%
1982	−5.5%	Lowest 20%
1983	2.1%	Second lowest 20%
Risk ranking	6.327	Second highest 20%
% 1983 Closeouts long term	21.4%	Lowest 20%
% 1982 Closeouts long term	18.8%	Second lowest 20%

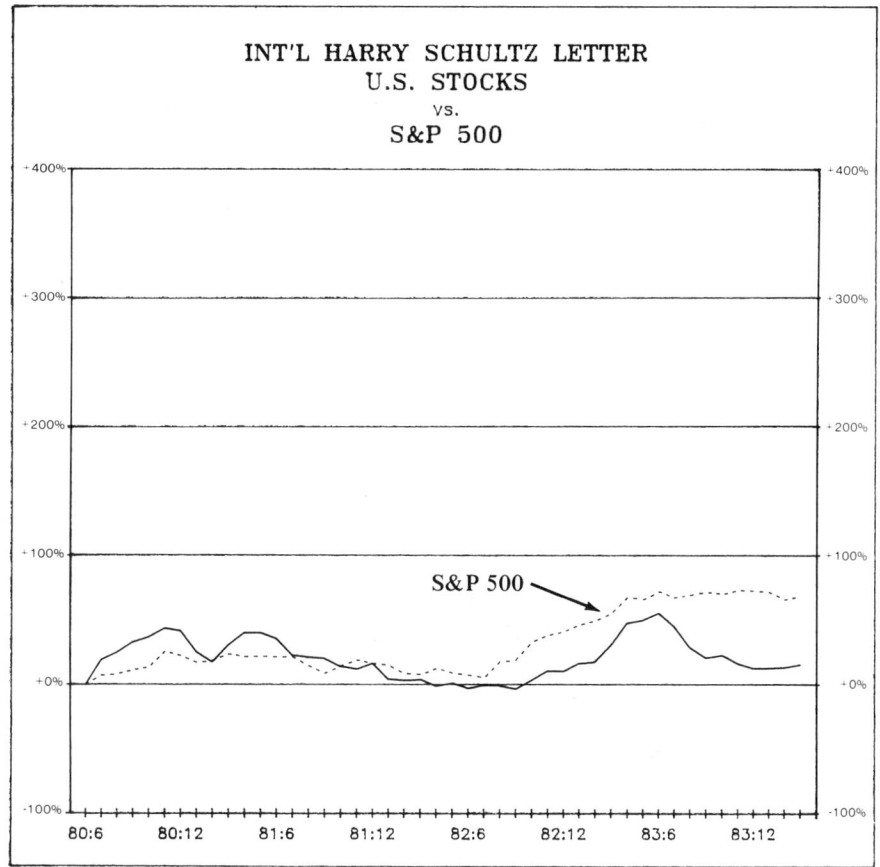

MARKET LOGIC®
from THE INSTITUTE FOR ECONOMETRIC RESEARCH
3471 NORTH FEDERAL HIGHWAY, FORT LAUDERDALE, FLORIDA 33306
NORMAN G. FOSBACK, PRESIDENT GLEN KING PARKER, CHAIRMAN

Issue No. 192   February 18, 1983

INSIDE MARKET LOGIC
- Models still bullish.................... 1, 2
- Options on futures: Big leverage, limited risk 2
- Brokerage stocks to lead market 3
- Cyclicals strong, defensive sectors weak 4
- Sell Syntex March 45 call position....... 6
- Rating the market letters: Special study reveals flaws in popular system 7, 8

CURRENT HOT LINE NUMBERS
PRIME: 305-564-8663
Backups: 305-564-0511, 305-564-0533, 305-564-0544
(Updates: 6 p.m. Eastern Time every Tuesday and Friday)

CURRENT FORECASTS
(From The Institute's Econometric Models of the U. S. Stock Market)

Projections of Standard & Poor's 500 Index
Three Months:	6%	HIGHER
Six Months:	9%	HIGHER
One Year:	15%	HIGHER
Two Years:	5%	HIGHER
Three Years:	22%	HIGHER
Five Years:	65%	HIGHER

Projections of the NYSE Total Return Index:
Three Months:	6%	HIGHER
Six Months:	7%	HIGHER
One Year:	20%	HIGHER
Two Years:	4%	HIGHER
Three Years:	10%	HIGHER
Five Years:	53%	HIGHER

The Major Trend Model is BULLISH at 1.15

SUMMARY & RECOMMENDATION

Practically every leading market index has reached a new all-time high during the past two weeks. Investors who are fully committed to equities continue to reap more benefits from this bull market than those on the sidelines awaiting corrections. Remain fully invested in recommended stocks, options, and mutual funds.

CURRENT POSITION

In the fifteen weeks since the Dow Industrials first broke out to close at a new all-time high, further progress by blue chips has been erratic, leading to widespread fears that a major top was forming. During those same fifteen weeks, however, the broad market has continued to forge ahead, with our all-inclusive NYSE Total Return Index gaining 14% and the more volatile American Stock Exchange Total Return Index running up 30%. Such strong breadth is symptomatic of ongoing bull markets, not major topping areas.

The Major Trend Model is super-bullish at 1.15, and mandates against liquidating recommended stocks. Remain fully invested and enjoy the bull market.

INDICATOR REVIEW

Although the long term outlook remains bullish, the indicators are diverging as the uptrend progresses. Monetary measures can safely be called bullish, but fundamental indicators are now just neutral in tone and technical indicators are mixed.

Perhaps more than any other factor, the great rally over the last six months was fueled by sharply declining interest rates. The chart on Page 2 shows how steep the rate of decline was last summer and *[Continued on Page 2]*

Market Logic's NYSE Total Return Index provides an unsurpassed view of the breadth and performance of the market. It is the only index that furnishes a complete historical record of the total return from both price change and dividends of every Big Board listed stock. By equally weighting all issues, the TR Index is the best indicia of average equity returns accuring to individual investors. (See the Total Return Indexes box elsewhere in this issue for the latest daily readings.) The current cyclical advance extending from the low in 1974, and interrupted only by several sharp intermediate corrections, represents one of the great bull markets of the 20th century.

Market Logic

Market Logic is published 24 times a year by The Institute for Econometric Research, which also publishes *New Issues*, reviewed elsewhere in this book, as well as three other investment advisories. The president of the institute is Norman G. Fosback and the chairman is Glen King Parker. An annual subscription to *Market Logic* is offered by The Institute for $195, and individual issues are sold for $9 each. The address is 3471 North Federal Highway, Fort Lauderdale, Florida 33306. Its telephone number is (305) 563-9000.

Each eight-page issue of *Market Logic* is clearly written and contains an abundance of investment information and advice. The first page of the newsletter provides the current forecasts by the Institute for Econometric Research of expected stock market behavior over various periods ranging from the next three months to the next five years. Based on these projections, *Market Logic* advises subscribers on how to distribute their assets available for investment. The second page of the newsletter reviews a number of fundamental, monetary, sentiment, and technical trend indicators. Another page is devoted to a research report summarizing a recent article of interest in the academic journals concerning research in the areas of finance and portfolio theory. *Market Logic's* 1984 research reports have discussed the effects of the presidential election cycle, stock splits, composite spin-offs and NYSE Listings on stock prices. Two pages or so of each newsletter issue summarize all open positions in *Market Logic's*

Master Portfolio, provide earnings and sales updates for stocks that are currently recommended, and make new recommendations.

Market Logic also rates all stocks that are the subject of exchange-traded options and makes specific recommendations for its Actual Option Portfolio. Other regular columns rank 60 industry groups, list those companies with the heaviest recent insider buying or selling, review a dozen or so no-load stock mutual funds, and present a gold price model. The final page of *Market Logic* gives a one-sentence summary of the current investment attitude of each of 20 or so widely read investment newsletters.

Performance

The HFD has calculated the performance of *Market Logic's* Master Portfolio since July 1, 1980. On a total return basis, this portfolio ranks fourth best of the portfolios tracked for the 45-month period ending March 31, 1984. On a risk-adjusted basis, *Market Logic* ranks third over the same period, having done about 75% better than the S & P 500 with only about 10% greater volatility. (See the appendices at the end of the book that rank letters on both absolute and risk-adjusted performance.) The Master Portfolio gained 18.9% in the second half of 1980, added 8.6% in 1981, surged 41.0% in 1982, and gained 19.8% more from the beginning of 1983 through the first quarter of 1984, for an aggregate gain of 118.2%.

Making this gain even more impressive is that almost all of it would qualify for long-term capital gains treatment. *Market Logic* takes a long-term approach to the markets, not attempting to trade in and out in hopes of avoiding a correction. In 1982, out of a portfolio size of about 35, five issues were sold having an average holding period of over five years since initial recommendation. In 1983, only one issue was sold from the Master Portfolio, though its holding period was just nine months.

Catching the Bull

In a study conducted by the HFD at the beginning of the bull market in 1982, we identified *Market Logic* as having come closer than any of the other newsletters we monitor in having forecast it. Over the first half of 1982, the Master Portfolio gradually increased its market exposure, moving to a fully invested posture in mid-1982 of that year, only about two months early as it turned out. In late July, two weeks before the market took off, they wrote that "one hundred million share days are ahead"—a phenomenon which at that time was still unheard of. They concluded that "the risk of a buying panic continues to far outweigh the risk of renewed heavy selling."

MARKET LOGIC

Period	Gain	Quintile
7/1 to 12/31/80	+18.9%	Third highest 20%
1981	+8.6%	Second highest 20%
1982	+41.0%	Second highest 20%
1983	+28.0%	Highest 20%
Risk ranking	4.544	Third highest 20%
% 1983 Closeouts long term	100%	Highest 20%
% 1982 Closeouts long term	100%	Highest 20%

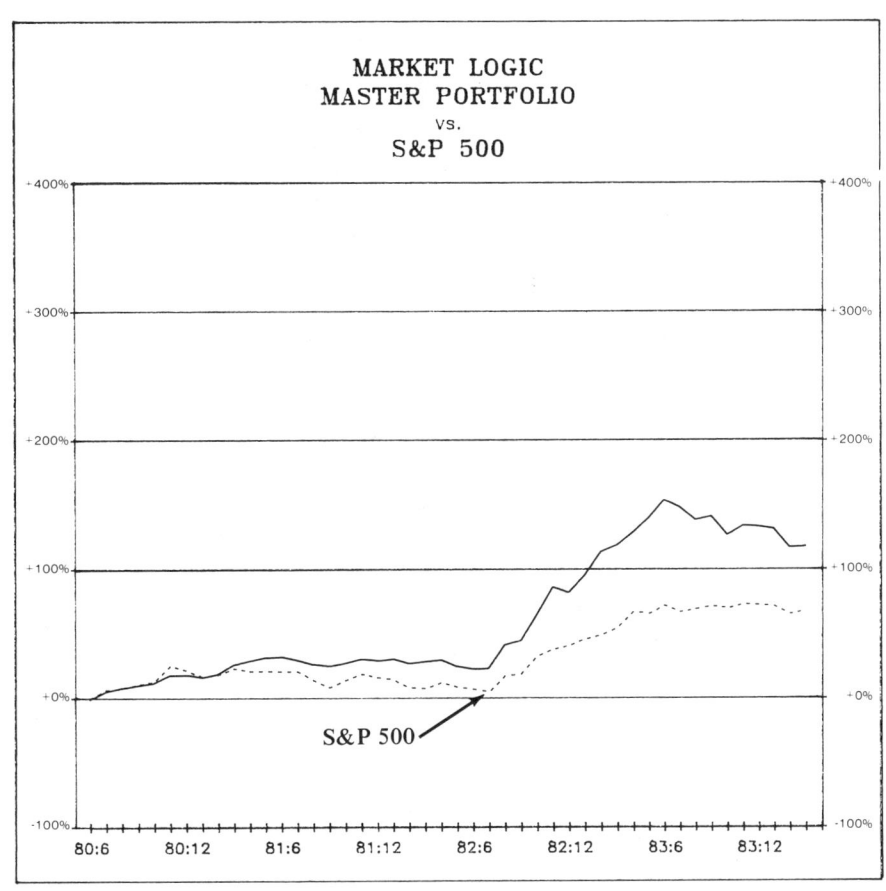

new issue investor

A monthly publication of Standard & Poor's Corp. April 18, 1983

New issue market review

•

Roster of major upcoming offerings

•

Spotlight recommendation
The MacNeal-Schwendler Corporation

•

Prospective new issues highlighted
Care Enterprises   LyphoMed
Combined Network   Telerate
Trak Auto

•

Reports on
new issues in the aftermarket
ACCO World   On-Line Software
Automatix   Rodime PLC
Genex   Silicon Valley Group
InteCom   TeleVideo Systems

Volume 2
Number 4

New Issue Investor

New Issue Investor is one of the relatively new newsletters that has been created to track (and hopefully profit from) the market for initial public offerings. Published by Standard & Poor's Corporation since 1982, its address is 25 Broadway, New York, New York 10004. An annual subscription costs $130. It is edited by Robert Natale, and a weekly telephone hotline is made available to all subscribers free of charge. A publication of S & P's Equity Research Department, this newsletter has no access to information obtained by the bond-rating arm of S & P.

Each issue of *New Issue Investor* gives a one-paragraph review of the prospects for the new issue market, reviews recently completed offerings, provides a roster of major upcoming offerings (recommending a select few for purchase), summarizes previously recommended issues and gives current buy-hold-sell advice for those issues, and provides a directory of new issue underwriters. The newsletter discusses the investor potential of new offerings under two categories, one entitled "New & Noteworthy," and the other entitled "Spotlight Recommendation." While the analysis under the "New & Noteworthy" category may well suggest purchase, *New Issue Investor* makes it clear that only the stocks mentioned in the "Spotlight Recommendation" category are formal recommendations. The newsletter does not recommend the proper division of your portfolio between stocks and cash, so you will have to decide for yourself how much money you wish to risk in the new issues market.

Performance

Since its inception in early 1982, according to *New Issue Investor's* own records, a portfolio that purchased 100 shares of each of the stocks in the "Spotlight Recommendation" category at the initial offering price would have gained 26% by May 1984. The S & P 500, in contrast, from January 31, 1982, to April 30, 1984, gained 33%—not counting dividends, which would have added another 5 to 10% to this total. We should note that this record assumes that an investor would have been able to purchase each issue at its initial offering price, which can be quite unrealistic when there is a large demand for the new issue. (See discussion of this issue in the write-up about *New Issues* elsewhere in this volume.)

The HFD has tracked the performance of *New Issue Investor* since Janauary 1983. During 1983, according to HFD's figures, *New Issue Investor* gained 6.6%, in contrast to the S & P 500's 22.5%. During the first quarter of 1984, the portfolio dropped by 17.8% while the S & P 500 was giving up 2.4%. Cumulatively over this 15-month period, *New Issue Investor* lost 12.4%, compared to an increase of 19.6% by the S & P 500 and an 11.6% return obtainable from Treasury bills. Despite underperforming the S & P 500, the newsletter's risk was triple that of the broad market; on a risk-adjusted basis, therefore, the service substantially underperformed the market.

NEW ISSUE INVESTOR

Period	Gain	Quintile
1983	6.6%	Second lowest 20%
Risk ranking	8.589	Highest 20%
%1983 Closeouts long term	100%	Highest 20%

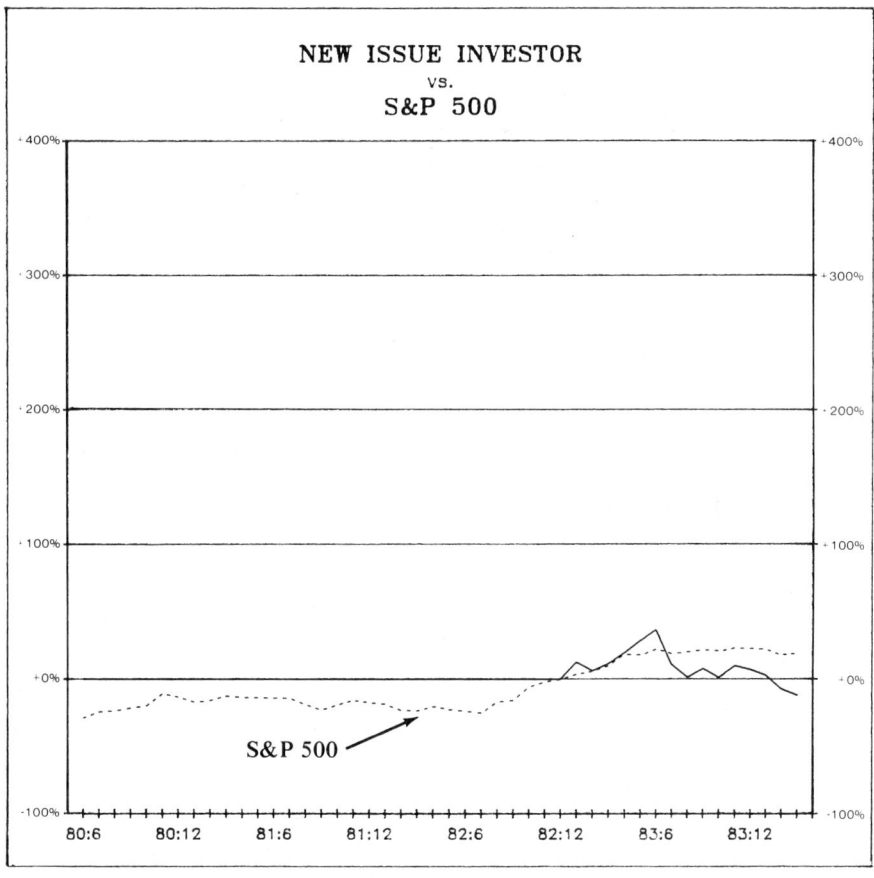

New Issues

The Investor's Guide to Initial Public Offerings

Norman G. Fosback, Editor • 3471 North Federal Highway, Fort Lauderdale, Florida 33306 • Glen King Parker, Publisher

Disk Drive Firms Highlight NCC Show

Issue No. 57   May 27, 1983
ACTION LINE NUMBER: 305-564-8699
Updated at 6 p.m. EDT Fridays with all recommendations.
Backups: 305-564-0622, 305-564-0645 and 305-564-0648.

Buy Giga-tronics

GIGA-TRONICS will offer 850,000 shares at $12 to $14 a share. We recommend purchase of this small, well sponsored offering when it comes to market in early June.

Giga-tronics manufactures instruments used to generate and measure microwave signals. Such products are used in a broad variety of electronic warfare, radar, and telecommunications systems. Approximately half of Giga-tronics sales have been to U.S. defense agencies, principally the U.S. Navy. Other major customers include Sperry, Loral Electronics, GTE Systems, Westinghouse, TRW, Itek, Honeywell, Ford Aerospace, and Harris Corporation.

The Reagan Administration has budgeted large increases for military hardware outlays. Much of that spending is only now beginning to come down the pipeline, and we expect it to benefit companies such as Giga-tronics. In fact, Giga-tronics' order backlog of $13.6 million (of which $10 million will be shipped within the next year) is nearly twice the company's latest fiscal year's net sales. This insures excellent

GIGA-TRONICS INCORPORATED — 2495 Estand Way, Pleasant Hill, CA 94523; (415) 680-8160.
Offering of 850,000 common shares @$12-$14 per share; 383,000 shares (45%) by the company and balance by existing stockholders. Managing Underwriters: Robertson, Colman & Stephens, 100 California St., San Francisco, CA 94111; (415) 781-9700; and Alex. Brown, 135 E. Baltimore St., Baltimore, MD 21202; (301) 727-1700.
After the offering, 3,678,920 shares will be outstanding and book value will equal $1.75 a share. Revenues equal $1.95 a share. 46 employees. No dividend. Proposed symbol: GIGA.

Year Ended	Revenues	Net Income	Prof. Margin	Earn./Shr.
Mar. 31, 1981	$ 72,000	$(349,000)	nil	$ (.29)
Mar. 31, 1982	992,000	(6,000)	nil	---
Mar. 31, 1983	7,174,000	1,271,000	17.7%	.38*
Quarter Ended				
June 30, 1982	$1,041,000	$ 130,000	12.5%	$ .04
Sept. 30, 1982	1,369,000	208,000	15.2%	.06
Dec. 31, 1982	2,179,000	433,000	19.9%	.13
Mar. 31, 1983	2,585,000	500,000	19.3%	.15†

(*$.35 pro forma; †$.14 pro forma; both reflect shares to be sold in current offering.)

operating gains into the foreseeable future.

We are also impressed with the underwriting sponsorship. The co-underwriters, *[Continued on Page 3]*

New Issues dispatched two analysts to the National Computer Conference in Anaheim earlier this month, to survey new technology developments and to interview top executives of both previously recommended companies and firms that are planning public offerings.

Without question, the predominant theme of NCC '83 was computer disk drives. Dozens of companies have developed or are developing new products in the booming disk drive market. Two that were particularly impressive at NCC are scheduling initial public offerings for the week of May 30 to June 3, **Priam** and **Micropolis**. The intensely competitive nature of the disk drive market makes both of these offerings extreme speculations, and frankly, there is very little way of telling which of the two firms is more likely to rise to the top. Based on a comparative analysis of these two firms and discussions with both chief executive officers, we are formally recommending Priam for purchase. Though not formally recommended, Micropolis is an appropriate purchase for aggressive accounts.

PRIAM will offer 3,500,000 shares between $14 and $16 per share. L.F. Rothschild, Unterberg, Towbin and Hambrecht & Quist, the nation's leading new issue sponsors, will co-underwrite the deal.

Priam manufactures high performance (i.e., high capacity) 8 inch and 14 inch Winchester disk drives, a market that is growing from 50% to 100% per year. Priam is also developing a line of smaller high performance 5-1/4 inch Winchester disk drives which it intends to start delivering within a year.

The high capacity end of   *[Continued on Page 2]*

WHAT TO DO NOW

Our featured Buy recommendations in this issue are: **Priam** (see above) and **Giga-tronics** (at left). In addition, we like **Burlington Coat Factory Warehouse** (Page 3) at $25 or below. Several other attractive offerings are discussed elsewhere in this issue, including a new Buy recommendation on previously recommended **Altos Computer** (Page 8). Because of the enormous volume of new offerings, we are once again scheduling a special mid-month bonus edition. It will be mailed June 10 to all current subscribers. Meanwhile, tune in to the *Action Line* each week for new recommendations and revised offering dates.

New Issues

New Issues is one of several investment newsletters that were founded to track (and hopefully profit from) investing in initial stock offerings. *New Issues* is edited by Norman G. Fosback and is published monthly by the Institute for Econometric Research, the publisher of *Market Logic* (reviewed elsewhere in this book), *The Insiders* (a compilation of trading activity by corporate insiders), *Trend Scan* (a computerized analysis of technical and fundamental data on more than 2,500 stocks), and *Money Fund Safety Ratings* (a guide to money market funds). The address is 3471 North Federal Highway, Fort Lauderdale, Florida 33306. The telephone number is (305) 563-9000. An annual subscription costs $150, although charter subscriptions were recently offered for $95 for one year and $55 for six months. A weekly telephone hotline is included with each subscription.

Each monthly eight-page issue of *New Issues* includes a comprehensive list of forthcoming issues priced above $1 per share giving the size, price, expected offering date, name of business, and underwriter for each upcoming new issue. A brief summary of operating history and business prospects of several of these initial public offerings (IPOs) is presented, and a few are recommended for purchase. Sometimes, *New Issues* recommmends that its subscribers purchase a recent IPO whose price has dropped in aftermarket trading. *New*

Issues rarely recommends the purchase of stocks whose price has risen above the initial offering price. The newsletter also reviews IPOs priced at $1 per share or less, commonly known as "penny stocks."

Long-Term Record

According to *New Issues'* own figures, 51% of the stocks (70 of the 138) recommended since September 19, 1978, and not subsequently recommended for sale were trading in February 1984 at a price higher than their initial offering prices; 49% of such stocks were trading at a lower price. The average change in price reported was an increase of 58%. In addition, 12 previously recommended new issues had been closed out at a profit. These figures assume that a subscriber who sought to purchase a recommended IPO would have been able to do so at the initial offering price. It is worth noting that this assumption is frequently unrealistic during new issue booms, when demand for many "hot issues" outstrips supply, brokers funnel the scarce stock to favored customers, and aftermarket trading begins at a sometimes substantial premium. For example, in March, 1983, *New Issues* recommended Information Resources, an IPO whose offering price was $23 per share. Demand for the issue was so strong that it never traded in the aftermarket for less than $36 per share. It closed the first day of trading at $43, at which point *New Issues* recommended selling it. The newsletter credits itself with the entire 87% "gain" from $23 to $43, even though many or most of its subscribers had no opportunity to participate in the reported "gain." An investor's ability to obtain the profits claimed by *New Issues* may well require having an on-going relationship with a broker at each of several firms that frequently participate in the syndicates that underwrite (bring to market) the new issues recommended. Even if an investor has a good broker at a "full service" brokerage house, it will not do the investor any good unless that brokerage firm is an underwriting participant.

Performance

The HFD has only tracked the performance of stocks recommended in *New Issues* since the beginning of 1983. In 1983, the newsletter's recommendations increased in value 11.6%, but in the first quarter of 1984 the selections dropped sharply, losing 13.9%, resulting in an aggregate 15-month loss of 3.9%. These figures assume that a subscriber purchased each recommended issue at the average of the high and low price for the first day of aftermarket trading, unless a price limit is specified in the newsletter.

If the price bulge that frequently occurs at the start of new issues trading were included in *New Issues'* performance ratings (as their own figures do), the above-reported figures would be dramatically improved. For example, instead of the 17.2% gain for the first 11 months of 1983 as calculated by the HFD, a 74.6% gain would have resulted. (This disparity again points out the importance of the methodology employed by any service that rates investment newsletters.) In comparison, the S & P 500 gained 22.5% in 1983 and gave up 2.4% in the first three months of 1984, for an aggregate gain of 19.6%. The portfolio of stocks recommended for purchase by *New Issues* was more than three times as risky (volatile) as the broad stock market, as measured by the S & P 500. Hence, over the 15-month period covered by the HFD, this portfolio has had a negative return on a risk-adjusted basis.

NEW ISSUES

Period	Gain	Quintile
1983	+11.6%	Third highest 20%
Risk ranking:	9.067	Highest 20%
% 1983 Closeouts long term	80.0%	Second highest 20%

New Issues

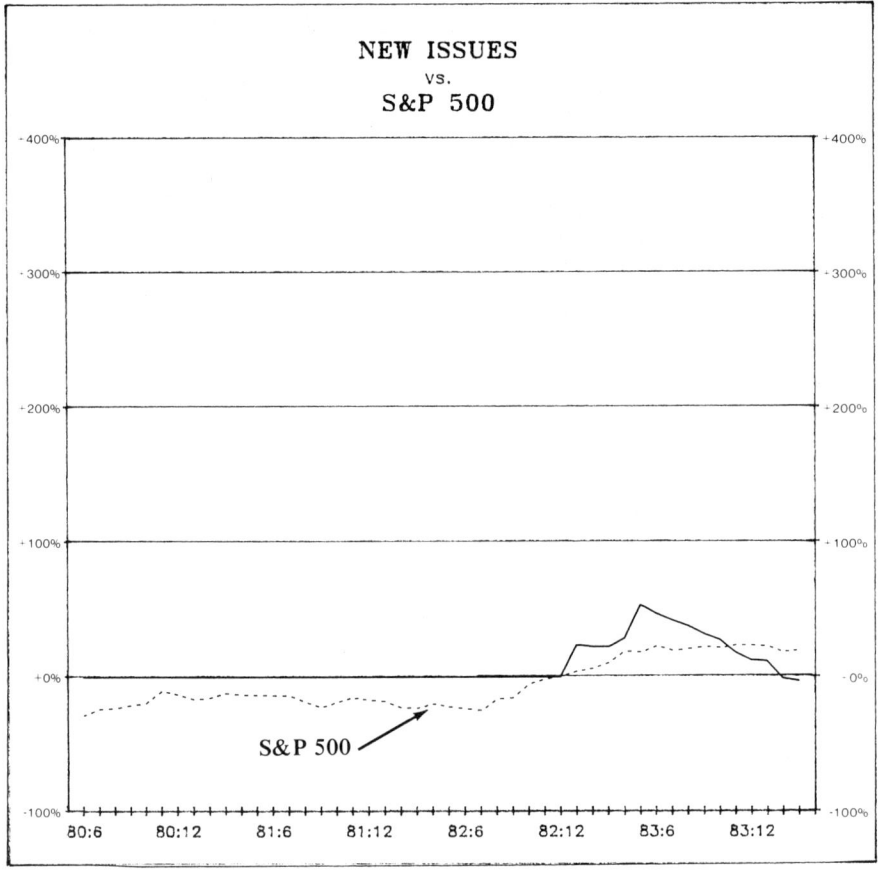

Part One: *Commentary*
Issue No. 141   August 8, 1983

The Nicholson Report
Stock Market Timing, Strategy and Discipline

Bounce!

The lines were so neat! A double-top at 1260 and a firm triple-bottom at 1180! A well-established, three-month-long trading range, which could mount at least one more rally to its top. Or, so we thought!

If the Dow had even touched 1180, we were ready to suggest that you do some selective buying and ride the wave up for 80 points—at a minimum. But, last Thursday, as you know, the market plunged right through our cherished support level at 1180, plummeting to 1166, intra-day.

We are forced now to recognize that a trading range usually fits into the technical description of a "rectangle". It is a common formation, from which the market eventually breaks out. But, there's no way of telling from the formation, itself, which direction the break will take.

One thing that is known, however, is that the move above or below the rectangle, once the break is firmly established, can be expected to proceed for a distance at least equal to the width of the formation. In this case, that would be 80 points. Thus, reasonable—though theoretical—objectives would be 1340 on an upside break or 1100 if the break were down.

Now, technical theory is absolutely wonderful in extending hope whenever a break goes against one's expectations. For instance, there are "false break-outs", moves outside the perimeter of the rectangle that point one way when the market really intends to go the other. The break below the rectangle last Thursday could be one of those, and maybe investors can look for a reversal, a move north that would break the top boundary line and proceed past 1300. Who knows?

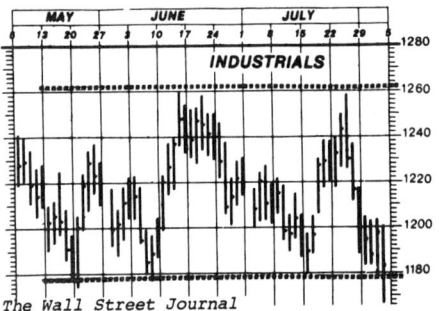

The Wall Street Journal

If we were pure formation-reading technicians, we'd have to wait for a move down to the 1140 area to get confirmation that the down-break was for real. Instead, for the near-term, we look for other clues of most-probable market action. And, there are quite a few. Many of them point to a substantial bounce up at this juncture. In fact, the evidence is sufficiently convincing that we think you should consider the market's recent negative action as an opportunity to do some selective buying. Here's what we see:

(please turn page)

The Nicholson Report

The Nicholson Report is published twice monthly by Robert Nicholson. An annual subscription costs $170; each individual issue is available for $7. A twice-weekly telephone hotline is provided without extra charge to regular subscribers. It is available separately for $75 per year. The address is 5901 Mariposa Court, Coral Gables, Florida 33146. The telephone number is (303) 665-7445. The newsletter was founded in 1979.

Each eight-page issue provides its readers with technically based stock market commentary and predictions. Much of the newsletter is devoted to reviewing the portfolios of stocks recommended "for the longer term investor" and "for the aggressive trader," profiling new stock recommendations, and recommending positions in individual stock options and in industry and market index options. *The Nicholson Report* focuses its attention on the stocks now listed on the options exchange—stocks that tend to be highly liquid with large market capitalizations. This enables subscribers frequently to buy or write call options on individual stocks recommended in this service.

Nicholson also reports on his short-term market timing indicator, the "Market Mood Indicator" (MMI) in each issue and on his hotline. According to Nicholson, the MMI is a gauge of investor sentiment, designed to indicate when it is and is not a good time to buy or sell stocks. The average time between MMI buy and sell signals is relatively short; during the first six months of 1984, for example, there were 13 such signals—slightly more than twice a month on average.

It sometimes is unclear how you should interpret MMI buy and sell signals. Nicholson himself has maintained a fully invested posture over the past two years, in spite of numerous MMI sell signals. Instead of selling, Nicholson has chosen only to hold off new purchases of stocks during MMI sell signals or to purchase stock index puts as a hedge. It appears that the MMI is not intended so much as the basis for deciding whether you should be long or short the market but instead as the basis for deciding when to buy or sell what you have otherwise determined you should buy or sell.*

Performance

Since the beginning of 1983, the HFD has compiled performance figures for the two Nicholson Report portfolios mentioned above. During the 15 months from January 1, 1983, through March 31, 1984, Nicholson's stock recommendations for the longer term investor fell 17.5% and his selections for the aggressive trader dropped 18.8%. In contrast, the S & P 500 gained 19.6% over the same period, while an investor staying solely in Treasury bills could have made 11.6%.

On a risk-adjusted basis, Nicholson's portfolios are also ranked low. His portfolio of stocks for investors is slightly more risky than the S & P 500, while his portfolio of stocks for traders is about 10% more so. Because both portfolios achieved a sub-market return despite this greater risk, this means they underperformed the market. And because their return was lower than the Treasury bill rate, their return per unit of risk was negative.

The Asterisk

The Nicholson Report places asterisks next to those stock recommendations that it considers "Best Buys Now!" Typically, 30–40% of the stocks recommended have asterisks at any given time. This presents one of the many difficult methodological issues faced by in-

---

* For this reason, the HFD has not compared the performance of the MMI with other timing indicators. However, we did track the performance of the MMI over the first six months of 1984 on the assumption that you went 100% long in the NYSE Composite on MMI buys and 100% short on MMI sells. Such a portfolio (assuming no commissions) would have appreciated by 0.9% over the period as compared to a 7.1% drop in the NYSE Composite itself. This 0.9% gain would have placed the MMI in seventh place out of the 28 timing portfolios tracked by the HFD in 1984.

vestment newsletter rating services. Should Nicholson's performance be measured with respect to the complete list of all his stock recommendations or only with respect to those stocks recommended most highly (and hence those most purchased by subscribers) at any given time? In August 1983, Nicholson made it clear that although "an asterisked stock may have more 'potential' than other stocks on the list," in order to reduce portfolio volatility and to diversify properly, an investor's portfolio should encompass all stocks recommended. The HFD ratings are based on the performance of Nicholson's asterisked recommendations until August 1983 and all stocks on the two lists of recommended stocks thereafter.

How, in fact, did Nicholson's asterisked selections compare to his complete portfolio of recommended stocks during the seven-month period from January through July 1983? During that period, his entire list of stocks recommended for "investors" increased in value 7.4% whereas his asterisked selections from that list plummeted 10.2%. An investor would actually have done far better avoiding those recommendations flagged as "best buys" by Nicholson. In contrast, during the first seven months of 1983, Nicholson's recommended list for traders dropped 7.6%, but his "best buys" on that list eked out a 1.2% gain. These differing performance figures again should alert a potential subscriber to the fact that his actual results may well differ from those reported by a rating service, depending on how quickly he or she acts on the advice given, how many of the recommended stocks he indeed purchases and at what prices, what commissions he or she pays, and whether the subscriber chooses to follow all or just the most highly recommended stocks.

NICHOLSON REPORT

Stocks for Investors

Period	Gain	Quintile
1983	−12.9%	Lowest 20%
Risk ranking	2.965	Lowest 20%
% 1983 Closeouts long term	57.1%	Third Highest 20%

Stocks for Traders

Period	Gain	Quintile
1983	−9.0%	Lowest 20%
Risk Ranking	3.306	Second lowest 20%
% 1983 Closeouts long term	0.0%	Lowest 20%

Average of Both

Period	Gain	Quintile
1983	−11.0%	Lowest 20%

The Nicholson Report

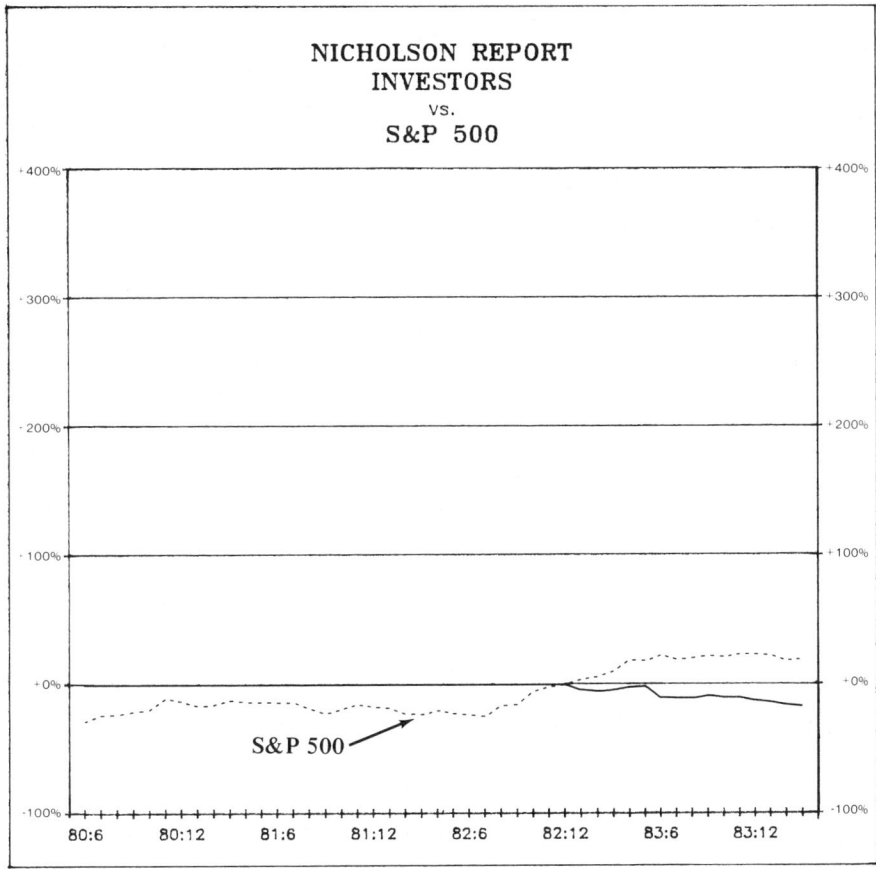

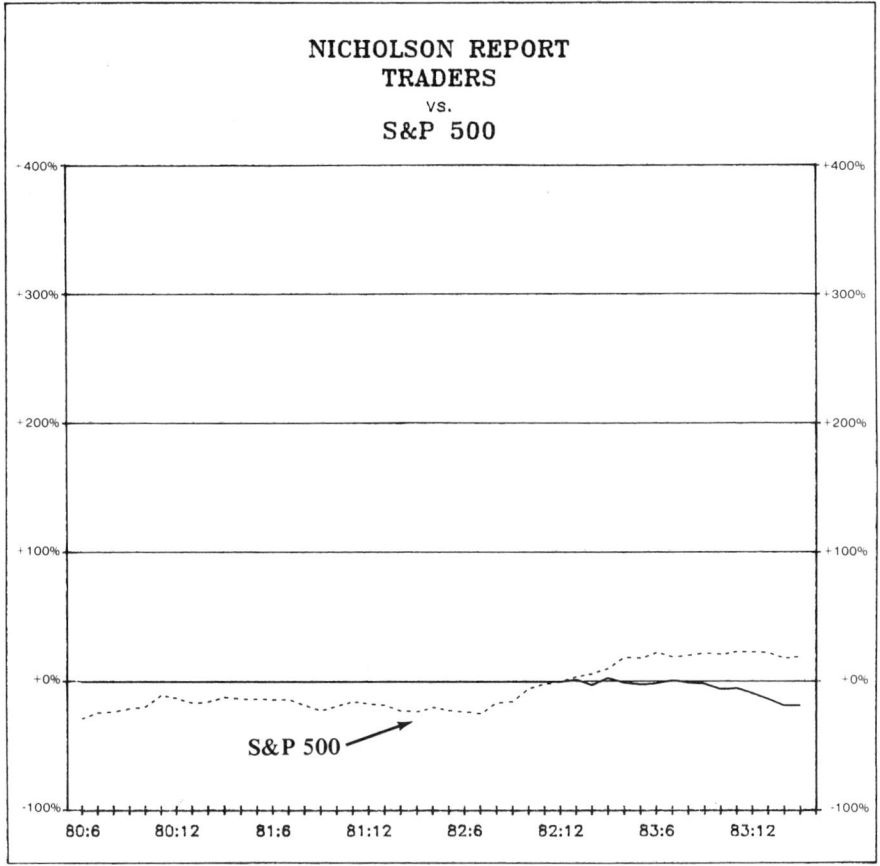

A publication of the Investment Research Institute, Inc.

September, 1983/Volume 3, Issue 9

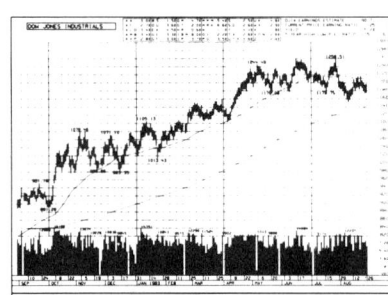

All charts courtesy: **Daily Graphs**
P.O. Box 24933, Los Angeles, CA 90024

THE MARKET

Tuesday, August 30
Closing DJIA 1196.04

The summer doldrums have descended upon an already lackluster market, with recent trading volume settling in the 50-60 million share range. The Dow Industrials remain locked into a narrow four-month trading range. Recent rally attempts have been feeble (only two closes above 1200 in the past month) yet there has been no major breakdown. All in all, a very difficult period for options traders. But the rewards will be bountiful when the inevitable breakout (or breakdown) occurs.

RECOMMENDATIONS AT A GLANCE

STOCK RE-CAP / OPTION RE-CAP

	Underlying Stock	Ticker Symbol	Closing Price 8/30	Momentum Index	Expiration Month	Striking Price	Closing Price 8/30	Maximum Entry Price	Option Profile	Volume/Liquidity Class	Track #
C A L L S	Ford Motor	F	54-3/4	+1.64	Sep.	55	1-9/16	1-7/8	I	B2	4.5
	Lockheed	LK	108-5/8	+1.35	Sep.	110	3	3-1/2	I	B2	9.5
	Mary Kay Cosm.	MKY	25-1/4	+1.89	Sep.	25	1-1/8	1-7/16	I	C2	3.3
	McDonald's	MCD	59-1/2	+2.37	Sep.	60	1-3/8	1-13/16	I	B3	4.0
P U T	S & P 100	OEX*	163.83	N/A	Sep.	165	2-3/4	N/A	II	A1	

* To be purchased by new subscribers only; others should hold positions in XMI October 120 puts. The total dollars to be invested in the OEX put should equal the total dollars to be invested by new subscribers in the above call recommendations (see page 3 for details).

Box 11321, Cincinnati, OH 45211

Copyright, Investment Research Institute, Inc. 1983

The Option Advisor

The Option Advisor is a highly volatile investment newsletter dedicated exclusively to options trading. It is edited and published monthly by Robert D. Bergen and Bernard G. Schaeffer. An annual subscription costs $225 and can be ordered by writing to P. O. Box 46709, Cincinnati, Ohio 45246. A weekly telephone hotline is provided to each subscriber at no extra cost. In addition to the 12 monthly issues, approximately six special bulletins are mailed to subscribers each year when there are "unusual profit opportunities." For an additional $300 per year, *The Option Advisor* also offers subscribers a "Wire Alert Service" that provides subscribers with a written copy of the recommendations made on the telephone hotline. *The Option Advisor* has been published since 1981.

    The Option Advisor currently offers recommendations in two different categories—one for "conservative" subscribers and the other for "aggressive" subscribers. In 1983, in contrast, *The Option Advisor* maintained three portfolios—the two above plus one for subscribers looking for a "moderate risk" strategy. In 1983, these three portfolios differed only in the recommended stop-loss points and profit objectives. In 1984, in addition to deleting the moderate risk category altogether, the conservative portfolio changed its orientation to focus exclusively upon option spreads (a spread involves the purchase of an option and the simultaneous sale of another option on the same security). The aggressive portfolio in 1984 continued the focus it had in 1983.

Performance

According to HFD performance figures, the conservative portfolio lost a whopping 83.5% of its value in 1983, but in a sharp reversal of fortune, it is second only to the aggressive portfolio among the newsletters tracked by the HFD in 1984, showing an 99.4% gain in just the first quarter.* As the accompanying graph reveals, this amounts to a cumulative loss of these 15 months of 67.0%. The aggressive portfolio recorded a similar performance, shedding 83.1% of its value in 1983 but recovering 121.6% in the first three months of 1984 for a cumulative loss of 62.6%. Twelve-month performance alone is available for the moderate risk portfolio, and its 1983 loss was almost identical to the others.

These cumulative performance figures illustrate well the hazards of simply adding percentage gains and losses together. A drop of 83.5% followed by a gain of 99.4% does not result in a 15.9% gain (99.4% minus 83.5%) but rather a 67.0% loss.

As these sharply fluctuating performance figures suggest, these portfolios are by far the riskiest of the 77 portfolios whose performance is assessed by the HFD. Both *Option Advisor* portfolios are more than 12 times as volatile as the stock market in general, as measured by the Standard & Poor's Composite Average of 500 stocks.

---

* One of the dilemmas facing any newsletter rater is how to treat instances where the newsletter has changed its investment strategy so dramatically that it calls into question whether the portfolio is the "same" portfolio. *The Option Advisor*, for example, complained when the HFD treated its 1984 conservative portfolio as the same as its 1983 conservative portfolio, pointing out that the portfolios were dissimilar. For the purposes of this book, however, the authors have treated the *Option Adivsor's* recommendations for "conservative" investors as one continuous portfolio (on the assumption that a subscriber looking for a conservative approach to trading options would have followed what was called the conservative portfolio in 1983 as well as what it was called in 1984).

OPTION ADVISOR

Conservative Risk Portfolio

Period	Gain	Quintile
1983	−83.5%	Lowest 20%
Risk ranking	28.895	Highest 20%

Aggressive Risk Portfolio

Period	Gain	Quintile
1983	−83.1%	Lowest 20%
Risk ranking	35.909	Highest 20%

Average of Two Portfolios

Period	Gain	Quintile
1983	−83.3%	Lowest 20%

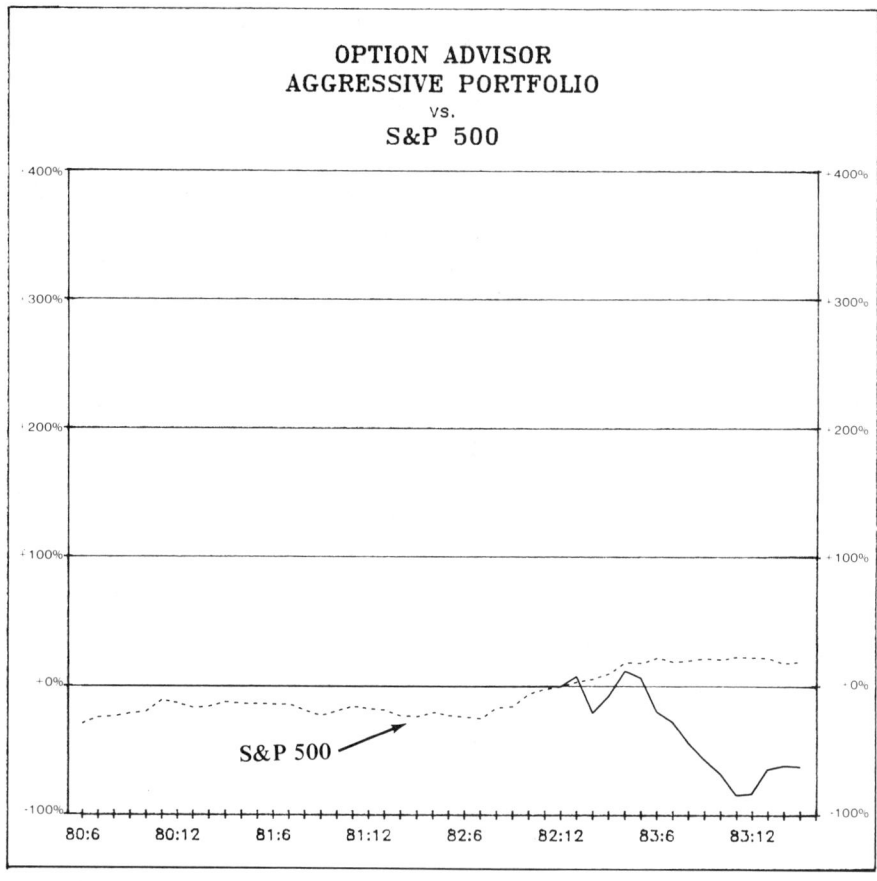

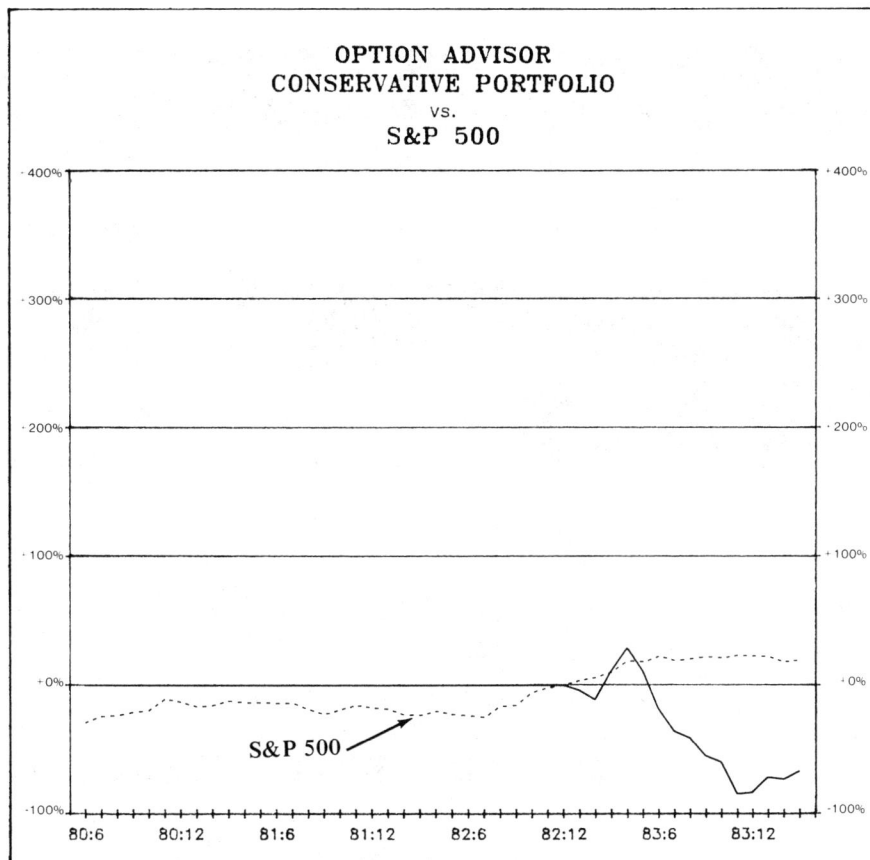

Building a
Diversified Portfolio

Beneficiaries of
Capital Spending Pickup

Dividend
Actions

Master List:
Group 2

Six-Month
Follow-Ups

In the
Limelight

Vol. 55, No. 43   Pages 482-492   2 SECTIONS, SECTION 1   **November 9, 1983**

Standard & Poor's
The Outlook

ANALYZES AND PROJECTS BUSINESS AND MARKET TRENDS

The Market Last Week

Rally attempts fell flat, owing to institutional apathy and to tax-loss selling by individuals. The S&P 500-stock index suffered its fourth consecutive weekly loss.

S&P 500 Index	
Close	Change
162.44	−0.93

The Current Outlook

The market could give some further ground before underlying demand for stocks reasserts itself. With the longer-term risk-reward ratio still highly positive, we would take advantage of the current weakness to accumulate sound issues in an unhurried manner.

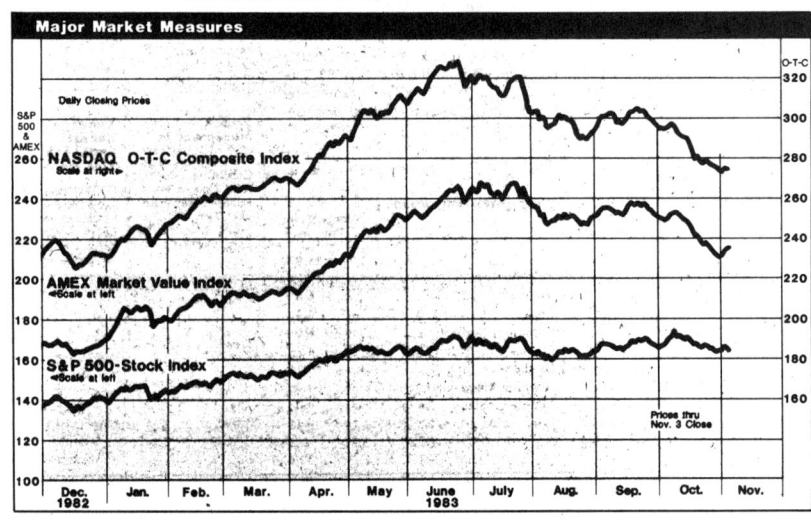

Standard & Poor's Corporation

The Outlook

The Outlook, published by Stephen Sanborn and edited by Arnold Kaufman, is a weekly publication of Standard & Poor's Equity Research Department. An annual subscription costs $185 and a quarterly subscription is offered for $55. The newsletter is not supplemented by a telephone hotline. The address is 25 Broadway, New York, New York 10004. This widely followed investment newsletter has been published weekly by Standard & Poor's Corporation for over 50 years and has one of the widest followings of any in the newsletter industry.

The Outlook maintains four "Supervised Master Lists of Recommended Issues": foundation stocks for long-term gain, growth stocks, cyclical/speculative stocks, and income stocks with inflation protection. Stock recommendations appear to be based entirely on fundamental analysis, with technical factors not playing a role. *The Outlook* up through late 1982 advised subscribers as to what percentage of their investable assets should be in the market and what percentage in cash. Since then, however, no such specific allocation advice has been provided. The market timing advice that is provided is nonspecific—such as, "we continue to recommend a policy of accumulation of sound stocks."

The HFD has tracked the performance of these four portfolios since mid-1980. Up until late 1982, the portfolios included a cash portion in line with the specific advice *The Outlook* provided, and since then, the portfolios have been fully invested (per the HFD's established methodology; see the methodological prologue for an in-depth discussion.) Even when *The Outlook* did offer specific allocation advice, however, they did not take a short-term trading approach, changing their market exposure relatively infrequently and in small increments. Consistent with their fundamental approach to security analysis, they purchase stocks for the longer term; the average holding periods of positions they have closed out over the past two years have been well in excess of six months.

The Outlook's Master Lists typically include from 10 to 15 stocks each, and in each issue they indicate which stocks on each list are "best situated among the group currently." Pursuant to its established methodology, the HFD follows the subset of each list which is "best situated."

Performance

Performance has been roughly in line with that of the market for each of the portfolios; the average performance for all four portfolios for the period beginning mid-1980 and ending March 31, 1984, was 62.2%, while the increase in the S & P 500 (including dividends) for this same period was 68.2%. The portfolios' performance has also been consistent. Of 32 portfolios tracked since mid-1980, only 10 have shown a gain in each of the following four periods: July to December 1980, calendar year 1981, calendar year 1982, and January 1983 to March 1984. These 10 included three of the four S & P portfolios (and, but for a 1.6% loss in 1981 in the fourth, would have included all four of the S & P portfolios).

As the accompanying chart shows, the "foundation stocks" portfolios surged in value 18.1% during the second half of 1980, gained an additional 8.8% in 1981, added another 19.9% in 1982, and increased 2.3% more from January 1, 1983, through March 31, 1984, for an aggregate gain over the 3-3/4-year period of 57.6%. In comparison, the Standard & Poor's 500 stock average gained 21.7% in the last six months of 1980, dropped 4.9% in 1981, increased 21.6% in 1982, and added another 19.6% from the start of 1983 through the first quarter of 1984, for an aggregate gain of 68.2%. A portfolio of Treasury bills would have gained 49.5% over the same period.

The Outlook's Master List of Growth Stocks gained 17.6%, 19.6%, 11.0%, and 1.4% over the same four periods, for a cumulative gain of 58.4%. The recommended list of income stocks increased in value 17.9%, 10.8%, 10.6%, and 13.5% during these four time periods for a cumulative gain of 63.9% over the 45-month period. The portfolio of speculative and cylical stocks showed the best performance of the four *Outlook* portfolios, gaining 19.6%, −1.6%, 31.0%, and 9.6% for an aggregate gain of 69.0%.

Risk-Adjusted Performance

The performance of the four *Outlook* portfolios—which about equals the market over this period—was achieved with higher volatility (and risk) than that associated with the market itself. In fact, the measure of the four's volatility shows them tightly bunched in a narrow range (see accompanying tables), all with about 33% greater volatility than that of the S & P 500.* Because they earned no greater profit in return for the greater risk, they have underperformed the market on a risk-adjusted basis. Because they outperformed the Treasury bill rate, however, the *Outlook* portfolios are some of the few which did achieve a positive return per unit of risk during the period the HFD has been tracking newsletters.

---

* One of the reasons for their greater-than-market volatility, no doubt, is the fact that they were constructed by the HFD to include just the subset that The Outlook at any given time recommends to be best situated. In general, one would expect that the subset will be more volatile than the overall list.

THE OUTLOOK

Master Lists of Foundation Stocks

Period	Gain	Quintile
7/1 to 12/31/80	18.1%	Third highest 20%
1981	8.8%	Second highest 20%
1982	19.9%	Third highest 20%
1983	12.3%	Third highest 20%
Risk rating	4.434	Third highest 20%
% 1983 Closeouts long term	100%	Highest 20%
% 1982 Closeouts long term	100%	Highest 20%

Master List of Growth Issues

Period	Gain	Quintile
7/1 to 12/31/80	17.6%	Third highest 20%
1981	19.6%	Highest 20%
1982	11.0%	Second lowest 20%
1983	10.4%	Third highest 20%
Risk rating	4.446	Third highest 20%
% 1983 Closeouts long term	100%	Highest 20%
% 1982 Closeouts long term	100%	Highest 20%

Master List of Speculative Issues

Period	Gain	Quintile
7/1 to 12/31/80	19.6%	Third highest 20%
1981	−1.6%	Third highest 20%
1982	31.0%	Second highest 20%
1983	21.4%	Second highest 20%
Risk rating	4.895	Third highest 20%
% 1983 Closeouts long term	100%	Highest 20%
% 1983 Closeouts long term	100%	Highest 20%

Master List of Income Issues

Period	Gain	Quintile
7/1 to 12/31/80	17.9%	Third highest 20%
1981	10.8%	Second highest 20%
1982	10.6%	Second lowest 20%
1983	28.0%	Highest 20%
Risk rating	4.135	Second lowest 20%
% 1983 Closeouts long term	[No positions closeout]	
% 1982 Closeouts long term	75.0%	Third highest 20%

Average of Four Lists

Period	Gain	Quintile
7/1 to 12/31/80	18.3%	Third lowest 20%
1981	9.4%	Second highest 20%
1982	18.1%	Second lowest 20%
1983	18.0%	Second highest 20%

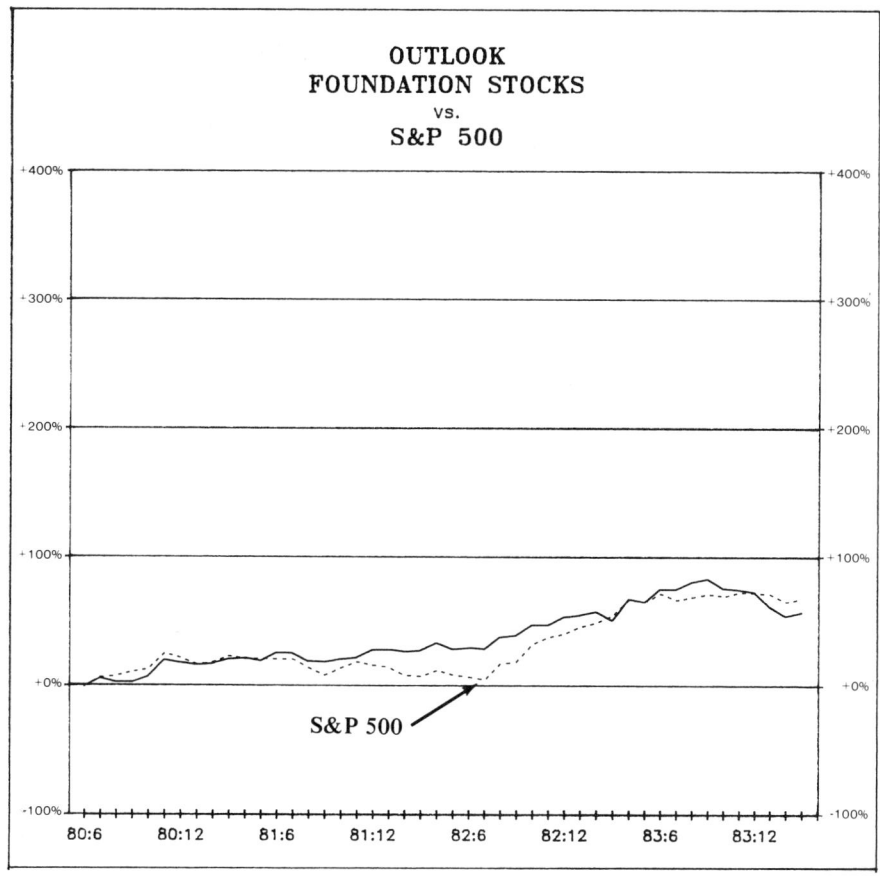

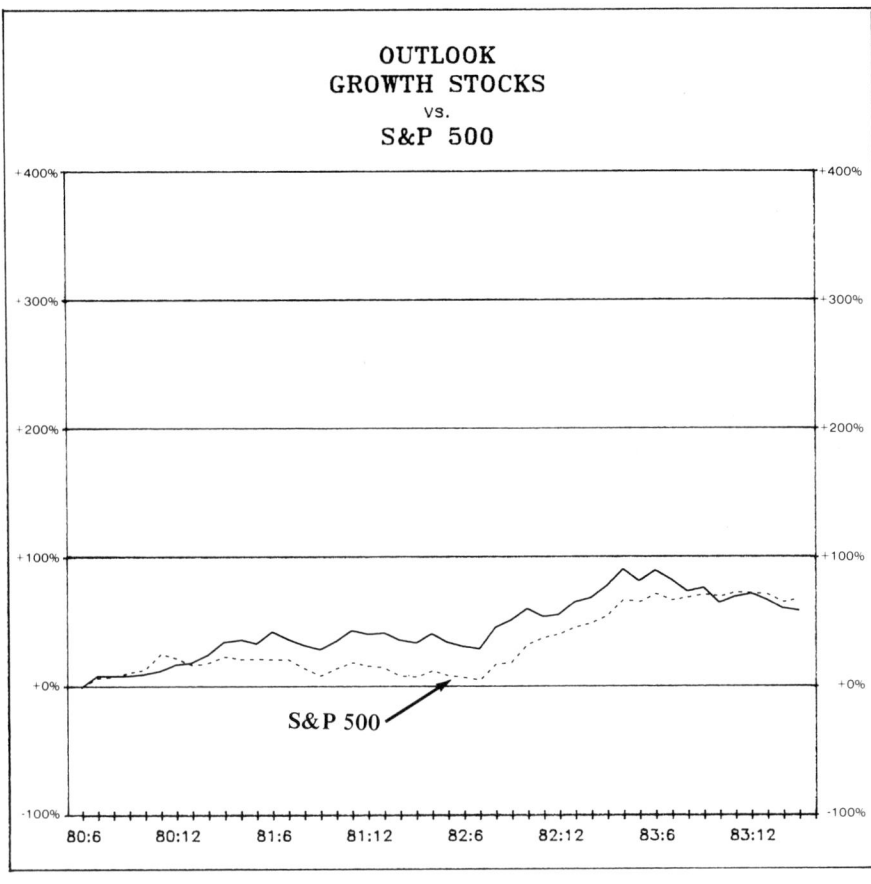

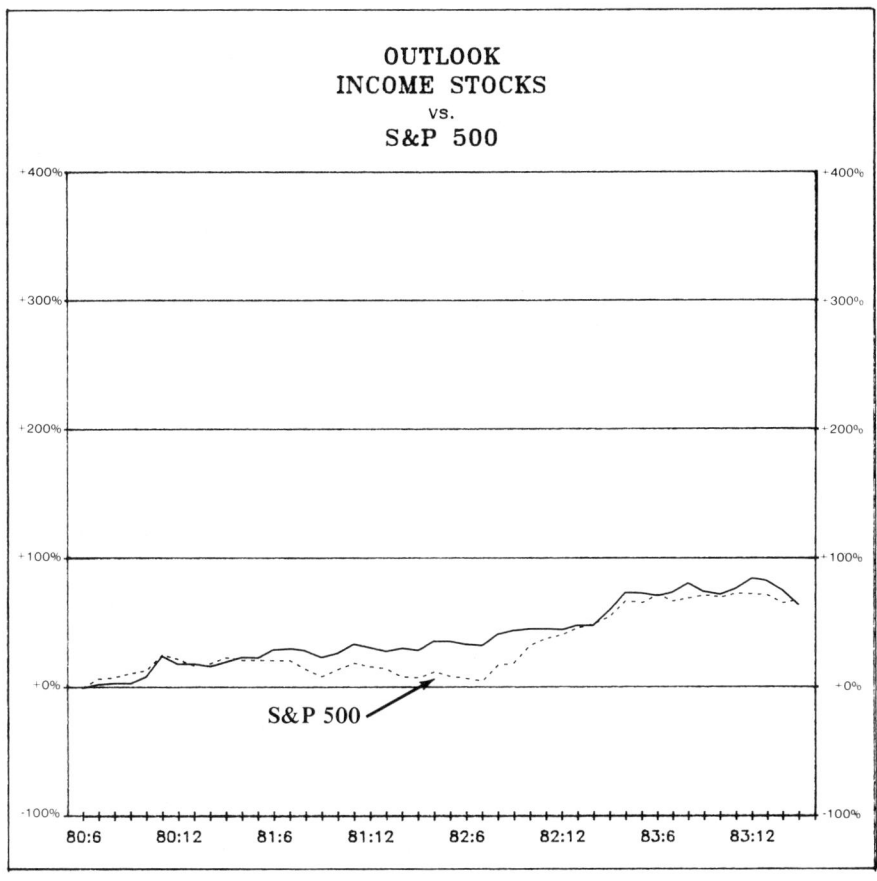

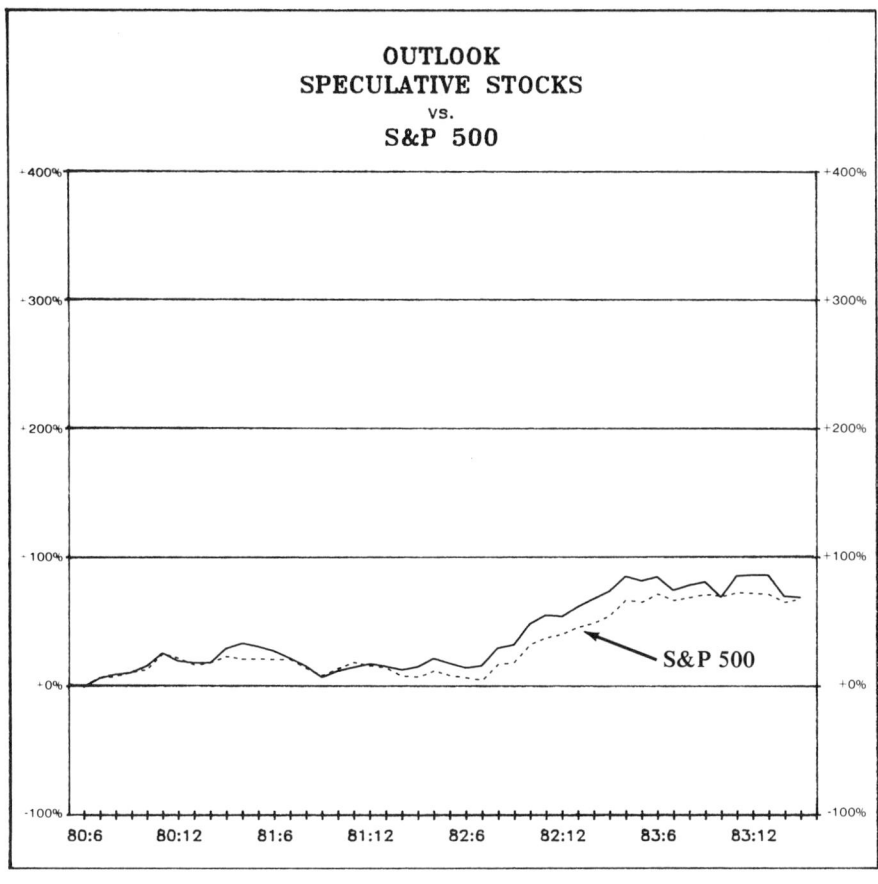

The Peter Dag Investment Letter

Vol. 83 No. 6   April 25, 1983   65 Lake Front Dr., Akron, Ohio 44319

INVESTMENT SCENARIO

As anticipated, short-term interest rates remain uncomfortably high in the 8-9% range, contrary to the consensus which expects lower rates. The economy seems to be willing to grow in response to the enormous monetary stimulus of the past 9 months. But its growth remains below average when compared to prior expansions.

Stock prices moved sharply higher, with the Dow Jones Industrial average closing at 1196.30, up 5.9%. A strong performance was also displayed by the Transportation average, which finished at 527.24 from 507.39, up 3.9%. The Utilities jumped to 127.17 from 124.54, up 2.1%. The Dow Jones Industrial average is up 14.3% so far this year, while the NYSE and S&P500 rose 13.7% and 14.1% respectively during the same period.

Outlook: A buying opportunity is likely to present itself during the second half of the year.

Short-term interest rates declined and are locked in the 8-9% range. The rate on prime commercial paper (90 days) - corporate IOUs - declined from 8.8% to 8.5%, while the rate on bankers acceptances (90 days) - bank-backed credit instruments - finished at 8.45%, down from 9% three weeks ago. The rate on federal funds - reserves traded among commercial banks - declined from 8.8% to 8.7%. Yields on Treasury bills declined to 8.1% from 8.6%.

Outlook: Do not expect major declines in short-term rates at this time. The likely range remains 8-9%.

The economy is expanding at a below average pace. The most positive element was that industrial output soared 1.1% in March, but still down 1.8% from a year earlier. Retail sales rose a slim 0.3%, while personal income was up 0.6%. Factory orders for durable goods rose 0.3%, and capacity utilization - still below 1974 levels - jumped 0.7 percentage points to 69.4, reflecting widespread increases in activity among manufacturing industries. An important vote of confidence in our economic strength is that the dollar is up against all major currencies since the beginning of the year. And now the bad news. Housing starts declined 9.2%. Building permits - a harbinger of housing activity - declined 4%. Business Week Index has been declining since February.

Outlook: Business will continue to improve at a below average pace.

Inflation continues to subside. Producer prices - i.e. prices at the wholesale level - for finished goods declined 0.1% in March, up 2.2% from a year earlier. Producer prices for intermediate materials sagged 0.7%, while prices of crude materials rose 0.6%. Consumer prices rose 0.1% in March, up 3.6% from a year earlier. Raw material prices continue to rise, up 12% from December 1982.

Outlook: Inflation, as measured by the rise in consumer prices, will continue to subside and will remain in the 3-4% range.

Bonds were strong. The Dow Jones 20 Bonds average jumped 2.4%, closing at 75.94, up from 74.18. Utility bonds rose 3.9%, while industrial bonds were up 0.9%. Yields on best grade bonds are 10.7%, while yields

The Peter Dag Investment Letter

The Peter Dag Investment Letter (PDIL) is published every three weeks by, not surprisingly, Peter Dag. An annual subscription costs $250, and a three-month trial subscription is available for $75. The address is 65 Lake Front Drive, Akron, Ohio 44319. The newsletter is not supplemented by a telephone hotline service.

Each six–eight page issue of PDIL summarizes Dag's current views of the outlook for stocks, the economy, short-term interest rates, inflation, bonds, and precious metals. Approximately one page of the newsletter is devoted to a discussion of each of these topics. Dag then specifically recommends what percentage of a subscriber's investment portfolio should be allocated to stocks, bonds, gold stocks, and money market instruments, respectively. He does not typically recommend specific stocks or bonds, but instead recommends no-load stock and bond mutual funds.

Model Portfolio

PDIL established a Model Portfolio in January 1979 to attempt to demonstrate that a prudent strategy attentive to current business trends and cycles can outperform the broad stock market averages. According to PDIL's records, in its first five years (through December 31, 1983) the Model Portfolio gained 81.3%, including stock dividends and interest paid on bonds and money market instruments. Over the same period, the S & P 500 gained 71.6%, excluding dividends—which, if included, would have comfortably exceeded the Model Portfolio's performance of 81.3%.

The HFD has been following Dag's Model Portfolio since the beginning of 1983, and calculated its gain to be 10.3% for the 15 months through March 31, 1984. This compares to a 19.6% increase in the S & P 500 and a 11.6% gain in a Treasury bill portfolio over the same period.

Expecting Too Much?

Over this 15-month period, Dag's model portfolio was the least risky of the 69 portfolios the HFD monitored for that period of time, incurring just a third of the risk experienced by the S & P 500. Given that low level of risk, Dag may be expecting too much when he writes that his goal is for the portfolio to "outperform broad stock market averages." At least during a bull market, such as the one experienced during 1983, it would be surprising if Dag's portfolio outperformed the more risky S & P 500.

During a down market, in contrast, such as what the market experienced in early 1984, one would be surprised if his portfolio did not outperform the market. And, true to form, during the first three months of 1984, when the S & P 500 gave up 2.4% in value, Dag's model portfolio gained 3.9%. Dag's goal of outperforming the market averages over long periods of time would be realistic only in the event that he expects the market to do poorly.

A more realistic goal would be to outperform the stock market averages on a risk-adjusted basis. Unfortunately, however, for the 15-month period the portfolio was monitored, it underperformed the S & P 500 on a risk-adjusted as well as a performance basis. Furthermore, because a better performance could have been achieved with riskless Treasury bills, his Model Portfolio's return per unit of risk was negative.

PETER DAG INVESTMENT LETTER
(Model Portfolio)

Period	Gain	Quintile
1983	6.1%	Second lowest 20%
Risk rating	0.994	Lowest 20%
% 1983 Closeouts long term	71.7%	Third highest 20%

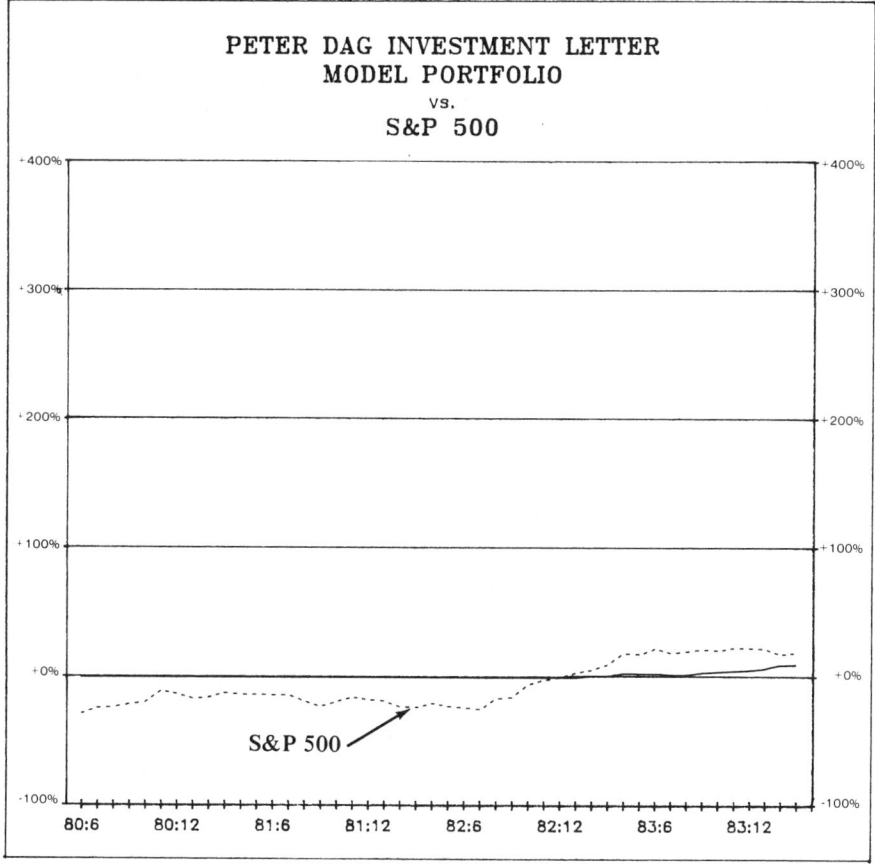

The Financial Magazine Designed To Be Better!

THE PROFESSIONAL INVESTOR ®

LYNATRACE, INC.   P. O. BOX 2144   POMPANO BEACH, FLORIDA 33061

Vol. 13, Issue 11   *A Financial Magazine Sold By Subscription Or On Newsstands At $5.00 Each*   Friday, February 18, 1983

Services quoted here for news value; no correlation with PI is implied

SCANNING ANOTHER SERVICE

Marketrend [Technical Market Opinion] is prepared by Richard J. Yashewski and Joseph H. Barthel, and is published by Butcher & Singer Inc., 1615 Northern Boulevard, Manhasset, NY 11030. Call: (516) 627-1600 or (212) 895-4915. Ask for Lucille Finnigan, technical assistant. Will sample.

Within the trade, we normally refer to this service simply as Dick & Joe, as in "What do Dick & Joe say?" The reason is simple. There are only seven living people (the same ones that fully understand Einstein) that can properly pronounce Dick's last name.

Despite being published by a brokerage house, this is one of the very best market letters in the world if you are technically-oriented. Dick and Joe are sometimes wrong on the intermediate trend [as are we all at times!], but they always have more good technical reasons for being wrong than anyone else we know. And they are just new enough in the market letter business that they haven't learned to lie when they make a mistake. They don't even dissimulate. We are sure that given a little time and experience they will become omniscient like all the great gurus, but in the meantime — enjoy!

They are long term bulls and have been for some time. They began making bullish noises in June or July of last year, and only faltered [as did just about everyone] for a few days when the bottom near 785-790 was briefly penetrated on the downside.

In any case within days, they had recovered their equilibrium, and have been long term bulls ever since.

But, they do fear a sizable correction is near, and they offer a plethora of evidence to support this thesis. We shall present a portion of it.

Continued On Page Two

COPYRIGHT © 1983, LYNATRACE, INC.

ARC	T	X	ASA	DD	N
3s51½	42	50¼	3s41¾	216	

WE MAY BE GETTING SENILE,

but we still can't find that Big Correction in our indicators that all those guest "analysts" on Financial News Network keep telling us is imminent.

Today, especially (Thursday), we heard one after the other tell us that "every" indicator was in gear for an almost immediate steep correction. We hasten to point out that this coterie of Cassandras did not include any of the really top technicians regularly listed in our Advisory Letters Scan.

But what to our surprise when we carefully worked over our own indicator scan and found out that the intermediate term indicators even improved a smidgin from two weeks ago — and they weren't that bad then! Don't misunderstand; they are not towers of strength. They are simply not bad enough to demand an imminent, deep correction.

Certainly, we could have one. The market can do anything it wants at any time. But based on our own technical work, which has treated us pretty well over the years, we stick with what we have been saying for a couple of months now.

That is, that this market will cross 1120 before we are in serious trouble. It then may go as high as 1150. During the period when it is in between 1120 and 1150, I say we are vulnerable to a big correction. That is, we could have one as large as 150 points. I do not say we must have one. Not at all. We could easily go through another round of rotational, so-called internal correction. Frankly, at this point, I don't know. We'll face that one when we get to it.

The Sentiment Indexes, especially including the amount of cash in mutual funds and INDATA's all-equity portfolio does need refurbishing. A big correction could take care of that. But internally, the market is actually strengthening right now.

Editor: Robert T. Gross   Continued On Page Two

The Professional Investor

The Professional Investor, a bi-weekly investment newsletter edited by Robert T. Gross, a noted technical analyst, was first published in 1971. An annual subscription costs $150; a six-month subscription is offered for $90; and a single issue is available for $15. The address is P. O. Box 2144, Pompano Beach, Florida 33061. A weekly telephone hotline service is provided to each subscriber at no additional cost. Specific stock recommendations are usually made through the newsletter, however, not over the hotline.

In Each Issue

In each eight-page issue, Gross devotes part of the first two pages to a technical analysis of recent stock market behavior. The conclusion of this analysis is usually Gross's unhedged classification of the major and intermediate trends as either bullish or bearish. (Gross does not translate his analysis into a specific percentage allocation of his subscribers' portfolios between stocks and cash, however.) On the first two pages of each issue, Gross also either analyzes (or unveils) a new technical indicator, reviews another investment newsletter, or discusses a new stock recommendation. An additional three pages of *The Professional Investor* are devoted to reviewing and updating three lists (he calls them "Scans") of Gross's recommended stock positions (either purchases or short sales), one list each for the NYSE,

Amex, and OTC markets. These lists are fairly large; for example, in February 1984, Gross recommended positions in 50 NYSE stocks, 58 Amex stocks, and 53 OTC stocks.

Gross takes a short- to intermediate-term perspective when recommending stocks for these Scans; the average holding period for positions closed out from these Scans over the past two years is about six months—which under the new tax law is the cut-off between short- and long-term capital gains treatment.

An interesting one-page feature in *The Professional Investor* is Gross's review of the intermediate- and long-term investment outlooks of 54 other investment newsletters, along with his summary of their current advice in a few words. A seventh page of *The Professional Investor* tracks 49 different market averages and technical indicators and rates each of them as bullish, bearish, or neutral for both the intermediate- and long-term outlook. Gross comments on trends in these indicators and their import. On the last page of each issue, Gross updates advice with respect to a handful of investment grade recommendations, tracks a portfolio of six gold stocks (the composition of this portfolio has remained unchanged, despite the fluctuations of gold bullion and stocks, in more than four years), advises switch fund traders, and makes specific recommendations for options traders.

Performance

The HFD has rated the advice given in T*he Professional Investor* since July 1, 1980, with respect to four different portfolios: the NYSE Scan, the Amex Scan, the OTC Scan, and the Investment Grade Stocks Scan. The four accompanying graphs depict the performance of each of these portfolios in comparison to the Standard & Poor's 500 (including dividends), the Amex Market Value Index (without dividends), and the NASDAQ OTC Composite (without dividends), and the DJIA (including dividends), respectively.

The Professional Investor's NYSE Scan gained 14.4% in the second half of 1980, underperforming the S & P 500 gain of 21.7%. In 1981, the S & P 500 shed 4.9%, while the NYSE Scan lost 6.1%. The following year witnessed a powerful bull market carrying the S & P 500 up 21.6%. The NYSE Scan in 1982 outperformed this with a 34.5% gain. From January 1, 1983, through March 31, 1984, the NYSE gained another 5.1%, falling short of the S & P 500's gain of 19.6%. The aggregate gain of the Gross's NYSE Scan over the 45-month period was 51.9%, as compared to 68.2% for the S & P 500. The volatility (risk) of Gross's NYSE Scan was very similar to that of the broader market, so on a risk-adjusted basis it slightly underperformed the market. Since it outperformed the Treasury bill rate, however, it did achieve a positive return per unit of risk.

The Professional Investor's Amex Scan scored the most impressive gains of the four portfolios. In the latter half of 1980, it surged 34.0%, outstripping the Amex Market Value Index's gain of 18.9%. In 1981, the Amex Scan lost 6.9%, but even this performance bettered the Amex Index's loss of 8.1%. In 1982, Gross' Amex Scan scored impressively, gaining a sharp 39.1%, while the usually volatile Amex Index lagged with a lowly gain of 6.2%. The 15-month period from January 1983 to March 1984 brought more success: the Amex Scan picked up 41.6% while the Amex Index surged 24.1%. The aggregate gain of the Amex Scan over this 45-month period was 145.8%, compared to a 44.0% gain in the Amex Market Value Index. On a risk-adjusted basis, this portfolio's performance was also impressive—more than tripling the return on the Amex Index with less volatility and risk. Looked at individually (and not averaged with the performance of the other *Professional Investor* portfolios), the Amex Scan was the third-best performing portfolio on a risk-adjusted basis among the portfolios monitored by the HFD for this 45-month period.

The portfolio of over-the-counter stocks also did well, gaining 30.8% in the second half of 1980, giving up 4.4% in 1981, but then strengthening 21.6% in 1982 and another 24.8% from January 1983 through March 1984. The NASDAQ OTC Composite, in contrast, gained 28.2%, lost 3.2%, gained 18.7%, and gained 7.9% over the same four time periods. The aggregate gain for *The Professional Investor* OTC Scan was 89.6% over the 3-3/4 year period in comparison to a gain of 58.9% in the NASDAQ OTC Composite stock index. Gross's OTC Scan outperformed the NASDAQ Composite with less volatility and risk and thus was one of the better performers on a risk-adjusted basis.

The Investment-Grade Stocks Scan

The fourth *Professional Investor* portfolio tracked by the HFD is the Investment Grade Stocks Scan. This portfolio, although more than twice as volatile as the DJIA or the S & P 500, on the whole has proven to be a disappointment, recording gains of 12.5%, 3.0%, and 23.7% in July–December 1980, 1981, and 1982, respectively, but losing 24.5% over the 15 months from January 1983 through March 1984. In comparison, the DJIA (including dividends) gained 14.8% in the last six months of 1980, lost 3.7% in 1981, recovered 23.9% in 1982, and added on another 20.1% in the 15 months since then. This unusual underperformance of the market in 1983 by an astonishing 40% or so is attributable in large part to an unfortunate error in recommending the purchase of too large a number of puts on the Amex Major Market Index in August 1983, a recommendation that caused this portfolio to lose approximately 25% of its value in less than two months!* Compounding these results over the time periods surveyed yields an aggregate gain of 8.2% for the Investment Grade Stocks Scan while the DJIA gained 64.5% over the same period.

---

* In the issue of his newsletter following the errant recommendation, Gross wrote that his ratio of puts to the stock portion of his portfolio "was all wrong. Frankly, I don't know what was going on in the head of the author when he suggested buying ten puts for each $5,000 of long exposure." This is another example of the dilemmas that a newsletter rater must confront. Should a rater do what he thinks the newsletter editor meant to say, or what an average subscriber thinks the editor meant to say, or what the editor actually said? The HFD felt that it had no choice but to follow the specific recommendation that was made.

PROFESSIONAL INVESTOR

NYSE Scan

Period	Gain	Quintile
7/1 to 12/31/80	14.4%	Second lowest 20%
1981	−6.1%	Second lowest 20%
1982	34.5%	Highest 20%
1983	14.1%	Third highest 20%
Risk ranking	3.415	Second lowest 20%
% 1983 Closeouts long term	17.3%	Lowest 20%
% 1982 Closeouts long term	5.4%	Lowest 20%

AMEX Scan

Period	Gain	Quintile
7/1 to 12/31/80	34.0%	Highest 20%
1981	−6.9%	Second lowest 20%
1982	39.1%	Highest 20%
1983	48.2%	Highest 20%
Risk ranking	5.097	Third lowest 20%
% 1983 Closeouts long term	42.3%	Second lowest 20%
% 1982 Closeouts long term	40.0%	Third highest 20%

OTC Scan

Period	Gain	Quintile
7/1 to 12/31/80	30.8%	Highest 20%
1981	−4.4%	Third highest 20%
1982	21.6%	Third Highest 20%
1983	29.3%	Highest 20%
Risk ranking	4.335	Third lowest 20%
% 1983 Closeouts long term	53.6%	Second lowest 20%
% 1982 Closeouts long term	23.4%	Second lowest 20%

Investment Grade Stocks Scan

Period	Gain	Quintile
7/1 to 12/31/80	12.5%	Second lowest 20%
1981	3.0%	Second highest 20%
1982	23.7%	Second highest 20%
1983	−18.5%	Lowest 20%
Risk ranking	6.335	Second highest 20%
% 1983 Closeouts long term	21.4%	Lowest 20%
% 1982 Closeouts long term	18.8%	Second lowest 20%

Average of Four Portfolios

Period	Gain	Quintile
7/1 to 12/31/80	22.9%	Second highest 20%
1981	−3.6%	Third highest 20%
1982	29.7%	Second highest 20%
1983	18.3%	Second highest 20%

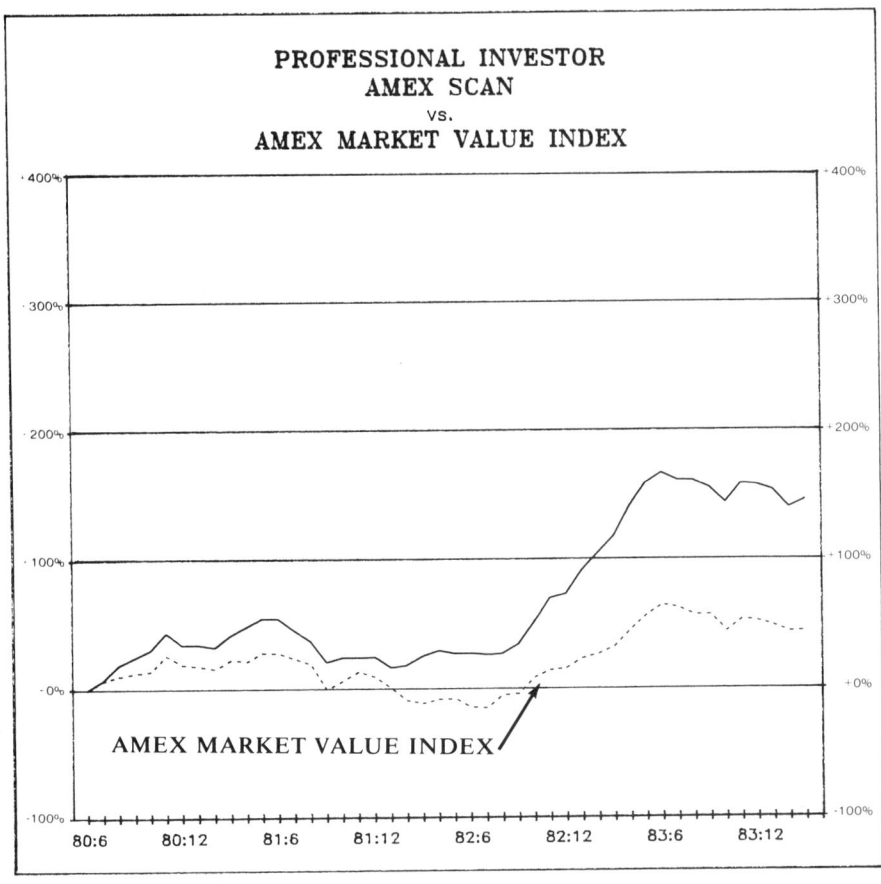

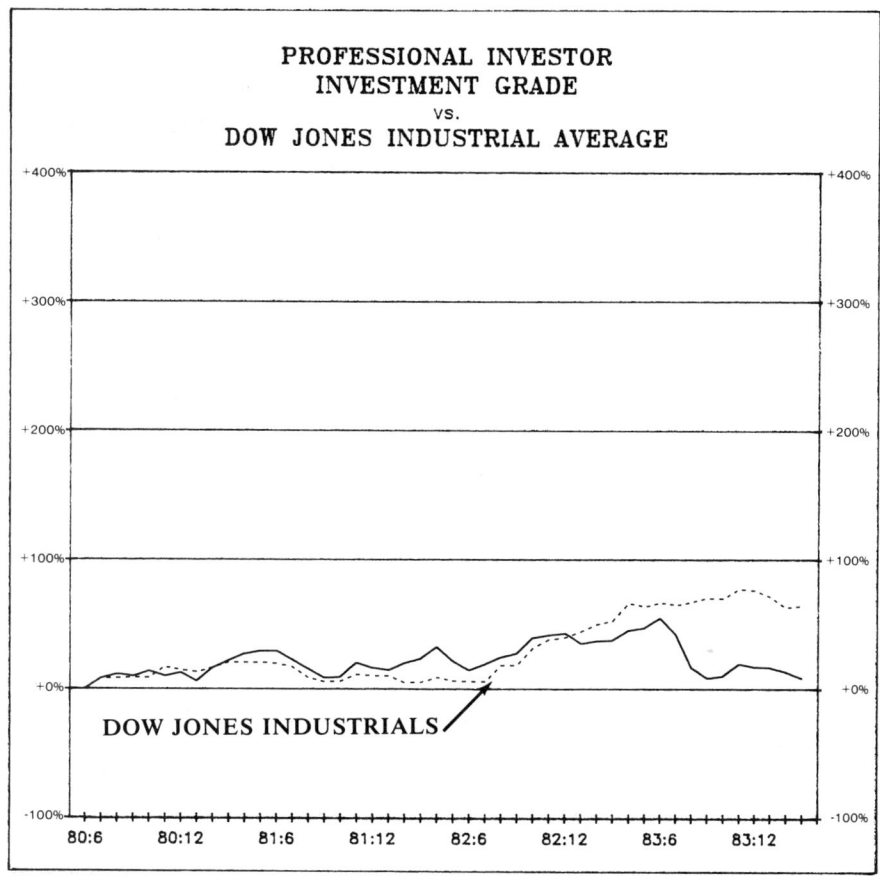

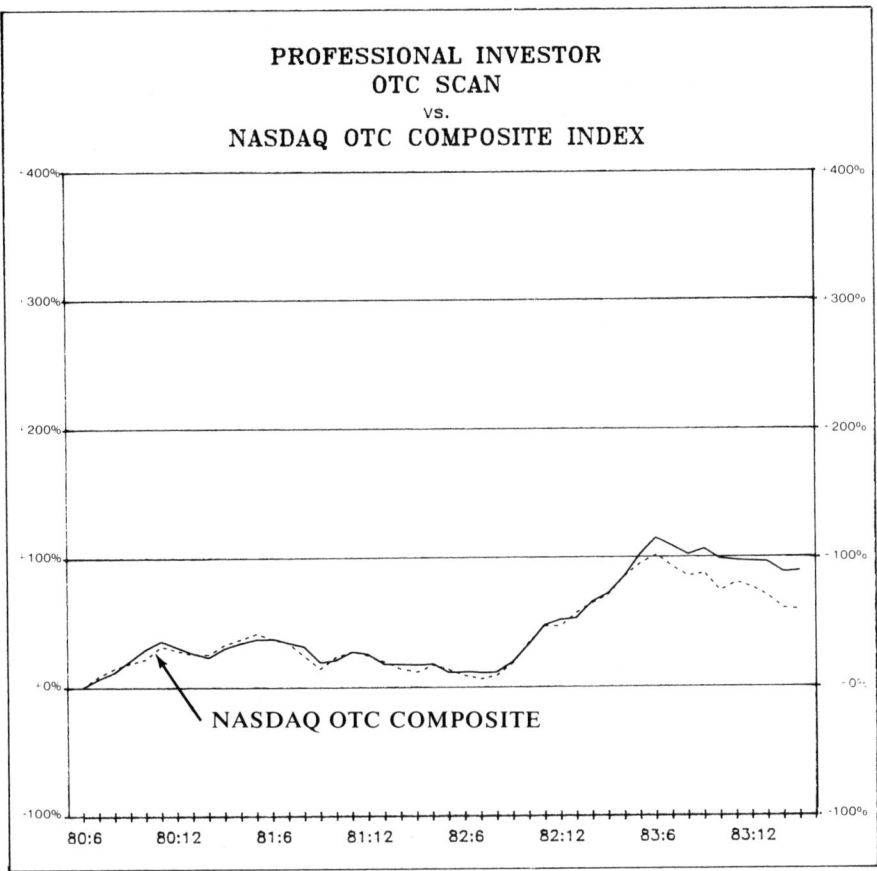

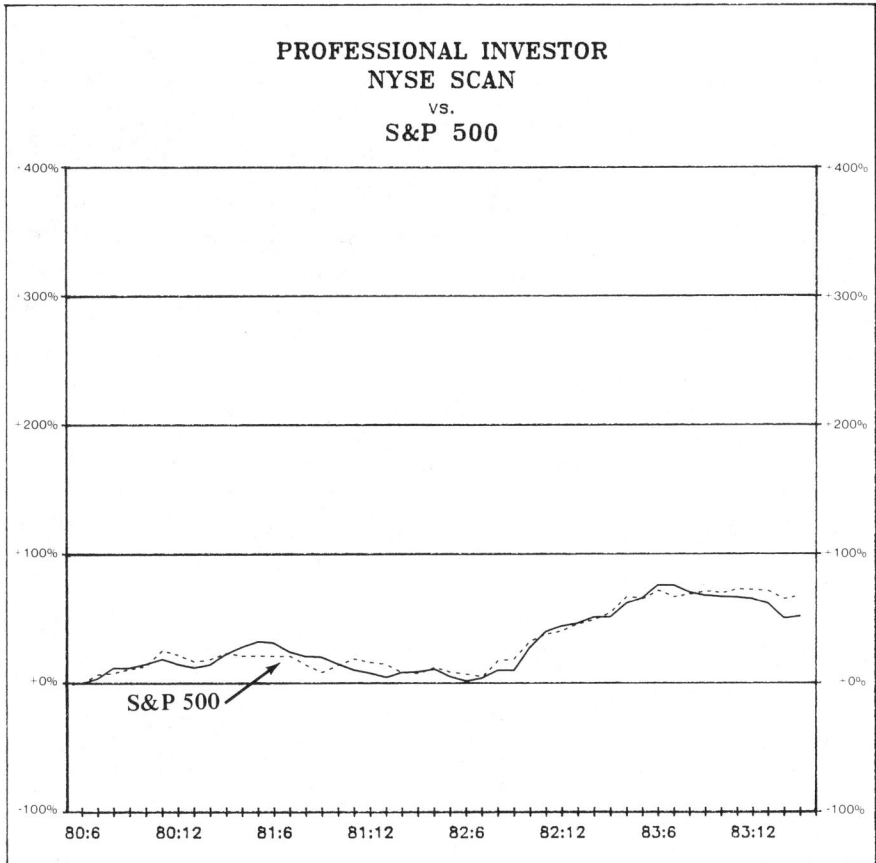

"The Tape Tells All"   Published & Edited by: *STAN WEINSTEIN*

THE PROFESSIONAL TAPE READER®

RADCAP, Inc.   P.O. Box 2407   Hollywood, Fla. 33022

Issue No. 282   REGISTERED WITH THE S.E.C. AS AN INVESTMENT ADVISOR   September 1, 1983

BETTER BUT...

There has been *some* near term improvement in the indicators, but *not enough* (by far) to give the 'all clear' for the intermediate term trend. Therefore, caution is still very much indicated. To see just why we feel as we do, let's examine the market's 3 trends, one by one.

First of all, the short term outlook improved when on Monday (August 29th) the market once again sold off sharply (on the disappointing money supply news) and quickly dropped near the key 1180 support level. Instead of breaking down, it made a short term reversal and closed on the upside. Then on Wednesday, the DJI jumped 20 points and completed a small 'W' formation. In addition, many of the weakest and most bombed out areas (such as Airlines, Hospital Management, Technology, etc.) finally staged sharp oversold rallies. And lastly, the Stock Index Futures have been acting better than the market averages in recent sessions.

So what's bothering us intermediate term? Plenty! As we said on last week's (Aug. 26th) Hotline: "The market is oversold near term, so there can be some sudden sharp upside bounces. However we don't expect them to run far as there is heavy resistance just overhead". Wednesday's sharp upmove fit that description to a 'T' and this morning, the market already neared its resistance zone that starts at 1220. But there's much more than resistance that calls for caution. One glance at this accompanying chart points out an important fact that we haven't seen mentioned anywhere else: *the quality of this rally is very poor!* There are times that the DJI runs ahead 50–60 points and the move can be played very profitably since many individual stocks chalk up far better gains. Those are healthy upmoves, and if they are broad, they are usually sustainable for many weeks. Then there are so-so rallies where some stocks zoom, while others advance quietly. These aren't as healthy, but if played selectively can be profitable. And then there are deceptive rallies, where the Dow masks weakness in the overall market. These moves are dangerous to play because they are so extremely selective, and also because they often give way suddenly to renewed weakness. Unfortunately, the latest advance has all of the characteristics of the latter type.

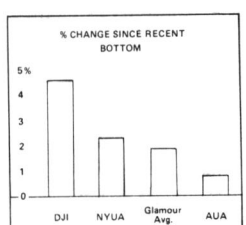

On a healthy rally, our Glamour Average, as well as NYUA and AUA (our NY and Amex unweighted Averages) should far outperform the Dow on the upmove since they are far more volatile. On a so-so rally, they usually move in line with the DJI. However on a sub-par rally that smacks of sub-surface weakness, they badly lag the Dow. This is exactly what appears to be shaping up on this latest oversold rally. While the DJ Industrials have rallied close to 5% from their recent low point, NYUA has only done half as well (about 2½%) which is terrible. And to make matters worse, the usually-frisky Glamour stocks that on healthy rallies move ahead about twice as much as the Dow, are up *less than* 2%. And finally, AUA is going nowhere fast, having moved ahead less than 1%. To say the least, this is *not* the profile of a technic-

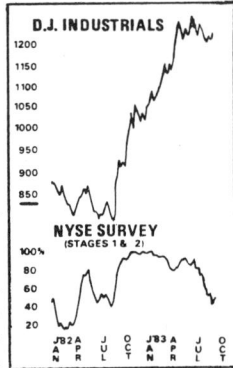

continued on page 8

COPYRIGHT © 1983 RADCAP, INC. Reproduction in whole or in part prohibited except by written permission. All rights reserved.

The Professional Tape Reader

Professional Tape Reader (PTR) has been published and edited by Stan Weinstein since 1975. It is printed every two weeks and is supplemented by a weekly hotline, which is made available to all nontrial subscribers at no extra charge. The subscription price is $250 per year and $150 for six months. A three-issue trial is available for $30. The address is P. O. Box 2407, Hollywood, Florida 33022.

Weinstein, a 1964 graduate of Hofstra University in economics, was an account executive with Walston & Co. for several months in 1969 and 1970. He quit that job to become the head of technical research for *Indicator Digest*, which job he held until assuming the role as editor of PTR in June 1975. He is perhaps best known for a number of technical indicators that he has developed, such as "stage analysis" (which classifies a stock or the market as a whole in one of four stages, according to whether it is in a consolidation phase, uptrend, topping phase, or decline) and "group intensity" (which is an intermediate timing indicator for the market based on Weinstein's analysis of the prospects for each of a number of industry groups).

Each eight-page issue of PTR includes the following features: a two-page analysis of the market's major, intermediate, and short-term trends; a one- to two-page discussion of which stocks currently are most and least attractive; a one- to two-page review of Weinstein's model portfolio (which includes the name of each stock, its current price and suggested stop loss, and a several-sentence comment by Weinstein); an "Option Scan," which lists the stocks upon which the most favorable and unfavorable calls and puts could be purchased; and a two-page review of several dozen technical indicators. Weinstein's weekly hotline briefly reviews his beliefs about the market's trends and makes any changes in his model portfolio. Weinstein is a trader, and he changes his portfolio exposure relatively frequently. The average length of time he held stocks in his portfolio, in both 1982 and 1983, was about 2-1/2 months.

Weinstein's advice for his model portfolio became more precise in early 1984. Before that, he would recommend the proper percentage allocation for a portfolio between long positions, short sales, and cash and also recommend particular securities to be purchased or sold. Which you bought or sold to bring your own portfolio into line with Weinstein's recommended overall allocation was in large part up to you. Since early 1984, however, Weinstein has assigned a particular weight to each of his recommended positions, and when he recommends that you increase or decrease market exposure, he also says which securities to purchase or sell. The HFD now rates it highest in clarity.

Performance

The HFD has calculated the performance since mid-1980 for both PTR's model portfolio and a timing portfolio based on Weinstein's Group Intensity. According to the HFD, Weinstein's model portfolio gained 22.9% over the last six months of 1980 (when the S & P 500 was increasing 21.7%); it fell 6.7% in 1981 (when the S & P 500 was declining 4.9%); surged 30.0% during 1982 (outperforming the S & P 500's 21.6%); and over the next 15 months, declined 18.6% (the S & P 500 was up 19.6% over the same period). The cumulative 45-month gain for PTR's model portfolio was 21.4%, as compared to 68.2% for the S & P 500 and 49.5% for a Treasury bill portfolio. Over this period, the portfolio incurred only slightly less risk than the S & P 500, so on a risk-adjusted basis, it also underperformed the market.

Part of this portfolio's performance was attributable to the fact that its stock selections underperformed the market. According to the analysis discussed in Section V, a portfolio constructed identically to PTR's model portfolio—substituting the NYSE Composite for the stock portion—would have gained 49.8% over this period, as compared to the 21.4% actually turned in by that portfolio. This 49.8%, furthermore, would have been in excess of the 40.3% by which the NYSE

Composite itself increased over this period.

Group Intensity

Also measured in this book's section on timing is a portfolio based on Group Intensity, Weinstein's proprietary indicator for calling intermediate turns in the market. Based on "investing" in the NYSE Composite when that indicator was bullish and staying in cash when that indicator was bearish (but for a few occasions when Weinstein recommended a 50%/50% split between the market and cash), Group Intensity would have allowed you to realize a 40.3% profit over this 45-month period, equal to the gain on the NYSE Composite over the same period. Weinstein recommends that subscribers use Group Intensity for their IRAs, switching to and from equity and money market funds according to the indicator's signals. While Group Intensity varies its market exposure less frequently than does PTR's model portfolio (and thus may be preferable to those who do not want to spend much time tracking their investments), this analysis suggests that you might do better trading your switch program according to the allocations Weinstein uses for his model portfolio.

PROFESSIONAL TAPE READER
Model Portfolio

Period	Gain	Quintile
7/1 to 12/31/80	22.9%	Second highest 20%
1981	−6.7%	Second lowest 20%
1982	30.0%	Second highest 20%
1983	−9.8%	Lowest 20%
Risk ranking	3.253	Second lowest 20%
% 1983 Closeouts long term	4.1%	Lowest 20%
% 1982 Closeouts long term	8.3%	Second lowest 20%

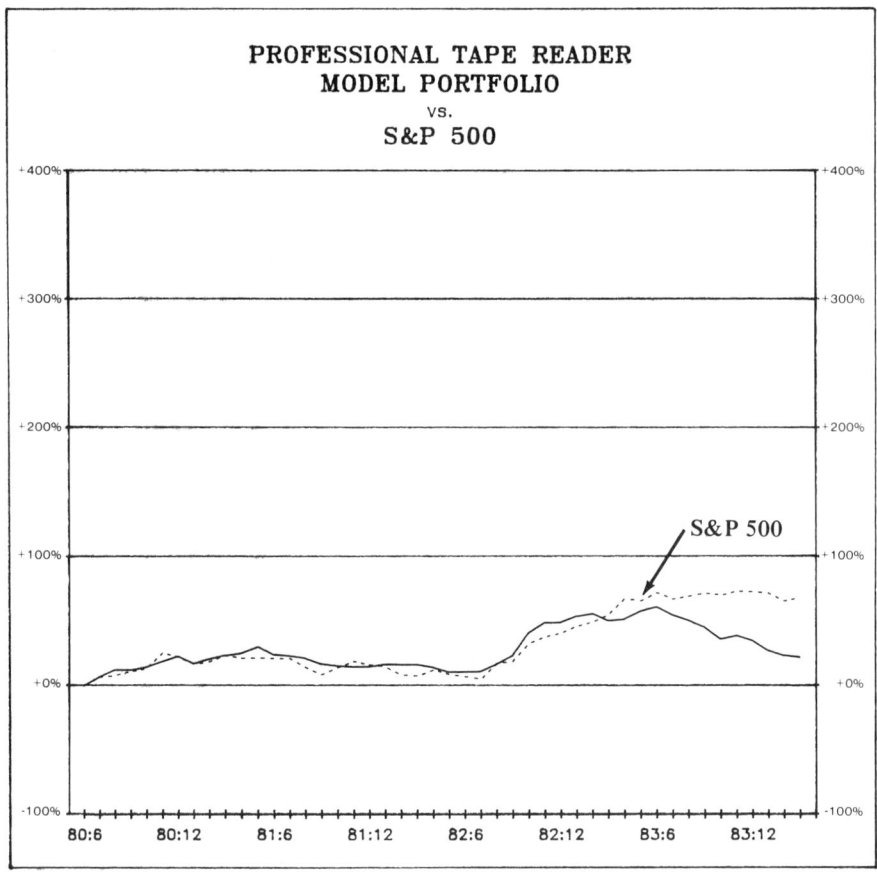

PROFESSIONAL TIMING SERVICE
P.O. BOX 7483, MISSOULA, MONTANA 59807
$150 A YEAR • MARKET REPORT TUESDAY & THURSDAY

#8307/7-1-83

THE LONG TERM--TOXIC WASTE DUMP SYNDROME TO PERSIST

Last month's advice was clear: "be out of all long positions by June 24." During the following two market sessions, the Dow plummeted over 30 points. Now sorry to say - there's more to come.

NOTHING IS FOREVER---Even strong bull markets do not extend on forever. If they did, we wouldn't need food stamp programs, or investment advisors. We would all just buy stocks, hold on, and borrow against them when we needed money.

ON THE SURFACE---one could point out all the sell signals being given by market excesses - the gargantuan number of secondaries, the diminishing number of new daily highs, the consistently huge amount of short selling by Exchange members, and the miniscule level of odd lot short selling just prior to this week's crash.

These are technical indicators which are <u>excellent</u> to measure trading extremes in the market; but they are not nearly as serious or long-lasting as the <u>negative</u> signals we see from the interest rate and monetary data.

TALL PAUL, HAPPY HENRY AND LITTLE LARRY---Volcker was reappointed; Kaufman turned bullish on bonds; and about 40 market sessions ago <u>I warned you</u> that "interest rates look higher." On May 5, we said:

> "I know - it flys in the face of all you've seen in the national media, but our interest rate model remains negative, warning that higher rates are more likely than lower - we suggest you prepare accordingly."

It is not amazing that from our Rocky Mountain high vantage point we have a better feel for interest rates than the Big Apple crowd. In fact, it's <u>not based on feel</u> at all, but <u>close study</u> of the markets.

I first went public in a late March interview with Dan Dorfmann stating interest rates were about to go up, causing bonds to fall. Even he expressed a not so small amount of disbelief. I went on to tell him that later on the stock market would also tumble.

LATER ON IS NOW---This, then, is the scenario at hand. Rates have gone up, so stock prices must go down. Higher rates will draw money <u>out of</u> the market, and the market will <u>stay</u> down until there is a fundamental change in the interest rate infrastructure. When will that happen? It is far too early to tell for sure.

DO NOT GET LED BACK INTO THIS MARKET---by those who say the "technical correction" has spent itself. What is about to unfold is not a technical correction, but a <u>mini-bear</u>. It will consist of at least four precise down legs. <u>The point is this</u>: You will want to buy, and many will cajole you to nibble at a few of the big fish that have swam back to shore.....<u>DON'T!</u>

LONG TERM ADVICE---*Long term investors, be fully invested in <u>cash</u>. Stay-with short term interest bearing accounts and - <u>above all</u> - stubbornly avoid getting back into the market.*

There is no guarantee that future performance will conform to that of the past, nor that it will be profitable.

Professional Timing Service

Professional Timing Service, a confidently and boldly written investment newsletter now in its eighteenth year of publication, is edited by Larry Williams and Curtis J. Hesler. Williams is the 42-year-old author of *The Secret of Selecting Stocks* (1969) and *How to Prosper in the Coming Good Years* (1982). He has twice run unsuccessfully as the Republican candidate for United States Senator from Montana. An annual subscription costs $150 and is available from P. O. Box 7483, Missoula, Montana, 59807. Beginning in February 1984, the newsletter has been supplemented with a two-page "Mid-month update." A twice-weekly telephone hotline is provided to subscribers at no additional charge.

Long-Term Bull

Professional Timing Service generally has a long-term bullish orientation to the market and appears to view this opinion as an obvious fact, having proclaimed in one issue that "[t]he missing ingredient in most economic theories is that they fail to realize the universal law of economics is: things get better." In his August 6, 1982, issue, Williams wrote that he anticipated "the best buying opportunity in 40 years," a near- perfect call. But, paradoxically, his proprietary timing indicator—termed the "Supply/Demand Formula"—did not divert from a "Sell Short" posture on the Dow Industrials until November

23, 1982, four months after the bull market began and the market, as measured by the DJIA, had gone up by some 200 points. (Indeed, on September 17 and October 28, 1982, his formula reissued and reconfirmed its sell short signal on the Dow Industrials.) Williams explains that he believed a correction during the first few months of the bull market would give investors a second buying opportunity and that his indicators were waiting for such a correction before flashing a "buy."

As the discussion in the previous paragraph suggests, Williams does not let his generally bullish long-term outlook prevent him from recommending that you be out of the market or aggressively sell it short. A typical conclusion to Williams' analysis of the market's trend will mention that the long-term is bullish but that the best buying point is not yet upon us. The December 1982 issue of *Professional Timing Service*, for example, was headlined "The Long Term–Bullish......But"—not too dissimilar to the headline of the May 1984 issue, which was "The Long Term–Little Darlin', The Ice is Slowly Melting" (which Williams interprets to mean "here comes the sun. It's not here yet, but it is coming.")

Performance

In addition to giving buy and sell signals on the market as a whole, the *Professional Timing Service* also reports on buy and sell signals for individual stocks. The HFD has tracked the performance since January 1982 of both Williams' market timing and his stock selections. The calculation of his market timing calls was based on trading the NYSE Composite index. In 1982, a portfolio that went long or short the NYSE Composite according to PTS's timing signals would have lost 24.5%[*] as compared to a 14.0% gain in the Index itself. This ranked *Professional Timing Service* at the bottom of the list of the newsletters monitored in 1982. In 1983, conversely, PTS was the top-ranked newsletter with a gain of 25.7% (as compared to a 17.5% increase in the NYSE Composite). The cumulative gain for the 27-month period from January 1982 through March 1984 was 2.6%, as compared to a 28.9% gain for the NYSE Composite.

---

[*] This 24.5% loss in 1982 is about twice as large as the 12.9% loss turned in by the Granville Market Letter, which remained bearish throughout the year. Because many people ask, "how could someone's timing have been worse in 1982 than a consistent bearish policy?" we want to respond. PTS's market timing advocated buying the market up through March 31, 1982, at which point it switched to a bearish stance—which it maintained until switching to a buy mode in November (as discussed above). Such a timing strategy was clearly worse than remaining bearish throughout, since PTS compounded the unprofitability of being short during the beginning of the bull market by being long during the first quarter's steep market decline.

The performance of PTS's stock selections over this period was almost the same (1.1% vs. 2.6%). In 1982, according to HFD calculations, PTS's stock selections lost 2.4% (the S & P 500 gained 21.6%), and in 1983 his stock selections gained 22.4% (as compared to the S & P 500's 22.5%). In contrast to the stock selections' 1.1% cumulative gain from January 1982 through March 1984, the S & P 500 gained 45.4% and a portfolio of Treasury bills gained 23.7%.

PROFESSIONAL TIMING SERVICE
Stock Selections

Period	Gain	Quintile
1982	−2.4%	Lowest 20%
1983	22.4%	Second highest 20%
Risk ranking	6.254	Second highest 20%
% 1983 Closeouts long term	20.0%	Lowest 20%
% 1982 Closeouts long term	38.1%	Second lowest 20%

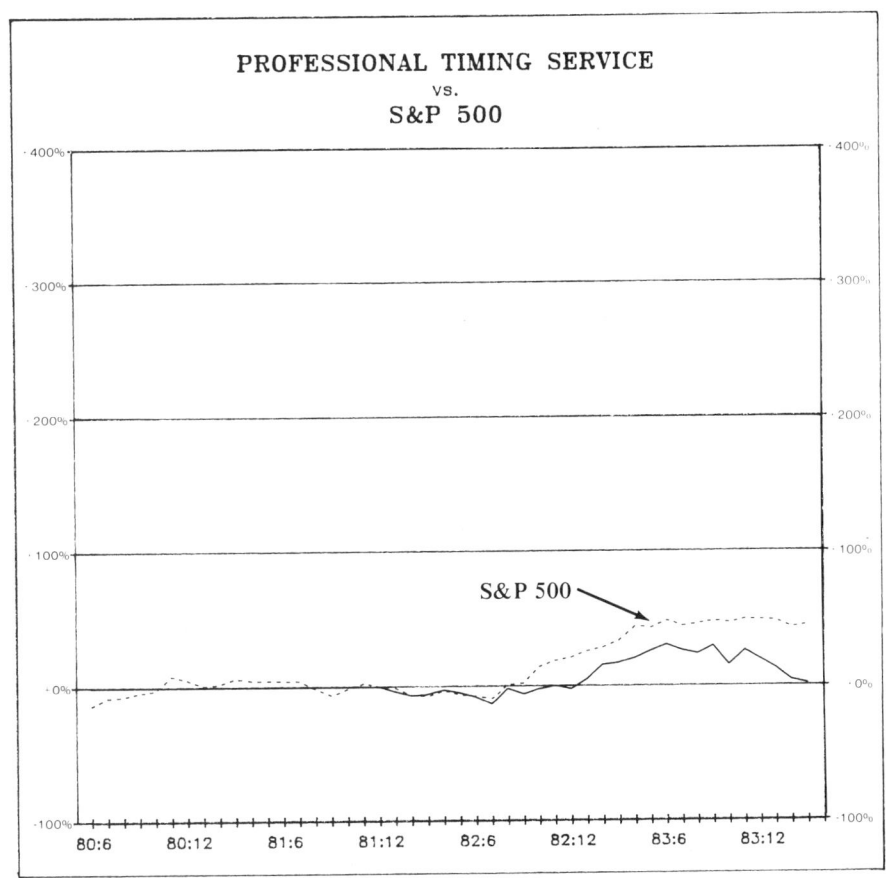

The Prudent Speculator

P.O. Box 1767, Santa Monica, California 90406

TPS 157, September 21, 1983

CURRENT APPROACHES

Up and up she goes, and where she stops, nobody knows. The Dow Jones Industrial Average (DJIA) has just made an all-time high, fascinating the layman and professional alike. We must consider this a positive event, although the higher the stock exchange indicators get without significant corrections, the more vulnerable "the market" becomes.

I have continued to buy more shares on margin, with the hope that most undervalued stocks will be significantly higher one year from now, even though we may well see a sickening correction (market-wide decline) or two along the way. BOLD SPECULATORS may still take additional margined positions, with the awareness that there is a good chance for shortterm, market-wide erosion in stock prices. MODERATE SPECULATORS may still augment their portfolios, even employing margin modestly. CONSERVATIVE INVESTORS may remain sensitive to risk, buying selected issues in order to balance widely diversified, longterm capital gains portfolios, yet retaining 20% or so in cash equivalent reserves.

REVIEW OF INDEXES	Dow Jones Industrials*	Composite Index*	TPS Portfolio Share Common*	TPS Portfolio Equity Analysis
For the past three weeks:				
Close 9/16/83	1225.71	96.17		
Close 8/26/83	1192.07	93.80		
Changes	+ 33.64	+ 2.37	+$ .40	+ $ 6,262
Percentages	+ 2.82%	+ 2.53%	+ 1.81%	+ 4.49%
For the past 38 weeks:				
Close 12/31/82	1046.54	81.03		
Changes	+179.17	+15.14	+$ 7.55	+ $58,205
Percentages	+ 17.12%	+18.68%	+ 36.48%	+ 135.94%
For the life of TPS:				
Close 3/11/77	947.72	54.72		
Changes	+277.99	+41.45	+$26.19	+ $96,190
Percentages	+ 29.33%	+75.75%	+160.02%	+1173.59%

*These "averages" do not include dividends paid during the various periods. TPS Portfolio is Al Frank's actual common stock and convertible bond portfolio. Equity Analysis accounts for margin expenses, dividends, and paid commissions.

RECENT STOCK MARKET ACTIVITY

The New York Stock Exchange (aka "the stock market") continues to surprise, amaze and please me. I mean, how long can this be goin' on? Well, why not for another 12 months or so, "on balance." Since the previous issue of TPS, we have had two lovely weeks, one terrible week, and two strong advancing days to the aforementioned record-high DJIA. With all this "buying"--isn't it buying

The Prudent Speculator is a stock market advisory service edited and published by Al Frank, an Investment Advisor registered with the Securities & Exchange Commission, and the State of California. Al Frank manages stock portfolios for individuals. Information in The Prudent Speculator is obtained from publications believed reliable, but accuracy, completeness and interpretations are not guaranteed. All comment and opinion are subject to change without notice. Al Frank or his clients may hold or trade issues recommended or mentioned. Recommendations may not be profitable or equal previous performance. Subscriptions: $100, 17-issues; $20, 3-issue trial; $10 overseas airmail; and are not assignable.

The Prudent Speculator

The Prudent Speculator (TPS) is published and edited every three weeks by Al Frank, who is a former graduate student in the philosophy of education at UCLA and a former college assistant professor and stockbroker, now 53 years old with a growing reputation. An annual subscription costs $125, and a three-issue trial subscription is available for $25. The address is P. O. Box 1767, Santa Monica, California 90406. Although published continuously since March 12, 1977, according to Al Frank, TPS experienced phenomenal growth in subscriptions in 1983—attributable in large part to TPS's impressive performance during most of 1983. (It ranked at the top of the HFD's ratings.) This performance led to articles in major financial publications such as *Barron's* and *Money*, a write-up by Dan Dorfman in his nationally syndicated column, and an appearance on Public Television's "Wall Street Week."

In each issue, Frank advises subscribers concerning the proper allocation of their investable assets between the market and cash. He frequently advocates purchasing stocks on margin, and his is one of the few investment newsletters monitored by the HFD whose advice contains specific recommendations on the percentage margin with which various purchases should be made. Although Frank attempts to time the market using technical indicators, at heart, he is an unabashed fundamentalist, "following in the footsteps of Graham, Dreman, and Templeton."

In many respects, Frank may be viewed as more "prudent" and less of a "speculator." His self-proclaimed goal is to purchase "undervalued stocks in a widely diversified portfolio held for long-term appreciation." TPS typically recommends stocks with low price-earnings ratios, high book values, high cash flows, and high earnings on net worths. Though most of TPS's recommended stocks are listed on the New York Stock Exchange, they typically have relatively small market capitalizations. Frank stresses that "diversity is probably the most important principle of prudent speculating."

Long-Term Approach

Because TPS seeks to ferret out "undervalued" stocks and to hold them until they become "fully valued," the newsletter often takes a multi-year time frame in examining and reviewing its recommendations. This approach leads to a relatively long average holding period. Virtually all of TPS's recommendations that appreciate in value are held long enough to qualify for long-term capital gain treatment. In 1983, TPS recommended the sale of only one stock, and it had been held for more than four years.

Each issue of TPS is written in a refreshingly low-key, forthright, humble, easy-to-read, understandable style. Frank imparts some of his investment philosophy to his subscribers while reviewing the performance of the market and his actual portfolio in the preceding three weeks. He mentions any changes that he has made in his personal portfolio and lists which of the stocks that he currently holds he recommends for purchase by subscribers.

The portfolio reported in each issue is Frank's actual stock portfolio, for which he claims a 720% gain in the last seven years, including the leverage obtained and the expense incurred by the frequent and aggressive use of margin, dividends received, and commissions paid. Of the 238 stocks recommended in TPS since 1977, only 39 declined in value since the date of first recommendation. A remarkable 84% of the stocks recommended appreciated. The HFD calculated its 1983 gain to be 72.8%, which placed it at the top of the list of the newsletters monitored by the HFD that year.* During the first three

---

* The gains reported by the HFD for *The Prudent Speculator* differ from those reported by Frank for his portfolio primarily because of the different margin rates used. As an on-going portfolio, Frank need only keep the value of the equity portion of his portfolio above 30% of total value, though a new subscriber would be unable to purchase new recommendations on anything less than 50% margin. With the lower margin figure, Frank's 1983 gain, for example, was 122.7% instead of 72.8%. For the purposes of tracking the letter, the HFD assumes that the portfolio starts each year at 50% margin.

months of 1984, Frank's portfolio gave up 9.6%, for an aggregate 15-month gain of 56.7%.

Investment Philosophy

Because the model portfolio reported in TPS is Frank's personal portfolio, transactions in it are sometimes made to raise money for personal expenses such as to purchase a house or make a venture capital investment. Frank indicates if the stocks sold for these personal reasons are still recommended. While this may be disconcerting to a subscriber who is mimicking Frank's portfolio, Frank's reasons for using his personal portfolio as a model are part and parcel of his investment philosophy. "There are no obvious or precise answers to the art of stock portfolio management," Frank has written. "One may be guided by statistical analyses, but at the moment of decision, intuition and idiosyncratic choice are the determining factors. All the stock advisory letters in the world cannot reflect each individual's unique personality with its tolerance for risk, optimism, patience, and intellectual and economic understanding. The art of stock speculating, like most arts, is almost ineffable; it cannot be described or taught, although it can be learned and practiced. This is the reason that I am so personal in TPS, because the best I can do, I believe, is report on what I am thinking and doing."

THE PRUDENT SPECULATOR

Period	Gain	Quintile
1983	72.8%	Highest 20%
Risk ranking	8.552	Second highest 20%
% 1983 Closeouts long term	100%	Highest 20%

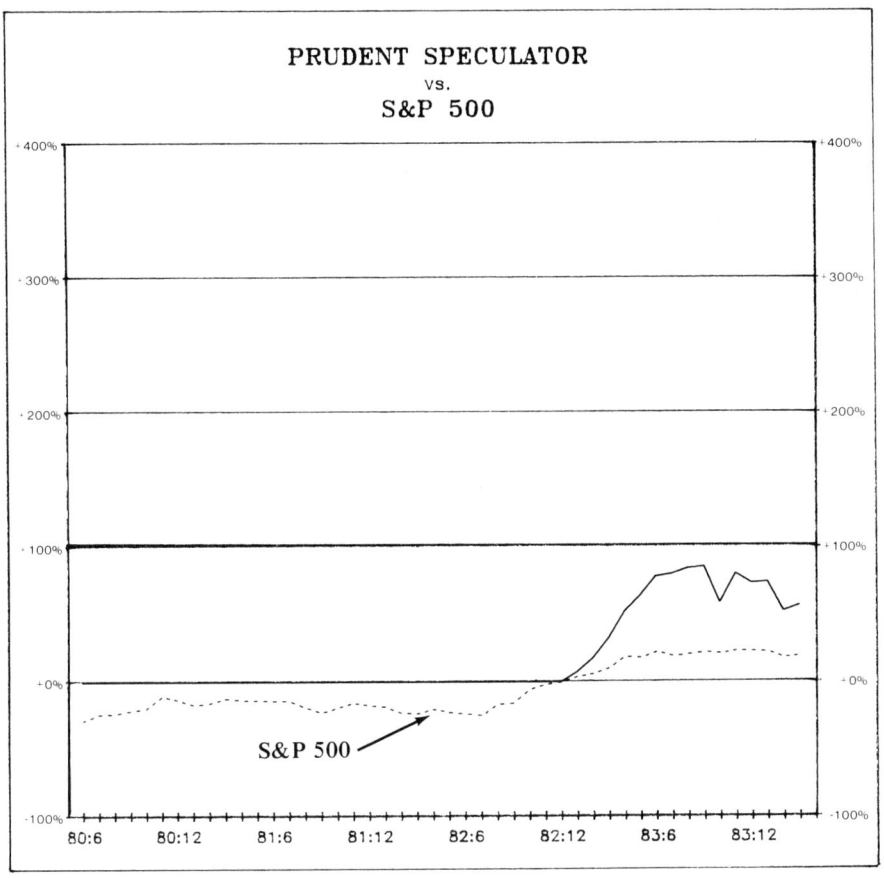

THE R·H·M SURVEY of WARRANTS · OPTIONS & LOW-PRICE STOCKS

VOL. XXXII, No. 27 — **Warrants on Listed Stocks** — July 15, 1983

NAME	EXERCISE TERMS	TDD.	OUTSTG 000	RECOM.	PRICES COM.	WT.
AMR Corp***	14.00 to 8-12-1983	S-S	5,000		35.75	21.62
Co has accelerated exp date to 8-12-83.						
APL Corp '88	14.00 to 12-31-1988	S-O	320		10.37	2.50
Acton Corp '86	1.05 shs at 18.05/sh to 6-2-1986	A-A	387		10.87	5.25
Alleghany Corp	3.75 Perpetual	S-A	75		63.75	59.00
Altex Oil Corp "A" '83	7.15 to 6-7-1984	A-A	1,100		2.50	.50
Altex Oil Corp "B" '84	7.50 to 12-7-1984	A-O	1,100		2.50	.37
American Express Company	1.333 shs for a total of 55.00 to 2-28-1987	S-A	1,000		67.50	38.50
Co may accelerate exp date if the daily closing price of com is at least $71.25 for 10 consec. tdg. days. Redeemable after 3-1-84 at 40.00 per Wt.						
Atlas Corp	31.25 Perpetual	S-A	1,000		25.75	7.00
Audiotronics Corp '85	12.42 to 1-21-1985	A-O	350		8.00	1.12
Bally Manufacturing '88	40.00 to 1-4-1988	S-A	860	Buy	25.12	10.75
Co has right to accelerate exp date of Wt. on 30 days written notice if daily closing price of com is at least $72.50 for 10 consec. tdg. days. After 6-2-85 the Co has right to redeem the warrants at $32.50.						
Beltran Corp	13.92 to 6-1-1986	A-A	208		4.62	1.62
Caesars World '85	24.50 to 8-1-1985 SS	S-O	875	Hold	15.75	5.62
Charter Company	10.00 to 9-1-1988 SS	S-S	3,750		11.75	5.75
Exp date may be accelerated to as early as 9-1-83 if com closes 120% above exer price for 60 consec. tdg. days; Wt may be exch for $1.25 during 10 tdg. days prior to 9-1-83 and 9-1-88, unless already expired.						
Chrysler Corp '85	13.00 to 6-15-1985	S-S	5,000		29.50	19.12
Exp date may be accelerated to 7-1-83 if com is 150% of exer price for 60 consec. tdg. days.						
Commonwealth Oil Refining '90	5.50 to 7-24-1990	P-P			.43	.22
Conquest Exploration Co '87	5.26 to 1-15-1987	A-A	3,500		10.87	7.50
Co may accelerate exp date of Wt as soon as 1-15-85 if com stk closes at or above $25 per sh for 60 consec. tdg. days.						
Consol Oil & Gas '84	30.00 to 6-30-1986 OL	A-A		Buy	8.75	1.62
11-1/2's '93 usable at face value + $800 cash in each 60 Wt exercise.						
Custom Energy Svc '85	.5 sh at 14.28/sh to 11-17-83; increases 50 cents each 6 mos thereafter to 11-17-1985	A-O	500		13.87	2.18
Damson Oil Corp	14.715 to 3-31-1985	A-A	275		11.75	6.62
Co may at its option extend exp date of Wt for 1 year.						
Digicon Inc '88	16.50 to 6-15-1988 SS (after 9-26-83)	A-O	945		16.50	6.25
Diversified Industries	9.25 to 5-14-1986	S-P	603		4.62	1.37
Dome Petroleum '84	18.91 to 12-31-1984	A-O			4.68	.11
Eastern Airlines June '87	10.00 to 6-1-1987	S-O	2,200		11.12	5.37
Eastern Airlines Oct '87	10.00 to 10-15-1987 SS	S-S	4,500		11.12	6.37
Co may accelerate exp to 10-15-85 if com trades above $15 for 45 consec. tdg. days.						
Elect Mem & Magnetics '88	12.00 to 6-1-1988 SS (after 9-1-83)	S-O	1,453		9.62	4.00
Callable at 3.00 per Wt on or after 6-1-86 if closing price of com stk has been in excess of 18.00 per sh for stated period of time.						
Evaluation Research '85	4.00 to 12-12-1985	A-O	300		13.37	11.62
Financial Corp '83***	3.295 shs at 6.07/sh to 11-1-1983 SS	S-P	76		40.50	186.00
Frontier Airlines	9.42 to 3-1-1987 SS (Frontier Holding)	A-A	576		20.62	13.87
Fuqua Industries "1988"	2.280 shs at 13.50/sh to 6-30-1988 SS (est.)	S-O	672		34.00	46.25
GEICO Corp***	2.08 shs at 24.00/sh to 8-1-1983	S-O	507		56.50	68.25
GTI Corp '86	4.50 to 11-15-1986	A-O	400		8.12	4.93
Redeemable after 11-15-83 at $1.00 per Wt if the closing price of com equals or exceeds $7.50 for 20 consec. tdg. days.						

(Continued on Page 679)

Explanatory Notes—See First Page, "Green Section"

PUBLISHED WEEKLY BY R.H.M. ASSOCIATES, INC. —677— 172 FOREST AVE., GLEN COVE, NEW YORK 11542

Copyright 1983 R.H.M. Associates

$120 PER ANNUM, $66 HALF-YEAR
+ Postage   + Postage

The R.H.M. Survey of Warrants, Options & Low-Price Stocks

The R.H.M. Survey of Warrants, Options & Low-Price Stocks is published weekly by R.H.M. Associates, Inc. and is edited by Sidney Fried, the author of several books on convertible securities. An annual subscription costs $120, and a six-month subscription is available for $68. The newsletter is not supplemented with a telephone hotline service. The address is 172 Forest Avenue, Glen Cove, New York 11542. *RHM Survey* now is in its thirty-third year of publication—one of the longest records of continuous publishing in the investment newsletter industry.

Each 12-page issue of *RHM Survey* presents a comprehensive list of all outstanding warrants on stocks that are listed on a national securities exchange, traded over the counter or in Canada. The prices of each warrant and its underlying stock are set forth in each issue, along with the warrant's full conversion terms, expiration date, and call features, if any. There is only one exception to this comprehensive coverage in each issue. Because of the unprecedented outpouring of new warrants since 1982 and the newsletter's space limitations, Fried has recently begun to give only the full terms of each warrant on an OTC stock in every other issue.

Each Issue

In each issue, Fried recommends that his subscribers buy or hold certain warrants, low-price stocks, or options. Most of the stocks in recent years have been of silver or gold mining or other natural resource companies. Editor Fried has stated that *RHM Survey's* interest in a particular warrant as a prospective investment increases when the issuing company runs into problems and its warrants fall to a low price. Fried employs technical analysis to forecast general market direction but opines that "it is much more rewarding to apply the insights of Technical Analysis to the stock market as a whole, rather than to individual stocks." Fried also writes two articles for each issue of *RHM Survey*, containing market commentary, general advice with respect to the use of various types of convertible securities, and particular options recommendations. In recent months, Fried has increasingly recommended stock index options positions.

Although *RHM Survey* is a very useful compilation of information relating to warrants and is generally well written, it sometimes suffers from a lack of clarity, especially with respect to market timing. Fried never specifies how a subscriber should allocate his or her investable assets, even though his market outlook shifts considerably over time. During 1981 and early 1982, for example, Fried periodically advised subscribers to reduce market exposure "to the point of comfort," which he defined to mean that exposure where "a pronounced market decline" would not affect "financial stability." Subscribers were also told to invest those proceeds in the ratio of 90% in Treasury bills and 10% in call options. Needless to say, the return you would have achieved by following *RHM Survey* would have depended to a large degree on how you defined what the "comfort level" was. A subscriber needs to determine what level of risk he is willing to undertake and deploy part of his funds in less risky alternative investments.

Performance

The HFD has calculated the performance of the stocks, warrants, and options recommended in *RHM Survey* since the beginning of 1981. The newsletter's picks suffered a calamitous 1981, losing 50.1% largely because Fried recommended many precious metals securities during a period when bullion prices fell. *RHM Survey* gained 23.2% in 1982 and added 10.6% more from January 1, 1983, through March 31, 1984. The portfolio's composite loss for this 3-1/4-year period was 32.0%. The S & P 500 advanced 38.3% over the same period, and a Treasury bill portfolio would have gained 41.3%. Not surprisingly, in light of the types of securities in which this service specializes, *RHM Survey's* selections were more than twice as volatile as the S & P 500, making it among the 10% most risky of the 35 portfolios tracked by the HFD over this 39-month period.

RHM SURVEY OF WARRANTS, OPTIONS & LOW-PRICE STOCKS

Period	Gain	Quintile
1981	−50.1%	Lowest 20%
1982	23.2%	Third highest 20%
1983	8.6%	Third highest 20%
Risk ranking	9.700	Highest 20%
% 1983 Closeouts long term	93.8%	Second highest 20%
% 1982 Closeouts long term	40%	Third highest 20%

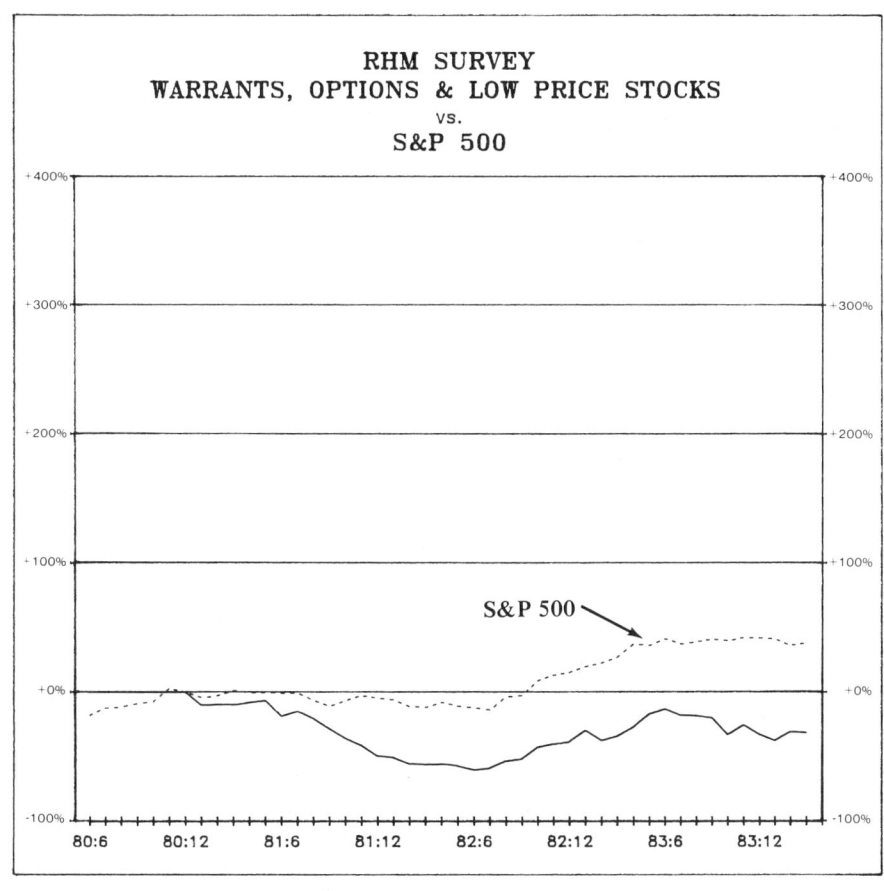

Robert Kinsman's
LOW RISK ADVISORY LETTER
"Making Your Money Make Money In Tough Times"

APRIL 22, 1983, VOL. FIVE, NO. 6

THE "IDES" OF SPRING

In the Roman calendar, the word ides referred to specific dates of the month: the 15th of March, May, July, and October and the 13th of other months. It was immortalized, of course, by a soothsayer's famous admonition to Caesar, "beware the ides of March."

The Romans may not have felt the pattern of ides was important, but recent bull markets seem to have taken something from it. The April-July period has been a bull tamer in each of the strongest upswings of the past decade. More about this in a moment. First, let's look briefly at what's just happened in our key markets since last Letter and then see where we go from here.

My Apr. 1 Letter description of the stock market as "two-faced" couldn't have been more apt. The next week the DJI dropped to within a hair of my 1109 mental stop point, closing on Apr. 6 at 1113, before rallying to four consecutive new highs and ending Apr. 20 at 1192. The broader S&P 500 and the AMEX and OTC composite indexes also made a string of new highs. Thus, my conclusion last time that **"we're on the right course to allow the market to move higher if it wishes but to tighten our mental stops just below it"** obviously worked out. Letting internally deteriorating "two-faced" markets have their head is an important low risk concept. (See R.K. Comments, p. 4.)

Also in my last Letter, I pointed out that 9 of 22 prominent advisory letter writers tracked by *Market Logic* were bearish on stocks (41%), but 12% of the universe of advisors surveyed by *Investors Intelligence* fit the same mode. That was certainly "two-faced" too.

That split seemed to be reflected behind the averages where carnage was developing. Not only was the DJ Utility Average more than a month away from its most recent high (set the week of Mar. 4), but several high-flying stocks had the props cut out from under them. To wit: Prime Computer fell 10 from its late March high, to 32-1/4; Paradyne plunged 12, to 25-1/4; and NBI crashed 15, to 26-1/2, before recovering half the loss. Those were huge percentage declines. True, specific news affected those stocks, but this still shows the sort of risk that now exists in some segments of the market.

Metals

In the gold market, prices held in the $400 to $410 range, which I'd noted as an important test level, and moved above the $435 March rebound highs. Meanwhile, silver completed its winter dive and rebound with an impressive move through the earlier $11.42 recovery level to above $12.50/oz. This does

INSIDE

Portfolio Changes . . . ACTION NOW. Read immediately . . . p. 7.

A Sellout and New Plans . . . Miss our Apr. 30 seminar? Two substitution ideas . . . p. 4.

A Hand for Mental Stops . . . How this low risk technique works . . . p. 4.

New Property Perspectives . . . The annual Stanford Symposium brings out contrasting opinions, investment protection methods . . . p. 5.

Dollar Dilemmas . . . The query answered: Why not add a zero to our gold's value? . . . p. 7.

not repair all the technical damage done in late February, but it could be the start of something significant.

Short term interest rates made an interim peak the week of Apr. 1, with the three month T-bill hitting 8.67% discount before dropping to 8.10% on Apr. 15, which still leaves my MCI above its 26 week moving average (MA), but barely. More interesting is how this pair looks when plotted as a deviation from trend in Chart 1.* Note that the rise through the 1.0 mark stopped just short of the descending trendline that dates back to May 1981.

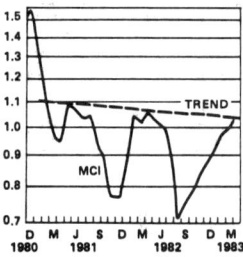

CHART 1. MCI DEVIATION FROM TREND

*Trend deviation is a very useful statistical technique that divides the current index number by its MA, thus showing clear changes in trend above or below the 1.0 unchanged levels. A trend change of two or more weeks is usually significant. (The chart shows a monthly plot except for two weeks in April.)

Robert Kinsman's
Low Risk Advisory Letter

Robert Kinsman's Low-Risk Advisory Letter is a tri-weekly investment newsletter edited by Robert Kinsman, the author of three books on finance and an adjunct professor of financial planning at San Francisco State University. An annual, 17-issue subscription is available for $125 from Kinsman Associates, Inc., 70 Mitchell Boulevard, San Rafael, California 94903. In March 1984, the newsletter added a weekly telephone hotline service. In addition, at no extra charge, Kinsman sends special one-paragraph bulletins to subscribers who sell covered call options on stocks recommended in the newsletter. The newsletter was founded in mid-1979.

Kinsman outlines somewhat varying asset allocations for different groups of investors. He maintains a Model Portfolio for persons with $20,000 to $100,000 to invest, but he also gives switch-fund advice for smaller investors and suggests portfolios with tax-sheltered aspects for persons investing more than $100,000.

Well-Named

Robert Kinsman's Low-Risk Advisory Letter lives up to its name. Its Model Portfolio had the second-lowest volatility of the 69 portfolios tracked by HFD for the last 15 months, through March 1984, incurring only 45% of the risk of the S & P 500. This low volatility is largely due to the fact that, since the start of 1983, Kinsman has had a minimum of 38% of assets invested in money market funds, T-Bills, or other cash equivalents. His average cash level has been 63.5%, a relatively high level.

What kind of performance has Kinsman achieved in light of this low-risk approach to investing? Quite good, according to both the HFD's performance ratings and Kinsman's own figures. In 1982, according to the HFD, Kinsman's Model Portfolio gained 18.3% in value (Kinsman's own figures show a 20.3% gain*); the S & P 500 was up 21.6% and a portfolio of Treasury bills was up 10.9%. From the beginning of 1983 through the first quarter of 1984, the Model Portfolio achieved another 9.1% advance (Kinsman claims 11.3%*) while the S & P 500 rose 19.6% and a Treasury bill portfolio would have gained 11.6%. Kinsman's aggregate gain for this 27-month period was 29.0%, as compared to a 45.4% gain for the S&P 500 and a 23.7% gain for Treasury bills.

Risk-Adjusted Performance

On a risk-adjusted basis, the performance of Kinsman's model portfolio is about equal to that of the market. Though the model portfolio gained 29.0% compared to 45.4% for the S&P 500, it did so with significantly less risk. In fact, though Kinsman's model portfolio is one of the lowest risk of those the HFD monitors, over the 27-month period beginning January 1, 1982, it outperformed 50% of the newsletters with higher risk.

KINSMAN'S LOW-RISK ADVISORY LETTER
(Model Portfolio)

Period	Gain	Quintile
1982	18.3%	Third highest 20%
1983	9.0%	Third highest 20%
Risk ranking	1.286	Lowest 20%
% 1983 Closeouts long term	33.3%	Second lowest 20%
% 1982 Closeouts long term	50.0%	Third highest 20%

---

* The discrepancies between the HFD's figures and Kinsman's own figures are due to (1): differences in the prices used to calculate the results; (the HFD uses prices on the date the newsletter is received), and (2) differences in the portfolio weight given to each element. Kinsman's own figures are based upon an actual portfolio, but the advice he gives is couched in percentage terms. As the value of each member of the portfolio changes over time, the actual weight each enjoys in the portfolio will deviate from the percentage assigned to it. The HFD's figures are based on a portfolio which is frequently rebalanced to keep each element in line with its assigned percentage. (See the methodological prologue for an in-depth discussion of these issues.)

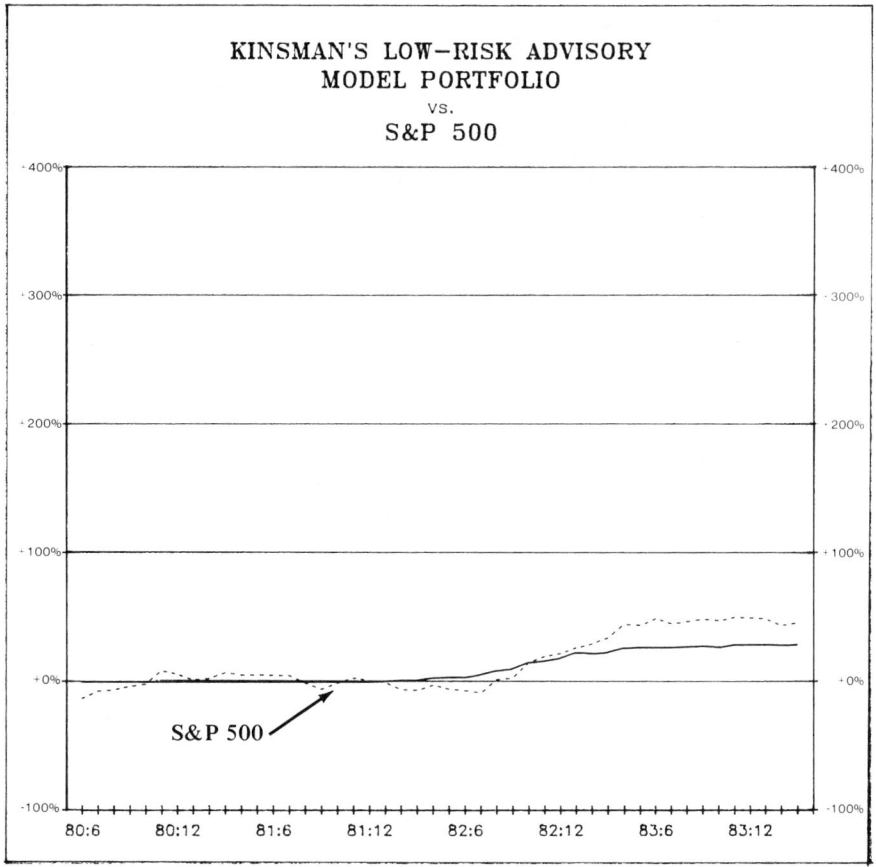

THE Speculator

EXPERTISE IN LISTED STOCKS UNDER $20 SINCE 1968

INSIDE • • •

As of close 5/26/83

Capital goods should add capital to investors in STEEGO. Drilling for profits? Try TRICO.
Pg. 2

GEMCO has constructed a base for future growth. TOROTEL is on line for a big profit rebound. A palatable acquisition is boosting profits at UNITED FOODS   Pg. 3

Strong defense telecommunications market lends super growth status to DECOM SYSTEMS, our OTC choice.   Pg. 4

Insiders, recognizing value, have been buying one of our "Selected Stocks of the Week," WATSCO. A bull spread on SEARLE offers speculators leverage of about 7:1.   Pg. 5

Auto production pick-up means an uphill ride for our "SOW"   Pg. 9

GENTLE REMINDER

We almost feel compelled to remind subscribers that stocks, unlike deposits in savings banks, have the capacity to move both up and down and that if you take the trouble to look at stock market prices, at the end of May, 1982, you'll see that they not only have a capacity to go down in price, but that they, in fact, did so. We also need to remind you that once a stock does make its move up in price, it doesn't go up forever. It goes through periods of consolidation, profit-taking and, depending upon technical and fundamental considerations, could very well return to its lower levels. Many stocks do, in fact, fluctuate within a designated range over a period of years. We need to mention all of the above because right now it looks as if there isn't going to be any end to this upward trend and that all one has to do is buy most any stock to make a profit. We need to remind you that these are the times we've been waiting for, but that the rules that we have been following over the years have not changed at all.

With the market continuing strong and the economy showing solid signs of potential growth, we have extended a number of our targets, but we've also called for profit-taking in AMERICAN FAMILY, OHIO-SEALY, THRIFTY CORP., BELL INDUSTRIES, ARMATRON and FLAGG INDUSTRIES during recent times. Just as we indicated in our last issue,*GEMCO,*VARO and*EDO did, in fact, have solid breakouts with VARO a major winner with over 9 points to 19-1/2. All three of the above still remain attractive. Furthermore, we would again add to positions in LA POINTE, WELDOTRON CORP., which just introduced a new high-speed automatic shrink packaging system for citrus fruit, and now that we are seeing signs of life in the oils, add to positions in *INEXCO,*DAMSON,*TRITON and*RANGER.

In the works is an extra special bonus to all subscribers highlighting the domestic oil and gas stocks that we've been bringing to your attention during the last five years.

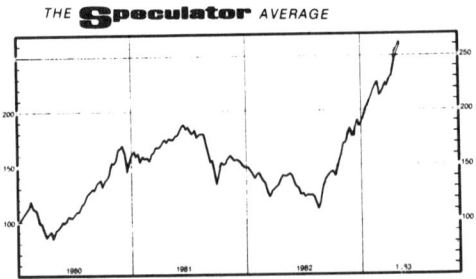

THE Speculator AVERAGE

Our Speculator Average (SA) continues to score big nominal and relative gains. During the past two weeks, SA tacked on about 3% against much smaller gains in the major popular averages. Unfortunately, the gains have been coming on heavy AMEX volume, a sign the market remains a little frothy.

Money Growth Institute, Inc., 108 Columbus Drive, Jersey City, N.J. 07302 (201) 432-8900

The Speculator

The Speculator is published bi-weekly by Money Growth Institute, Inc., 37 Van Reipen Avenue, Jersey City, New Jersey 07306. Money Growth Institute privately manages a number of portfolio accounts. The telephone number is (201) 792-0802. An annual subscription costs $175; a six-month subscription is available for $95; and a three month trial subscription is offered for $49.50. The newsletter added a free telephone hotline service in 1982.

The Speculator has specialized in ferreting out attractive opportunities in listed stocks trading at a price of less than $20 per share since 1968. Most of the stocks recommended in this service are traded on the American Stock Exchange (Amex). Each eight-page issue presents a market commentary and a short general summary of the technical status of the market. Approximately three stocks traded on the NYSE or Amex are reviewed in detail in each issue. Many of these write-ups are updates of previously recommended low-priced stocks. In addition, one stock that is traded over the counter is highlighted in each issue. One column of this newsletter reports insider trading activity, another provides corporate earnings and sales results for currently recommended issues, and another feature suggests low-priced option strategies. An additional page of *The Speculator* reviews in detail and recommends a "Selected Stock of the Week."

Selected Stocks of the Week

According to *The Speculator's* figures, since May 5, 1977, 76 of the newsletter's 152 "Selected Stock of the Week" recommendations have been closed out at an average profit of almost 100%, and 39 of the other 76 recommended stocks that have not been closed out have increased in price (as of June 21, 1984). Beginning in early 1983, *The Speculator* began to narrow its subscribers' focus from the entire list of open positions to a handful of asterisked selections "favored for current buying." These asterisks disappeared in February and early March 1984 (presumably because none was currently favored for buying), but they reappeared in late March 1984.

The HFD has calculated *The Speculator's* performance since the beginning of 1981 for all issues previously recommended as "Selected Stocks of the Week" and not yet closed out of the newsletter's portfolio. When a subset of stocks was specified as "favored for current buying," the HFD tracked these stocks only, consistent with its methodology. which aims to value an investment adviser's most highly recommended selections. According to the HFD's performance ratings, *The Speculator's* stock picks dropped 10.8% in 1981, surged 45.3% in 1982, added 8.8% in 1983, but gave up 10.4% in the first quarter of 1984. The newsletter's aggregate performance for this 3-1/4-year period shows a gain of 26.3%. In comparison, the Amex Market Value Index declined 8.1% in 1981, moved ahead just 6.2% in 1982, but soared 31.0% in 1983, before dropping back 5.2% in the first three months of 1984. The Amex Index's aggregate gain for this period was 21.1%, while the S & P advanced 38.3% and a Treasury bill portfolio advanced 41.3% over the same 39-month period.

Over this period, *The Speculator's* portfolio had a mixed record on a risk-adjusted basis. Even though it was riskier than the Amex Market Value Index, for example, it earned sufficiently more than the AMEX Index to outperform it on a risk-adjusted basis. But it underperformed the S & P 500 despite having 84% more risk, and thus underperformed on a risk-adjusted basis this broader market average.

Trading Portfolio

Beginning in mid-1983, *The Speculator* established a portfolio for traders, as contrasted with long-term speculators. The HFD calculcates that this portfolio fell 3.2% in the first three months of 1984, slightly better than the 5.2% drop in the Amex Market Value Index and slightly worse than the 2.4% drop in the S & P 500.

THE SPECULATOR
Selected Stocks of the Week

Period	Gain	Quintile
1981	−10.8%	Lowest 20%
1982	45.3%	Highest 20%
1983	8.8%	Third Highest 20%
Risk ranking	8.255	Second highest 20%
% 1983 Closeouts long term	93.3%	Second highest 20%
% 1982 Closeouts long term	100%	Highest 20%

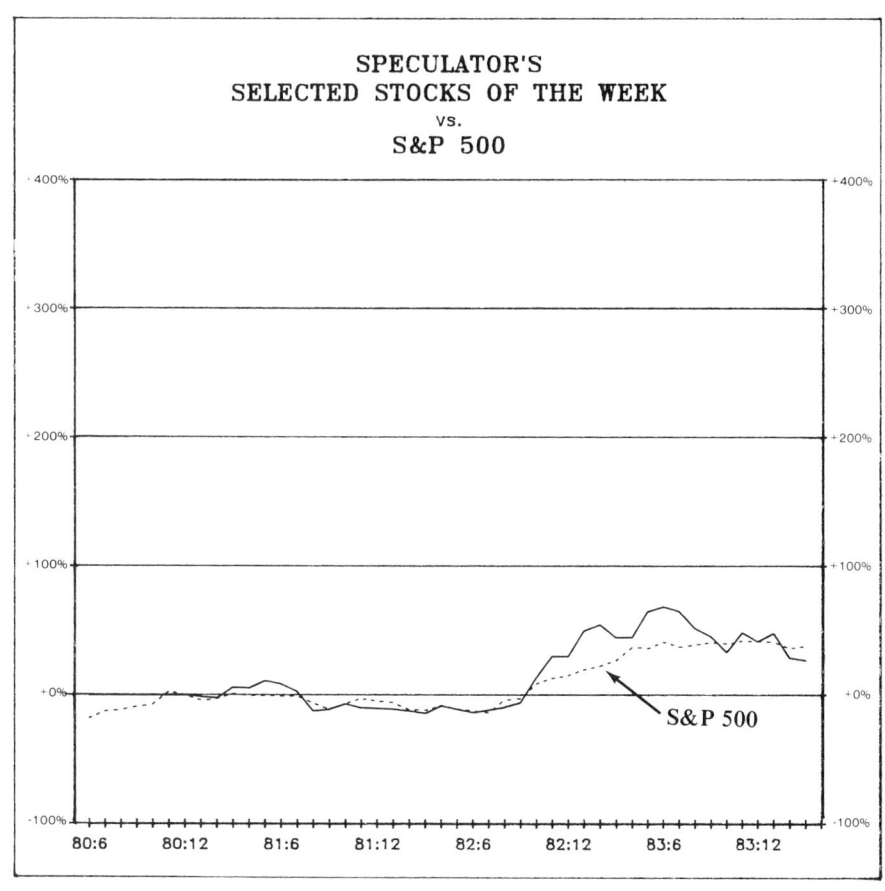

PORTFOLIO REVIEW
July 25, 1983

Dow Jones Industrials
Average: Market Close
7/25/83: **1232.87**

SUCCESSFUL OPTIONS INVESTING THE MOST OUTSTANDING INVESTMENT ADVISOR FOR THE MONTH OF JUNE ACCORDING TO THE HULBERT FINANCIAL DIGEST

According to the widely respected Hulbert Financial Digest, which tracks the records of some 44 leading investment advisory services, Successful Options Investing posted a record of an advance of 19.2% for the month of June. This information was set forth on pages 4 and 5 of the Hulbert Financial Digest for July of 1983. Those pages show that SOI was by far the most outstanding performer for the month of June. In making these calculations, the Hulbert Digest uses the SOI Hedged Portfolio—wherein the investor is invested in selected calls and puts at the same time, so as to be able to profit from a market move in either direction.

Indeed, remarkably enough, the next best performer for the month of June was The Prudent Speculator, which advanced 8.7%; followed by the New Issue Investor +6.3% and the Market Logic's Master Portfolio up 5.8%.

Thus it can be seen that this Service far outdistanced its leading competitors.

We attribute this to hard work and to proof positive once again on the tremendous power of options investing. Investors will find tremendous leverage power in options, as the material in this service discussing the background of options indicates.

A major problem for the first-time investor is just becoming familiar enough with what options really are and how they work. In the interest of providing this information SOI provides in every issue basic background information on what options are and how they work. We also discuss some of the background of our own sophisticated mathematical information that we provide in each issue. (It is not necessary for the reader to grasp all or even very much of the material. It is provided for those who may be interested.) But you can do very well by just following our recommendations.

Which takes us back to Hulbert. We can, perhaps, be permitted to pat ourselves on the back a little at this latest achievement of SOI. As readers will recall, SOI was one of the leading performers for the month of March in the Hulbert sweepstakes.

What makes this all particularly gratifying is that we have the potential of making these kinds of profits in a down market as well as an up market.

But, enough of this chit-chat. There are some big investment winners (and a few losers) chronicled on the pages within. We continue to recommend that readers be invested in selected calls and puts from our list of recommendations found on the following pages—i.e. form a hedged portfolio. Let us turn the page, and, during the dog days of July and August, let us make some money...

NEW TECHNICAL DATA

Continuing our efforts to provide the most outstanding options service available to our readers, we with this issue begin a more expanded reporting of the already very detailed technical data that we have been publishing in the past. These data, provided on selected options each issue, are designed to provide an in-depth sophisticated look at the potential and risks of the particular option under analysis. The particular new items that we will now be providing are explained in full in the back pages of this issue (and every issue). It is not necessary for a subscriber to this service to understand any or all of this information. This information is provided for the use of the market professional and those who wish to learn more in depth about options. However, a subscriber to this service can do just fine simply by following the recommendations provided herein without worrying at all about the technical data. The results are what counts. This service provides an analysis of options that is generally only available to market professionals.

But let us tarry no longer. The results since last issue plus the latest recommendations, including options on two very widely held stocks, are provided in the pages within...

Successful Options Investing

Successful Options Investing (SOI) is published twice monthly by Martin Juman, Options Strategy Associates, 100 Ring Road West, Garden City, New York 11530. The telephone number is (516) 248-1666. (As we go to press, we should note, the newsletter is listing its address as 5818 Lover's Lane, Suite 227B, Dallas, TX 75225; we are unsure whether the change is permanent). An annual subscription costs $160. A six-week trial subscription is offered for $25. The newsletter is not supplemented by a telephone hotline. The newsletter was founded in 1982.

As its name suggests, this newsletter seeks to provide investment advice solely with respect to options. In each bare-bones issue, *Successful Options Investing* recommends calls, puts, a hedged portfolio of calls and puts, a portfolio of call spreads, and a portfolio of covered call writing. (The latter two first appeared in early 1984.) For several months during 1983 (up until the end of September 1983), the newsletter recommended that its subscribers sell any option if it declined more than 30% from the price at which it was originally recommended. That stop-loss policy has been discontinued. Some follow-up advice is provided concerning previous recommended positions. One problem subscribers to this newsletter have apparently experienced is large price changes in recommended options between the time the issue is written and the date on which it is actually received by subscribers. The newsletter recognizes this problem but advises subscribers to disregard those fluctuations.

Successful Options Investing appears to base its recommendations upon the Black/Scholes option-pricing model. Yet the fact that SOI stands behind their original recommendations, regardless of price fluctuations during the time it takes a subscriber to receive the newsletter, makes us suspect that their recommendations have a basis beyond the Black/Scholes model. That model assigns a theoretical value to each option, and it is an open question whether a recommended option is still undervalued by the time a subscriber receives the newsletter. Evidently, their call option recommendations are based on a conviction that the underlying stock is undervalued, and their put recommendations are based on a belief that the underlying stock is overvalued.

Performance

The HFD has tracked the performance of this investment advisory service's extremely volatile hedged portfolio of calls and puts since the beginning of 1982, and it has been a wild ride. Their hedged portfolio lost 19.8% in 1983 and dropped 29.8% more in just the first quarter of 1984. As the accompanying graph illustrates, this aggregate loss of 43.7% compares to a 19.6% gain in the S & P 500 over the same period.

This portfolio was one of the most volatile and risky of the portfolios HFD monitored for this period. Seven times in that 15-month period the portfolio lost more than 10% in a single month. On three occasions, this portfolio gained more than 10% in a single month. Only once did the portfolio change less than 6% in value in a given month. The extraordinary risk undertaken by this hedged options portfolio is reflected in its volatility—more than seven times that of the S & P 500 over the same period.

SUCCESSFUL OPTIONS INVESTING
Hedged Portfolio of Calls and Puts

Period	Gain	Quintile
1983	−19.8%	Lowest 20%
Risk ranking	20.976	Highest 20%

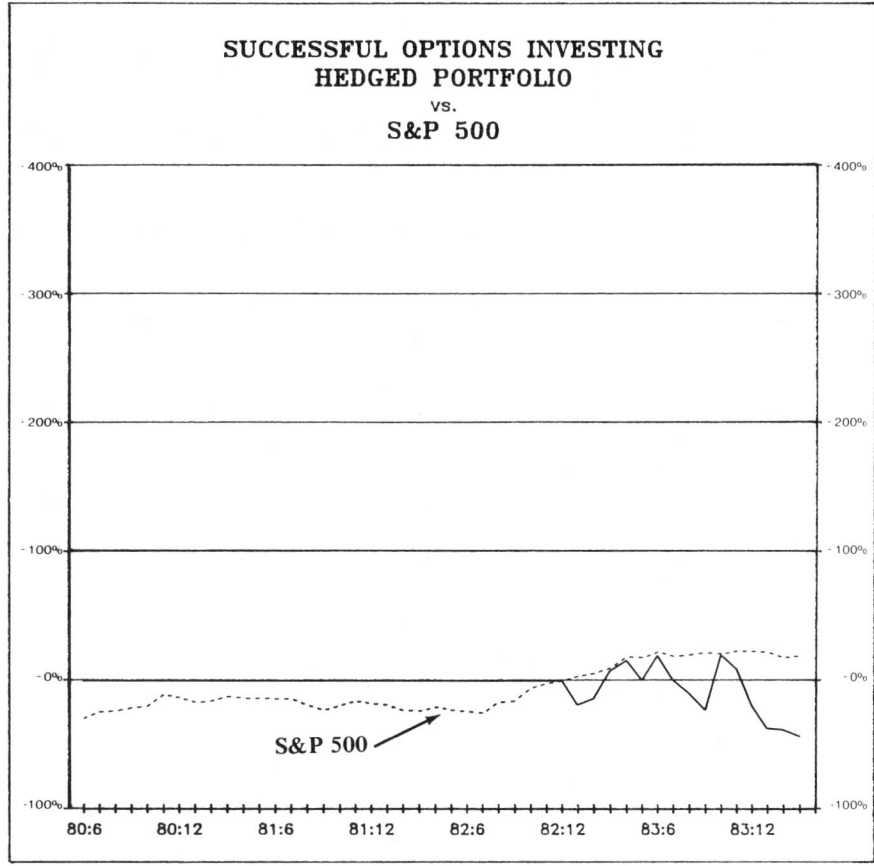

SWITCH FUND ADVISORY

"PRUDENT STRATEGY FOR TRADING THE MUTUAL FUNDS"

January 1983

1983: In A Volatile Market, Flexibility Remains The Key

During December the stock market continued to advance but not at the blistering pace of previous months. Investors apparently have fully discounted future drops in interest rates, as the market hardly reacted when the Discount Rate was lowered half a percentage point on December 10th. The Federal Reserve at the moment seems content to let rates remain low, and may even let rates drop a little bit further. But most economists do not see dramatic drops in interest rates during the coming year akin to what we saw last summer, partly because rates are not at a peak but at a trough.

As a result, many analysts believe that bonds have made their major moves, although some profits perhaps remain to be made. With rates not dropping as sharply as before, it is unlikely that bonds will be able to match their 1982 performances this year. (Note from the table below that the bonds categories are ranked #2 and #3 for the year 1982). The greater potential for future capital gains would appear to lie with equity (stock) funds.

As we move further into 1983 there are three major trends in the economy which you should keep your eye on. These trends are important because they will affect the stock market and therefore your equity investments. First, the economy is at a cyclical low and is primed to start trending upward. The housing and auto industries are enjoying increasing sales, and this strength should spillover to other sectors of the economy. So long as rates stay low, the probabilities remain high that business activity will turn around, thus providing further fuel for the stock market.

Second, taxes are on the rise, especially at the Federal level, as our political leaders are attempting to grapple with the seemingly uncontrollable budget deficits. Social security, too, will likely be a cause of higher taxes, even though benefits will probably remain at current levels or even decline some. This is bad news for the stock market because the extra monies taken away from individuals reduces the pool of dollars available for investing. (continued on page 2)

CURRENT YIELD AND PERFORMANCE RECORD OF MUTUAL FUND CATEGORIES
AS OF DECEMBER 31, 1982

PERF RANK	LAST MO.	MUTUAL FUND CATEGORY	6 MO. RELATIVE % PERF.	1 MO.% PERF.	6 MO.% PERF.	12 MO.% PERF.	% INCOME YIELD	TOTAL % RETURN
1	1	Gold Funds	+75.5	+12.7	+104.0	+36.0	3.6	+39.6
2	4	Tax-Exempt Bonds	-10.4	+3.6	+18.1	+24.3	9.2	+33.5
3	2	Bonds, Non Tax-Exempt	-13.7	+1.3	+14.8	+14.2	11.9	+26.1
4	5	Growth with Current Income	+0.1	+0.9	+28.6	+19.1	5.2	+24.3
5	3	Maximum Capital Gains	+8.2	+0.5	+36.7	+21.9	2.1	+24.0
6	6	Income, Stocks &/or Bonds	-9.6	+1.1	+18.9	+14.8	9.1	+23.9
7	7	Balanced Funds	-4.6	+1.8	+23.9	+15.3	6.6	+21.9
8	8	Income, Stocks Only	-7.6	0.0	+20.9	+13.2	4.8	+18.0
9	10	Long Term Growth	+1.0	+1.5	+29.5	+14.1	2.9	+17.0
10	9	Taxable Money Market	-23.5	+0.7	+5.0	+12.6	N/A	+12.6
11	11	Tax-Exempt Money Market	-25.5	+0.4	+3.0	+7.2	N/A	+7.2
		S & P 500 Composite	-0.2	+1.5	+28.3	+14.8	4.9	+19.7
		Dow Jones Industrials	+0.4	+0.7	+28.9	+19.6	5.3	+24.9

Published and Copyrighted 1983 by Schabacker Investment Management, 8943 Shady Grove Court, Gaithersburg, Md 20877. Annual subscription is $105 for 12 monthly issues. Rights of reproduction and distribution are reserved by the publishers. Schabacker Investment Management is registered with the SEC as an investment advisor. Pursuant to SEC regulations, it is not our intent to state, indicate or imply in any manner whatsoever that any charts, formulas, theories or methods can guarantee profitable results in the future and/or equal past performance. All material presented is compiled from sources believed reliable, but accuracy cannot be guaranteed. Before buying any mutual fund, you should read its prospectus carefully. Mutual funds exchanging, like a redemption, is a taxable event.

Switch Fund Advisory

Switch Fund Advisory (SFA) is one of several investment newsletters geared to subscribers who desire to invest in mutual funds rather than individual securities. This easy-to-read newsletter is published by Schabacker Investment Management, 8943 Shady Grove Court, Gaithersburg, Maryland 20877, which also publishes *Retirement Fund Advisory*, a newsletter aimed at IRA and Keogh Plan investors. An annual subscription to *Switch Fund Advisory* costs $125 for 12 monthly issues, each of which is supplemented by three weekly four-page advisory bulletins. The newsletter is not supplemented with a telephone hotline service. *Switch Fund Advisory* was founded in 1977.

Each 18-page monthly issue of *Switch Fund Advisory* contains a lead article briefly reviewing recent economic news and providing market commentary. A table summarizes the current yield and performance record of 11 different mutual fund categories (for example, gold funds, taxable money market funds, tax-exempt money market funds, bond funds, funds made up only of income stocks, funds seeking maximum capital gains, etc.).

The newsletter specifically advises subscribers "what to do now": what portion of their investable assets should be placed in equity funds and what portion in money market funds. *Switch Fund Advisory* recommends several funds for investors to consider in each of four categories, depending on their investment objective: aggressive growth, quality growth, income with moderate growth, and secure income.

259

The newsletter also tries to forecast changes in the S & P 500 and in the prices of gold stocks over the next month and the next six months. Two pages of the newsletter are devoted to a descriptive summary of a particular mutual fund "family," given paragraph reviews of each of the affiliated funds.

A useful table continuously updates the performance of the 40 best-performing mutual funds, irrespective of category, over the last five- and ten-year periods, respectively. Another table divides 108 no-load stock and bond mutual funds into eight groups according to the stated objective of the fund and then rates their performance and yield over the last one-, six-, and twelve-month periods. Four pages of graphs depict the performance over the last 15–18 months of 24 of the most volatile funds. Another table rates 151 load mutual funds by category and performance.

Model Portfolio

Switch Fund Advisory established a Model Portfolio in June 1979, which, according to the newsletter's own figures, had increased 134.1% by March 30, 1984, a compounded 19.5% annual rate over that 4-3/4-year period. The S & P 500 advanced 54.7% over the same period (not including dividends, which would add about 25% more to this total). Although the HFD has tracked this model portfolio's performance only since the start of 1983, we have found their performance calculations and ours to match very closely and thus see no reason to disbelieve their claims.

In 1983, according to HFD performance data, SFA's Model Portfolio gained 16.4% (the newsletter's own figures also credit it with a gain of 16.4%), while the S & P 500 gained 22.5%. During the first quarter of 1984, the Model Portfolio gained 0.6%, bucking a 2.4% decline in the S & P 500. For this 15-month period since the start of 1983, according to the HFD, SFA's Model Portfolio increased 17.1%, compared to a 19.6% advance in the S & P 500.

While SFA's Model Portfolio slightly underperformed the S & P 500 over this period, it did so with 25% less volatility and risk. On a risk-adjusted basis, therefore, its performance is just about equal to the market, and the portfolio is one of the better low-risk newsletters among those monitored by the HFD. In fact, SFA's model portfolio was one of the least risky of those monitored by the HFD for this 15-month period—yet it outperformed all but 7 of the other newsletters tracked by the HFD.

SWITCH FUND ADVISORY
Model Portfolio

Period	Gain	Quintile
1983	16.4%	Second highest 20%
Risk ranking	2.168	Lowest 20%
% 1983 Closeouts long term	100%	Highest 20%

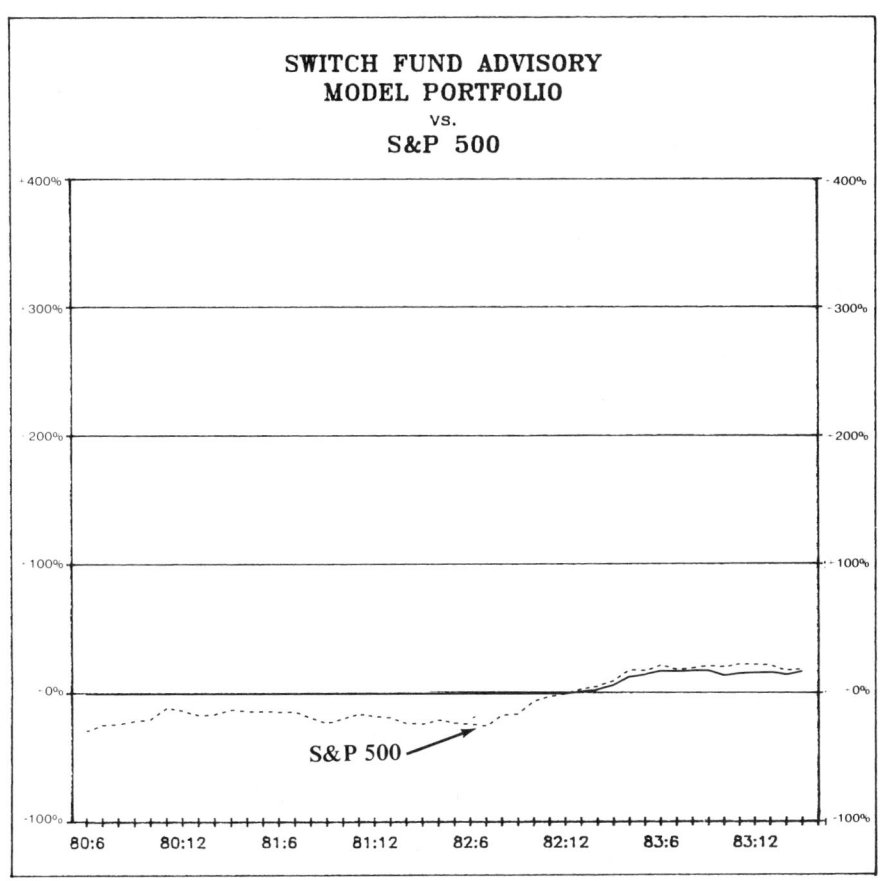

SYSTEMS and FORECASTS

SIGNALERT CORPORATION   185 GREAT NECK ROAD   GREAT NECK, N.Y. 11021

Volume XI   REGISTERED WITH THE S.E.C. AS AN INVESTMENT ADVISOR   Number 9

October 3, 1983

THE SCIENTIFIC INVESTMENT SYSTEMS RESEARCH GROUP:

A number of subscribers have written in to inquire as to the composition of the Scientific Investment Systems Research Group (SISRG).

This group was formed by Scientific Investment Systems, Inc., of Toronto, which prepares and publishes reports dealing with long, intermediate and short term technical analysis and trading systems. Reports are issued at intervals of from 4-7 weeks, when SISRG has arrived at something of use, and are mailed to members as they are prepared.

In the past, such reports have been from 16-32 pages in length, generally documented with 10-12 years of market back data and history.

Among the topics covered in the past have been our Market Thrust Indicator, several studies relating to Wilder's Relative Strength, the Dual-70 trading system, The Major Swing Deviation Indicator, short term commodity trading systems (for the stock index futures), intermediate filtering of short term trading devices, composite market cycles and trading range penetration devices.

Membership for the first 12 reports is available at $300. Reports are sold separately for between $50 - $75.

Report #9 will be issued shortly.

The response from current members has been almost universally enthusiastic. If you own a computer, you will find the studies quite compatible. They can be readily programmed with Compu-trac. For more information, write in.

THE STATE OF THE MARKET: The August Advance Has Probably Come to An End, Although Short Term Cyclical Strength Is Due to Arrive Shortly. The Strength of Any Rally That Develops Will be Decisive.

THE BIG MOVE COMPOSITE IMPROVED LAST WEEK TO +6, WHICH IS STILL A NEUTRAL RATING. We Continue to Look for a Sluggish and Indecisive Market for the Coming Months.

The Time-Trend buy signal of August 31 remains intact at this time, but the market is moving into a position from which a sell signal could develop shortly if strength does not re-appear. Certain other trading models such as Dual-70 and MACDTM have already generated sell signals, but these are whippier than Time-Trend, the model with the best long term track record.

THE BIG MOVE COMPOSITE has generated a cover short signal, largely because of favorable sentiment indicators, but has not generated a BUY signal. Its components are not in position to generate an important buy anywhere in the near future. We have been suggesting as a result that any rally was likely to prove only moderate at best. The recent advance met our expectations of new highs in the major averages (in this case, the Dow) or a near miss (the NYSE Index). Other measures of market action did not challenge their June highs.

Historic precedents suggest that further corrective action is likely. This can take the form of a fairly sharp market decline into late November, perhaps following a very limp rally attempt from the next short term cyclical low, or the corrective action can take the form of a trading range, probably between 1160 - 1180 at the low end and 1250 at the high end. Industry groups would rotate in their corrective action during such a pattern. Similar action took place during 1972 and 1976. Our best guess is that a very severe decline will not take place, at least not in the primary sector of the marketplace. (The secondary sector seems more vulnerable), but we would follow any Time-Trend sell signal by reducing our long exposure to no more than 50%.

There is a time to buy, a time to sell aggressively, and a time to sit on the sidelines collecting interest until the ingredients for a good market move fall into place. We believe that we are now at a juncture where prudent investors will simply stand aside until clearer signals develop.

Systems and Forecasts

Systems and Forecasts is a technically oriented investment newsletter edited by Gerald Appel, a practicing psychologist. Appel is the author of several books on the stock market and other investments, including *Winning Market Systems*, *99 Ways to Make Money in a Depression*, *Winning Stock Selection Systems*, *Double Your Money Every Three Years*, *New Directions in Technical Analysis* (co-authored with Martin E. Zweig, editor of *Zweig Forecast*, reviewed later in this book), *The Stock Option and No-Load Switch Fund Scalper's Manual*, *Stock Market Trading Systems* (co-authored with Fred Hitschler), and a number of other trading manuals and articles. *Systems and Forecasts* is published 24 times per year by Signalert Corporation at an annual subscription cost of $140. The address is 150 Great Neck Road, Great Neck, New York 11021. The newsletter is supplemented twice weekly with a telephone hotline service at no extra cost.

Each bi-weekly, eight-page issue contains several regular features. The first page provides general market commentary and an overview of the key technical indicators followed by *Systems and Forecasts*. The next two pages are devoted to feature articles highlighting a particular indicator or array of indicators, a synopsis of work of other advisers, or the review of books, computer programs, or research that *Systems and Forecasts* is completing in the areas of options, hedging, futures, or market timing. The fourth page portrays a daily based chart of the DJIA, the S & P 500, the NYSE advance-decline line, and NYSE daily volume and analysis of that data. Page five of the newsletter assesses the implications given of current readings of various techical indicators. The next page seeks to quantify the trend in relative strength and the risk-reward characteristics for each of 36 no-load stock mutual funds. Next, in a feature entitled "Sampling the Services," Appel reviews and analyzes the current market views of a handful of major newsletters. The final page of each issue of *Systems and Forecasts* sets forth specific portfolio advice: what percentage of a subscriber's investable assets should be invested at any given time and in what stocks, bonds, options, or convertible securities the equity portion should be invested.

Two Track Records

The HFD has been tracking *Systems and Forecasts* since January 1983 and has performance data for two different portfolios, one being the portfolio recommended on the back page of the newsletter and the other based on one of Appel's proprietary timing indicators, entitled "Time Trend." According to HFD's figures, the former portfolio lost 6.9% in 1983 (when the S & P 500 was up 22.5%) but gained 6.9% during the market slump in the first quarter of 1984 (when the S & P 500 was down 2.4%). For the 15-month period, *Systems and Forecasts'* recommended portfolio declined by 0.5%, while the S & P 500 gained 19.6%. Because this portfolio underperformed the S & P 500 with about 20% more risk and volatility, it has substantially underperformed the market on a risk-adjusted basis.

A portfolio trading the NYSE Composite on the basis of signals given by Appel's Time Trend did better. In 1983, a portfolio that went 100% long on Time Trend "buys" and 100% into Treasury bills on Time Trend "sells" would have gained 18.7%, as compared to 17.5% for the NYSE Composite itself. For the 15-month period, such a portfolio would have bettered the NYSE Composite by a 16.4% to 13.1% margin.

Divergence Between the Performance of the Two Portfolios

Appel by and large varied the market exposure of the portfolio tracked on the back page of his newsletter according to Time Trend's signals, so the fact that the timing portfolio did better than the actual one means that Appel's stock, option, and convertible bond selections underperformed the market by a fairly wide margin. This poor average performance of Appel's securities is in large part due to some option recommendations that did not pan out. Because Appel typically did not recommend a specific portfolio weight for his option recommendations, the HFD gave them the same portfolio weight enjoyed by his other recommendations. (See the discussion of methodology in the prologue.)

As this suggests, potential subscribers to *Systems and Forecasts* should also be aware that Appel's recommendations are sometimes less than clear with respect to how much of the portfolio should be allocated to any given investment. In September 1983, for example, Appel recommended the purchase of a call on the S & P 100 Index over his telephone hotline. The HFD called the hotline twice, and on one occasion, the option recommendation was accompanied by advice to purchase one such call for each $10,000 to $12,000 of stocks you owned in your portfolio. On the other occasion, the recording included no mention of this weighting. It was unclear what advice Appel intended subscribers to follow. These ambiguities create difficulties for newsletter rating services such as the HFD which seek to accurately record the likely results achieved by persons following such advice.

SYSTEMS AND FORECASTS

Period	Gain	Quintile
1983	−6.9%	Lowest 20%
Risk ranking	3.388	Second lowest 20%
% 1983 Closeouts long term	12.7%	Lowest 20%

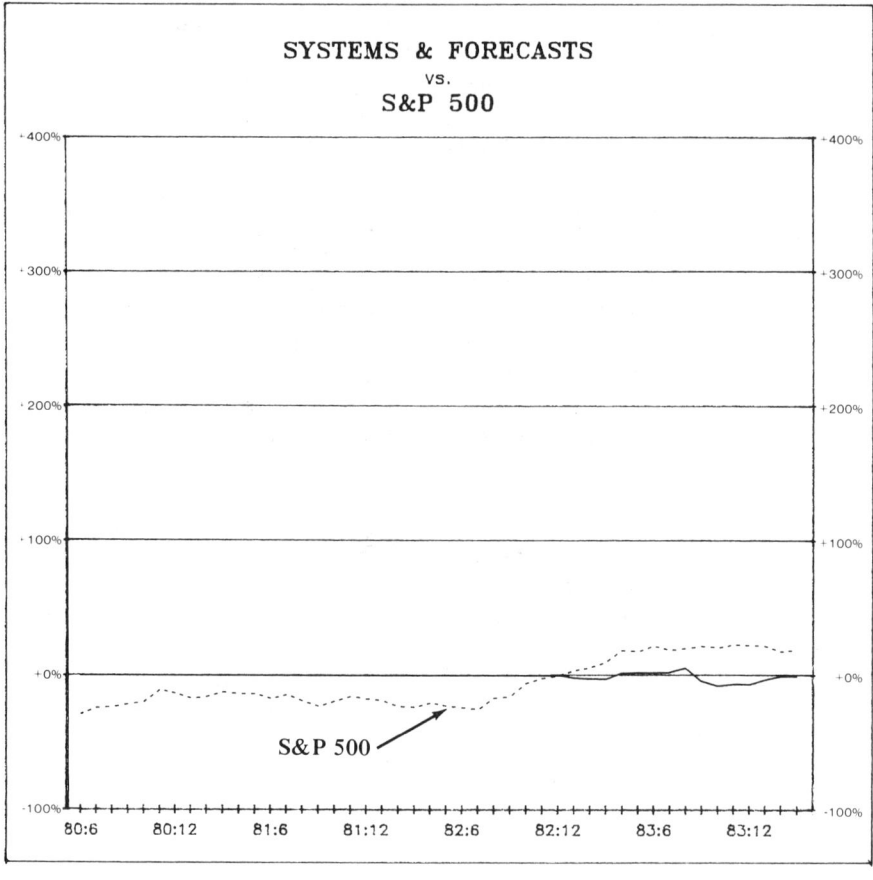

DICK FABIAN - Editor
DOUGLAS FABIAN - Co-Editor
P.O. Box 2538
Huntington Beach, CA 92647
(714) 840-4747

Telephone Switch Newsletter

The Simple Approach to Mutual Fund Trading

Date Mailed: August 10, 1983

GENERAL MARKET: At the close of the market on Friday August 5th, the Mutual Fund Composite (MFC) has declined by 10.8% from its alltime high reading of 17734 which was reached on 6/24/83. Its reading on 8/5/83 was 15815 which is 9.23% above its 39 week average reading (WAR) of 14479.

The indicators which measure the general market are closer to their individual 39WAR than those indicators which measure the secondary markets. (It is in the secondary markets where the Mutual Funds we use have the majority of their holdings.) Specifically: DJ Industrials are 4.3% above their 39WAR, DJTransportations are 6.8% above, Wilshire Index 6.5% above, New York Composite 5.5% above and S&P 500 5.3% above. At the same time the American Stock Exchange Index is 14.2% above and the O-T-C Industrials are 10.6% above their 39WAR.

Two points of interest: 1-The most often mentioned reason for the recent pullback in the market is based on negative expectations for the direction of interest rates. The DowUtilities, the most interest rate sensitive indicator we monitor, is still 3% above its 39WAR. 2-It has been difficult to read any comment about the market over the past four or five months without being warned to "stay away from" the Technology Stocks. Reviewing our currently recommended group of Mutual Funds, Fidelity Select Technology has declined the least from its June high for the 5 Funds which make up this group.

Quoting from the August 5th Hot-Line message: "...It is during trying times such as these that it is most important to have **firm** trading rules available AND then to have the discipline to stick to them." I know that many mutual fund traders have already "switched" into money funds. I am sure that the majority of them had also switched out of the equity funds at least once or twice before since last August. It would be interesting to know what the price was when they bought back in from their previous trades. In talking with subscribers we sense that during trying times, emotionally people just **want** to bail out... their only reason is so that they will "feel better". On the day they do get out, they do feel better. **BUT**..then they must answer the very difficult question: "When do I buy back in?" The really tragic consequence of this "feel better" approach to trading is the fact that many investor/traders after a few whipsaws find the emotional strain so great, they just give up on the investment and walk away. Their shortcoming was the fact that they continually focus in on the wrong part of the picture.

Wouldn't it seem reasonable that a very large percentage of investors would have said on August 27, 1982 (49 weeks ago exactly) they would be very satisfied if their investment would grow over 60% and they would only be 3 weeks away from a long-term capital gain eleven months later? I am sure they would have. Now that we have arrived at that point in time, instead of looking at what they have gained to date they insist on focusing on the unrealized gain that has been removed since the high in June.

RECOMMENDED TOP PERFORMING AGGRESSIVE EQUITY TYPE TELEPHONE-SWITCH MUTUAL FUNDS							
					PERFORMANCE		
PRICES AS OF 08/05/83	CURRENT SHARE PRICE	39 WEEK AVERAGE READING	08/27/82 TO ** 08/05/83	05/23/80 TO *** 07/23/81	11/16/79 TO *** 03/18/80	03/28/79 TO *** 10/23/79	11/10/76 TO *** 10/23/78
##-FID/SEL TECHNOLOGY	$25.05	#$21.36	+142.9%	N/A	N/A	N/A	N/A
##-FOUNDERS SPECIAL	33.02	29.97	+84.6%	+44.1%	N/A	N/A	N/A
##-STEIN ROE CAP OPPORT	30.40	28.20	+82.9%	+41.5%	+ 4.9%	+ 4.2%	+23.4%
##-44 WALL STREET	19.13	18.06	+77.1%	+48.6%	- 4.5%	+ 9.2%	+68.3%
##-R/P NEW HORIZONS	19.36	17.60	+76.8%	+49.8%	+ 3.7%	+ 5.0%	+42.0%
MUTUAL FUND COMPOSITE	15815	14478	+69.0%*	+45.1%*	+ 2.3%*	+ 3.5%*	+54.0%*
DJ INDUSTRIALS	1183.29	1134.07	+33.9%	+ 8.7%	- 1.7%	- 6.9%	-11.5%
DJ TRANSPORTATIONS	542.43	508.00	+55.0%	+51.1%	+ 5.7%	+ 1.2%	+ 1.3%

#THE COMPUTATION OF THE 39WAR HAS BEEN ADJUSTED FOR CURRENT DISTRIBUTIONS.
##-FIVE RECOMMENDED EQUITY AGGRESSIVE FUNDS.

*PERFORMANCE SHOWN FOR THE MFC IS BASED ON THE ACTUAL MUTUAL FUNDS WHICH MADE UP THE MFC DURING EACH PERIOD SHOWN.
**PERFORMANCE FOR THE FUNDS SHOWN FOR THE MOST RECENT PERIOD WHEN WE RECOMMENDED THE USE OF EQUITY FUNDS.
***PERFORMANCE SHOWN FOR PREVIOUS PERIOD WHEN WE RECOMMENDED THE USE OF EQUITY FUNDS.
NOTE: INTEREST EARNED WHILE IN THE MONEY FUNDS IS NOT SHOWN. IT SHOULD NOT BE ASSUMED THAT RECOMMENDATIONS MADE IN THE FUTURE WILL BE PROFITABLE OR WILL EQUAL THE PERFORMANCE OF THE MUTUAL FUNDS LISTED ABOVE.

Telephone Switch Newsletter

Telephone Switch Newsletter is one of several market timing investment newsletters begun in recent years in an effort to advise subscribers when they should have their money invested in no-load stock mutual funds and when they should "switch" the money to a related money market fund within the same family of funds. *Telephone Switch Newsletter* is published monthly and is edited by Richard J. Fabian and co-edited by Douglas Fabian. Before becoming a financial adviser, Dick Fabian sold mutual funds as a stockbroker during the late 1960s. An annual subscription costs $117 and is available from P. O. Box 2538, Huntington Beach, California 92647. The newsletter's telephone number is (714) 840-4747. A telephone hotline service is provided without extra charge to regular subscribers. Special hotline bulletins are mailed free of charge to subcribers whenever equity fund switch signals are given. *Telephone Switch Newsletter* was founded in 1977.

    Telephone Switch Newsletter bills itself as "the simple approach to mutual fund trading," and its goals and approach are indeed simple. The goal is simple: to accumulate capital at a 20% compounded growth rate over an extended period of time. The approach is also simple: to switch assets from money market funds to aggressive, volatile stock mutual funds whenever current price exceeds the 39-week average price for a given fund or group of funds and at the same time the current DJIA or Dow Jones Transportation Average or both exceed their respective 39-week moving averages (20-week moving average in the case of gold funds). This simple timing device has generated just nine switch recommendations over the past 7-1/4 years. Commissions are reduced or eliminated because only no-load or low-load mutual funds are recommended as investment vehicles.

Performance

How has this trading system fared? The HFD has tracked the performance of two *Telephone Switch Newsletter* portfolios since the beginning of 1983. One, which concentrates upon switching in and out of aggressive stock funds and money market funds, gained 15.2% from January 1, 1983, through March 31, 1984. In comparison, the S & P 500 (including dividends) gained 19.6% over this same period—with only slightly more than half the risk. Therefore, TSN's equity-cash switch plan for this 15-month period underperformed the market on a risk-adjusted basis.

The second TSN portfolio tracked by the HFD concentrates on gold share mutual funds. This portfolio, when a sell signal on gold funds was issued by TSN's trading system, switched either into equity funds or money market funds depending upon whether TSN's trading signal for equity funds was on a buy or a sell. This portfolio lost 3.6% over the same 15-month period, with volatility and risk more than twice as high as that experienced by the S & P 500.

Long-Term Record

Telephone Switch Newsletter's longer-term record, at least with regard to the equity funds, appears to be better than the record for these 15 months. According to an analysis conducted by Lipper Analytical Services for *The Wall Street Journal*, TSN's switch signals since 1977 could have been the basis of strategy that significantly outperformed the market. Since then, according to Lipper, a strategy of remaining 100% invested in the average growth-oriented mutual fund would have gained 129% as of March 6, 1984 (including reinvestment of dividends and interest on money market funds). In contrast, a strategy of trading in and out of the average growth-oriented mutual fund according to TSN's timing signals would have brought a return of 179% over the same period.

TELEPHONE SWITCH NEWSLETTER

Equity-Cash Switch Portfolio

Period	Gain	Quintile
1983	19.0%	Second highest 20%
Risk ranking	5.479	Third highest 20%
% 1983 Closeouts long term	(No positions were closed out)	

Gold/Equity/Cash Switch Portfolio

Period	Gain	Quintile
1983	−7.8%	Lowest 20%
Risk ranking	6.786	Second highest 20%
% 1983 Closeouts long term	50.0%	Second lowest 20%

Average of Two Portfolios

Period	Gain	Quintile
1983	+5.6%	Second lowest 20%

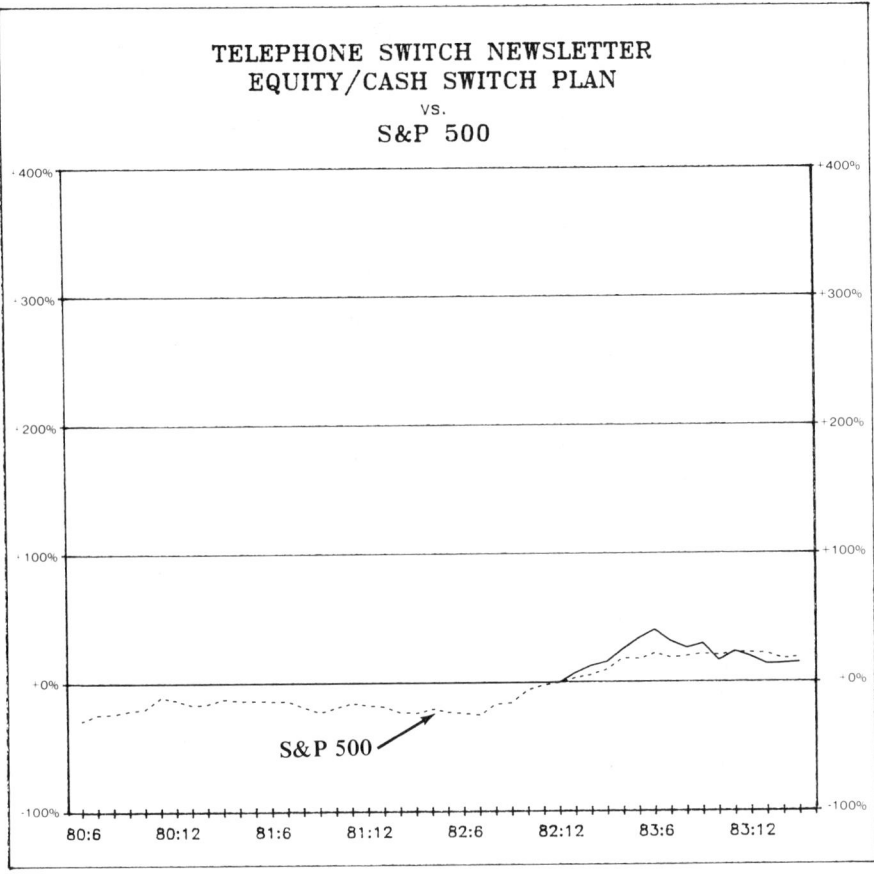

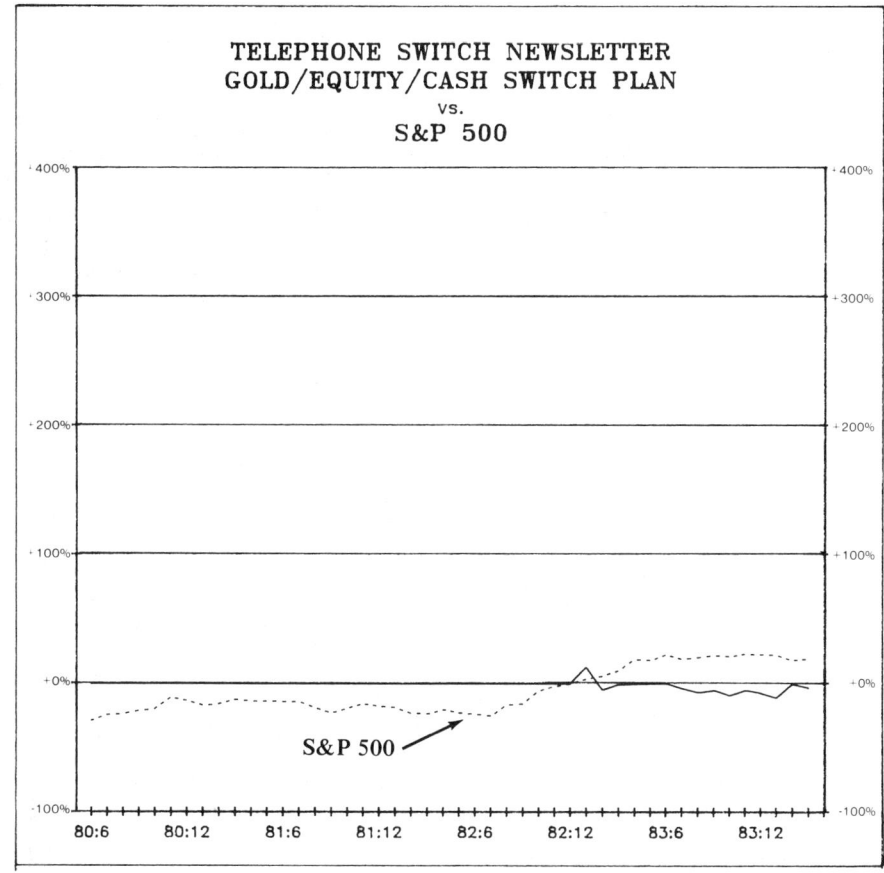

TONY HENFREY'S gold letter

No. 162 THURSDAY, 24 NOVEMBER, 1983

	Latest Price	Intermediate Direction	Resistance or Support	Intermediate Objective	Major Direction	Resistance or Support	Major Objective
Gold (London fix)	$376	To Rally ?	380 R 374 S		Down	400 R 350 S	
Silver (London spot)	$8.61	To Rally ?	8.80 R 8.30 S		Down	12.00 R 6.00 S	
Platinum (London spot)	$386	To Rally ?	390 R 375 S		Down	450 R 375 S	
RDM Gold Index	726	To Rally ?	770 R 660 S		Down	920 R 660 S	
DJIA	1275.81	Up	Broken 1200 S		Up	1290 R 1190 S	
US 3 Months Euro-rate	9.64%	To edge down	9.90 R 9.20 S		Basing	10.6 R 6.0 S	
DJ 20 Bond Index	70.81	Neutral	71.0 R 70.0 S		Down	76.0 R 60.0 S	
CRB Futures Index	269.2	To Rally	275 R 264 S		Up	283 R 260 S	
US Dollar (To Swiss franc)	2.183	Down	2.19 R 2.15 S		Down	2.22 R 2.04 S	

THE FORCES AT WORK : United States M1 could respond to short term upside cyclical pressure with rises over the next few weeks. But the overall slowdown in annualised growth rate should still continue. Industrial production index is on the verge of going through to a new high which could mean the US economic expansion is still on course. However high 'real' interest rates so early in the business cycle should suppress the desire by business to borrow. As it is business borrowings are declining. US inflation rate ought to move higher in coming months in response to the sustained growth rate in M1 and the rise in industrial production. The forces at work are in the favourable mode to support a turnaround in the gold price . (Page 2)

PRECIOUS METALS : The performance of precious metals will be determined to a large extent by the speed of the rise in the US inflation rate. Big resistance overhangs the precious metal markets which could well inhibit the ability to break upside in the shorter view. Gold needs to break above the $400 resistance level in order to reverse the current bearish outlook. Short term signals from ratio indicators suggest that there could soon be a better relative performance from silver in the short term (long term silver to behave least well) which may be indication of at least a rally in the precious metals. (Page 5)

GOLD SHARES : The gold price in rand terms has hardly budged whilst in dollar terms it has fallen over 10 percent in recent weeks (see chart on page 6). The reason is the drop in the rand/dollar rate. This cushion effect could well support a rally in the short term as GL's indicators continue to read oversold. On page 9 GL looks at E T Cons which should continue to outperform the market if gold moves higher. The Investment and Relative Strength Rankings on page 11 highlight the shares which could respond favourably to a rally. The fact that gold bullion has made a new low whereas gold shares have not confirmed gives rise to hopes of an important turnaround soon.

WORLD MARKETS : The Dow Jones index has bounced nicely off the 1200 support level but we still get non-confirmations on many indicators which is not supportive of a wildly bullish outlook. Resistance is evident around the 1290 level which if broken will allow the index to move to a new high in the face of negative indications.

US INTEREST RATES : The big basing action in the 3 months US Euro-rate continues although in the immediate term rates could fall slightly. However there appears to be very little possibility of a drop below the massive support levels around the 9 percent level.

US DOLLAR : Has moved up to encounter significant resistance against the Swiss franc which extends from 2.18 to 2.22. It is technically inconceivable that the dollar will succeed in pushing through to new highs at this time. The dollar has more downside than upside potential.

COMMODITIES : The (London) Reuters Commodity index has broken upside through resistance in rising to 1910 indicating that in pound terms at least commodities are headed higher on a broad front. The DJ Futures index needs to penetrate the 143 resistance level in order to reverse the 13 week long downtrend - the 36 week cyclical low could have been seen last week. Commodities to move higher into December.

Tony Henfrey's Gold Letter

Tony Henfrey's Gold Letter, edited by Tony Henfrey, is published 26 times per year by Indexia (Pty) Ltd., Suite 816, NBS Building, 300 Smith Street, Durban, P. O. Box 5577, Durban 4000, South Africa. The telephone number in South Africa for subscription information is (31) 742566. An annual subscription costs $185; a six-month subscription is offered for $100; and a three-month, six-issue trial subscription is available for $50. The newsletter is supplemented by a telephone hotline service at no additional charge. However, Henfrey does make additional recommendations through a Telex service for which investors must subscribe separately. The *Letter* has been published since 1977.

    This newsletter, one of the few tracked by the HFD that has its base outside the United States, presents a technical analysis of precious metals, principally gold and South African gold mining shares, the American stock market, U. S. inflation statistics, money supply figures, and interest rates and also looks at the strength of the dollar relative to the Swiss franc.

    The *Gold Letter* also maintains a number of different portfolios. The *Letter*'s "South African Gold Share Portfolio", also referred to as the "Long Term Gold Share Portfolio," appears to be the longest-lived of the portfolios and is the one the HFD has tracked since the beginning of 1982. This portfolio takes a fairly long-term perspective and does not attempt to trade short-term swings in the gold share markets;

since 1982, for example, the portfolio has made two round-trips in and out of the shares. In March 1983, Henfrey added a "Gold Trader" portfolio to his letter, which purchases or sells gold bullion on the basis of Henfrey's short-term trading signals. Henfrey has recently added a "U. S. Stock Market Portfolio," which gives "buy" or "sell" signals on the market as a whole and for industry groups but does not recommend specific stocks to buy or sell short. In addition, Henfrey recommends specific gold shares to be purchases by the aggressive trader—usually via his telex and telegram service (which he terms his "TT Traders Portfolio") but sometimes in the letter itself (which he terms "GL traders portfolio"). Potential subscribers should be aware that Henfrey does not update each one of these portfolios in every issue and that, at times, a bit of textual analysis is required to ascertain which portfolio Henfrey may be referring to when he mentions, for example, "traders."

Performance

The HFD reports that, in 1982, Henfrey's portfolio of gold shares surged 93.3%, outperforming all other portfolios tracked that year by the HFD. The S & P 500 was up 21.6% over the same period. From January 1983 through March 1984, Henfrey's long-term portfolio of gold shares climbed 36.1%, compared to the S & P 500's gain of 19.6% over the same period. Over the 27-month period, Henfrey's gold share portfolio gained 163.0%, compared to 45.4% for the S & P 500.

Part of this impressive return is due to the portfolio's high risk—which would lead one to expect it to do better than the market in a bullish period. In fact, Henfrey's portfolio was the third most risky portfolio of those monitored by the HFD over this period, incurring risk more than three times as great as the S & P 500. Even factoring out the risk, however, Henfrey's gold-share portfolio outperformed the S & P 500.

In 1984, the HFD also began tracking the performance of Henfrey's "Gold Trader" portfolio. For the first quarter of 1984, the portfolio gained 4.2%. The S & P 500 shed 2.4% over the same period.

TONY HENFREY'S GOLD LETTER
South African Gold Share Portfolio

Period	Gain	Quintile
1982	93.3%	Highest 20%
1983	6.9%	Third highest 20%
Risk ranking	11.476	Highest 20%
% 1983 Closeouts long term	100%	Highest 20%
% 1982 Closeouts long term	[No positions were closed out]	

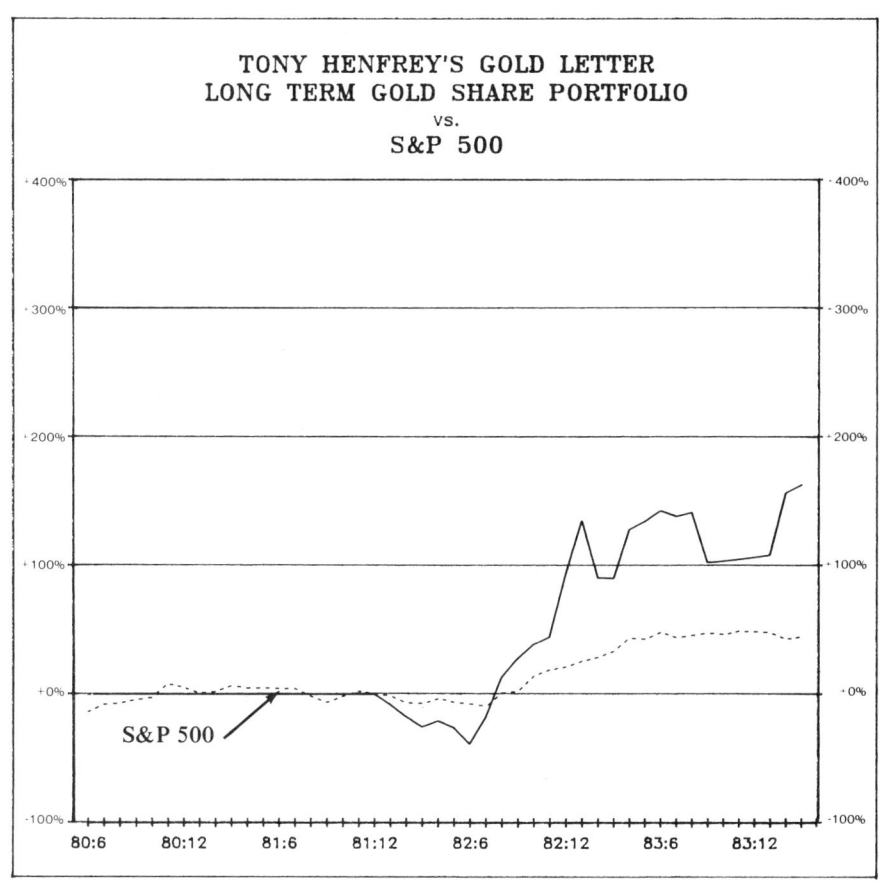

February 6, 1984

A man's judgment is no better than his information

UNITED.
Business & Investment
REPORT.

Current Situation at a Glance

Contents

Monthly Follow-Up of Supervised List

Trade Restriction — A Case Study

The Budget: Defense Gets Top Billing

Municipal Bonds — The Investor's Delight

Commodity Price Forecasts

Stocks People Are Asking About

Stock Market Advices

Active Stocks on the American Exchange

And from the Over-the-Counter Market

News and Advice on Supervised Issues

Favorable Factors

Leading Economic Indicators—This barometer of future activity rebounded in December; the 0.6% rise presages continued expansion.

Unemployment—Declined further in January, dropping to 8% from 8.2% in December; all major categories fell except black youth.

Real Estate—Sales of new single-family homes climbed 28.5% in December from November; the 1983 total (625,000) was highest since 1979.

Unfavorable Factors

Government Red Ink—Won't shrink much over the next three years, according to President Reagan's budget forecasts (see page 54).

Merchandise Trade Deficit—Soared to $69.4 billion in 1983 from $42.7 billion in 1982; this year's shortfall could top $100 billion.

Lebanon Quagmire—Continued to be a major source of concern, with new casualties and mounting Congressional sentiment for an early U. S. exit.

Summary and Forecast

The index of leading economic indicators rose for 14 uninterrupted months before stumbling in November (when revised data show that it slipped 0.2%, less than originally reported). But this composite barometer moved back into the plus column in December. The 0.6% advance from November was not as impressive as the typically large monthly moves of 1983. However, last year was one of rapid recovery as the economy rebounded from a deep recession; it would be illogical to expect the trend of king-size leading indicator jumps to continue over a protracted period. The index is certainly not an infallible guide, but its latest reading adds to evidence that the economy will follow a path of moderate growth.

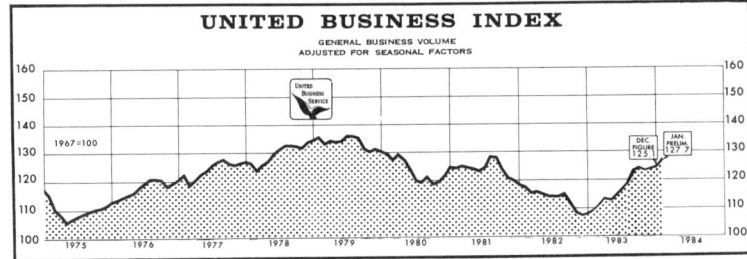

WEEKLY INDEX	
THIS WEEK	127.2
5th wk. Jan.:	127.3
4th wk. Jan.:	127.4
3rd wk. Jan.:	128.3
Feb. 1983:	111.9
Feb. 1982:	115.5

VOL. LXXVI No. 6   © UNITED BUSINESS SERVICE CO., 1984 — ALL RIGHTS RESERVED.   Pages 52 to 61

United Business and Investment Report

Published since 1919, *United Business and Investment Reports* ("United") is one of the oldest and most-subscribed to services in the newsletter industry. United is published weekly by United Business Service Company, 210 Newbury Street, Boston, Massachusetts 02116. The telephone number is (617) 267-8855. An annual subscription costs $170; a six-month subscription is offered for $95. The newsletter is not supplemented with a telephone hotline.

Each 12-page issue of *United Business and Investment Reports* contains the following feature articles: "Opinion From Washington," "Special Study," "Commodity Price Forecasts," "Stock Market—Performance and Prospect," and "Common Stock Recommendations." Recent "Special Studies" have discussed convertible securities, high-technology stocks, money market funds, municipal bonds, and the AT & T divestiture. In many respects, United is as much a business report as an investment advisory newsletter. Other articles concern industry surveys, news, and advice on supervised issues, financial planning, and articles on general business topics such as inventories, labor, and antitrust developments. No specific market timing advice is given.

Prediction Record

At the start of each year, United makes several predictions with respect to the forthcoming course of the stock market and the economy in general. Its predictions for 1983 were among the best of the many predictions made by the more than 50 investment newsletters monitored by the HFD. For example, for 1983, United predicted a high of 1300 for the DJIA (the actual high was 1287), a GNP gain of 3.2% (the actual gain was 3.4%), and an increase in the Consumer Price Index of 4.0% (the actual figure turned out to be just 3.2%).

United maintains three "Supervised Lists" of stocks: growth stocks; cyclical stocks; and income stocks. The stocks included on these lists tend to be companies with relatively large capitalizations. The average capitalization, even among speculative stocks, is larger than that of most other investment newsletters. Each list is reviewed and revised in the first issue of each month. Unlike the case with some other newsletters with multiple portfolios, the volatility and risk of the stocks selected for lists accords with the self-designation of these stock groups; in other words, their cyclical stocks are, in fact, riskier than their growth stocks, which in turn are riskier than their income stocks. United also recommends stocks that are not included on the Supervised Lists—98 such stock recommendations were made during the last six months of 1983.

One-third to one-half of the stocks included on United's Supervised Lists are marked with an asterisk, indicating that these stocks "are considered relatively best situated at present for new buying based on current market prices and other factors." Because these asterisked selections represent United's top choices for price appreciation at any given time, the HFD has tracked the performance of these stocks in computing performance ratings for United's three portfolios. (See the discussion in the methodological prologue.) Although the stocks included on the three Supervised Lists remain relatively constant, the selection of stocks highlighted with asterisks is marked by relatively high turnover.*

Performance

The HFD has tracked the performance of United's three supervised

---

* The HFD charges a 1% commission on all purchases and sales from each of the portfolios, per its established methodology. The portfolio constructed out of just the asterisked stocks thus was charged with more commissions than would have been charged against a portfolio that statically remained in the entire list. But insofar as the average asterisked stock outperforms the average unasterisked stock by more than 2%, the smaller portfolio will perform better (apart from taxes, which the HFD does not take into account). The HFD presumes that when the United Business Service (or any service, for that matter) designates one stock to be a better bet than another, it has in mind a performance differential greater than 2%.

lists since mid-1980. According to the HFD, United's "Supervised List of Stocks for Long-Term Growth" gained 15.8% during the second half of 1980, dropped 14.1% in 1981, tacked on another 6.7% in 1982, but gave up 4.7% from the beginning of 1983 through the first quarter of 1984. The aggregate gain over the 45-month period from July 1, 1980, to March 31, 1984, was 1.2%. United's "Supervised List of Cyclical Stocks for Profit" performed better, surging 28.2% in the last six months of 1980, declining 12.9% in 1981, thrusting ahead another 15.6% in 1982, and retreating 8.3% in the 15-months beginning January 1983, for an aggregate 3-3/4-year gain of 18.5%. United's "Supervised List of Stocks for the Income-Minded" performed the best over this period, growing 4.6% from July 1, 1980, through December 31, 1980; giving up 3.8% in 1981; moving ahead 13.8% in 1982; and adding another 8.5% in the succeeding 15 months. This portfolio shows an aggregate gain of 24.2% over the 45-month period for which performance figures have been calculated. For purposes of comparison, the S & P 500 gained 21.7% during the last six months of 1980, lost 4.9% in 1981, gained 21.6% in 1982, and added another 19.6% in the period from January 1, 1983, through March 31, 1984, for an aggregate gain of 68.2%. A Treasury bill portfolio would have gained 49.5% over the same period.

On a risk-adjusted basis, the income stocks formed the best performing portfolio. Not only did this outperform the other two United portfolios, it did so with less risk. Nevertheless, all three portfolios underperformed the S & P 500 on a risk-adjusted basis.

UNTIED BUSINESS & INVESTMENT REPORT

Supervised List of Growth Stocks

Period	Gain	Quintile
7/1 to 12/31/80	15.8%	Second lowest 20%
1981	−14.1%	Lowest 20%
1982	6.7%	Lowest 20%
1983	1.7%	Second lowest 20%
Risk ranking	3.221	Second lowest 20%
% 1983 Closeouts long term	100%	Highest 20%
% 1982 Closeouts long term	100%	Highest 20%

Supervised List of Cyclical Stocks

Period	Gain	Quintile
7/1 to 12/31/80	28.2%	Second highest 20%
1981	−12.9%	Lowest 20%
1982	15.6%	Second lowest 20%
1983	7.0%	Second lowest 20%
Risk ranking	5.341	Third highest 20%
% 1983 Closeouts long term	100%	Highest 20%
% 1982 Closeouts long term	85.7%	Third highest 20%

Supervised List of Income Stocks

Period	Gain	Quintile
7/1 to 12/31/80	4.6%	Lowest 20%
1981	−3.8%	Third highest 20%
1982	13.8%	Second lowest 20%
1983	14.7%	Third highest 20%
Risk ranking	2.488	Lowest 20%
% 1983 Closeouts long term	(No positions were closed out)	
% 1982 Closeouts long term	100%	Highest 20%

Average of Three Lists

Period	Gain	Quintile
7/1 to 12/31/80	16.2%	Second lowest 20%
1981	−10.3%	Second lowest 20%
1982	12.0%	Second lowest 20%
1983	7.8%	Third highest 20%

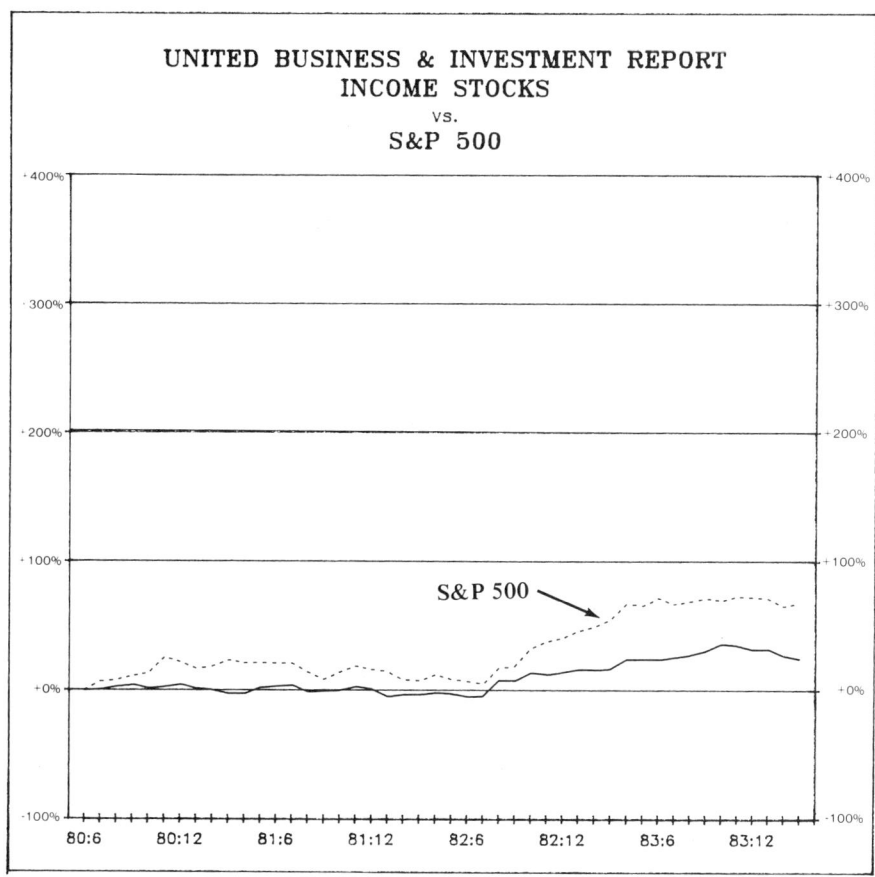

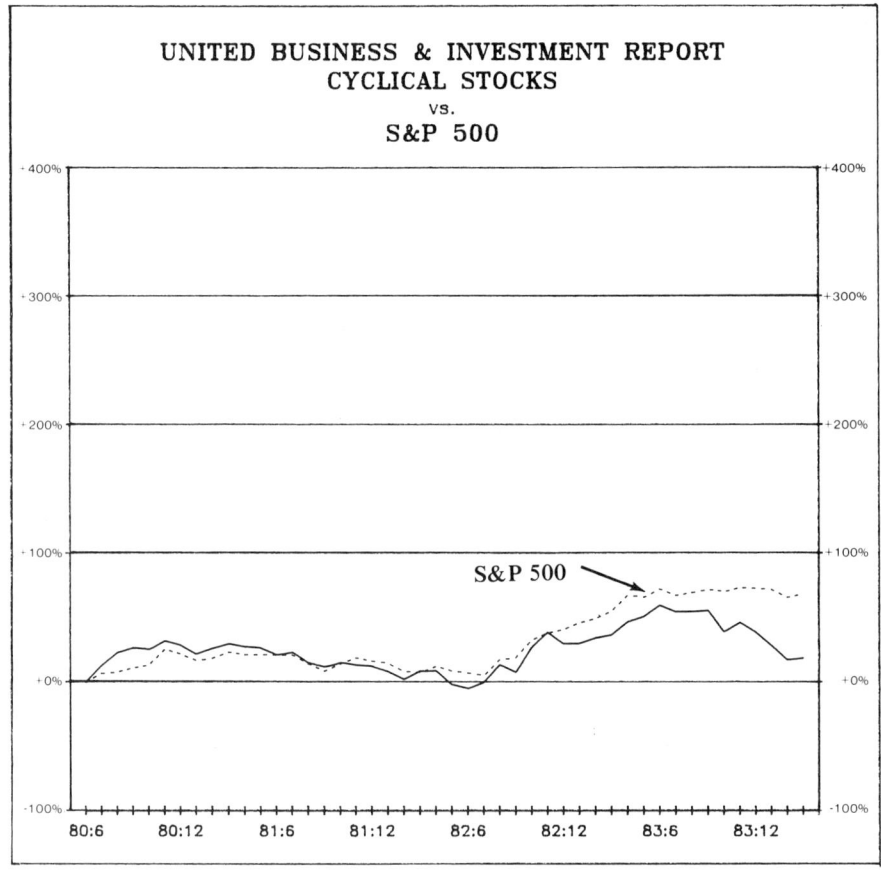

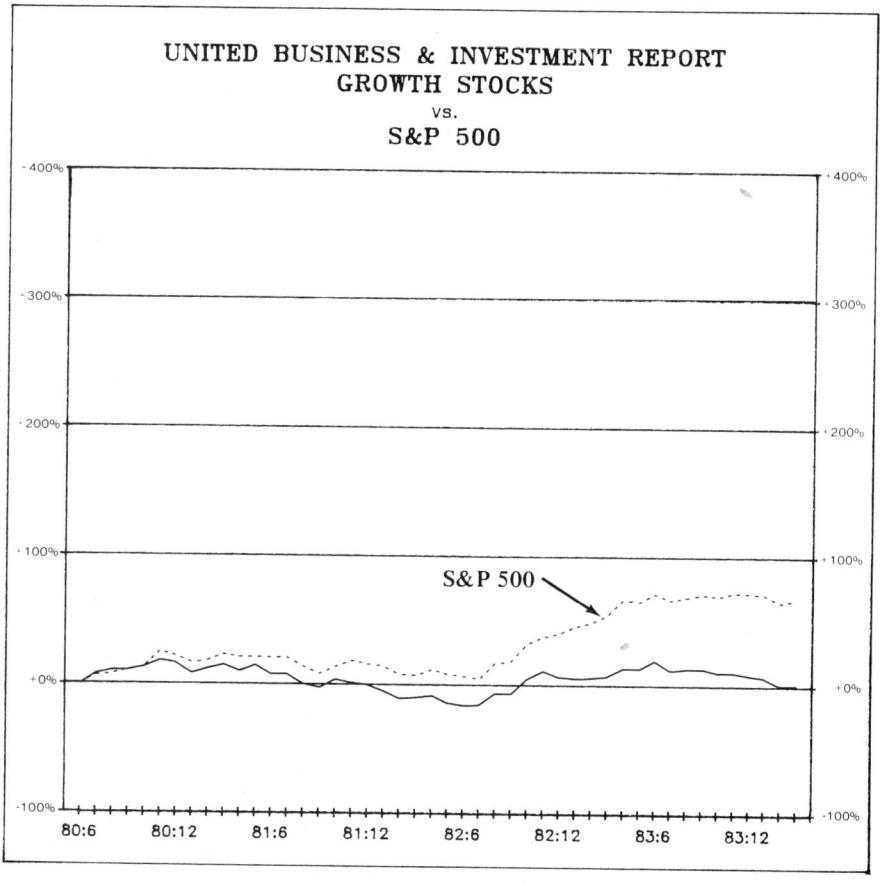

THE VALUE LINE Investment Survey

Part 1 — Summary & Index

January 6, 1984

File at the front of the Ratings & Reports binder. Last week's Summary & Index should be removed.

TABLE OF SUMMARY-INDEX CONTENTS

Summary-Index Page Number

Industries, in alphabetical order 1
Stocks—complete list with latest prices, Timeliness and Safety ranks, Betas, estimated earnings and dividends; also references to pages in Ratings & Reports carrying latest full-page reports 2–22
Industries, in order of Timeliness rank 23

SCREENS

Timely stocks (1 & 2 for Performance) 23-25	High P/E stocks 31
Conservative stocks (1 & 2 for Safety) 26-27	High total return stocks 32
High yielding stocks 28	High 3- to 5-year dividend returns 32
High 3- to 5-year appreciation 28	Companies with high return on capital 33
Cash generating companies 29	High yielding non-utility stocks 34
Best performing stocks last 13 weeks 29	Untimely stocks (5 for Performance) 34
Poorest performing stocks last 13 weeks 29	High growth stocks 35
Stocks below book value 30	Stocks below liquidating value 36
Low P/E stocks 31	Option information 36-39
	Stock market averages 40

The Median of Estimated PRICE-EARNINGS RATIOS
of all stocks with earnings

11.5

26 Weeks Ago*	Market Low 12-23-74*	Market High 12-13-68*
13.1	4.8	19.0

The Median of ESTIMATED YIELDS
(next 12 months) of all dividend paying stocks under review

3.4%

26 Weeks :o*	Market Low 12-23-74*	Market High 12-13-68*
3.2%	7.8%	2.7%

The Estimated Median APPRECIATION POTENTIAL
of all 1700 stocks in the hypothesized Economic environment 3 to 5 years hence

85%

26 Weeks Ago*	Market Low 12-23-74*	Market High 12-13-68*
75%	234%	18%

*Estimated medians as published in The Value Line Investment Survey on the dates shown.

ANALYSES OF INDUSTRIES IN ALPHABETICAL ORDER WITH PAGE NUMBER
Numeral in parenthesis after the industry is rank for probable performance (next 12 months).

PAGE	PAGE	PAGE	PAGE
Advertising (80) 1816	*Distilling/Tobacco (22) 330	Insurance-Diversified (62) 2064	Petroleum-Producing (66) 2084,1824
Aerospace/Diversified (34) 551	Drug Industry (15) 1249	Insurance-Life (19) 1187	Precision Instrument (65) 151
Agric. Equip./Diversified (6) ..1432	Drugstore (2) 772	Insurance-Prop./Cas. (74) 637	Publishing (41) 1783
*Air Transport (86) 251	Electrical Equipment (70) 1001	Investment Company (49) 2083	*Railroad (58) 304
Aluminum (46) 1209	Electric Utility-Cent. (16) ★ ★ .. 701	Iron Ore (78) 1209	Railroad Equipment (88) 603
Apparel (29) 1601	Electric Utility-East (14) ★ ★ ... 178	Lead, Zinc Minor Mtls. (51) 1140,622	Railroad/Resources (10) 1231
Auto & Truck (4) 101	Electric Utility-West (39) ★ ★ .1721	Machinery (84) 1301	Real Estate (42) 680
Auto Parts-OEM (21) 791	Electronics (33) 1033	Machinery-Const. (85) 1359	REIT (26) 671,1163
Auto Parts-Replacement (13) ... 110	*Fast Food Service (48) 312	Machine Tool (83) 1343	Recreation (59) 1751
Bank (32) 2001	Financial Services (20) 2045	Manu. Housing/Rec. Veh. (35) ..1562	Retail-Special Lines (57) 1698
Bank (Midwest) (38) 648	Food Processing (18) 1451	*Maritime (91) 294	Retail Store (11) 1647
Bank (Southwest) (81) 648	Food Wholesalers (9) 1536	*Medical Services (37) 360	Savings & Loan (27) 1151
Brewing (1) 1139,1554	Foreign Stocks (European) (28) . 818	Metal Fabricating (67) 584	Securities Brokerage (87) 1176
*Broadcasting/Cable TV (45) .. 373	Foreign Stocks (Japanese) (8) ..1573	Metals & Mining-Gen'l (69) ..1209	Shoe (79) 1683
Building (56) 851	Furn./Home Furnishings (23) 915	Multiform (55) 1378	Soft Drink (43) 1548
Canadian Energy (64) 438	Gold/Diamond (S.A.) (—) ... 1200	Natural Gas (Diversified)(40) .. 452	Steel-General (75) 609
Cement (90) 907	Gold (No. American) (77) ... 1209	Natural Gas (Utility)(47) 473	Steel-Integrated (53) 1418
Chemical-Basic (24) 1237	Grocery (30) 1509	Newspaper (12) 1807	Steel-Specialty (60) 2104
Chemical-Diversified (72) ... 1890	Health Care/Hosp. (36) 214	Office Equip. & Supplies (61) ..1114	Telecommunications (68) ..402,750
Chemical-Specialty (25) 510	Home Appliance (3) 140	Oilfield Services (89) 1843	Textile (7) 1629
Coal/Uran./Geothermal (17) ..1878	Hotel/Gaming (52) 1770	Packaging & Cont. (73) 954	Tire & Rubber (44) 126
Comp. and Peripherals (63) ..1076	Household Products (82) 979	Paper & Forest Prods. (50) 926	Toiletries/Cosmetics (31) 801
Computer Services (76) 1129	*Industrial Services (54) 340	Petroleum-Integrated (71) .2140,401	Toys & School Supplies (93) .. 783
Copper (92) 1209			*Trucking/Trans Lease (5) 278

*Reviewed in this week's edition

In three parts: This is Part I, the Summary & Index. Part II is Selection & Opinion. Part III is Ratings & Reports. Volume XXXIX, No. 15.

Published weekly by VALUE LINE, INC. 711 Third Avenue, New York, N.Y. 10017
For the confidential use of subscribers. Reprint by permission only. Copyright 1984 by Value Line, Inc.

Value Line Investment Survey

The *Value Line Investment Survey* is perhaps the best known source of investment information and advice of any of the newsletters monitored by the HFD; most libraries and brokerage offices, for example, subscribe to the Survey. Evidence of this wide recognition is the fact that Arnold Bernhard & Co. was able to sell $30,000,000 of its stock to the public in 1983. The Survey is published weekly by Arnold Bernhard & Co., 711 Third Avenue, New York, New York 10017, at an annual price of $365, with a ten-week trial sold for $37. The service is not supplemented by a telephone hotline. Arnold Bernhard & Co. also publishes a number of other newsletters, one of which—the *OTC Special Situations Survey*—is reviewed later in this book.

The Survey is broken into three parts: "Ratings & Reports," which distills a huge amount of statistics and other information about each of 1700 companies into a one-page review and analysis; "Summary & Index," which, in addition to an index to the "Ratings & Reports" provides a breakdown of the 1700 *Value-Line*-rated companies into various categories; and "Selection & Opinion," in which *Value Line* offers its analysis of the prospects for the economy, interest rates, and the stock market; selects and discusses a stock for its "Stock Highlight" section; and reviews the progress of the market.

The Value Line Rating System

The heart of *Value Line's* investment advice is its rating system, which for both safety and timeliness ranks its 1700 companies from "Group I" (the safest or most timely) to "Group V" (the least safe or timely). The distribution of stocks within these groups places the most stocks in the middle so that, at any time, there are 100 Group I and Group V stocks, 300 Group II and Group IV stocks, and 700 Group III stocks. A stock rated Group I for timeliness, of course, may or may not be rated Group I for safety.

Much to the consternation of those who believe that the market is a random affair—and thus cannot be beaten over time—the *Value Line* ranking system has consistently and significantly beaten the market. *Value Line* has tracked the performance of their five groups of stocks since inception in 1965, assuming that the portfolio of Group I stocks changed composition each week, adding those stocks newly rated "I," and selling those that were downgraded.

Value Line's results, which have been verified by academic researchers, show that the rating system consistently beat the market. Over the 21 years since 1965 through the end of 1983, the Group I stocks gained 6627%, the Group II stocks gained 625%, Group III stocks gained 82%, Group IV stocks lost 39%, and Group V stocks lost 88%—perfectly in line with *Value Line's* ranking system. In each year, furthermore, the stocks rated I or II for timeliness outperformed stocks rated III, IV, or V. And in 19 of the 21 years, the breakdown of the yearly returns for each group has been in perfect order from I down to V.

Fischer Black, who used to be a professor at the Massachussetts Institute of Technology (and who now works for Goldman Sachs) and is one of the strongest proponents of the random walk theory, has admitted that the *Value Line* ranking system is an exception to his theory. Though Black continues to believe in the random walk theory, he has said that most investment management organizations would improve their performance if they fired all but one of their security analysts and then provided the remaining analysts with the *Value Line* service.

Other Features in Value Line

In addition to rating 1700 stocks from "I" to "V," *Value Line* also attempts to analyze the market's trend, offering intermediate- to long-term timing advice. This advice typically comes in a recommendation to either remain in common stocks or to stay out of stocks and in bonds. *Value Line* does not recommend how you should divide your

The Value Line Investment Survey

portfolio between cash, bonds, and stocks, however. The conclusion in their June 29, 1984, issue, for example, was "stay predominantly invested in common stocks with favorable Timeliness ratings."

There are an indefinite number of ways in which you can use *Value Line's* rating system to build your own portfolio. You could look at just those stocks rated "I" for timeliness, for example, selling out when they are downgraded to "II" or waiting until they are downgraded to "III" and so forth. Or you could insist on just those stocks that are rated "I" for both timeliness and safety. In fact, *Value Line* each week provides you with a number of "screens" that identify those stocks satisfying a certain criterion. The screens published each week include "High Yielding Stocks," "Biggest 'Free-Flow' Cash Generators," "Widest Discounts From Book Value," "Lowest P/Es," and "Highest P/Es," among others. There are 12 pages of such screens in each week's "Summary & Index."

Performance

Since January 1983, the HFD has tracked the performance of the 100 stocks *Value Line* rates "I" for timeliness. The portfolio the HFD constructed sells a stock when its rating drops below "I" and buys a stock when it first appears in that grouping. Pursuant to its established methodology, the HFD uses the closing price on the day the issue of *Value Line* arrives in the mail (usually Friday).* During 1983, the portfolio gained 34.8%, compared to 22.5% for the S & P 500, making it the third-best performing newsletter for the year among those tracked by the HFD. During the first quarter of 1984, however, during which the S & P 500 dropped by 2.4%, the 100 Group I stocks dropped by 13.1%, for a cumulative gain for the 15-month period of 17.1% — slightly less than the S & P 500's 19.6% gain. On a risk-adjusted basis, however, this portfolio underperformed the market by a greater degree because the portfolio was twice as volatile (risky) as the market as a whole.

---

* *Value Line's* calculations of the performance of their stocks is based on Wednesday's closing price each week, instead of Friday's. For this reason, its performance data will be higher than the HFD's, which uses prices that already have been bid up by *Value Line's* recommendations.

VALUE LINE INVESTMENT SURVEY
Stocks Rated "1" for Timeliness

Period	Gain	Quintile
1983	34.8%	Highest 20%
Risk ranking	5.952	Second highest 20%
% 1983 Closeouts long term	38.8%	Second lowest 20%

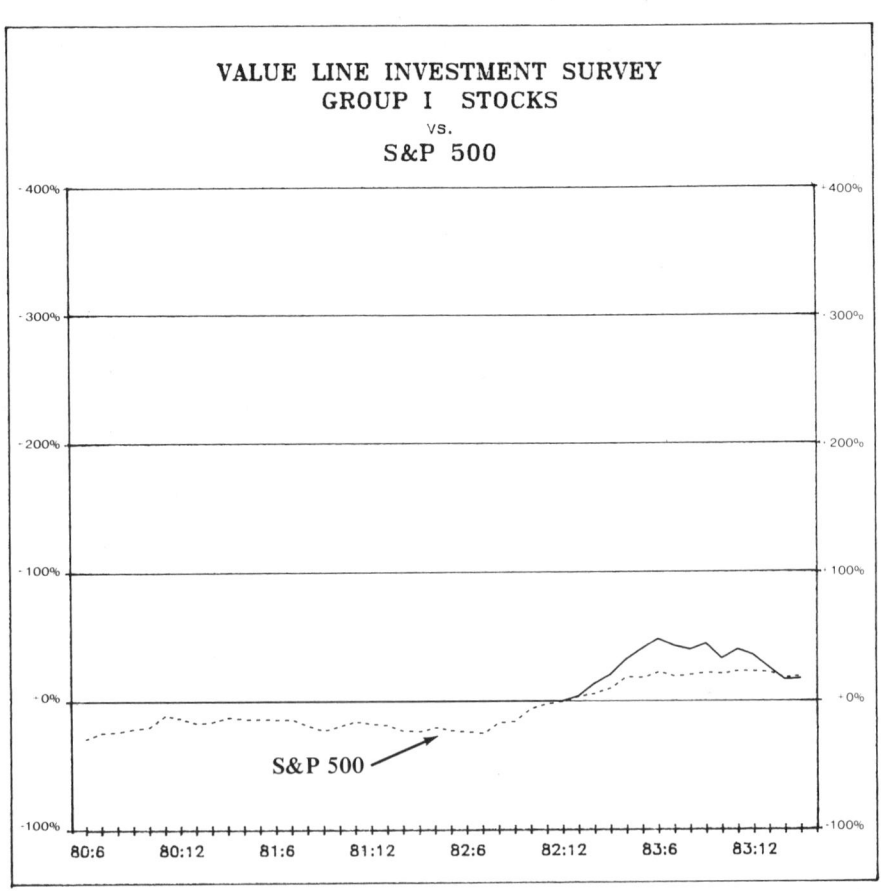

MAY 23, 1983

THE VALUE LINE OTC SPECIAL SITUATIONS SERVICE

Published and Copyrighted 1983 by VALUE LINE, INC., 711 Third Avenue, New York, N.Y. 10017.

The Value Line Special Situations Service is published 24 times a year, on the second and fourth Monday of each month, by Value Line, Inc., 711 Third Ave., New York, N.Y. 10017. Subscription rate: $300 a year. Rights of reproduction and distribution are reserved for those with express permission, in writing, from the publishers.

Editor & Publisher .... Peter A. Shraga
Assistant Editor .... Robert E. Upton
Analyst .... Elizabeth B. Ehrlich
Analyst .... Royal F. Shepard
Analyst .... Robert C. Herz
Analyst .... John A. Conlon

SUPERVISORY REVIEWS • S-566 to S-577
PREVIOUSLY RECOMMENDED SPECIAL SITUATIONS REVIEWED IN THIS ISSUE

Page		Current Recommendation	Price
S-577	Anacomp, Inc.	Hold	19⅝
S-576	Analog Devices, Inc.	Buy/Hold	28⅞
S-567	Analogic Corp.	Buy/Hold	54⅝
S-568	Andrew Corp.	Hold	39¼
S-569	Data Switch Corp.	Hold	56⅛
S-576	Datascope Corp.	Hold	31¾
S-570	Diagnostic Products Corp.	Buy/Hold	27½
S-576	Dynatech Corp.	Hold	35⅝
S-576	Fluke (John) Mfg. Co., Inc.	Hold	30½
S-571	HBO & Co.	Hold	32¾
S-575	Intelligent Systems Corp.	Hold	30⅛
S-575	National Data Corp.	Hold	23⅝
S-572	Radiation Systems, Inc.	Buy/Hold	34⅝
S-575	Scientific-Atlanta, Inc.	Hold	17⅝
S-573	TIE/communications	Buy/Hold	62⅛
S-574	The Ultimate Corp.	Esp. Rec.	21½
S-577	Recent Earnings Reports		

Each supervisory review in this section is a quarterly follow-up to an original recommendation and is not necessarily sufficient by itself to form the basis for an investment decision. A subscriber interested in purchasing any of the securities currently rated "Buy/Hold" or "Especially Recommended", who does not have available Value Line's original four-page recommendation of the security, should feel free to request from us a copy of the original recommendation so that he will have more information on which to base a decision.

THE NEWSWIRE

.... **CGA Computer Associates, Inc.**, normally slated for review in this issue, will be reviewed in our June 13th issue.

.... **Chi-Chi's, Inc.** expects to report fiscal 1982 (ended April 30, 1983) earnings of greater than $9 million (about 60¢ a share) on sales of $90 million.

.... **Community Psychiatric Centers** has agreed to acquire Personal Care Health Services Corp., a provider of home health care services, in exchange for common stock in a pooling-of-interests transaction.

.... **Computer Consoles, Inc.** announced that it will be supplying a $30 million computerized directory assistance system to British Telecom, through its U.K. distributor, Standard Telephone and Cables, plc. The system, the world's largest, will be installed over a two-year period.

.... **Computer Products, Inc.** announced the receipt of an order from Scientific Systems Services, Inc. for measurement and data acquisition equipment valued at up to $4 million. The equipment will be used in the Prairie Island Nuclear Power Plant in Red Wing, Minn.

.... **Electrospace Systems, Inc.** has received three contracts totaling $5.1 million. The first was awarded by Delco Electronics for the design, engineering, and modification kits for installing Fuel Savings Advisory/Cockpit Avionics Systems in KC-135 aircraft. The second, also from Delco, is to support modification of the KC-135 aircraft for inertial navigation systems previously delivered. And the third, from Radiation Systems, Inc., is for an Antenna Servo Control System for positioning of a large diameter antenna.

.... **Haemonetics Corp.**, has announced that it has had discussions with several suitors regarding the possible sale of the company.

.... **Infotron Systems, Inc.** has filed a proposed public offering of 650,000 common shares. Proceeds will be used for debt repayment, working capital, capital expenditures, and for possible acquisitions.

.... On April 1st, **Lumex, Inc.** completed the acquisition of Eagle Performance Systems, Inc., a manufacturer of weight stack exercise equipment. The acquisition, which was for 105,000 shares of Lumex common, is not expected to have a significant impact on 1983 results.

.... **Sensormatic Electronics Corp.** will redeem on June 17th all of its 10% convertible debentures due 2007, at 109.33% of the principal amount plus accrued interest. Each debenture is convertible into Sensormatic common at a rate of $25.37 a share. There are currently $49.8 million of debentures outstanding .... The company also announced the purchase of certain patents and assets from privately owned Rail-Management Communication Systems in order to add closed-circuit television security systems to its product line. Included is a patented rail carriage system that permits a micro-
(Continued on page S-576)

The Value Line OTC Special Situations Service is designed for the experienced investor who understands financial risk and who is able and willing to devote a portion of his portfolio to equities having above-average risk in the hope of realizing exceptional capital gains. (The Value Line OTC Special Situations Service is not a part of The Value Line Investment Survey, which is also published by Value Line, Inc.) Factual material is not guaranteed but is obtained from sources believed to be reliable.

Value Line
OTC Special Situations Service

Value Line OTC Special Situations Service has proven to be one of the best-performing newsletters monitored by the HFD. Published by Arnold Bernhard & Co. (see the write-up about the *Value Line Investment Survey* earlier in this book), its address is 711 Third Avenue, New York, New York 10017. It is priced at $300 per year and $29 for a three-month trial. The bi-weekly newsletter is not supplemented by a telephone hotline.

    Each clearly written and well-organized issue of the Service comes in three sections. The first, entitled "New Recommendation," is a four-page, in-depth analysis of their latest special situation (which almost always is traded over the counter, though occasionally on the American Stock Exchange). The second section is entitled "Summary-Index," and it gives a summary of all special situations that have been recommended in past issues and which have yet to be closed out and provides a list of all special situations currently "especially recommended." The third section, entitled "Supervisory Reviews," is comprised of one-page follow-up analyses on previously recommended situations. Though a few comments about the current stock market are provided in each issue, the Service does not attempt to time the market, nor does it recommend what percentage of your portfolio

The Value Line OTC Special Situations Service

should be in the market and which in cash. You will have to decide for yourself how much of your assets you wish to risk on special situations.

The OTC Service vs. the Investment Survey

Though the Special Situations Service looks at much the same factors in analyzing its companies as does the *Value Line Investment Survey*, the services are separate. The *Special Situations Service*, for example, does not rank its stocks from Groups I through V for either timeliness or safety. The ranking it does provide is on a scale from "Especially Recommended" to "Switch" (with intermediate steps "Buy," "Buy/Hold," and "Hold").

Pursuant to its established methodology, the HFD tracks this service on the basis of the performance of those stocks especially recommended. The number of stocks enjoying this status at any given time is a function of the market. During periods when bull market moves have been particularly strong and speculation is quite high (periods when the prices of their special situations have run up the most), the number of stocks especially recommended drops to less than ten. There were only seven, for example, during the first half of 1983. During bear markets, when special situations perform most poorly, the number grows. During the spring of 1984, for example, as this book goes to press and the bear market in secondary issues is quite severe, the number of stocks especially recommended has grown to 30.

Performance

The HFD has tracked the performance of the Service's especially recommended stocks since mid-1980. In the last six months of that year, they were the best-performing portfolio, gaining 72.3% when the NASDAQ OTC Composite Index was up 28.2%. In 1981, a year when the OTC index was down 3.2%, the Service was down 17.6%—making it the second worst-performing newsletter among those monitored by the HFD. In 1982, when the OTC index was up 18.7%, the Service was up 50.2%—making it the second best-performing letter among those monitored by the HFD. And over the next 15 months, when the OTC index was up 7.9%, the Service gained 2.2%. Over this 45-month period, the *Value Line OTC Special Situations Service* gained 118.1% as compared to 58.9% for the NASDAQ OTC Composite.

This extreme volatility, from being the best or nearly the best in one year to being near the bottom the next year, is indicative of the risk associated with the approach of the Service. The portfolio of the Service especially recommended stocks was more than twice

The Value Line OTC Special Situations Service

as volatile as the S & P 500 over this 45-month period, for example, and 85% more volatile than the NASDAQ Composite. Despite this increased volatility, though, on a risk-adjusted basis the Service nevertheless was almost twice as good a performer as the S & P 500 and almost three times better than the NASDAQ Composite.

VALUE LINE OTC SPECIAL SITUATIONS SERVICE
Especially Recommended Stocks

Period	Gain	Quintile
7/1 to 12/31/80	72.3%	Highest 20%
1981	−17.6%	Lowest 20%
1982	50.2%	Highest 20%
1983	24.1%	Highest 20%
Risk ranking	8.735	Highest 20%
% 1983 Closeouts long term	66.7%	Third highest 20%
% 1982 Closeouts long term	90.0%	Third highest 20%

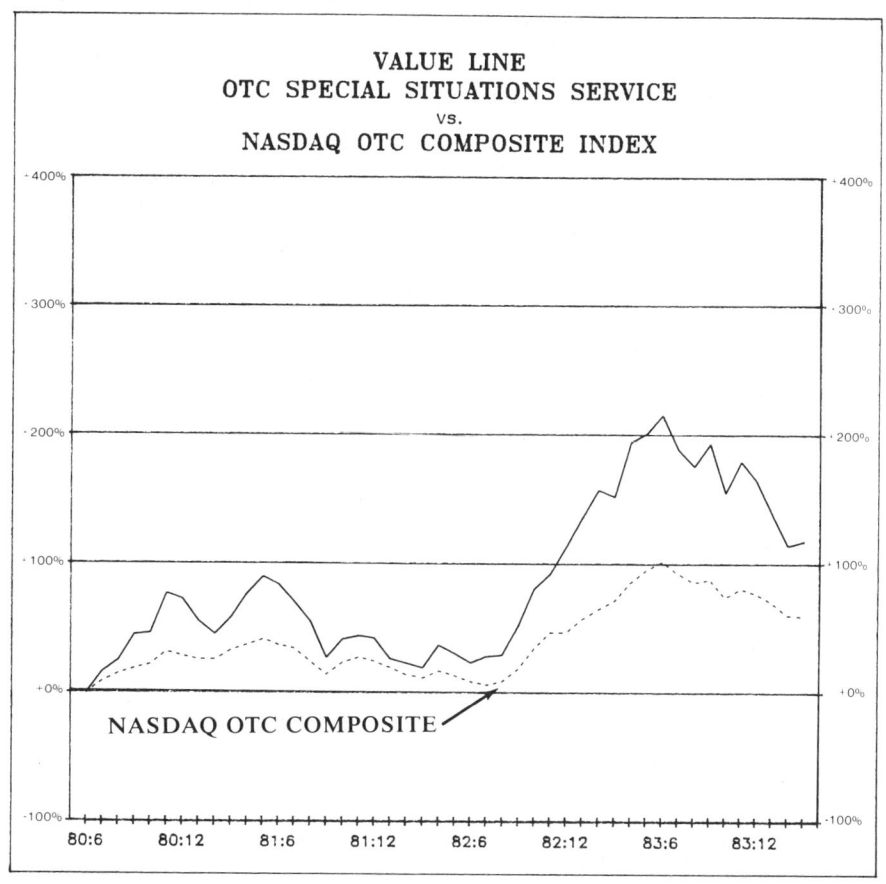

Vol. 13
Number 7
May 5, 1983

THE ZWEIG FORECAST

OUTLOOK AND STRATEGY

Unless Interest Rates jump, the odds of a major correction are low. The Tick shows good Tape action and several Short Selling numbers point to excessive pessimism. Stock & Bond Offerings are a minus but heavy Public buying of Funds is a strong plus.

Investors are 94% Long/6% Cash. Use STOPS (p. 4). Six new stocks were recently recommended (p. 3).

BIG CORRECTION DOUBTFUL

Zweig Unweighted Price Indices, May 3:
NYSE: 196.32
AMEX: 156.87
DOW: 1208

Rarely have so many called for a major correction - 100 to 150 Dow points, but rarely in Wall Street does a widely anticipated event occur. During the recent 113 point rally over a 17-day stretch, an average of 61% of the Advisory Services were either outright bearish or expected a large correction. The contingent was joined the other day by a large institutional brokerage house, news of which ignited a 22-point setback the same day. Certainly, a short-term dip of say 5% or 6% is possible almost anytime...but a careful examination of history shows the odds of a 10% or greater Dow correction are remote at this point.

Since World War II there were ten new Bull Markets prior to this one. The first 10% or greater correction came anywhere between 6 to 32 months after those Bulls began, with a median of 12 months. We're not quite 9 months into the present Bull Market. But the key is that not a single one of those corrections began until TREASURY BILL RATES had risen a minimum of 21% off their lows. The median advance was 32%. To date the low in T' Bill rates was 7.48% last October. A 21% rise implies that rates would have to climb to 9.05% (weekly average) in order to run even minimal risk of a large stock correction. A 32% uptick suggests that 9.87% T' Bill rates are needed even for 50-50 odds of a big correction. To date, the high on Bills was 8.64%, only 15.5% above the low, and that came just before that 113 point Dow surge a few weeks ago. T' Bill rates are now back down to only about 8%. Unless rates balloon, the odds of a major correction are very slim, especially since so many folks think a big drop is coming.

INTERMEDIATE INDEX of 36 technical indicators is a bullish 126. The MONETARY MODEL is neutral (consistent with 3% annualized stock gains since 1940) but is close to turning "extremely bullish" again 33% per year gains).

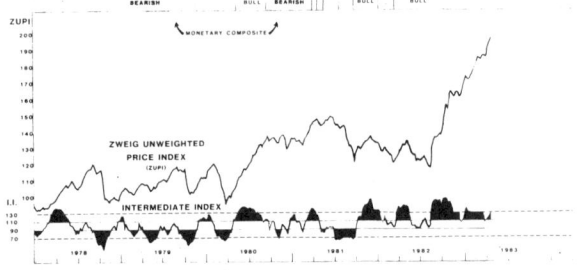

THE ZWEIG FORECAST • 747 THIRD AVENUE, NEW YORK, N.Y. 10017 • 212-644-0040
Published every 3 weeks plus special bulletins when conditions warrant. Includes twice-a-week phone service.
Subscriptions: 6 months $145; 1 year $245; 2 years $415. (unlisted number sent to you separately).

The Zweig Forecast

The Zweig Forecast is published every three weeks by Zweig Securities Advisory Service, Inc. Martin E. Zweig, the editor of *The Zweig Forecast* since its inception in 1971, was a professor of economics and finance at Baruch College of the City University of New York, and for seven more years he was a professor of finance at Iona College. Zweig has a B. S. E. from the Wharton School of Finance, an M. B. A. from the University of Miami, and a Ph. D. in Finance from Michigan State University. Since 1970, Zweig has been a frequent contributor to *Barron's*, and since 1974, he has been a regular rotating panelist on television's "Wall Street Week." Zweig is also director of research for Avatar Associates, an investment counseling firm with more than $300 million of assets under management. An annual subscription to Zweig Forecast costs $245; a six-month subscription is offered for $145. The newsletter is supplemented several times each week by a telephone hotline serice at no extra charge to subscribers. Zweig uses the telephone hotline to make market commentaries, to update his readings of an assortment of technical indicators, and to make almost all of his stock recommendations. The address is P. 0. Box 5345, New York, New York 10150. The telephone number is (202) 644-0040.

What Each Issue Contains

Each tri-weekly, four-page issue of *The Zweig Forecast* reviews a host of sentiment, monetary, and other technical and economic indicators

The Zweig Forecast

and reports Zweig's opinion about the near-term direction of the stock market. Zweig reports the current readings of both his proprietary "Intermediate Index," composed of 36 technical indicators, and his "Monetary Model." Often Zweig compares current stock market patterns and behavior to historical stock market data. For example, in January 1984, the Tick (the Tick is the difference between the number of NYSE stocks last traded on upticks and those last traded on downticks) closed at +300 or greater for three consecutive days. Zweig noted that such three-day strength has only occurred 13 times since 1966 and reported the average subsequent market movement in those instances.

In each issue, Zweig maintains a recommended portfolio of stocks. Frequently, this portfolio also contains stock index futures as a hedge against other positions or as a way of increasing his exposure on one side of the market. Zweig summarizes each recommendation, giving the date and price at which it was originally made, its current price, the recommended weight it is to have in the portfolio, the percentage change since recommendation, the recommended stop-loss point (which he frequently changes), the stock's Performance Rating (see the review in this book of the companion *Zweig Performance Ratings Report*) and its price-earnings ratio. Any changes in the recommended list made over the hotline since the preceding issue of the newsletter are specified.

Performance

The HFD has calculated the performance of investments recommended by *The Zweig Forecast* from July 1, 1980, through March 31, 1984. Zweig's picks gained 23.2% during the last six months of 1980, moved up 24.0% in 1981, and added on 24.6% more in 1982, but it has remained essentially even since the beginning of 1983. Zweig's aggregate gain of 90.3% compares with an advance of 68.2% in the S & P 500 over the same 45-month period. Because the portfolio of Zweig's recommendations outperformed the S & P 500 by 33% with just 25% more risk (volatility), it is one of the few among the letters monitored by the HFD with positive risk-adjusted performance. (See the ranking of all newsletters in the Appendix.)

Up through 1982, the HFD calculated newsletters' performance assuming no commissions, no dividends, and that stocks recommended over telephone hotlines could be bought or sold at the prices prevailing when the hotline was recorded. Since then, as described in the Methodological Prologue to this book, commissions and dividends have been taken into account and hotline recommendations are executed at the average of their high and low prices in trading following the hotline. The figures reported here for *The Zweig Forecast* (as well as for all letters in this book) reflect this second approach. See footnote 1 to the Prologue for a discussion of the impact this had on *The Zweig Forecast's* performance.

Patterns in Zweig's Performance

The decline in *The Zweig Forecast's* performance—from outperforming the market in 1980-2 to underperforming it in 1983-is no doubt attributable to a number of factors, two of which are worth noting here. The first is that, since early 1983, the stock market has not been of the type for which Zweig's methods are best suited. Zweig bases much of his strategy on a momentum model, which advises that a portfolio reorient itself at early signs that a major trend has begun. Some of the most profitable parts of a major trend can be at its initial, explosive stage, and the profits can indeed be large when his momentum model correctly pinpoints an imminent major move. (Zweig was net short the market just prior to the beginning of the bull market in August 1982, for example, but moved to a 70% invested position after the first day the market took off, and was fully invested within a few weeks—much to his subscribers' gain.) However, the price that must be paid for striving to catch the beginning of major market moves is being whipsawed out of the market—at a loss—when the expected move fizzles out. All the expected rallies during 1983 and early 1984 were fizzles, of course, with attendant losses for those following Zweig's recommendations.

The second factor worth noting in the decline in the performance of *The Zweig Forecast* is that the number of investors following its recommendations has grown dramatically—with correspondingly dramatic effects on the prices of recommended securities. When the HFD first began monitoring *The Zweig Forecast* in mid-1980, its recommendations had little noticeable impact on stock prices. By 1982 and 1983, however, a buy recommendation on a stock traded over the counter frequently pushed its price up by 10% or even 20%, with a sell recommendation having a similar effect on the downside. Needless to say, this reduced the probabilities that recommendations would be as profitable as they were when fewer investors were attempting to act upon Zweig's advice.

Changes

Zweig has changed somewhat his investment strategy in light of these factors. His stock recommendations have become more concentrated in relatively larger capitalization companies, for example, on whose stocks a buy or sell recommendation will have less effect. And increasingly, he is altering his portfolio's composition in light of market developments by hedging with stock index futures, not through the sale of stocks. Nevertheless, you should still expect that most all of the gains or losses will be short term. The average holding period for positions closed out in *The Zweig Forecast's* recommended portfolio in 1983 was 70 days, implying an annual turnover rate of 5.2. (This was down from a turnover rate in 1982 of 6.9.)

In addition, despite the greater concentration on companies with larger capitalization, you must still buy and sell recommended stocks with care. As a rule, do not place market orders to buy or sell recommended stocks at the opening following one of Zweig's hotlines. As described further in our introductory section on the use of telephone hotlines, the opening price is rarely the best price of the day. With portfolio turnover as high as it is in the case of *The Zweig Forecast*, the difference in profitability resulting from better prices quickly adds up.

THE ZWEIG FORECAST

Period	Gain	Quintile
7/1 to 12/31/80	+23.2%	Second highest 20%
1981	+24.0%	Highest 20%
1982	+24.6%	Third Highest 20%
1983	+1.5%	Second lowest 20%
Risk ranking	4.186	Second lowest 20%
% 1983 Closeouts long term	7.1%	Lowest 20%
% 1982 Closeouts long term	1.8%	Lowest 20%

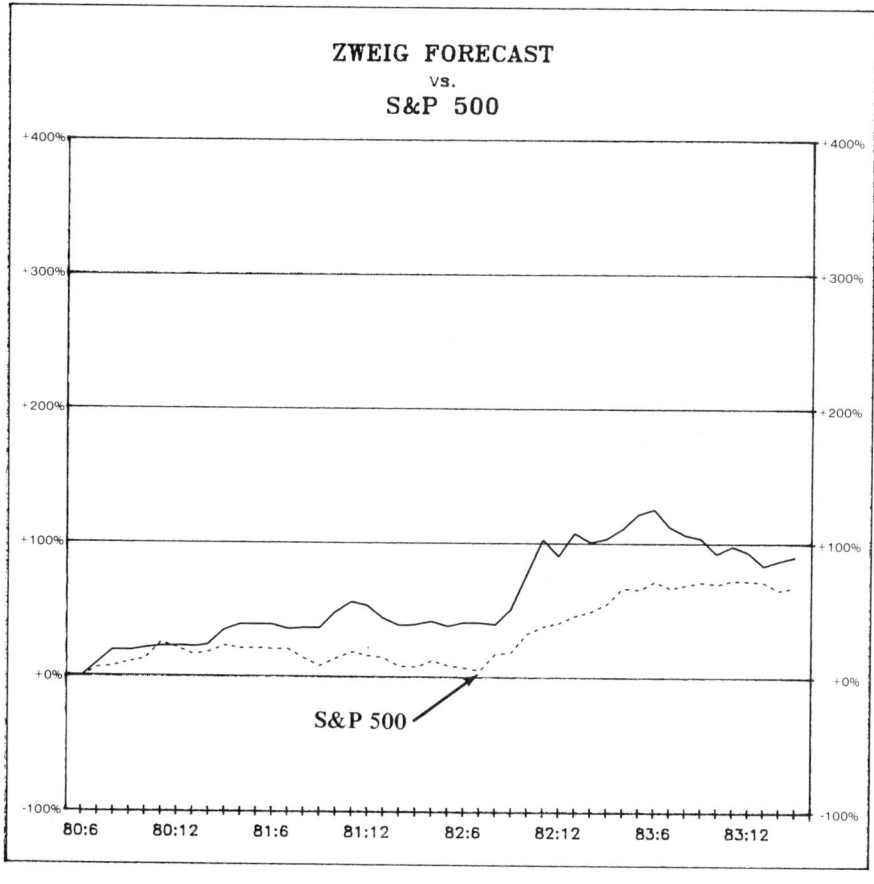

PUBLISHED TWICE A MONTH BY ZWEIG SECURITIES ADVISORY SERVICE, INC., 747 THIRD AVENUE, NEW YORK, N.Y. 10017
NYSE EDITION

Zweig Performance Ratings Report

$150 Annually   June 1983

Zweig's Performance Ratings are computer-generated estimates of how stocks are expected to perform over the next 6 to 12 months relative to each other. The scale runs from 1, the best 5%, down to 9, the worst 5%. As seen in the performance table, there are more stocks in the middle ratings—fewer at the extremes. The Performance Ratings are derived from numerous technical and fundamental variables — each weighted by our proprietary formula. The most significant factors are *Insider Trading, Earnings Trends, Price/Earnings Ratios* and *Rate of Return on Assets*. Other factors include Institutional Trading Activity, Short Interest, Money Flows (using price and volume data), Relative P/Es, "Unexpected" Earnings Changes, Debt/Equity, Book Value and Dividends.

The table shows the results that could have been earned since May 1976, by following the ratings published monthly in our companion service, THE ZWEIG SECURITY SCREEN. These results assume that one switched portfolios each month so as al-

PERFORMANCE RATING RESULTS

Performance Ratings	% of Stocks In Groups	Return 84 Months Since 5/76
1	5%	+639.3%
2	8%	+476.6%
3	12%	+450.7%
4	15%	+357.2%
5	20%	+279.1%
6	15%	+210.6%
7	12%	+174.2%
8	8%	+140.9%
9	5%	+122.3%
All Stocks:		+277.9%

ways to remain in the Number 1 stocks (or Number 2, etc.). The SCREEN publishes the above variables and many more such as Relative Strength, Beta and Industry Rating. In addition, the SCREEN runs numerous "Screens" each month including the Number 1 Performance Ratings; the Number 9's; all stocks with Insider "Buy" and "Sell" signals; best Relative Strength; Dividend Payers Selling Below Book Value; Low Price Stocks; Consistent Growth Stocks and more. Send $15 for a 2-issue trial or $125 for one year.

Also seen in the report you are holding are Insider Trades. They are the sum of all different corporate Insiders who bought or sold in the *last 6 months*. Studies over two decades have shown that stocks with multiple Insider buying tend to beat the market; stocks with multiple selling tend to lag. Data generally ignore transactions of less than 500 shares unless several Insiders make small trades. Insider data are courtesy of Stock Research Corp., 50 Broadway, N.Y., N.Y. 10004.

STOCKS OF INTEREST

CARLING O'KEEFE LTD. (CKB - $15) - CKB rates a 2, putting it in the top 13% of all stocks in the Performance Ratings. Carling O'Keefe is the third largest Canadian brewer. Among the brands it produces are Carling Black Label, Carlsberg and Colt 45. Earlier this year CKB won the right to brew Miller beer in Canada, which has greatly improved the company's competitive position in its home market. The new Miller brand, improving sales of its other brands, and aggressive pricing policies which are increasing its profit margins should ensure that Carling O'Keefe's recent excellent earnings record will continue. CKB reported EPS for the quarter ended March 31, 1983 at $.34, versus $.07 the same quarter the previous year. Annual earnings grew nearly 50% for the fiscal year ended March 31, 1982, while sales grew 22%. About 75% of Carling O'Keefe's EPS come from its brewing business, the remainder is from its wine and oil and gas subsidiaries. The only negative for CKB is its Star Oil and Gas subsidiary whose performance is being hindered by a still sluggish Canadian economy and by recently enacted tax hikes.

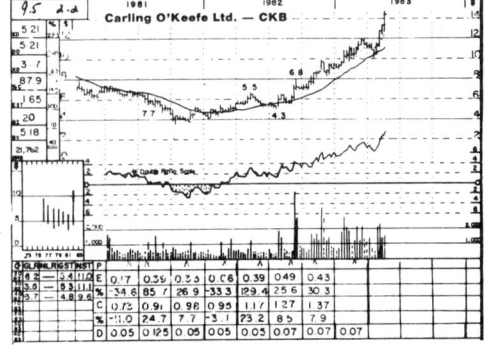
Courtesy: Mansfield

Nevertheless the earnings prospects for CKB appear excellent and the stock recently broke to a new high. The company has an excellent balance sheet with little debt. With a PE of only 9, CKB could be considered for purchase. A stop around $12.50 is recommended.

Zweig Performance Ratings Report

Zweig Performance Ratings Report (ZPRR) is published twice monthly by Zweig Securities Advisory Service, Inc., P. O. Box 5345, New York, New York 10150, the same firm that publishes *The Zweig Forecast*. The telephone number is (212) 644-0040. ZPRR is edited by Joe DiMenna and Carol Whitehead, using research and computer models created by Martin E. Zweig, editor of *The Zweig Forecast*. The subscription rate is $150 per year. A trial subscription is offered for $30. The service was founded in 1981.

The first ZPRR issue of each month reviews about 1400 stocks traded on the New York Stock Exchange. The other issue, which is mailed approximately two weeks later, surveys about 600 stocks traded on the American Stock Exchange and 1000 stocks traded over the counter. For each stock, ZPRR lists a Performance Rating, the stock price, and the number of reported purchase and sale transactions by insiders in the preceding six months. Any change in performance rating is noted. Those stocks ranked most highly and those rated the least promising are listed separately. In addition, those stocks which, in the last three months, have experienced three or more insider buyers and no sellers or three or more insider sellers and no buyers are reported separately. Three stocks are reviewed in greater depth in each issue and are recommended either for purchase or as short-sale candidates. Stop-loss points are specified for each recommendation. Unlike *The Zweig Forecast*, which often advises subscribers to place a particular percentage of their assets in cash equivalents, ZPRR assumes that its subscribers are fully invested at all times; market timing advice is provided by changing the ratio of buy recommendations to short sale selections.

Performance Ratings

The key data presented each month for the almost 3,000 stocks followed by ZPRR are the Performance Ratings. Zweig's Performance Ratings are computer-generated estimates of how stocks are expected to perform over the next six to twelve months relative to each other. The scale runs from "1," the best 5%, to "9," the worst 5%. The Performance Ratings are derived from numerous technical and fundamental variables, the most significant of which are insider trading, earnings trends, price-earnings ratios, and the rate of return on assets. Other factors include institutional trading activity, short interest, money flows, relative price-earnings ratios, "unexpected" earnings changes, debt-to-equity ratios, book value, and dividends.

According to ZPRR, these performance ratings, published in a comparison services, Zweig Security Screen, since May, 1976, have proven to be an accurate instrument for forecasting individual stock movements. ZPRR claims that stocks rated "1" have markedly outperformed those rated "2," which, in turn, have outperformed those rated "3," and on downward through nine levels of ratings. Stocks rated "1" have increased in price 2-1/2 times as much as the average stock, rated 5, which, in turn, has performed 2-1/2 times as well as stocks rated in the lowest category, "9".

In light of this historical performance data, it is perplexing that few of ZPRR's purchase recommendations are rated in the highest category at the time of recommendation. Similarly, only some of ZPRR's stocks recommended for short sale are given the lowest Performance Rating. In May 1984, for example, of 17 stocks recommended for purchase only two had performance ratings of "1." Three had "2" ratings, six had "3" ratings, two had "4" ratings, and three had "5" ratings (with one having no rating at all). In addition, of eight short sale recommendations, only one had a "9" rating.

Performance of Performance Ratings

The HFD has calculated the performance of stocks recommended for purchase or short sale in the *Zweig Performance Ratings Report* since the beginning of 1983. These stock selections advanced 17.4% in 1983 but gave up 12.6% in the first quarter of 1984, for an aggregate 15-month gain of 2.7%. In comparison, the S & P 500 gained 22.5% in 1983 but receded 2.4% in the first three months of 1984, for an aggregate gain of 19.6%. ZPRR's portfolio was twice as volatile as the S & P 500 over this period, so it underperformed the market on a risk-adjusted basis as well.

ZWEIG PERFORMANCE RATINGS REPORT

Period	Gain	Quintile
1983	17.4%	Second highest 20%
Risk ranking	5.662	Third highest 20%
% 1983 Closeouts long term	32.3%	Lowest 20%

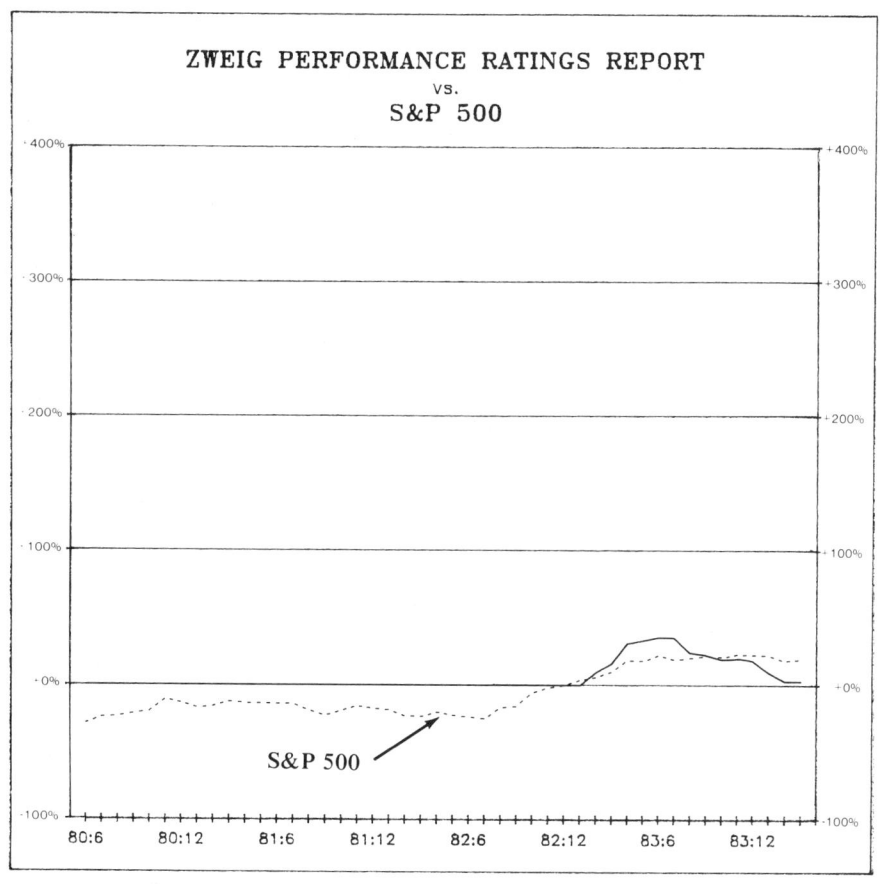

Appendix A

Newsletter Performance

The following tables rank newsletters on the basis of their aggregate performance. (The next appendix ranks them according to their risk-adjusted performance.) Because various newsletters were followed for various periods of time, this appendix is broken into eight different tables. They show cumulative portfolio performance over the following eight periods:

1. June 30, 1980, to March 31, 1984
2. January 1, 1981, to March 31, 1984
3. January 1, 1982, to March 31, 1984
4. January 1, 1983, to March 31, 1984
5. June 30, 1980, to December 31, 1980
6. Calendar year 1981
7. Calendar year 1982
8. Calendar year 1983

Also ranked in each of these eight tables is the performance of the Standard & Poor's 500 Index (adjusted to include dividends), as well as the performance of a portfolio that was fully invested in Treasury bills throughout. The figures in these tables were calculated by *The Hulbert Financial Digest* according to its established methodology. Please refer to the introduction to this book for a complete description of that methodology.

A-1. Performance from June 30, 1980 to March 31, 1984

1. Green's Commodity Market Comments +172.7%
   (Portfolio for Traders)
2. The Dines Letter (Average of 6 Portfolios) +139.3%
   a. List #6 (Trading Portfolio) +373.1%
   b. List #4 (Growth Portfolio) +183.5%
   c. List #2 (Speculative Portfolio) +177.3%
   d. List #3 (Income Portfolio) + 66.7%
   e. List #1 (Moderate Risk Port.) + 56.1%
   f. List #5 (Precious Metals Port.) − 20.9%
3. Growth Stock Outlook (Supervised Portfolio) +133.2%
4. Market Logic (Master Portfolio) +118.2%
5. Value Line OTC Special Situations Service +118.1%
6. Zweig Forecast + 90.3%
7. Professional Investor (Average of 4 Portfolios) + 73.9%
   a. AMEX Scan +145.8%
   b. OTC Scan + 89.6%
   c. NYSE Scan + 51.9%
   d. Investment Grade Stocks Scan + 8.2%

STANDARD & POOR'S 500 INDEX (Including Dividends) + 68.2%

8. Standard & Poor's Outlook (Average of 4 Portfolios) + 62.2%
   a. Speculative Stocks + 69.0%
   b. Income Stocks + 63.9%
   c. Growth Stocks + 58.4%
   d. Foundation Stocks + 57.6%
9. Dow Theory Forecasts (Average of 4 Portfolios) + 51.7%
   a. Investment Stocks + 65.5%
   b. Growth Stocks + 55.7%
   c. Income Stocks + 48.3%
   d. Speculative Stocks + 37.3%

RISK-FREE RATE OF RETURN (A T-Bill Only Portfolio) + 49.5%

10. Professional Tape Reader (Model Portfolio) + 21.4%
11. International Harry Schultz Letter + 15.9%
    (U.S. Stocks Portfolio)
12. United Business & Investment Reports + 14.6%
    (Average of 4 Portfolios)
    a. Income Stocks + 24.2%
    b. Cyclical Stocks + 18.5%
    c. Growth Stocks + 1.2%
13. Howard Ruff's Financial Success Report + 11.5%
14. Heim Investment Letter + 8.8%
15. Holt Investment Advisory − 16.2%
16. Granville Market Letter − 39.2%
    (Aggressive Traders' Portfolio)

A-2. Performance from January 1, 1981 to March 31, 1984

1. Green's Commodity Market Comments (Portfolio for Traders)		+124.8%
2. The Dines Letter (Average of 6 Portfolios)		+114.5%
a. List #6 (Trading Portfolio)	+296.4%	
b. List #4 (Growth Portfolio)	+167.8%	
c. List #2 (Speculative Portfolio)	+162.0%	
d. List #3 (Income Portfolio)	+ 57.5%	
e. List #1 (Moderate Risk Port.)	+ 41.7%	
f. List #5 (Precious Metals Port.)	− 38.7%	
3. Market Logic (Master Portfolio)		+ 83.5%
4. Growth Stock Outlook (Supervised Portfolio)		+ 74.0%
5. Zweig Forecast		+ 54.5%
RISK-FREE RATE OF RETURN (A T-Bill Only Portfolio)		+ 41.3%
6. Professional Investor (Average of 4 Portfolios)		+ 39.3%
a. AMEX Scan	+ 83.5%	
b. OTC Scan	+ 45.0%	
c. NYSE Scan	+ 32.7%	
d. Investment Grade Stocks Scan	− 3.8%	
STANDARD & POOR'S 500 INDEX (Including Dividends)		+ 38.3%
7. Standard & Poor's Outlook (Average of 4 Portfolios)		+ 37.1%
a. Speculative Stocks	+ 41.3%	
b. Income Stocks	+ 39.0%	
c. Growth Stocks	+ 34.7%	
d. Foundation Stocks	+ 33.4%	
8. Value Line OTC Special Situations Service		+ 26.5%
9. Speculator (Selected Stocks of the Week)		+ 26.3%
10. Dow Theory Forecasts (Average of 4 Portfolios)		+ 24.9%
a. Investment Stocks	+ 35.9%	
b. Income Stocks	+ 29.1%	
c. Growth Stocks	+ 27.1%	
d. Speculative Stocks	+ 7.7%	
11. Howard Ruff's Financial Success Report		+ 19.6%
12. Dow Theory Letters		+ 19.3%
13. Harry Browne's Special Reports (Variable Portfolio)		+ 18.5%
14. Cabot Market Letter (Model Portfolio)		+ 13.0%
15. Heim Investment Letter		+ 6.0%
16. United Business & Investment Reports (Average of 3 Portfolios)		− 0.5%
a. Income Stocks	+ 18.7%	
b. Cyclical Stocks	− 7.6%	
c. Growth Stocks	− 12.6%	
17. Professional Tape Reader (Model Portfolio)		− 1.2%
18. Holt Investment Advisory		− 10.7%

19. International Harry Schultz Letter (U.S. Stocks Portfolio)		− 18.0%
20. RHM Survey of Warrants, Options, & Low-Priced Stocks		− 32.0%
21. Granville Market Letter (Aggressive Traders' Portfolio)		− 45.1%

A-3. Performance from January 1, 1982 to March 31, 1984

1. Tony Henfrey's Gold Letter (Long-term Gold Share Portfolio)		+163.0%
2. The Dines Letter (Average of 6 Portfolios)		+122.5%
a. List #6 (Trading Portfolio)	+356.7%	
b. List #4 (Growth Portfolio)	+134.5%	
c. List #2 (Speculative Portfolio)	+126.8%	
d. List #1 (Moderate Risk Port.)	+ 78.0%	
e. List #3 (Income Portfolio)	+ 37.9%	
f. List #5 (Precious Metals Port.)	+ 1.2%	
3. Green's Commodity Market Comments (Portfolio for Traders)		+101.4%
4. Market Logic (Master Portfolio)		+ 69.0%
5. Chartist (Actual Cash Account)		+ 56.3%
6. Growth Stock Outlook (Supervised Portfolio)		+ 55.6%
7. Value Line OTC Special Situations Service		+ 53.6%
8. Professional Investor (Average of 4 Portfolios)		+ 45.9%
a. AMEX Scan	+ 97.0%	
b. OTC Scan	+ 51.7%	
c. NYSE Scan	+ 41.4%	
d. Investment Grade Stocks Scan	− 6.6%	
STANDARD & POOR'S 500 INDEX (Including Dividends)		+ 45.2%
9. Dessauer's Journal (International Portfolio)		+ 44.3%
10. Speculator (Selected Stocks of the Week)		+ 41.6%
11. RHM Survey of Warrants, Options, & Low-Priced Stocks		+ 36.3%
12. Dow Theory Forecasts (Average of 4 Portfolios)		+ 29.4%
a. Investment Stocks	+ 41.8%	
b. Income Stocks	+ 40.6%	
c. Growth Stocks	+ 20.8%	
d. Speculative Stocks	+ 14.4%	
13. Kinsman's Low-Risk Advisory Letter (Model Portfolio)		+ 29.0%
14. Harry Browne's Special Reports (Variable Portfolio)		+ 27.3%

15. Standard & Poor's Outlook (Average of 4 Portfolios)   + 26.1%
    a. Speculative Stocks   + 43.5%
    b. Income Stocks   + 25.5%
    c. Foundation Stocks   + 22.6%
    d. Growth Stocks   + 12.6%
16. Zweig Forecast   + 24.6%

RISK-FREE RATE OF RETURN (A T-Bill Only Portfolio)   + 23.7%

17. Howard Ruff's Financial Success Report   + 22.6%
18. United Business & Investment Reports   + 10.4%
    (Average of 3 Portfolios)
    a. Income Stocks   + 23.4%
    b. Cyclical Stocks   + 6.0%
    c. Growth Stocks   + 1.7%
19. Cabot Market Letter (Model Portfolio)   + 10.2%
20. Dow Theory Letters   + 8.3%
21. Professional Tape Reader (Model Portfolio)   + 5.9%
22. Professional Timing Service   + 1.1%
23. International Harry Schultz Letter   − 0.6%
    (U.S. Stocks Portfolio)
24. Heim Investment Letter   − 4.0%
25. Holt Investment Advisory   − 17.3%
26. Granville Market Letter   − 43.2%
    (Aggressive Traders' Portfolio)

A-4. Performance from January 1, 1983 to March 31, 1984

1. The Dines Letter (Average of 6 Portfolios)   +108.8%
   a. List #6 (Trading Portfolio)   +377.4%
   b. List #2 (Speculative Portfolio)   +107.8%
   c. List #4 (Growth Portfolio)   + 87.4%
   d. List #1 (Moderate Risk Port.)   + 54.6%
   e. List #3 (Income Portfolio)   + 14.8%
   f. List #5 (Precious Metals Port.)   + 10.6%
2. Prudent Speculator   + 56.7%
3. Addison Report (Average of 2 Portfolios)   + 51.3%
   a. Speculative Stocks   + 79.2%
   b. Conservative Stocks   + 23.3%
4. Tony Henfrey's Gold Letter   + 36.1%
   (Long-term Gold Share Portfolio)
5. Green's Commodity Market Comments   + 35.8%
   (Portfolio for Traders)
6. Growth Stock Outlook (Supervised Portfolio)   + 25.5%
7. Dessauer's Journal (International Portfolio)   + 20.1%
8. Market Logic (Master Portfolio)   + 19.8%

STANDARD & POOR'S 500 INDEX (Including Dividends)		+ 19.6%
9. Value Line Investment Survey (Stocks Rated I for "Timeliness")		+ 17.1%
10. Switch Fund Advisory (Model Portfolio)		+ 17.1%
11. Growth Fund Guide (Average of 4 Portfolios)		+ 15.0%
a. Quality Growth Funds	+ 18.9%	
b. Special Situations Funds	+ 18.9%	
c. Growth Funds	+ 16.0%	
d. Aggressive Growth Funds	+ 6.3%	
12. Professional Investor (Average of 4 Portfolios)		+ 11.8%
a. AMEX Scan	+ 41.6%	
b. OTC Scan	+ 24.8%	
b. NYSE Scan	+ 5.1%	
c. Investment Grade Stocks Scan	− 24.5%	
RISK-FREE RATE OF RETURN (A T-Bill Only Portfolio)		+ 11.6%
13. RHM Survey of Warrants, Options & Low-Priced Stocks		+ 10.6%
14. Peter Dag Investment Letter (Model Portfolio)		+ 10.3%
15. Chartist (Average of 2 Portfolios)		+ 19.9%
a. Actual Cash Account	+ 15.5%	
b. Traders' Stocks	+ 4.2%	
16. Kinsman's Low-Risk Advisory Letter (Model Portfolio)		+ 9.1%
17. Harry Browne's Special Reports (Variable Portfolio)		+ 8.6%
18. Dow Theory Forecasts (Average of 4 Portfolios)		+ 8.4%
a. Income Stocks	+ 17.0%	
b. Investment Stocks	+ 10.4%	
c. Growth Stocks	+ 5.1%	
d. Speculative Stocks	+ 0.9%	
19. Standard & Poor's Outlook (Average of 4 Portfolios)		+ 6.7%
a. Income Stocks	+ 13.5%	
b. Speculative Stocks	+ 9.6%	
c. Foundation Stocks	+ 2.3%	
d. Growth Stocks	+ 1.4%	
20. Charted Course (Model Portfolio)		+ 5.9%
21. Telephone Switch Newsletter (Average of 2 Portfolios)		+ 5.8%
a. Equities/Cash Portfolio	+ 15.2%	
b. Gold/Equities/Cash Portfolio	− 3.6%	
22. International Harry Schultz Letter (U.S. Stocks Portfolio)		+ 5.2%
23. Heim Investment Letter		+ 4.7%
24. Professional Timing Service		+ 3.7%
25. Zweig Performance Ratings		+ 2.7%
26. Value Line OTC Special Situations Service		+ 2.2%

27. Indicator Digest + 1.6%
28. Zweig Forecast + 0.0%
29. Systems and Forecasts − 0.5%
30. United Business & Investment Reports − 1.5%
    (Average of 3 Portfolios)
    a. Income Stocks + 8.5%
    b. Growth Stocks − 4.7%
    c. Cyclical Stocks − 8.3%
31. Speculator (Selected Stocks of the Week) − 2.5%
32. New Issues − 3.9%
33. Holt Investment Advisory − 6.3%
34. Dow Theory Letters − 9.1%
35. High Technology Investments − 9.9%
    (Average of 2 Portfolios)
    a. Long-term Portfolio + 0.6%
    b. "Trigger Price Advisory" − 20.4%
       Trading Portfolio
36. New Issue Investor − 12.4%
37. Howard Ruff's Financial Success Report − 14.7%
38. Cabot Market Letter (Model Portfolio) − 17.0%
39. California Technology Stock Letter − 17.1%
    (Model Portfolio)
40. Nicholson Report (Average of 2 Portfolios) − 18.1%
    a. Stocks for the Long-term Investor − 17.5%
    b. Stocks for the Aggressive Trader − 18.8%
41. Professional Tape Reader (Model Portfolio) − 18.6%
42. Granville Market Letter − 19.1%
    (Aggressive Traders Portfolio)
43. Successful Options Investing (Hedged Portfolio) − 43.7%
44. Option Advisor (Average of 2 Portfolios) − 64.8%
    a. Aggressive Portfolio − 62.6%
    b. Conservative Portfolio − 67.0%

A-5. Performance for Last 6 Months of 1980

1. Value Line OTC Special Situations Service + 72.3%
2. International Harry Schultz Letter + 41.2%
   (U.S. Stocks Portfolio)
3. Growth Stock Outlook (Supervised Portfolio) + 34.0%
4. Zweig Forecast + 23.2%
5. Professional Investor (Average of 4 Portfolios) + 22.9%
   a. AMEX Scan + 34.0%
   b. OTC Scan + 30.8%
   c. NYSE Scan + 14.4%
   d. Investment Grade Stocks Scan + 12.5%
6. Professional Tape Reader (Model Portfolio) + 22.9%

7. Dow Theory Forecasts (Average of 4 Portfolios)   + 21.7%
    a. Speculative Stocks   + 27.5%
    b. Growth Stocks   + 22.5%
    c. Investment Stocks   + 21.8%
    d. Income Stocks   + 14.9%

STANDARD & POOR'S 500 INDEX (Including Dividends)   + 21.7%

8. Green's Commodity Market Comments (Portfolio for Traders)   + 21.3%
9. Market Logic (Master Portfolio)   + 18.9%
10. Standard & Poor's Outlook (Average of Portfolios)   + 18.3%
    a. Speculative Stocks   + 19.6%
    b. Foundation Stocks   + 18.1%
    c. Income Stocks   + 17.9%
    d. Growth Stocks   + 17.6%
11. United Business & Investment Reports (Average of 3 Portfolios)   + 16.2%
    a. Cyclical Stocks   + 28.2%
    b. Growth Stocks   + 15.8%
    c. Income Stocks   + 4.6%
12. The Dines Letter (Average of 6 Portfolios)   + 12.6%
    a. List #5 (Precious Metals Port.)   + 28.9%
    b. List #6 (Trading Portfolio)   + 19.3%
    c. List #1 (Moderate Risk Port.)   + 10.2%
    d. List #2 (Speculative Portfolio)   + 5.8%
    e. List #3 (Income Portfolio)   + 5.8%
    f. List #4 (Growth Portfolio)   + 5.8%
13. Granville Market Letter (Aggressive Traders' Portfolio)   + 10.6%

RISK-FREE RATE OF RETURN (A T-Bill Only Portfolio)   + 5.8%

14. Heim Investment Letter   + 2.6%
15. Holt Investment Advisory   − 6.1%
16. Howard Ruff's Financial Success Report   − 6.8%

A-6. 1981 Gain

1. Zweig Forecast   + 24.0%

RISK-FREE RATE OF RETURN (A T-Bill Only Portfolio)   + 14.2%

2. Growth Stock Outlook (Supervised Portfolio)   + 11.8%
3. Green's Commodity Market Comments (Portfolio for Traders)   + 11.6%
4. Heim Investment Letter   + 10.5%
5. Dow Theory Letters   + 10.2%

6. Standard & Poor's Outlook (Average of 4 Portfolios)   + 9.4%
    a. Growth Stocks   + 19.6%
    b. Income Stocks   + 10.8%
    c. Foundation Stocks   + 8.8%
    d. Speculative Stocks   − 1.6%
7. Market Logic (Master Portfolio)   + 8.6%
8. Holt Investment Advisory   + 7.9%
9. Cabot Market Letter (Model Portfolio)   + 2.5%
10. Howard Ruff's Financial Success Report   − 2.4%
11. Dow Theory Forecasts (Average of 4 Portfolios)   − 3.3%
    a. Growth Stocks   + 5.2%
    b. Investment Stocks   − 4.2%
    c. Speculative Stocks   − 5.9%
    d. Income Stocks   − 8.2%
12. Granville Market Letter (Aggressive Traders Portfolio)   − 3.3%
13. Professional Investor (Average of 4 Portfolios)   − 3.6%
    a. Investment Grade Stocks Scan   + 3.0%
    b. OTC Scan   − 4.4%
    c. NYSE Scan   − 6.1%
    d. AMEX Scan   − 6.9%
14. The Dines Letter (Average of 6 Portfolios)   − 4.8%
    a. List #2 (Speculative Port.)   + 15.5%
    b. List #3 (Income Portfolio)   + 14.2%
    c. List #4 (Growth Portfolio)   + 14.2%
    d. List #6 (Trading Portfolio)   − 13.2%
    e. List #1 (Moderate Risk Port.)   − 20.4%
    f. List #5 (Precious Metals Port)   − 39.4%

STANDARD & POOR'S 500 INDEX (Including Dividends)   − 4.9%

15. Professional Tape Reader (Model Portfolio)   − 6.7%
16. Harry Browne's Special Reports (Variable Portfolio)   − 6.9%
17. United Business & Investment Reports (Average of 3 Portfolios)   − 10.3%
    a. Income Stocks   − 3.8%
    b. Cyclical Stocks   − 12.9%
    c. Growth Stocks   − 14.1%
18. Speculator (Selected Stocks of the Week)   − 10.8%
19. International Harry Schultz Letter (U.S. Stocks Portfolio)   − 17.5%
20. Value Line OTC Special Situations Service   − 17.6%
21. RHM Survey of Warrants, Options & Low-Priced Stocks   − 50.1%

Newsletter Performance

A-7. 1982 Gain

1. Tony Henfrey's Gold Letter (Long-term Gold Share Portfolio)	+ 93.3%
2. Value Line OTC Special Situations Service	+ 50.2%
3. Green's Commodity Market Comments (Portfolio for Traders)	+ 48.4%
4. Speculator (Selected Stocks of the Week)	+ 45.3%
5. Howard Ruff's Financial Success Report	+ 43.8%
6. Market Logic (Master Portfolio)	+ 41.0%
8. Chartist (Actual Cash Account)	+ 35.4%
7. Cabot Market Letter (Model Portfolio)	+ 32.8%
9. Professional Tape Reader (Model Portfolio)	+ 30.0%
10. Professional Investor (Average of 4 Portfolios)	+ 29.7%
a. Amex Scan + 39.1%	
b. NYSE Scan + 34.5%	
c. Invesment Grade Stocks Scan + 23.7%	
d. OTC Scan + 21.6%	
11. Zweig Forecast	+ 24.6%
12. Growth Stock Outlook (Supervised Portfolio)	+ 24.0%
13. RHM Survey of Warrants, Options & Low-Priced Stocks	+ 23.2%
STANDARD & POOR'S 500 INDEX (Including Dividends)	**+ 21.6%**
14. Dessauer's Journal (International Portfolio)	+ 20.1%
15. Dow Theory Forecasts (Average of 4 Portfolios)	+ 19.2%
a. Investment Stocks + 28.4%	
b. Income Stocks + 20.2%	
c. Growth Stocks + 14.9%	
d. Speculative Stocks + 13.4%	
16. Dow Theory Letters	+ 19.2%
17. Kinsman's Low-Risk Advisory Letter (Model Portfolio)	+ 18.3%
18. Standard & Poor's Outlook (Average of 4 Portfolios)	+ 18.1%
a. Speculative Stocks + 31.0%	
b. Foundation Stocks + 19.9%	
c. Growth Stocks + 11.0%	
d. Income Stocks + 10.6%	
19. Harry Browne's Special Reports (Variable Portfolio)	+ 17.2%
20. United Business & Investment Reports (Average of 3 Portfolios)	+ 12.0%
a. Cyclical Stocks + 15.6%	
b. Income Stocks + 13.8%	
c. Growth Stocks + 6.7%	
RISK-FREE RATE OF RETURN (A T-Bill Only Portfolio)	**+ 10.9%**
21. The Dines Letter (Average of 6 Portfolios)	+ 9.4%

Newsletter Performance

	a. List #4 (Growth Portfolio)	+ 25.1%	
	b. List #3 (Income Portfolio)	+ 20.1%	
	c. List #1 (Moderate Risk Port.)	+ 15.1%	
	d. List #2 (Speculative Portfolio)	+ 9.1%	
	e. List #6 (Trading Portfolio)	− 4.3%	
	f. List #5 (Precious Metals Port.)	− 8.4%	
22.	Professional Timing Service		− 2.4%
23.	International Harry Schultz Letter (U.S. Stocks Portfolio)		− 5.5%
24.	Heim Investment Letter		− 8.4%
25.	Holt Investment Advisory		− 11.8%
26.	Granville Market Letter (Aggressive Traders' Portfolio)		− 29.8%

A-8. 1983 Gain

1.	Prudent Speculator		+ 72.8%
2.	Addison Report (Average of 2 Portfolios)		+ 59.3%
	a. Speculative Stocks	+ 89.6%	
	b. Conservative Stocks	+ 28.9%	
3.	Value Line Investment Survey (Stocks Rated I for "Timeliness")		+ 34.8%
4.	Growth Stock Outlook (Supervised Portfolio)		+ 33.1%
5.	The Dines Letter (Average of 6 Portfolios)		+ 28.6%
	a. List #6 (Trading Portfolio)	+ 90.1%	
	b. List #1 (Moderate Risk Port.)	+ 43.5%	
	c. List #3 (Income Portfolio)	+ 13.2%	
	d. List #5 (Precious Metals Port.)	+ 9.1%	
	e. List #2 (Speculative Portfolio)	+ 8.6%	
	f. List #4 (Growth Portfolio)	+ 7.0%	
6.	Market Logic (Master Portfolio)		+ 28.0%
7.	Chartist (Average of 2 Portfolios)		+ 27.8%
	a. Traders' Stocks	+ 30.5%	
	b. Actual Cash Account	+ 25.1%	
8.	Growth Fund Guide (Average of 4 Portfolios)		+ 24.8%
	a. Special Situations Funds	+ 30.3%	
	b. Growth Fund	+ 24.2%	
	c. Aggressive Growth Funds	+ 22.4%	
	d. Quality Growth Funds	+ 22.4%	
9.	Value Line OTC Special Situations Service		+ 24.1%
	STANDARD & POOR'S 500 INDEX (Including Dividends)		+ 22.5%
10.	Professional Timing Service		+ 22.4%
11.	Dessauer's Journal (International Portfolio)		+ 21.0%
12.	Green's Commodity Market Comments (Portfolio for Traders)		+ 20.2%

13. Professional Investor (Average of 4 Portfolios)   + 18.3%
    a. AMEX Scan   + 48.2%
    b. OTC Scan   + 29.3%
    c. NYSE Scan   + 14.1%
    d. Investment Grade Stocks Scan   − 18.5%
14. Standard & Poor's Outlook   + 18.0%
    (Average of 4 Portfolios)
    a. Income Stocks   + 28.0%
    b. Speculative Stocks   + 21.4%
    c. Foundation Stocks   + 12.3%
    d. Growth Stocks   + 10.4%
15. Zweig Performance Ratings   + 17.4%
16. Switch Fund Advisory (Model Portfolio)   + 16.4%
17. Dow Theory Forecasts (Average of 4 Portfolios)   + 14.9%
    a. Income Stocks   + 20.5%
    b. Investment Stocks   + 15.6%
    c. Growth Stocks   + 11.7%
    d. Speculative Stocks   + 11.7%
18. Indicator Digest   + 11.8%
19. New Issues   + 11.6%

RISK-FREE RATE OF RETURN (A T-Bill Only Portfolio)   + 9.0%

20. Kinsman's Low-Risk Advisory Letter   + 9.0%
    (Model Portfolio)
21. Speculator's (Selected Stocks of the Week)   + 8.8%
22. RHM Survey of Warrants, Options, & Low-Priced Stocks   + 8.6%
23. Harry Browne's Special Reports   + 8.0%
    (Variable Portfolio)
24. United Business & Investment Reports   + 7.8%
    (Average of 3 Portfolios)
    a. Income Stocks   + 14.7%
    b. Cyclical Stocks   + 7.0%
    c. Growth Stocks   + 1.7%
25. Cabot Market Letter (Model Portfolio)   + 7.3%
26. Tony Henfrey's Gold-Letter   + 6.9%
    (Long-term Gold Share Portfolio)
27. New Issue Investor   + 6.6%
28. Peter Dag Investment Letter (Model Portfolio)   + 6.1%
29. Charted Course (Model Portfolio)   + 5.9%
30. Telephone Switch Newsletter   + 5.6%
    (Average of 2 Portfolios)
    a. Equities/Cash Portfolio   + 19.0%
    b. Gold/Equities/Cash Portfolio   − 7.8%
31. California Technology Stock Letter   + 4.6%
    (Model Portfolio)
32. Heim Investment Letter   + 2.6%
33. International Harry Schultz Letter   + 2.1%
    (U.S. Stocks Portfolio)

34.	Zweig Forecast		+	1.5%
35.	Dow Theory Letters		−	6.8%
36.	Systems and Forecasts		−	6.9%
37.	High Technology Investments		−	7.9%
	a. Long-term Portfolio	+ 3.5%		
	b. "Trigger Price Advisory" (Trading Portfolio)	− 19.3%		
38.	Holt Investment Advisory		−	8.2%
39.	Professional Tape Reader (Model Portfolio)		−	9.8%
40.	Nicholson Report (Average of 2 Portfolios)		−	11.0%
	a. Traders	− 9.0%		
	b. Investors	− 12.9%		
41.	Howard Ruff's Financial Success Report		−	14.9%
42.	Successful Options Investing (Hedged Portfolio)		−	19.8%
43.	Granville Market Letter (Aggressive Traders' Portfolio)		−	25.2%
44.	Option Advisor (Average of 2 Portfolios)		−	83.3%
	a. Aggressive Portfolio	− 83.1%		
	b. Conservative Portfolio	− 83.5%		

Appendix B

Risk-Adjusted Performance

Each of the four tables in this appendix covers periods similar to those in their corresponding tables in Appendix A (performance through the first quarter of 1984 as measured from (a) June 30, 1980; (b) January 1, 1981; (c) January 2, 1982; and (3) January 1, 1983). Instead of ranking newsletters on the basis of aggregate performance, however, this appendix ranks them on the basis of risk-adjusted performance.

The risk-adjusted figures allow you to compare newsletters on the basis of how much money they made per unit of risk. This facilitates comparisons between, on the one hand, extremely risky portfolios (for example, portfolios invested in options) and, on the other hand, portfolios with very little risk (for example, portfolios invested in high-yielding blue chip stocks). The options portfolio is quite likely in some periods to make more money than the blue-chip stocks portfolio, but does it make enough more to justify the much greater risk? The following tables are the basis of an answer to such questions.

For an in-depth discussion of risk and how it is measured, please refer to the chapter on the subject earlier in this book. Basically, risk is defined as volatility of performance; if a portfolio makes exactly 1.0% each and every month, it has no volatility and no risk. If, however, a portfolio makes 50% some months but loses that much in others, its volatility (and risk) is very high.

Because you can earn the Treasury bill rate without incurring any risk at all, the following tables credit a newsletter only for its performance (if any) above and beyond the Treasury bill rate. The "greater than T-Bill" premium that each newsletter earns for incurring risk is then compared with a statistical measure of risk known as the standard deviation. The ratio of the two figures—which shows how much is earned per unit of risk—is the basis of the rankings in the tables that follow.

As with the previous appendix, the figures are based on ratings calculated by *The Hulbert Financial Digest* according to its established methodology. Please refer to the introduction to this book for a full description of that methodology.

B-1. Risk-adjusted Performance June 30, 1980 to March 31, 1984
(Average monthly gain per unit of risk)

1. Growth Stock Outlook (Supervised Portfolio) .28%
2. Green's Commodity Market Comments .21%
   (Portfolio for Traders)
3. Market Logic (Master Portfolio) .21%
4. Value Line OTC Special Situations Service .14%
5. Zweig Forecast .13%
6. The Dines Letter (Average of 6 Portfolios) .12%
   a. List #4 (Growth Portfolio) .24%
   b. List #6 (Trading Portfolio) .21%
   c. List #3 (Income Portfolio) .16%
   d. List #2 (Speculative Port.) .15%
   e. List #1 (Moderate Risk Port.) .05%
   f. List #5 (Precious Metals Port.) −.08%

STANDARD & POOR'S 500 INDEX (Including Dividends) .08%

7. Professional Investor (Average of 4 Portfolios) .07%
   a. AMEX Scan .23%
   b. OTC Scan .14%
   c. NYSE Scan .03%
   d. Investment Grade Stocks Scan −.10%
8. Standard & Poor's Outlook (Average of 4 Portfolios) .06%
   a. Speculative Stocks .08%
   b. Income Stocks .07%
   c. Growth Stocks .05%
   d. Foundation Stocks .05%
9. Dow Theory Forecasts (Average of 4 Portfolios) .03%
   a. Investment Stocks .08%
   b. Growth Stocks .04%
   c. Income Stocks .02%
   d. Speculative Stocks −.01%

RISK-FREE RATE OF RETURN (A T-Bill Only Portfolio)		.00%
10. Howard Ruff's Financial Success Report		−.05%
11. International Harry Schultz Letter (U.S. Stocks Portfolio)		−.06%
12. Professional Tape Reader (Model Portfolio)		−.10%
13. United Business & Investment Reports (Average of 3 Portfolios)		−.11%
a. Cyclical Stocks	−.05%	
b. Income Stocks	−.12%	
c. Growth Stocks	−.17%	
14. Holt Investment Advisory		−.16%
15. Heim Investment Letter		−.30%
16. Granville Market Letter (Aggressive Traders' Portfolio)		−.30%

B-2. Risk-adjusted Performance January 1, 1981 to March 31, 1984

(Average monthly performance per unit of risk)

1. Green's Commodity Market Comments (Portfolio for Traders)		.19%
2. Growth Stock Outlook (Supervised Portfolio)		.17%
3. Market Logic (Master Portfolio)		.16%
4. The Dines Letter (Average of 6 Portfolios)		.11%
a. List #4 (Growth Portfolio)	.26%	
b. List #6 (Trading Portfolio)	.21%	
c. List #3 (Income Portfolio)	.17%	
d. List #2 (Speculative Portfolio)	.16%	
e. List #1 (Moderate Risk Port.)	.03%	
f. List #5 (Precious Metals Port.)	−.17%	
5. Zweig Forecast		.07%
6. Value Line OTC Special Situations Service		.02%
STANDARD & POOR'S 500 INDEX (Including Dividends)		.01%
7. Professional Investor (Average of 4 Portfolios)		.01%
a. AMEX Scan	.15%	
b. OTC Scan	.04%	
c. NYSE Scan	−.01%	
d. Investment Grade Stocks Scan	−.14%	
8. Standard & Poor's Outlook (Average of 4 Portfolios)		.00%
a. Speculative Stocks	.02%	
b. Income Stocks	.00%	
c. Growth Stocks	.00%	
d. Foundation Stocks	−.02%	
RISK-FREE RATE OF RETURN (A T-Bill Only Portfolio)		.00%
9. Speculator's (Selected Stocks of the Week)		−.00%
10. Howard Ruff's Financial Success Report		−.02%

11. Cabot Market Letter (Model Portfolio) −.04%
12. Dow Theory Forecasts (Average of 4 Portfolios) −.05%
    a. Investment Stocks −.00%
    b. Growth Stocks −.02%
    c. Income Stocks −.04%
    d. Speculative Stocks −.11%
13. Holt Investment Advisory −.13%
14. RHM Survey of Warrants, Options & Low-Priced Stocks −.17%
15. United Business & Investment Reports (Average of 3 Portfolios) −.17%
    a. Income Stocks −.12%
    b. Cyclical Stocks −.15%
    c. Growth Stocks −.24%
16. Dow Theory Letters −.18%
17. Harry Browne's Special Reports (Variable Portfolio) −.19%
18. International Harry Schultz Letter (U.S. Stocks Portfolio) −.20%
19. Professional Tape Reader (Model Portfolio) −.22%
20. Heim Investment Letter −.29%
21. Granville Market Letter (Aggressive Traders' Portfolio) −.37%

B-3. Risk-adjusted Performance January 1, 1982 to March 31, 1984
(Average monthly gain per unit of risk)

1. Green's Commodity Market Comments (Portfolio for Traders) .31%
2. Tony Henfrey's Gold Letter (Long-term Gold Share Portfolio) .26%
3. Growth Stock Outlook (Supervised Portfolio) .24%
4. Market Logic (Master Portfolio) .24%
5. The Dines Letter (Average of 6 Portfolios) .20%
    a. List #4 (Growth Portfolio) .32%
    b. List #6 (Trading Portfolio) .30%
    c. List #1 (Moderate Risk Port.) .23%
    d. List #3 (Income Portfolio) .20%
    e. List #2 (Speculative Portfolio) .19%
    f. List #5 (Precious Metals Port.) −.03%
6. Chartist (Actual Cash Account) .18%

STANDARD & POOR'S 500 INDEX (Including Dividends) .17%

7. Dessauer's Journal (International Portfolio) .18%
8. Value Line OTC Special Situations Service .13%
9. Professional Investor (Average of 4 Portfolios) .13%

	a. AMEX Scan	.36%	
	b. OTC Scan	.18%	
	c. NYSE Scan	.13%	
	d. Investment Grade Stocks Scan	−.14%	
10.	Kinsman's Low-Risk Advisory Letter (Model Portfolio)		.13%
11.	Speculator's (Selected Stocks of the Week)		.10%
12.	RHM Survey of Warrants, Options & Low-Priced Stocks		.08%
13.	Dow Theory Forecasts (Average of 4 Portfolios)		.07%
	a. Income Stocks	.16%	
	b. Investment Stocks	.14%	
	c. Growth Stocks	.01%	
	d. Speculative Stocks	−.03%	
14.	Harry Browne's Special Reports (Variable Portfolio)		.06%
15.	Howard Ruff's Financial Success Report		.04%
16.	Standard & Poor's Outlook (Average of 4 Portfolios)		.03%
	a. Speculative Stocks	.14%	
	b. Income Stocks	.03%	
	c. Foundation Stocks	.01%	
	d. Growth Stocks	−.05%	
17.	Zweig Forecast		.03%
	RISK-FREE RATE OF RETURN (A T-Bill Only Portfolio)		.00%
18.	Cabot Market Letter (Model Portfolio)		−.02%
19.	United Business & Investment Report (Average of 3 Portfolios)		−.06%
	a. Income Stocks	.01%	
	b. Cyclical Stocks	−.05%	
	c. Growth Stocks	−.13%	
20.	Professional Timing Service		−.10%
21.	International Harry Schultz Letter (U.S. Stocks Portfolio)		−.11%
22.	Professional Tape Reader (Model Portfolio)		−.11%
23.	Holt Investment Advisory		−.14%
24.	Dow Theory Letters		−.17%
25.	Heim Investment Letter		−.31%
26.	Granville Market Letter (Aggressive Traders' Portfolio)		−.42%

B-4. Risk-adjusted Performance January 1, 1983 to March 31, 1984
(Average monthly gain per unit of risk)

1.	Addison Report (Average of 2 Portfolios)		.39%
	a. Speculative Stocks	.54%	
	b. Conservative Stocks	.23%	

2. Prudent Speculator .31%
3. The Dines Letter (Average of 6 Portfolios) .27%
    a. List #6 (Trading Portfolio) .46%
    b. List #4 (Growth Portfolio) .38%
    c. List #1 (Moderate Risk Portfolio) .36%
    d. List #2 (Speculative Portfolio) .27%
    e. List #3 (Income Portfolio) .10%
    f. List #5 (Precious Metals Port.) .05%
4. Green's Commodity Market Comments .24%
   (Portfolio for Traders)
5. Growth Stock Outlook (Supervised Portfolio) .22%
6. Dessauer's Journal (International Portfolio) .21%

STANDARD & POOR'S 500 INDEX (Including Dividends) .18%

7. Tony Henfrey's Gold Letter .17%
   (Long-term Gold Share Portfolio)
8. Switch Fund Advisory (Model Portfolio) .16%
9. Market Logic (Master Portfolio) .13%
10. Growth Fund Guide (Average of 4 Portfolios) .09%
    a. Quality Growth Funds .20%
    b. Special Situations Funds .12%
    c. Growth Funds .09%
    d. Aggressive Growth Funds −.03%
11. Value Line Investment Survey .08%
    (Stocks Rated I for "Timeliness")
12. RHM Survey of Warrants, Options & Low-Priced .04%
    Stocks
13. Chartist (Average of 2 Portfolios) .02%
    a. Average Cash Account .07%
    b. Trader's Stocks −.03%

RISK-FREE RATE OF RETURN (A T-Bill Only Portfolio) .00%

14. Professional Investor (Average of 4 Portfolios) .02%
    a. AMEX Scan .34%
    b. OTC Scan .20%
    c. NYSE Scan −.10%
    d. Investment Grade Stocks Scan −.37%
15. Dow Theory Forecasts (Average of 4 Portfolios) −.02%
    a. Income Stocks .15%
    b. Investment Stocks −.00%
    c. Growth Stocks −.08%
    d. Speculative Stocks −.14%
16. Telephone Switch (Average of 2 Portfolios) −.02%
    a. Equities/Cash Portfolio .07%
    b. Gold/Equities/Cash Portfolio −.11%
17. Value Line OTC Special Situations Service −.02%
18. International Harry Schultz Letter −.03%
    (U.S. Stocks Portfolio)

19. Standard & Poor's Outlook   −.05%
    (Average of 4 Portfolios)
    a. Income Stocks   .05%
    b. Speculative Stocks   .00%
    c. Foundation Stocks   −.11%
    d. Growth Stocks   −.12%
20. Professional Timing Service   −.05%
21. Harry Browne's Special Reports   −.05%
    (Variable Portfolio)
22. Holt Investment Advisory   −.06%
23. New Issues   −.07%
24. Speculator's (Selected Stocks of the Week)   −.07%
25. Zweig Performance Ratings   −.07%
26. Peter Dag Investment Letter (Model Portfolio)   −.07%
27. Indicator Digest   −.08%
28. Option Advisor (Average of 2 Portfolios)   −.08%
    a. Aggressive   −.05%
    b. Conservative   −.11%
29. Charted Course (Model Portfolio)   −.09%
30. Kinsman Low-Risk Advisory Letter   −.11%
    (Model Portfolio)
31. Successful Options Investing (Hedged Portfolio)   −.12%
32. Howard Ruff's Financial Success Report   −.13%
33. New Issue Investor   −.14%
34. Zweig Forecast   −.15%
35. United Business & Investment Reports   −.20%
    (Average of 3 Portfolios)
    a. Income Stocks   −.06%
    b. Cyclical Stocks   −.22%
    c. Growth Stocks   −.31%
36. Systems & Forecasts   −.21%
37. Cabot Market Letter (Model Portfolio)   −.22%
38. California Technology Stock Letter   −.27%
    (Model Portfolio)
39. Heim Investment Letter   −.30%
40. Dow Theory Letters   −.41%
41. Granville Market Letter   −.47%
    (Aggressive Traders' Portfolio)
42. High Technology Investments   −.55%
    (Average of 2 Portfolios)
    a. Long-term Portfolio   −.16%
    b. "Trigger Price Advisory"   −.95%
       (Trading Portfolio)
43. Professional Tape Reader (Model Portfolio)   −.63%
44. Nicholson Report (Average of 2 Portfolios)   −.64%
    a. Stocks for the Aggressive Trader   −.62%
    b. Stocks for the Longer Term Investor −.66%

Appendix C

Newsletter Directory

This appendix lists the addresses and subscription rates for the investment newsletters that have been scrutinized in this book. If we have the information, we also list the name of the newsletter's editor, its phone number, and whether or not the newsletter supplements its issues with a telephone hotline.

As you will see, most letters have relatively inexpensive trial offers that allow you to become exposed to them at very little cost. As discussed earlier in this book, we recommend that, in the final stages of choosing between various newsletters, you take out a trial subscription to them. Only in that way can you be sure that you are comfortable with the investment philosophy and clarity provided in them.

Every effort was made to insure that the addresses and rates were current as of the press date (May 1984), but we do not guarantee that these rates will be the ones you can get. Some advertise more inexpensive offers, especially in the pages of the financial press (especially *Barron's*), and in many instances a little checking is all you will need to do to discover even cheaper trial offers to these newsletters.

Newsletter Directory

Newsletter Name	Subscription Cost			Phone Hotline
	Yr	1/2-Yr	Trial	
ADDISON REPORT (Andrew Addison) P. O. Box 425 Quincy, MA 02269 617-471-3343	$185	$100	$50/4 issues	X
CABOT MARKET LETTER (Carlton G. Lutts) P. O. Box 3044 Salem, MA 01970 617-745-5532	150	85		
CALIFORNIA TECHNOLOGY STOCK LETTER (Michael Murphy & Jim McCamant) 155 Montgomery St. San Francisco, CA 94104 415-982-0125	220		25/3 issues	X
CHARTED COURSE (Carl A. Cascella) P. O. Box 88 Westport, CT 06881 203-334-5102	180	95	25/3 issues	X
THE CHARTIST (Dan Sullivan) P. O. Box 3160 Long Beach, CA 90803	115	70		X
DESSAUER'S JOURNAL (John P. Dessauer) P. O. Box 1718 Orleans, MA 02653 617-255-1651	150	85	45/3 months	
THE DINES LETTER (James Dines) P. O. Box 22 Belvedere, CA 94920-2692 415-435-2314	150	85		
DOW THEORY FORECASTS 7412 Calumet Avenue Hammond, IN 46324	157			
DOW THEORY LETTERS (Richard Russell)	225		5/3 issues	

Newsletter Directory

Newsletter Name	Subscription Cost			Phone Hotline
	Yr	1/2-Yr	Trial	
P. O. Box 1759 LaJolla, CA 92038 714-454-0481				
GRANVILLE MARKET LETTER (Joseph Granville) P. O. Drawer 23006 Kansas City, MO. 64141 800-874-0977 (except Missouri) 816-474-5353	250	150	85/11 issues	
GREEN'S COMMODITY MARKET COMMENTS (Charles Stahl) P. O. Box 174 Princeton, NJ 08540 609-921-6594	240	150	65/3 months	
GROWTH FUND GUIDE Growth Fund Research Building Box 6600 Rapid City, SD 57709	79			
GROWTH STOCK OUTLOOK (Charles Allmon) P.O. Box 15381 Chevy Chase, MD 20815 301-654-5205	125		48/3 months	X
HARRY BROWNE'S SPECIAL REPORTS (Harry Browne) P. O. Box 5586 Austin, TX 78763 512-453-7313	225			X
HEIM INVESTMENT LETTER (Lawrence H. Heim) (Truman C. Pagh) 729 SW Alder, Suite 420 Portland, OR 97205 503-228-9555	150	80	10/1 month	

Newsletter Name	Subscription Cost			Phone Hotline
	Yr	1/2-Yr	Trial	
HIGH TECHNOLOGY INVESTMENTS (Michael Gianturco) 5925 Kirby Drive, Ste.219 Houston, TX 77005 713-529-1453	119	75 for weekly service alone 44 for monthly service alone		
HOLT INVESTMENT ADVISORY (Thomas J. Holt) 290 Post Road West Westport, CT 06880 203-226-8911	180	98	25/3 months	
HOWARD RUFF'S FINANCIAL SUCCESS REPORT (Howard J. Ruff) P. O. Box 25 Pleasanton, CA 94566-0625 415-463-2200	89		3/1 issue	X
INDICATOR DIGEST Indicator Research Group Palisades Park, NJ 07650 201-947-8800	125	75	7/1 issue	X
INTERNATIONAL HARRY SCHULTZ LETTER (Harry Schultz) PM & S, Park Tremeland 12 B-3120-Tremelo, Belgium Sub. Inquiries: 203-329-2066	258	152	20/1 issue	
KINSMAN LOW-RISK ADVISORY LETTER (Robert Kinsman) 70 Mitchell Blvd. San Rafael, CA 94903 415-479-1451	125			X
MARKET LOGIC (Norman G. Fosback, Pres. Glen King Parker, Chairman) 3471 North Federal Hwy. Fort Lauderdale, FL 33306 305-563-9000	195		9/issue	X

Newsletter Name	Subscription Cost			Phone Hotline
	Yr	1/2-Yr	Trial	
NEW ISSUE INVESTOR (Robert Natale) c/o Standard & Poor's 25 Broadway New York, NY 10004 212-208-8000	130		30/3 issues	X
NEW ISSUES (Norman G. Fosback, Pres. Glen King Parker, Chairman) 3471 North Federal Hwy. Fort Lauderdale, FL 33306 305-563-9000	150		15/issue	X
NICHOLSON REPORT (Robert Nicholson) 5901 Mariposa Court Coral Gables, FL 33146 305-665-7445	170		7/issue	X
OPTION ADVISOR (Bernard G. Schaeffer Robert D. Bergen) Box 46709 Cincinnati, OH 45246 513-772-2552	225			X
OUTLOOK (Stephen Sanborn) (Arnold Kaufman) c/o Standard & Poor's 25 Broadway New York, NY 10004 212-208-8000	185		55/Qtr.	
PETER DAG INVESTMENT LETTER (Peter Dag) 65 Lakefront Drive Akron, OH 44319	250		75/3 months	
PROFESSIONAL INVESTOR (Robert T. Gross) P. O. Box 2144 Pompano Beach, FL 33061 305-946-6353	200	75	18.95/1 issue	X

Newsletter Directory

Newsletter Name	Subscription Cost			Phone Hotline
	Yr	1/2-Yr	Trial	
PROFESSIONAL TAPE READER (Stan Weinstein) P. O. Box 2407 Hollywood, FL 33022	250	150	30/3 issues	X
PROFESSIONAL TIMING SERVICE (Larry Williams Curtis Hesler) P. O. Box 7483 Missoula, MT 59807	150			X
PRUDENT SPECULATOR (Al Frank) P. O. Box 1767 Santa Monica, CA 90406 213-395-5275	125		25/3 issues	
RHM SURVEY OF WARRANTS, OPTIONS & LOW-PRICE STOCKS (Sidney Fried) 172 Forest Avenue Glen Cove, NY 11542	120	68		
THE SPECULATOR (Stephen Leeb) 37 Van Reipen Jersey City, NJ 07306	175	95	49.50/3 months	X
SUCCESSFUL OPTIONS INVESTING (Martin Juman) 100 Ring Road West Garden City, NY 11530 516-248-1666	160		25/6 weeks	
SWITCH FUND ADVISORY (Jay Schabacker) 8943 Shady Grove Court Gaithersburg, MD 20877	125			
SYSTEMS & FORECASTS 150 Great Neck Rd. Great Neck, NY 11021 516-829-6444	140			X

Newsletter Name	Subscription Cost			Phone Hotline
	Yr	1/2-Yr	Trial	
TELEPHONE SWITCH NEWSLETTER (Richard Fabian) P. O. Box 2538 Huntington Beach, CA 92647 714-840-4747	117			X
TONY HENFREY'S GOLD LETTER (Tony Henfrey) P. O. BOX 5577 Durban 4000 South Africa (31) 742566	185	100	50/3 months	X
UNITED BUSINESS AND INVESTMENT REPORT 210 Newbury Street Boston, MA 02116	170	95		
VALUE LINE INVESTMENT SURVEY Arnold Bernhard & Co. 711 Third Avenue New York, NY 10017 212-687-3965	365		37/10 weeks	
VALUE LINE OTC SPECIAL SITUATIONS SERVICE Arnold Bernhard & Co. 711 Third Avenue New York, NY 10017 212-687-3965	300		29/6 issues	
ZWEIG FORECAST (Martin E. Zweig) P. O. Box 5345 New York, NY 10150 212-644-0040	245	145	50/3 months	X
ZWEIG PERFORMANCE RATINGS REPORT (Joe DiMenna Carol Whitehead) P. O. Box 5345 New York, NY 10150 212-644-0040	150			

Appendix **D**

A Short Guide to Using Discount Brokers

Having selected one or more investment newsletters to which to subscribe, and for whose advice you are willing to pay (because of its performance) from $75 to $350 or more per year, is there any reason to pay full-service commission costs? The answer in most cases is an emphatic, "no!"

A little history may be helpful here. Until May 1, 1975, the stock exchanges imposed fixed commission rates on their member firms. Therefore, the execution cost of a particular stock order would not vary whether you went to a national brokerage firm such as Merrill Lynch, Pierce, Fenner & Smith, or a local firm with its sole office in your community; whether you bought and sold stocks dozens of times annually or merely once when your great Aunt Minnie died leaving you five shares of ABC Nursing Homes & Funeral Parlors, Inc. The price you were charged was not dependent on whether your broker sent you his own firm's research reports, sent you copies of Standard & Poor's sheets, or made no recommendations at all. Whether you wanted or needed the many different services offered by a brokerage firm, you paid for all of them in one package price.

"May Day"

Beginning May 1, 1975, known on Wall Street as "May Day," the Securities and Exchange Commission declared this exchange-sanctioned price fixing as contrary to the public interest and illegal. Ironically, in an industry that purports to believe in the value of competition, the approach of May Day was widely viewed on Wall Street by most brokerage firms and stock brokers with fear, horror, dismay, and dire predictions of the ruin of the industry. Othermore innovative and entrepreneurial brokerage firms accepted the challenge of competition and inaugurated a new sub-industry, now widely known as discount brokers.

What Is A Discount Broker?

A discount broker is a firm that executes stock, option, and bond trades at a discount, often 50% to 90%, from the 1975 fixed commission rate schedule. Most do not provide research, although some reproduce widely respected investment reports from organizations such as Standard & Poor's and Value Line. Most discount brokers advertise on the basis of price, do not provide a personal account executive (although some do provide personalized service), and do not solicit orders from customers. All are covered by the same Securities Industry Protection Corporation (SIPC) federal insurance that the full-service brokers are.

The price savings of going to a discount broker can be substantial. According to Mark Coler and Ellis Ratner (whose book *70% Off* does an excellent job of comparing discount and full-service brokerage firms), the following table shows the average savings you can expect on transactions whose value is $10,000:

Average Savings Over Full-service Rates on $10,000 Transactions

Type of Broker	Average Commission	Percent Savings Over Full Service
Full-commission broker	$178	0%
Savings & loan discounter	134	25%
Average discount broker	85	52%
Average of big 3 discounters	76	57%
Average of big 5 discounters	71	60%
Average of 20 large firms	58	67%
Best single discounter	37	75%

Source: Coler, Mark, and Ellis Ratner, *70% Off: The Investor's Guide to Discount Brokerage* (New York, Facts on File, 1983, p. 92).

Discount brokers in many cases will be the logical choice of investment newsletter subscribers who are making their own investment decisions. Full-service commission rates are higher because they must compensate the firm not only for the execution of your orders but also for their research departments' budget. If you are not interested in the recommendations of their research departments—as many newsletter subscribers are not—then there is no reason to pay for them. Of course, if you value the opinions and recommendations of your full-service broker, by all means keep him. But if all you are looking for is execution of your buy and sell orders, then there is no reason to pay the higher rates. And if you are following the advice of a newsletter, all you are looking for is fast, efficient execution of your buy and sell orders.

Do Full-Service Brokers Execute Your Orders More Quickly?

Many full-service brokerage firms justify their higher rates by arguing that they can execute their orders more quickly and efficiently than discount brokers. But this argument often does not withstand scrutiny. Virtually all market orders of less than 600 shares of an NYSE-listed stock (and limit orders up to 500 shares)—regardless of broker—are routed to the floor of the exchange via the same computer system. And once to the floor they are executed without regard to their source. Other exchanges and the over-the-counter market have similar computerized order systems.

Many of the other arguments often advanced to justify higher commissions are also weak, according to Coler and Ratner. In fact, according to a 1981 survey cited in their book, "slightly more than half the investors who used both discount and full-commission firms found no real difference between them with respect to speed and executing orders or accuracy of confirmations and statements. But of those who did, two-thirds thought that discount brokers provided speedier executions, and about sixty percent thought they provided more accurate confirmations and statements."

Not all Discount Brokers Are Alike

One of the main themes of Coler and Ratner's book is that, though discount brokers have a distinct price advantage over full service brokerage firms, there is also a wide disparity between the commission schedules of different discount brokers. They divide the commission schedules of discount brokers into two categories: (1) "sharebrokers," whose schedules give the greatest discounts to transactions involving large numbers of shares, regardless of the price of those shares, and (2) "valuebrokers," whose schedules give the greatest discounts on the basis of the dollar size of the transaction, regardless of the number of shares involved. If you are purchasing a large number of very low-priced stocks, you should use a valuebroker—where the commission schedule charges you according to the relatively low dollar value of the transaction rather than the large number of shares. If you are purchasing high-priced shares, in contrast, chances are that a sharebroker would have the best price—where the commission schedule charges you according to the relatively low number of shares purchased, rather than the transaction's higher dollar value. According to Coler and Ratner, by using two discount brokers instead of one (one sharebroker and one valuebroker), and by dividing your transactions between them according to which is cheapest, you can increase the already substantial savings that accompany the move from full service to discount brokers.

Though some may feel that this is a lot of work for what appears to be relatively little savings, the fact of the matter is that commission savings quickly add up and can make the difference between profit and loss for strategies which trade frequently in and out of the market. As pointed out earlier in this book (see Section IV), some portfolios monitored by the HFD have annual turnover rates of six times or more. If you were to save 1.5% on each buy and sell order (1.5% is the approximate difference between the average full-service rate and the average discount rate), this could lead to a total of 18% greater performance over a year's time for a follower of such frequent trading newsletters!

For an in-depth discussion of the ways in which you can most profitably use discount brokers, we highly recommend *70% Off*. You may also be interested in a newsletter that is being published by Coler and Ratner, which is scheduled to first appear in October 1984, entitled "Discount Brokerage Advisory Service."[1]

In general, the lesson to learn in choosing between brokers is similar to that involved in the choice between investment newsletters—be an informed consumer. Classify the number and type of transactions you most frequently undertake, and choose the brokers best fitted to those needs and objectives.

Some of the Cheapest Discount Brokers

Just as there is no "best" investment newsletter, there is no "cheapest" discount broker. It depends upon the number of shares

---

[1] Discount Brokerage Advisory Service, 200 Park Avenue, Suite 303 East, New York, NY 10166.

being bought or sold and their price. In *70% Off*, Coler and Ratner list the 30 cheapest discount brokers for each of a wide variety of transactions. To give you a representative idea of who some of the cheapest discounters are in several representative categories, we have listed below the names and addresses of the three cheapest discount brokers in four separate categories. (More than three are listed if they all have equally low rates for the particular transaction.) Each of the categories involves transactions valued at $10,000, and the categories differ only in the price of the securities being purchased:

I. 1000 shares @ $10/share

1. Odd Lots Securities
   60 E. 42nd Street
   New York, NY 10017

2. Quick & Reilly
   120 Wall Street
   New York, NY 10005

3. York Securities
   44 Wall Street
   New York, NY 10005

4. Brown & Company
   7 Water Street
   Boston, MA 02109

II. 500 shares @ $20/share

1. Pacific Brokerage Services
   8200 Wilshire Blvd., Suite 314
   Beverly Hills, CA 90211

2. Brown & Company
   7 Water Street
   Boston, MA 02109

3. Seaport Securities
   19 Rector St.
   New York, NY 10006

III. 200 shares @ $50/share

1. Haas Securities
   120 Broadway
   New York, NY 10271

2. Pacific Brokerage Services
   8200 Wilshire Blvd., Suite 314
   Beverly Hills, CA 90211

3. Bevill, Bresler & Schulman, Inc.
   301 S. Livingston Avenue

Livingston, NJ 07039

IV. 100 shares @ $100/share

1. Burke, Christensen & Lewis Securities
   120 LaSalle Street, Suite 940
   Chicago, IL 60603

2. First National Brokerage Services
   119 S. 19th Street
   Omaha, NE 68102

3. Haas Securities
   120 Broadway
   New York, NY 10271

4. Pacific Brokerage Services
   8200 Wilshire Blvd., Suite 314
   Beverly Hills, CA 90211

5. Rose & Company Investment Brokers, Inc.
   Board of Trade Building
   Chicago, IL 60604

6. St. Louis Discount Securities, Inc.
   35 North Central Avenue
   Clayton, MO 63105